MW01698180

ThinkUp!™ MATH

STUDENT EDITION

Standards Mastery through Critical Thinking

Let's get started!

Publisher
Michael L. Lujan, M.Ed.

Editorial Director
Teresa Sherman, B.S.E.

Production Manager
Ashley Muniz, B.A.A.S.

Production Artists
Tammy Black
Nicole Langston
Sarah Poff, B.S.
Judy Bankhead, M.F.A.
Laura Adams, A.A.
Amber Bordelon, B.F.A.

Content Development Team
Marian Rainwater, M.Ed.
Erica Miller, B.S.E.
Teresa Sherman, B.S.E.
Karen Crawford, M.Ed.
Rachael Blackstone, B.S.E.
Jackie Cannon, M.Ed.
Kimberley Costanza, B.A.
Keri McIntosh, B.S.I.S.
Brooke North, B.A.

Content Editorial Team
Erica Miller, B.S.E.
Marian Rainwater, M.Ed.
Karen Reeves, M.Ed.
Allison Wiley, B.S.E.
Cathy Cutler, B.S.E.
Anne Altamirano, M.A.T.
Shae Connell, B.B.A.

MentoringMinds®
Critical Thinking for Life!™

P.O. Box 8843
Tyler, TX 75711

p800.585.5258 | f800.838.8186

For other great products from Mentoring Minds,
please visit our website at:
mentoring**minds**.com

ISBN: 978-1-62763-287-4

ThinkUp! Math™, Student Edition

Copyright infringement is a violation of Federal Law.

Trademarks used in this book belong to their respective owners.

©2019 by *Mentoring Minds, L.P.* All rights reserved. *ThinkUp! Math™* is protected by copyright law and international treaties. No part of this publication may be reproduced, translated, stored in a retrieval system, or transmitted in any way or by any means (electronic, mechanical, photocopying, recording, or otherwise) without prior written permission from *Mentoring Minds, L.P.* Unauthorized reproduction of any portion of this book without written permission of *Mentoring Minds, L.P.* may result in criminal penalties and will be prosecuted to the maximum extent of the law. Not for resale.

Printed in the United States of America

Mentoring Minds®
Critical Thinking for Life!®

Dear Student,

It's time to start your *ThinkUp! Math* journey!

You use math skills and critical thinking every day. We want you to enjoy learning and applying these skills. Your teacher will give you opportunities to learn in various ways that will allow you to think critically. Be an active listener and participant. Apply the "I will" statements below and you will be successful on your journey as a learner.

Your friends at Mentoring Minds

- I will think critically using the 9 traits.
- I will listen carefully in all situations.
- I will ask questions when I do not understand.
- I will use all available tools.
- I will apply what I learn to my everyday life.
- I will improve as a critical thinker.
- I will believe in myself!

ThinkUp!™ MATH

Table of Contents

Name: ______________________________

Getting Started

Unit 1 – Standard 1.2(A)

Unit 1: Recognize the Quantities of Structured Arrangements

TEKS LEARNING TARGETS

- I can identify how many objects are in a small set without counting.
- I can group objects in my mind to help determine the number of items.

Focus for 9 Traits of Critical Thinking™

Collaborate: *I work with others to achieve better outcomes.*

How does working with a partner or group help you complete a task quicker? How does it help you reach a correct answer?

____

____

Link: *I apply knowledge to reach new understandings.*

What did you learn last year that will help you with counting objects in your head?

____

____

Illegal to Copy

Listen to your teacher and work with your partner to follow directions.

A ____________

B ____________

C ____________

D ____________

E ____________

F ____________

G ____________

H ____________

I ____________

J ____________

How did you use the critical thinking trait ***collaborate*** in this activity?

____

____

How did you use the critical thinking trait ***link*** in this activity?

____

____

Illegal to Copy

eight (8)	**nine (9)**	**seven (7)**	**ten frame**
eleven (11)	**number**	**six (6)**	**three (3)**
five (5)	**numeral**	**tally marks**	**twelve (12)**
four (4)	**one (1)**	**ten (10)**	**two (2)**

Draw 2 examples and 2 non-examples of a structured arrangement.

Examples	Non-Examples

When working with others, why is it important to use the same vocabulary? Does it help make collaborating easier?

____

____

How does a tally mark represent a numeral?

____

____

Instruction

Name: ______________________________

Concept Development

Standard 1.2(A) – **Unit 1**

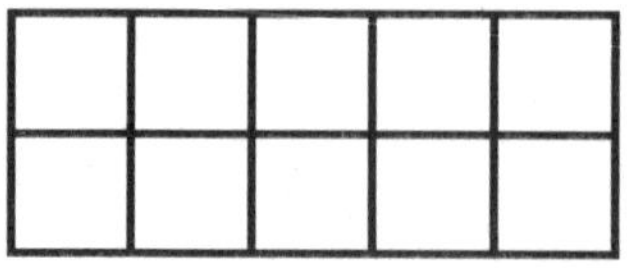

Place a number of circles in your ten frame.

What number did you make?

Answer ______________________

A ten frame is a math tool with 10 spaces used to build numbers. Each circle or counter in a ten frame is equal to 1.

This ten frame represents 3.

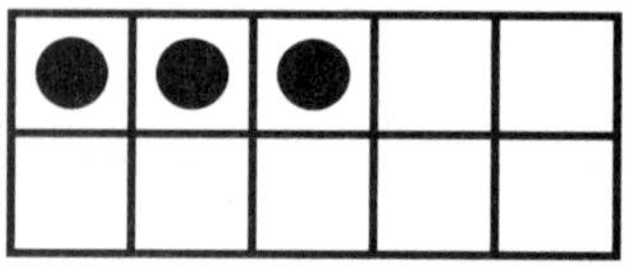

How many tally marks do you count?

Answer ______________________

Draw tally marks to show 12.

Tally marks are used to keep track of data being counted. Each mark is equal to 1.

This set of tally marks represents 4.

When you count 5 objects, the fifth mark is drawn across the group.

Try It!

1) Write the number.

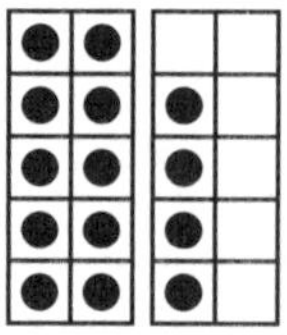 ____

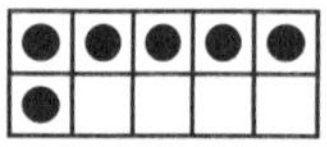 ____

Try It!

2) Write the number for each row.

Drinks	Votes
Juice	𝍸 𝍸 𝍸
Soda	𝍸 𝍷𝍷𝍷𝍷

Juice: ____

Soda: ____

Show 8 using tally marks.

____

Illegal to Copy

1 Tam held up fingers to show his age.

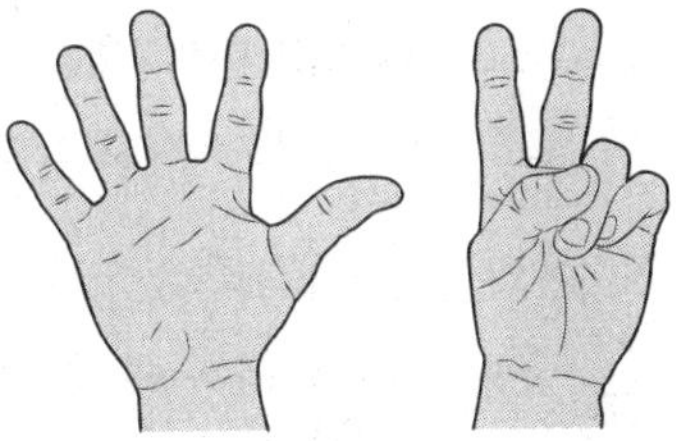

How old is Tam?

Answer ____________________

2 What number is shown on the ten frame?

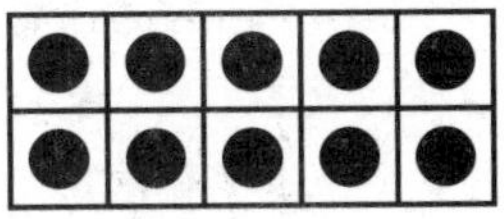

- ⬭ 6
- ⬭ 7
- ⬭ 10

3 Taylor's soccer team scores 9 goals. Which set of tally marks shows this score?

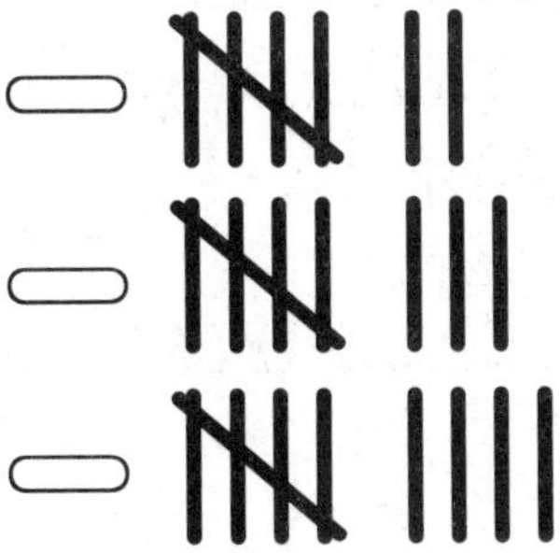

4 Circle the arrangements of 6.

5 The numbers on the cards are missing.

Write the missing numbers.

______ ______ ______ ______

6 Zack earned 8 stickers. Draw tally marks to show the stickers Zack earned.

Instruction

Name: ____________________

Concept Practice

Standard 1.2(A) – **Unit 1**

1 How many pepperonis are on the pizza?

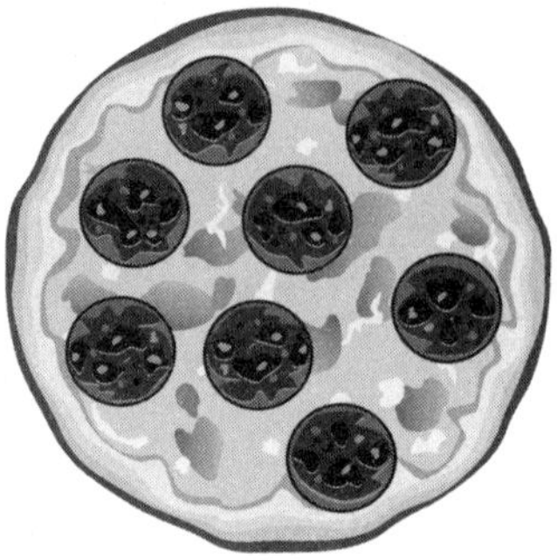

Answer ____________________

Write the answer in tally marks.

____

2 Draw lines to match the numbers to the dice.

2　　3　　5　　6

3 Color the circles that do NOT show the number 7.

4 Mrs. Brown made cupcakes for Mia's birthday.

How many cupcakes did Mrs. Brown make?

- 6
- 5
- 8

5 David has 9 crayons in his box. Which picture shows 9 crayons?

- 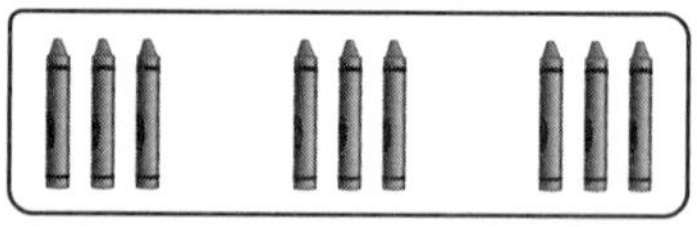
- 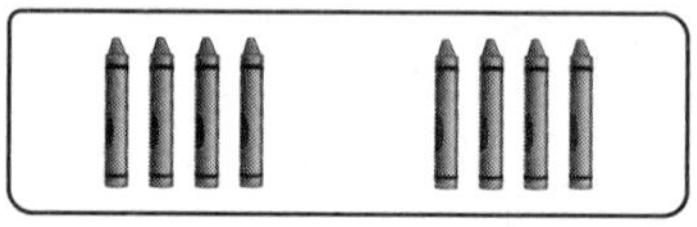
- 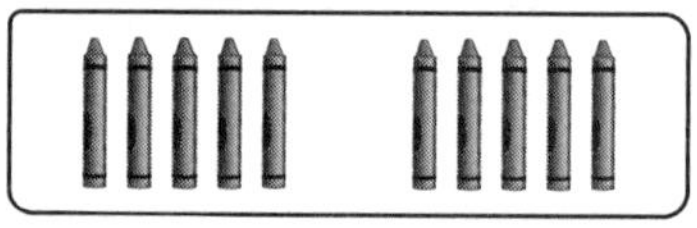

6 Draw tally marks to show the number ten.

Illegal to Copy

Count and Cover the Clock

Play *Count and Cover the Clock* with a partner. Each player needs 12 small tokens or centimeter cubes. Each pair of players needs two dice and the game board. In turn, each player rolls two dice and counts the number of dots. The player covers the number on the clock that equals the number of dots shown on the dice. Players pass if they roll a number that is already covered. To begin, players cover the number 1. The winner is the first player to cover all numbers on the clock.

Player 1

Player 2

Extension

Name: ______________________________

Standard 1.2(A) – **Unit 1**

Math Challenge

Sam shows his teacher the number 5 using fingers on two hands. Complete the chart to show the number of fingers Sam could have used.

Left Hand	Right Hand

Reflection on My Learning

Look at the domino.

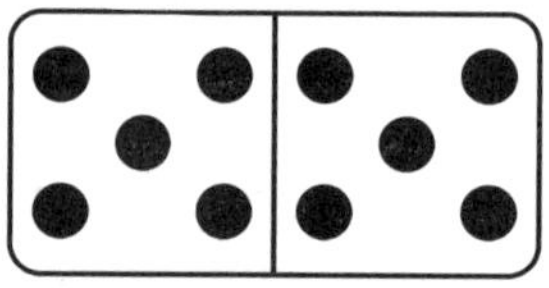

How can you tell the number of dots without counting each dot?

____

____

Reflection on Critical Thinking

Circle the traits you used most often in this unit.

I show ______________________ when I ______________________.

Illegal to Copy

Name: ______________________________ **Assessment**

Unit 1 – Standard 1.2(A) **Concept Check**

1 Write the numbers shown on the dice.

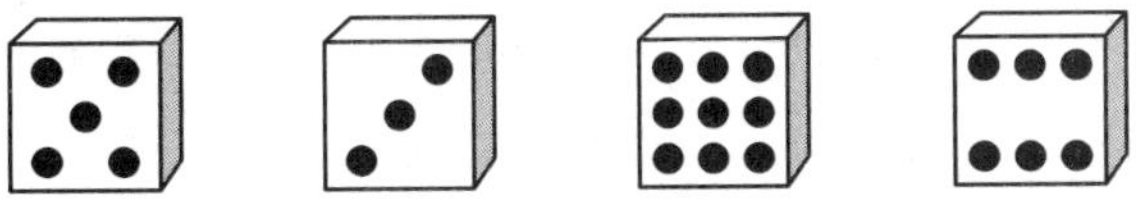

_____ _____ _____ _____

2 Theo turns over a domino with a total of six dots.

Circle Theo's domino.

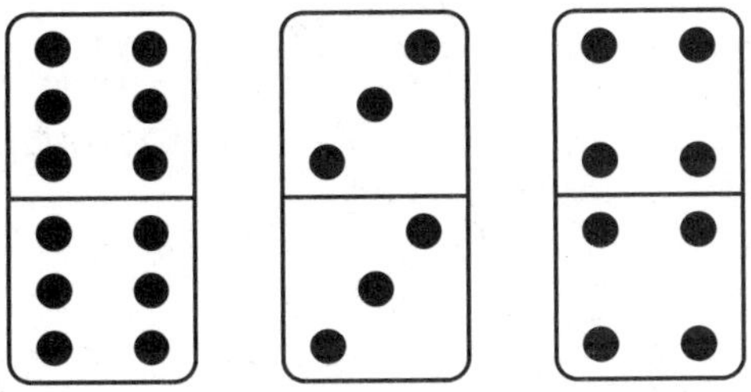

3 Draw a line to match each ten frame to the number word.

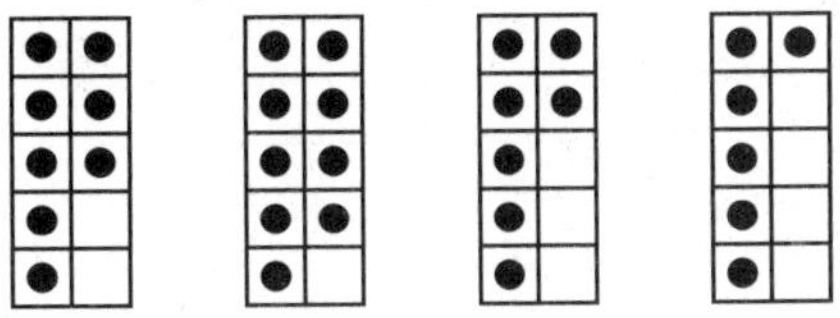

six eight nine seven

4 Al eats peas for dinner.

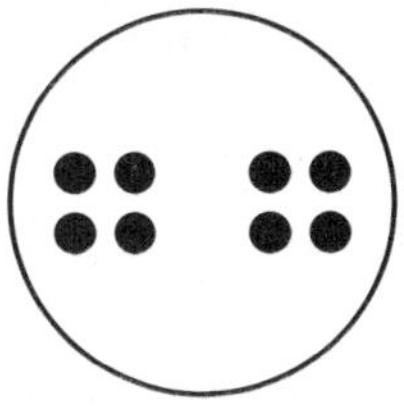

How many peas are on Al's plate?

Answer ______________________

5 Cleo collects marbles. She keeps her marbles in a bag.

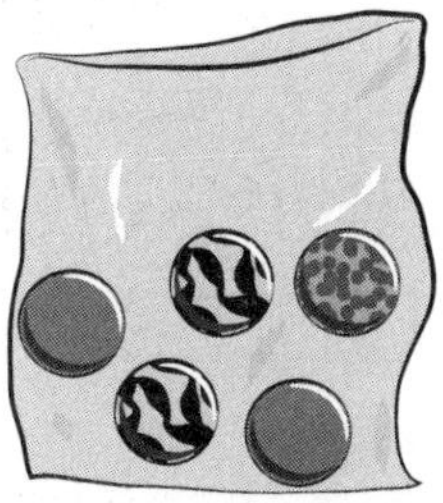

How many marbles are in Cleo's bag?

- ⬭ 6
- ⬭ 5
- ⬭ 9

6 How many fingers are up?

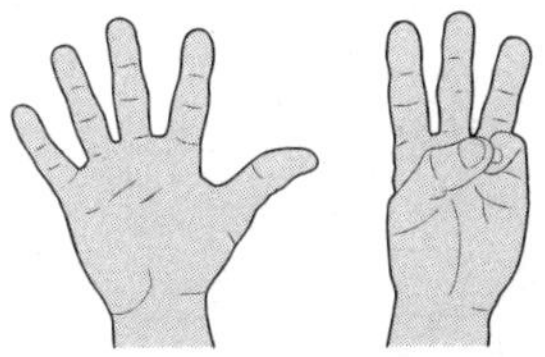

Answer ______________________

Assessment

Name: ____________________

Concept Check

Standard 1.2(A) – **Unit 1**

7 Maggie's family plays games. This week they played three games. One game used dice. One game used cards. One game used dominoes.

Show how these numbers could look in each game.

10 | 9 | 5

dice game | card game | domino game

8 Jackson keeps score in a game. He makes tally marks to show the score. What is the score in the game? Write the numbers.

__________ __________

9 Mario is 9 years old. Box the ten frame that shows Mario's age.

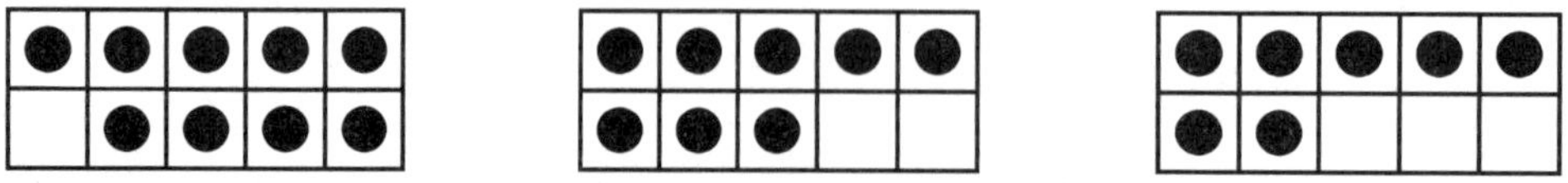

Illegal to Copy

Name: ____________________

Getting Started

Unit 2 – Standard 1.2(B)

Unit 2: Compose and Decompose Numbers to 120

TEKS LEARNING TARGETS

- I can explain the value of a digit as determined by its location in a number such as ones, tens, and hundreds.
- I can combine parts or smaller values to form a number.
- I can break a number into smaller parts or smaller values.
- I can compose and decompose a number in more than one way.

Focus for 9 Traits of Critical Thinking™

Adapt: *I adjust my actions and strategies to accomplish tasks.*

Have you ever taken more than one path to get to a destination such as to the store or park? How can the idea of more than one way to reach a solution apply to numbers?

____

____

Create: *I use my knowledge and imagination to express new and innovative ideas.*

A globe is a model that is made to help people understand the Earth. What model have you used in math that helped you better understand a concept?

____

____

Name: ____________________

Concept Exploration

____________   ____________

____________ tens   ____________ ones

____________   ____________

____________ tens   ____________ ones

How did this activity help you practice flexible thinking?

____

____

Is the ten frame a strategy that helps you demonstrate your learning? Explain how this strategy might be improved.

____

____

Illegal to Copy

Instruction

Vocabulary Mastery

compose	**hundreds**	**ones**	**tens**
decompose	**number**	**place value**	**zero**
digit	**numeral**		

34

Look at this number.

Use words, pictures, or numbers to show 2 ways to represent the number 34.

What is another way you can use pictures to represent the number 34?

____

____

Did your model of the number look the same as your classmates? How was it different?

____

____

113

1 hundred | 1 ten | 3 ones

118

_____ **hundred** _____ **ten** _____ **ones**

8 tens and 6 ones is the same as 86.

5 tens and 3 ones is the same as

______________________________.

71 is 7 tens and 1 one.

OR

71 is 6 tens and 11 ones.

The place the digit is in tells you the value of the number.

The different place values can be combined to make a new number.

Numbers can be formed in more than one way.

Try It!

1) Show the number 39.

How many tens? _________

How many ones? _________

Try It!

2)

Write the number. _________

How many tens? _________

How many ones? _________

Illegal to Copy

Name: ______________________________

Instruction

Unit 2 – Standard 1.2(B)

Concept Application

1 Devon has 112 blocks. Circle the blocks that show the value of the 2 in 112.

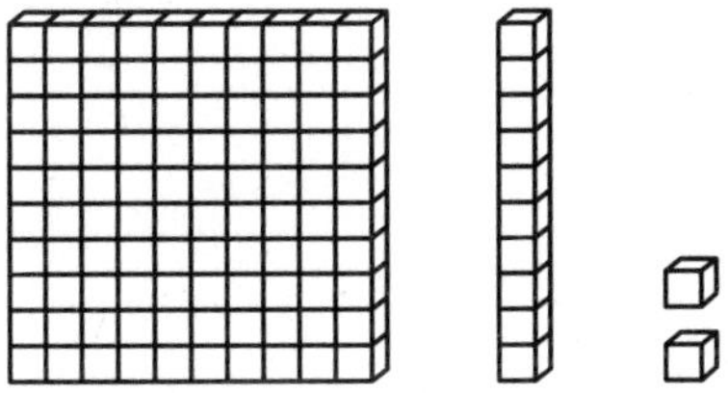

Answer ______________________

2 Coach Rice puts 10 balls in each bucket. How many balls does Coach Rice have in all?

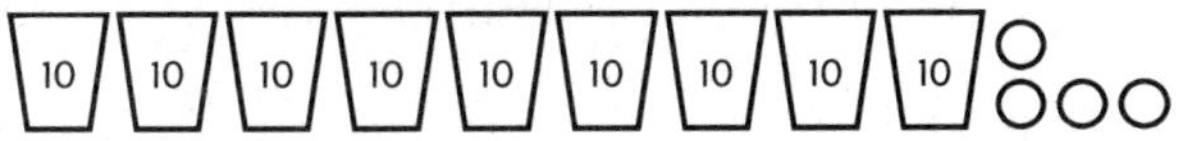

Answer ______________________

3 If Coach Rice adds 10 more balls in another bucket, how many balls will Coach Rice have?

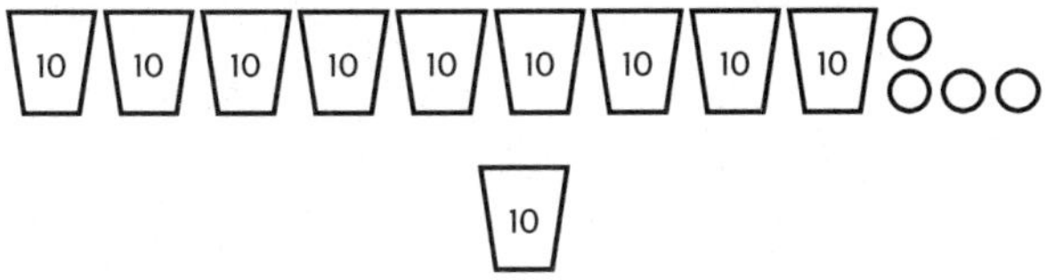

Answer ______________________

4 Lucy makes bracelets. She puts 10 beads on each bracelet.

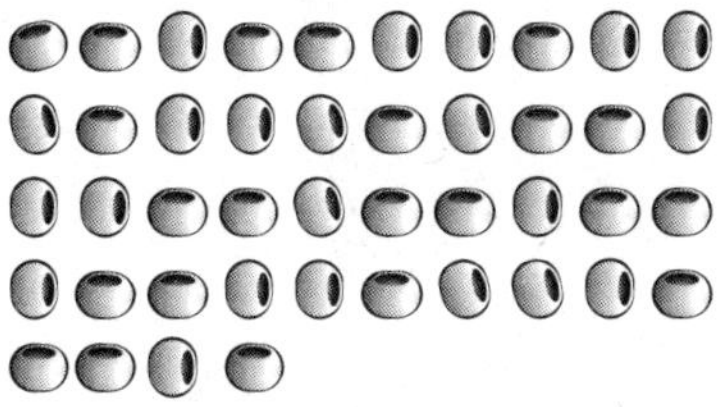

How many bracelets can Lucy make?

Answer ______________________

How many beads are not used?

Answer ______________________

5 Write the number shown as tens and ones.

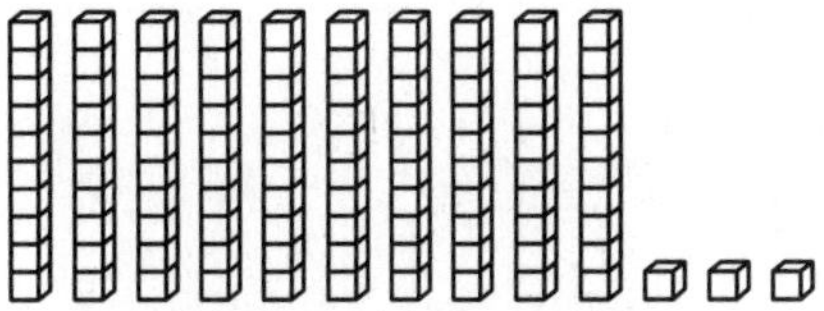

tens	ones

Write the number as hundreds, tens, and ones.

hundreds	tens	ones

1 Mrs. Brown's class collected 86 cans to recycle.

Which picture represents 86?

- ○ 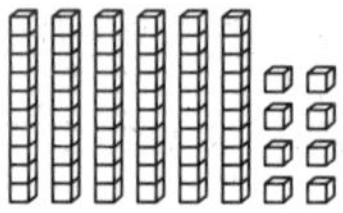
- ○ 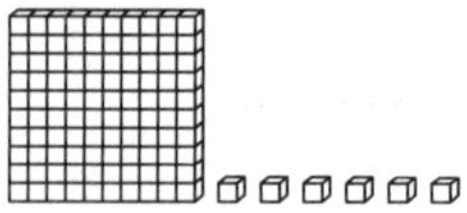
- ○ 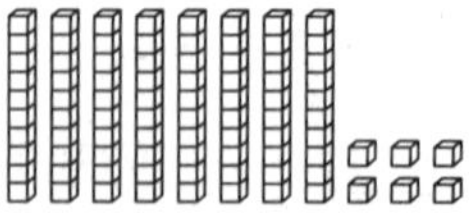

2 Dylan has 7 tens and 3 ones.

Draw a model of Dylan's number.

Write Dylan's number.

Answer ____________________

3

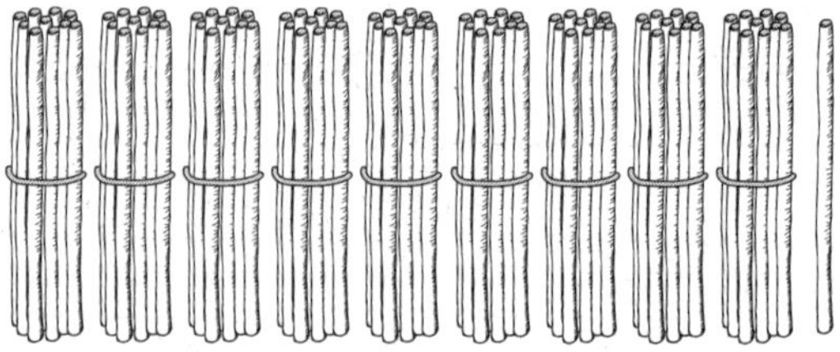

Which number tells how many straws in all?

- ○ 101
- ○ 90
- ○ 91

4 Lamar wants to see how many jelly beans he has.

Fill in the blanks to help Lamar count his jelly beans.

_____ tens and _____ ones

How many does Lamar have?

Answer ____________________

5 Look at the model.

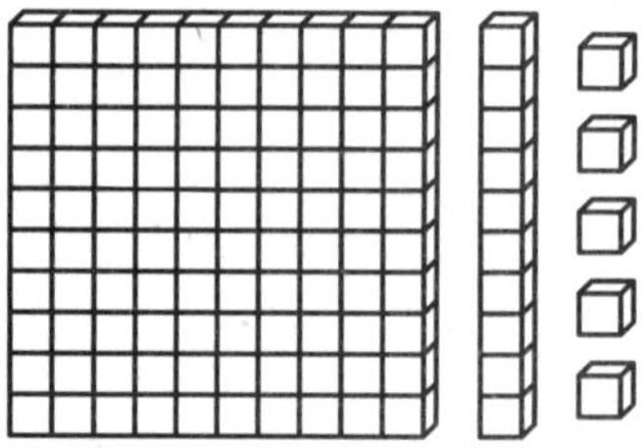

Circle all the ways to represent the number.

115

1 hundred 1 ten 5 ones

1 hundred 0 tens 15 ones

105

Illegal to Copy

Name: ____________________

Slip and Slide

Play *Slip and Slide* with a friend. Groups need 1 game board and 1 die or number cube. Each player needs a game token. The first player rolls the die or number cube and moves that number of spaces along the icy path. Players use the key to move forward, move backward, or stay in place. The first player to reach the ocean is the winner.

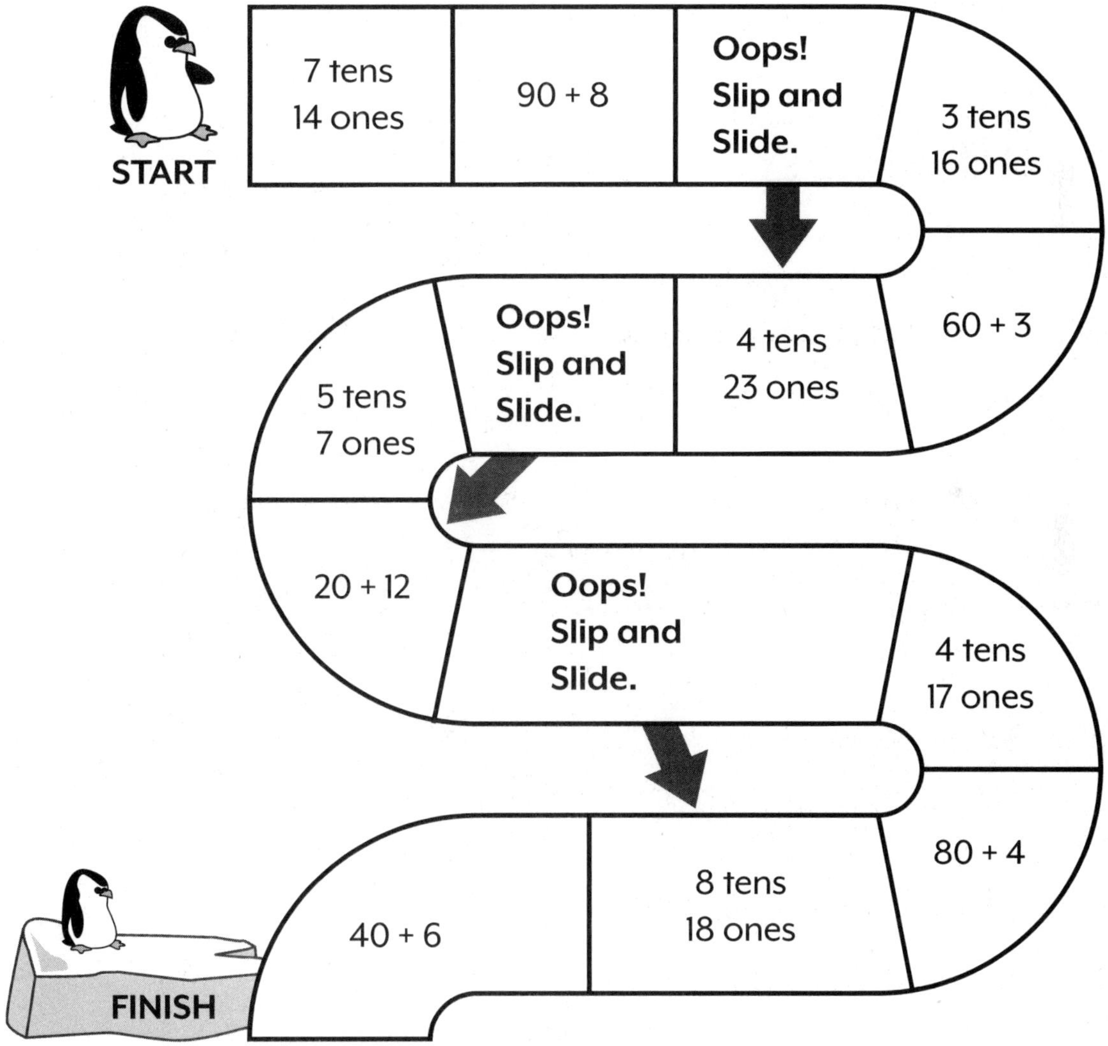

Key

If the space represents ...	46	32	98	63	84	57
... the player	moves 1 space forward	moves 1 space back	moves 2 spaces forward	moves 2 spaces back	stays in place	moves back to START

Name: ____________________

Math Challenge

Watson wants to decompose the number below in more than one way.

What are three ways Watson can decompose this number?

62

Reflection on My Learning

Look at the number.

107

Tell why the number 0 is important.

____

____

Reflection on Critical Thinking

Circle the traits you used most often in this unit.

I show ____________________ when I ____________________ .

Illegal to Copy

Name: ______________________________

Assessment

Unit 2 – Standard 1.2(B)

Concept Check

1 Corey has 115 pennies. Which picture shows 115?

- ○ 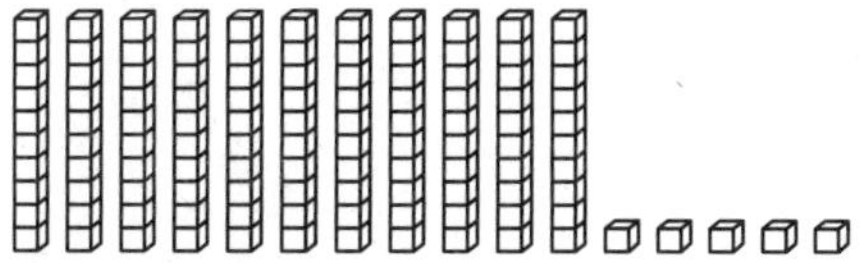
- ○ 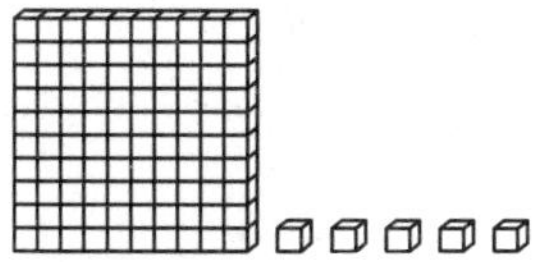
- ○ 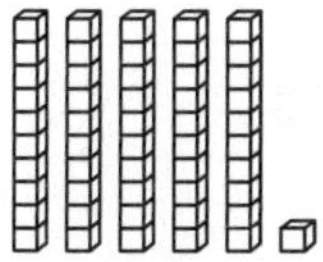

2 Look at the picture.

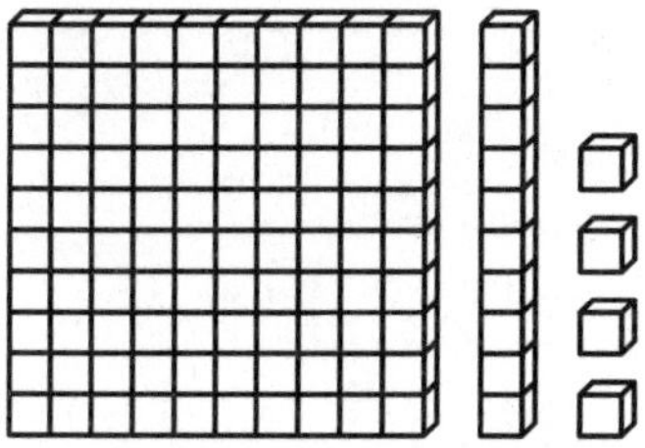

What is another way of showing the same number?

- ○ 10014
- ○ 1 hundred 14 tens 0 ones
- ○ 1 hundred 1 ten 4 ones

3 Look at the number and fill in the blanks.

92

____ hundreds ____ tens ____ ones

4 Brad has 113 blocks. Circle the blocks that show the value of the 3 in 113.

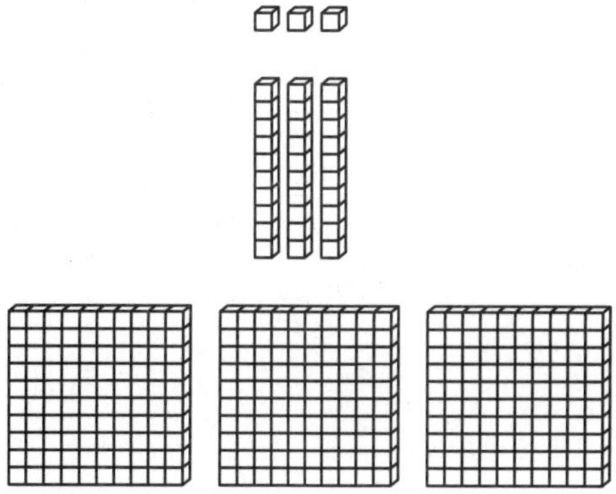

5 Choose the number that BEST represents the picture.

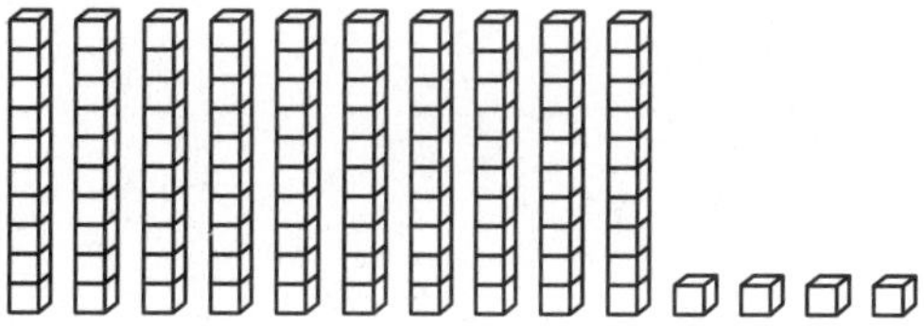

- ○ 114
- ○ 104
- ○ 94

6 Circle the picture that shows the number 101.

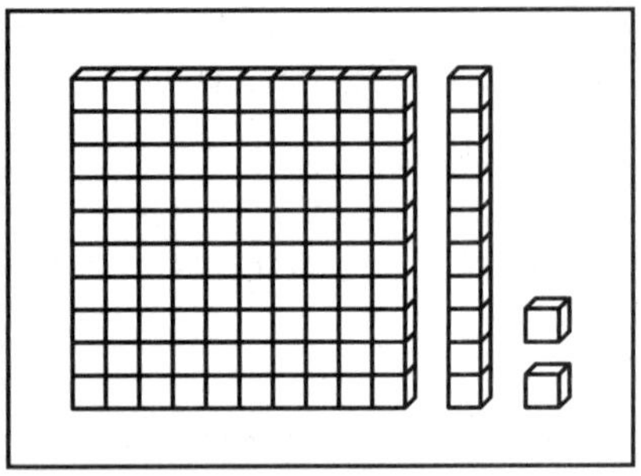

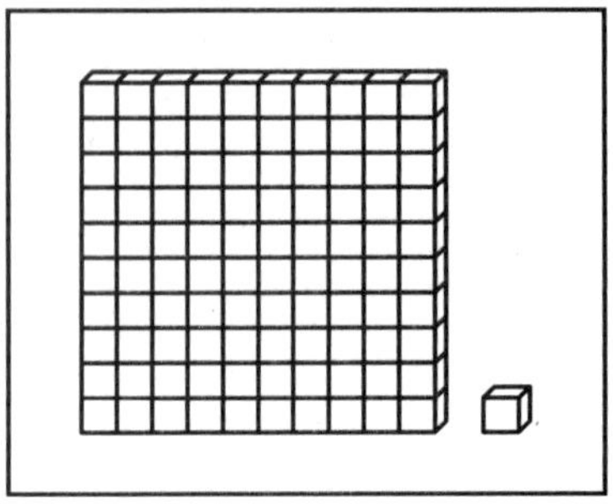

7 Circle True or False.

46 is 4 tens and 6 ones. It is also 2 tens and 21 ones.

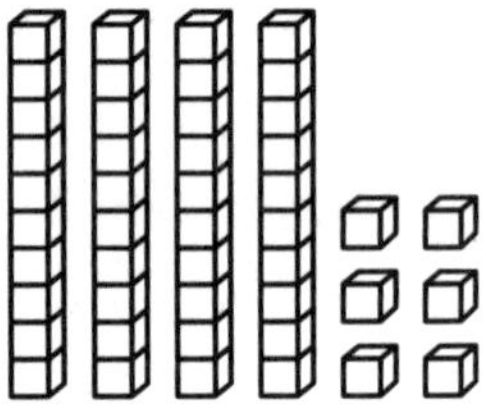

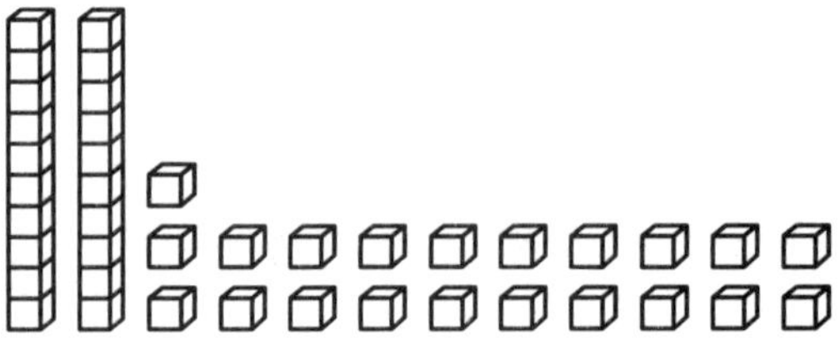

True False

8 Draw a picture of 118.

Name: ______________________________

Unit 3 – Standard 1.2(C)

Getting Started

Unit 3: Represent Numbers to 120 in Different Forms

TEKS LEARNING TARGETS

- I can explain the value of a digit by using its location in a number such as ones, tens, and hundreds.
- I can represent a number in multiple ways using word form, standard form, expanded form, or models.

Focus for 9 Traits of Critical Thinking™

Communicate: *I use clear language to express my ideas and to share information.*

Think about words that are different but have the same meaning. Can you give an example?

____

____

Inquire: *I seek information that excites my curiosity and inspires my learning.*

Why is it important to understand place value?

____

____

Instruction

Name: ______________________________

Standard 1.2(C) – **Unit 3**

Concept Exploration

1 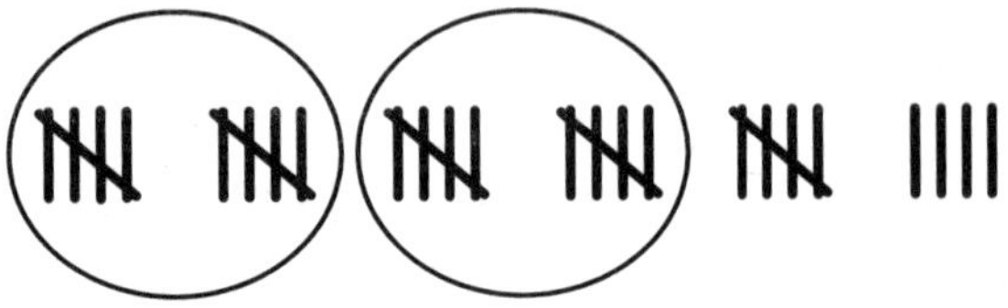

Standard Form:

____

Expanded Form:

______ tens ______ ones

______ + ______

2 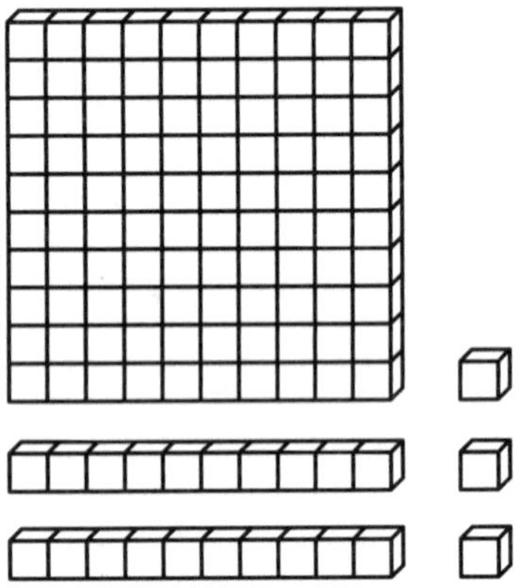

Standard Form:

____

Expanded Form:

______ hundreds ______ tens ______ ones

______ + ______ + ______

3 Draw a picture to show the number 53.

How is this number written in expanded form?

Answer ____________________

What questions do you have about representing a number in different ways?

____

____

Illegal to Copy

Name: ______________________________

Instruction

Unit 3 – Standard 1.2(C)

Vocabulary Mastery

compose	**expanded form**	**numeral**	**standard form**
decompose	**hundreds**	**ones**	**tens**
digit	**number**	**place value**	**zero**

Draw a line to match each word to the example.

standard form	100 + 10 + 3
hundreds	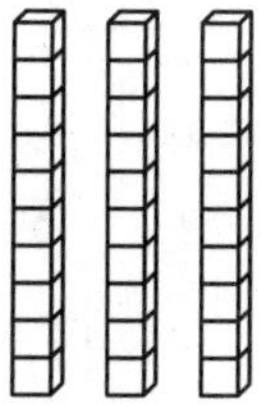
tens	78
expanded form	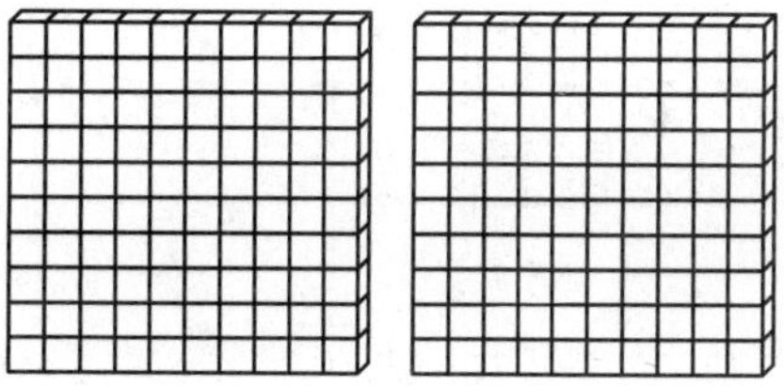
ones	

Why is it helpful to express numbers in different forms?

____

____

How is the expanded form of a number like the standard form? How is it different?

____

____

Hundreds	Tens	Ones
1	1	1

This is the same number as:

100 + 10 + 1

Hundreds	Tens	Ones
1	1	8

Write the expanded form of the number.

Answer ______

Hundreds	Tens	Ones
1	0	4

Write the expanded form of the number:

Answer ______

Expanded form is a way to write a number to show the place value of each digit.

Zero is very important in place value. It tells you that the digit in that place value is 0. The number 120 means there are 1 hundred 2 tens and 0 ones.

Try It!

1) Write the expanded form of 85.

______

Try It!

2) Write the expanded form of 109.

______

Name: ______________________________

Unit 3 – Standard 1.2(C)

Instruction

Concept Application

1 Look at the place value chart. What is the standard form of this number?

Hundreds	Tens	Ones
1	2	0

- ⬭ 10020
- ⬭ 100 + 20 + 0
- ⬭ 120

2 Circle the numbers that are written in standard form.

108	30 + 9
11 tens, 5 ones	74
22	40 + 1
fifty-seven	76

3 Complete the chart.

97	
Expanded Form	
Word Form	

4 Anne has 36 erasers.

How is this number written in expanded form?

________ + ________

5 Complete the chart.

Standard Form	Expanded Form	Picture
		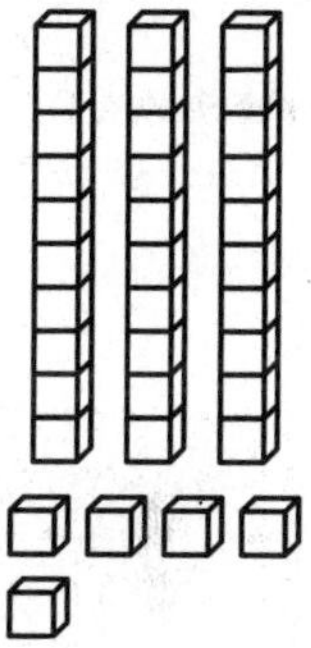

6 Shad has 87 blocks.

Complete the blanks for Shad's number.

________ tens + ________ ones

Write the number in word form.

____

1 Circle the numbers that are written in expanded form.

115

100 + 10 + 1

100 + 20 + 1

One hundred eighteen

119

60 + 2

2 What is the expanded form of 104?

- ⬭ One hundred four
- ⬭ 100 + 40 + 0
- ⬭ 100 + 00 + 4

3 What is the standard form of this number?

Hundreds	Tens	Ones
	9	9

- ⬭ 9
- ⬭ 99
- ⬭ 109

4 What is the standard form for the number shown?

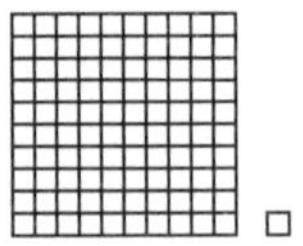

- ⬭ 110
- ⬭ 10
- ⬭ 101

5 Draw lines to match the standard form and the expanded form of each number.

400 + 70 + 2	541
67	980
900 + 80 + 0	60 + 7
500 + 40 + 1	472

6 Circle sets of 10. Write the number of butterflies.

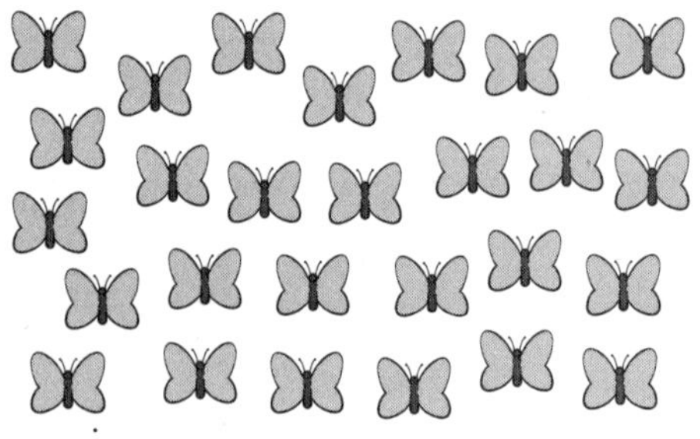

Answer ______________________

Write the number in expanded form.

____

Number Race

Play *Number Race* with a partner. Take turns rolling a number cube and moving your token the number of spaces rolled. After landing on a space, read the number in the space and say the number of tens and ones. Then say the number as a sum of a tens number and ones. For example, if you land on 14 say "fourteen; 1 ten 4 ones; 10 + 4." If you are correct, stay on the space. If you are not correct, go back to "Start." The first player to land on "Finish" wins.

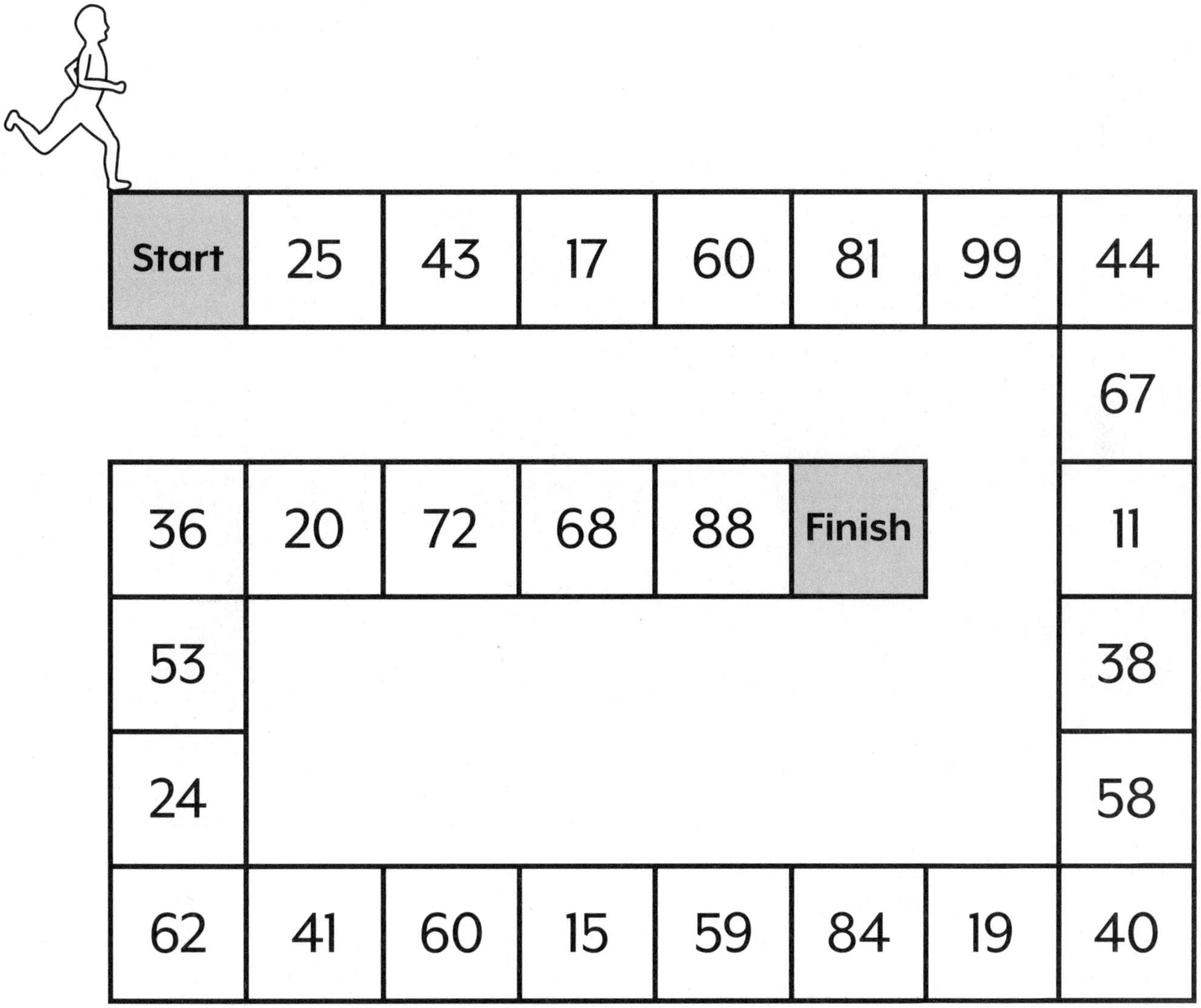

Extension

Name: ______________________________

Standard 1.2(C) – **Unit 3**

Math Challenge

Collette says that the expanded form of 117 is 10017.

Is Collette correct? ______________________________

Use words or pictures to explain your answer.

Reflection on My Learning

Use your words to explain the expanded form of a number.

____

____

Reflection on Critical Thinking

Circle the traits you used most often in this unit.

I show ______________________ when I ______________________.

Illegal to Copy

Name: ______________________

Assessment

Unit 3 – Standard 1.2(C)

Concept Check

1 Choose the number that BEST represents the picture.

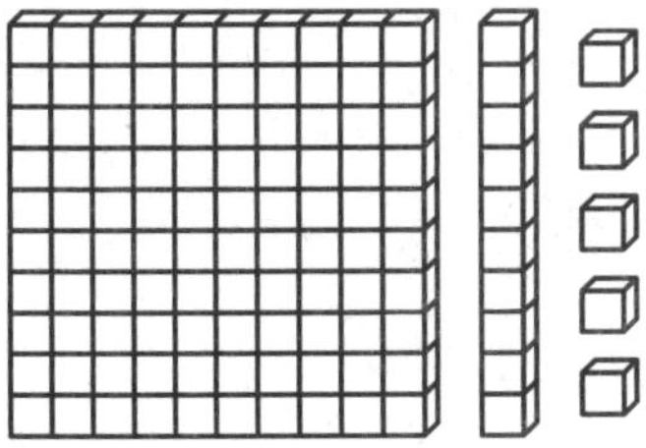

- ⬭ 115
- ⬭ 105
- ⬭ 51

2 Adelie has 92 pennies.

How is this number written in expanded form?

____

3 A number is shown using bundles of 10 sticks.

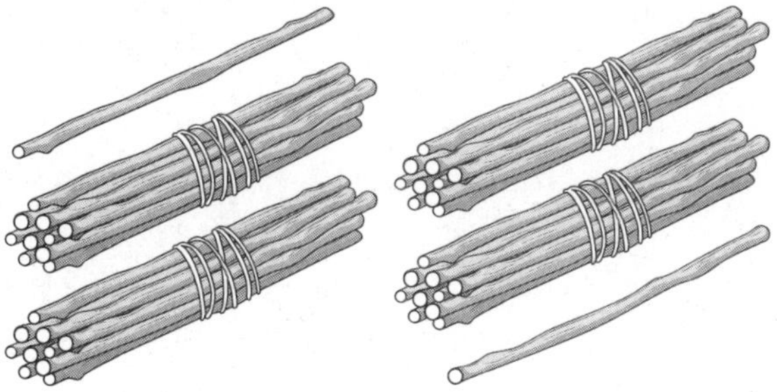

Which number represents the expanded form of the number of objects?

- ⬭ 4 + 2
- ⬭ 40 + 2
- ⬭ 400 + 0 + 2

4 What is the standard form of this number?

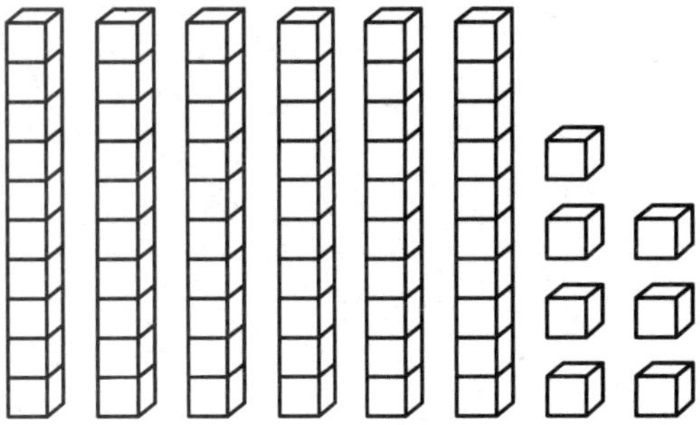

- ⬭ 6 tens + 7 ones
- ⬭ sixty-seven
- ⬭ 67

5 Look at the picture.

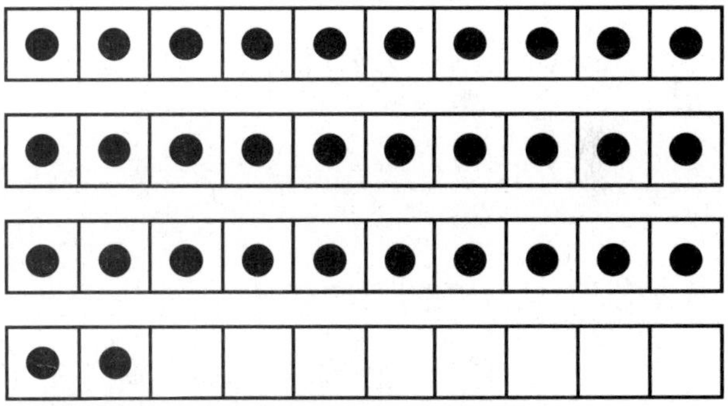

How many dots are there?

____

Write the expanded form of the number.

____

Name: ______________________________

Concept Check

6 Draw a line to match each number in standard form to its expanded form.

52	100 + 0 + 7
115	50 + 2
107	100 + 10 + 0
110	100 + 10 + 5

7 Diana says the expanded form of 111 is 100 + 10 + 0.

Is Diana correct? ______________________________

Use words or pictures to explain your answer.

8 Look at the picture.

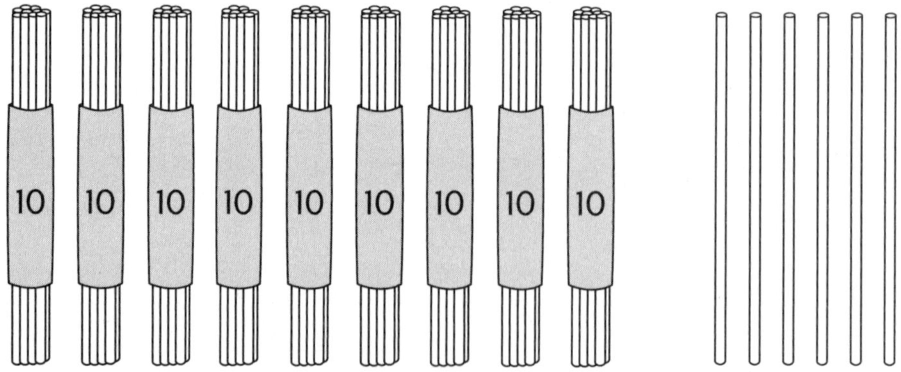

Write the number in expanded form.

____

Illegal to Copy

Name: ______________________________

Getting Started

Unit 4: Generate Numbers to 120

TEKS LEARNING TARGETS

- I can generate a number that is greater than a given number up to 120.
- I can generate a number that is less than a given number up to 120.

Focus for 9 Traits of Critical Thinking™

Examine: *I use a variety of methods to explore and to analyze.*

What do you do when you are not sure about something? How do you figure out the unknown?

____

____

Collaborate: *I work with others to achieve better outcomes.*

How do you use the ideas of others to help you learn? Give an example.

____

____

Instruction

Name: ______________________________

Concept Exploration

Standard 1.2(D) – **Unit 4**

ones	
tens	
hundreds	

What if the digits in your number are all the same? Does that change the place value of the digits? Explain your answer.

____

____

During the activity, did you offer your partner any suggestions? Did your suggestions help in a positive way?

____

____

Illegal to Copy

Name: ______________________________

Unit 4 – Standard 1.2(D)

Instruction

Vocabulary Mastery

compare	**greater than**	**less than**	**place value**
equal	**hundreds**	**ones**	**tens**

Choose between *greater than*, *less than*, or *equal* and complete the graphic organizer.

Word: ______________________________

What does the word mean?	Draw a picture of the word.
Use the word in a sentence.	Write a word that has the same meaning.

Where did you get the information to complete your graphic organizer correctly?

____

____

How does using the vocabulary words during group work help you understand the words better?

____

____

Instruction

Name: ____________________

Concept Development

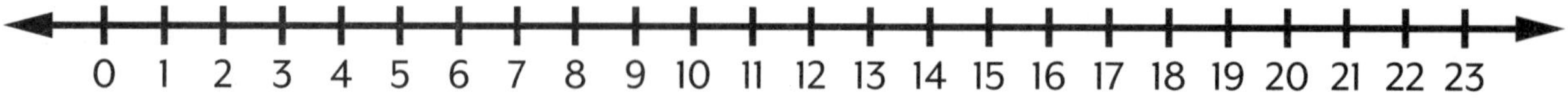

Look at the number line above.

What are 5 numbers on this number line that are greater than 18?

____

As you move right on the number line, the numbers grow larger. Numbers greater than 18 are to the right of 18 on the number line.

What are 5 numbers on this number line that are less than 18?

____

As you move left on the number line, the numbers grow smaller. Numbers less than 18 are to the left of 18 on the number line.

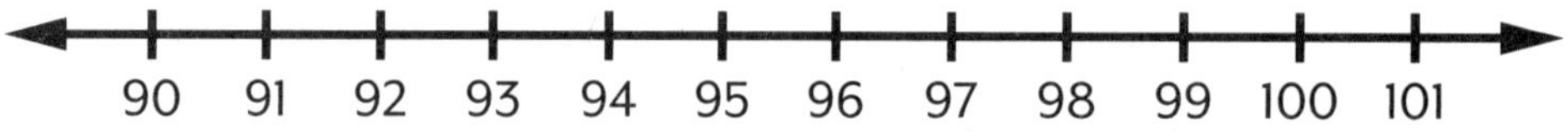

Look at the number line above.

What numbers on this number line are greater than 96?

____

100 is greater than 99. In the set of whole numbers, a number with 3 digits is always larger than a number with 2 digits.

Try It!

1) Picture a number line in your mind.

What is a number that is greater than 75?

____

Try It!

2) Picture a number line in your mind.

What is a number that is less than 50?

____

Illegal to Copy

1 Which number is less than 76?

- ⊂⊃ 86
- ⊂⊃ 72
- ⊂⊃ 77

2 Sue has 118 pennies. Kim has 109 pennies. Nam has 115 pennies.

Who has a number of pennies that is less than 110?

- ⊂⊃ Sue
- ⊂⊃ Kim
- ⊂⊃ Nam

3 Look at the numbers in the box.

54	95	40	26
87	23	11	44

Circle the numbers with more than 4 tens.

Put an X on the numbers with less than 4 ones.

4 Farmer Dale picked these apples from his tree.

Write a number that is greater than his number of apples.

____

5 Build 37 with base 10 blocks. Use blocks to complete.

1 more than 37 is ____________.

Name a number less than 37.

____

6 Zeke has 88 baseball cards. Tim has a greater number of cards than Zeke.

Circle the number that tells how many cards Tim might have.

45 88 92

Instruction

Name: ____________________

Concept Practice

Standard 1.2(D) – **Unit 4**

1 Adam buys 50 pieces of gum. Lex buys less gum than Adam.

Box the numbers that show how many pieces of gum Lex might have.

51 46 22 55

2 Lin has 87 rocks. Kamisha has 97 rocks. Keetay has 99 rocks.

Who has a number of rocks that is greater than 98?

- Lin
- Kamisha
- Keetay

3 Write a number that is less than the number shown by the base 10 blocks.

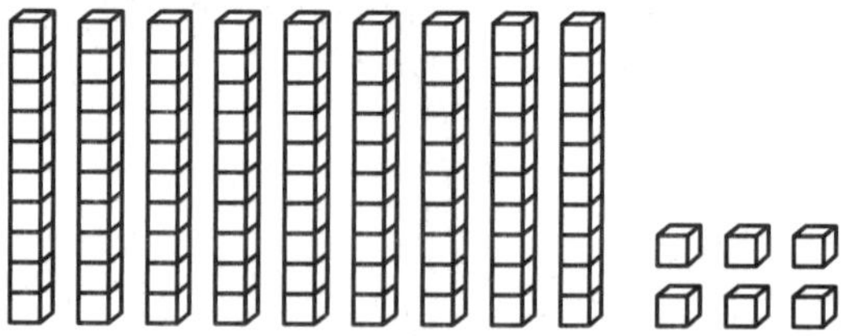

____

4 Look at the number line below.

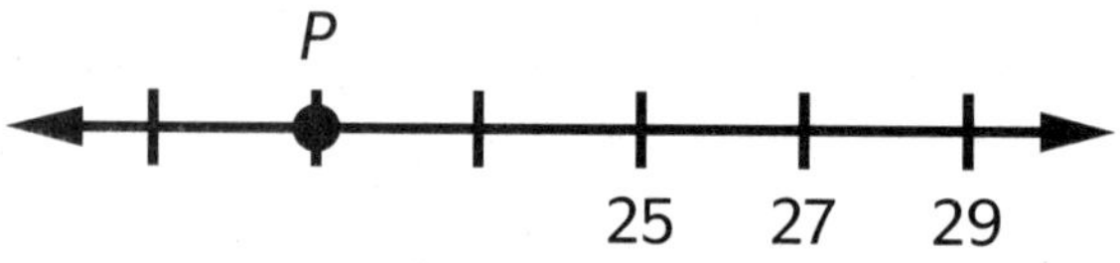

Circle the correct answer.

P is less than 25.

P is greater than 25.

5 Look at the set of blocks.

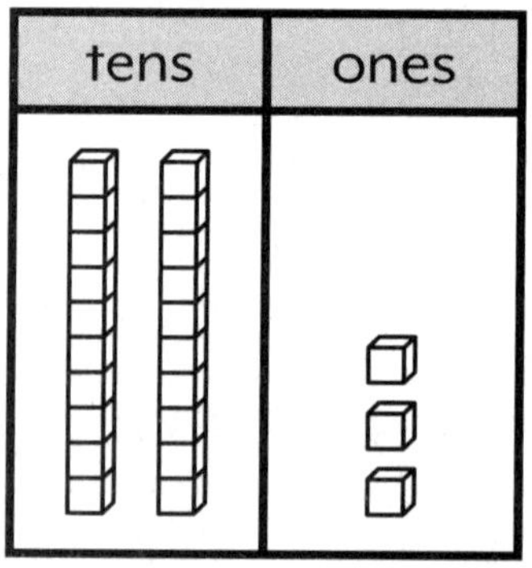

Write the number of blocks on the line.

____

Write a number that is greater than the number of blocks.

____

Write a number that is less than the number of blocks.

____

Illegal to Copy

Straight Six

Play *Straight Six* with a partner. Each pair of players needs a game board. Each player needs 25 counters (a different color for each player) and two dice (0–9 if available). Each player rolls two dice and states a two-digit number. Players compare numbers. The person with the greater number places a colored counter on the game board. Play continues until one player has six counters in a row going across, up, down, or diagonally.

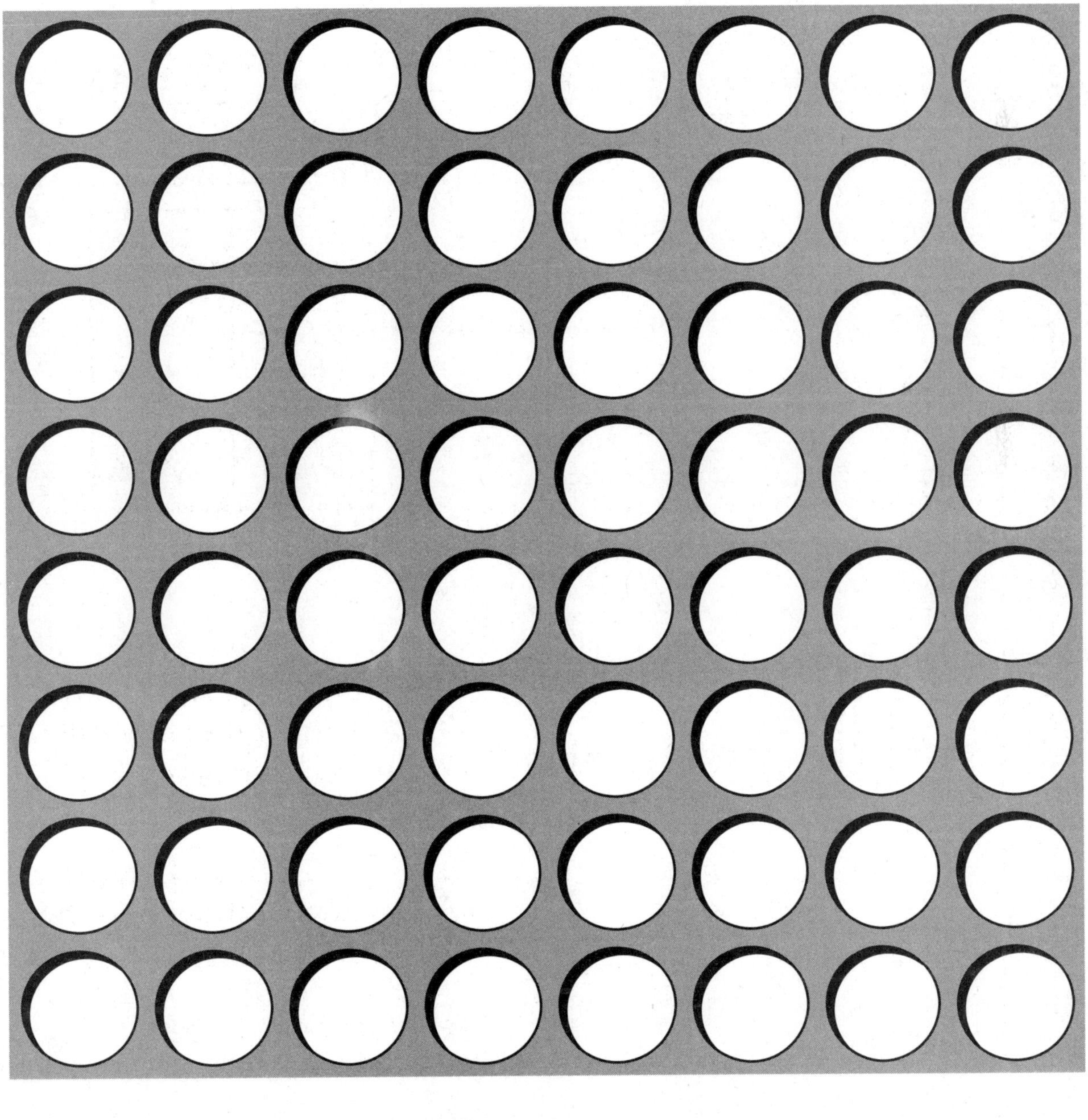

Extension

Name: ______________________________

Standard 1.2(D) – **Unit 4**

Math Challenge

Use the clues to find the number.

- The number is greater than 60.
- The number is less than 70.
- The digit in the tens place is one less than the digit in the ones place.

Write the number on the soccer shirt.

Reflection on My Learning

Mr. Miller's first-grade class has a marble jar. There are 45 marbles in the jar. Mrs. Gray also has a marble jar. Her jar has a number of marbles with less tens but more ones than Mr. Miller's jar. How many marbles could be in Mrs. Gray's jar?

Answer ______________________________

Use numbers, words, or pictures to explain your answer.

Reflection on Critical Thinking

Circle the traits you used most often in this unit.

I show ______________________________ when I ______________________________.

Illegal to Copy

Name: ______________________________

Assessment

Unit 4 – Standard 1.2(D)

Concept Check

1 The picture shows bundles of 10 sticks and single sticks.

Circle the numbers that are greater than the number of objects shown.

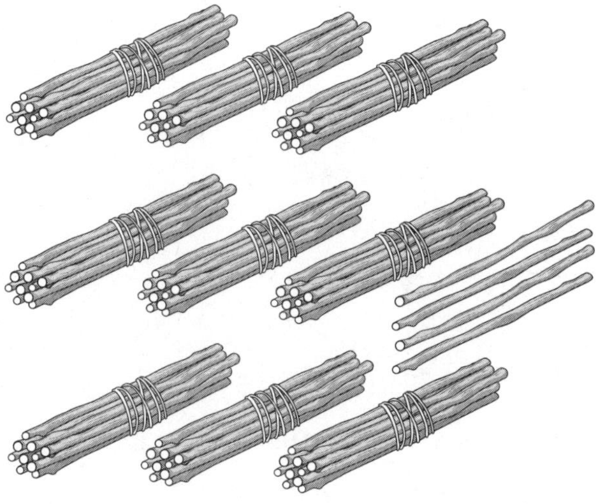

94 99 120

2 Rosa is making a necklace with cereal.

She needs more cereal pieces to make the necklace.

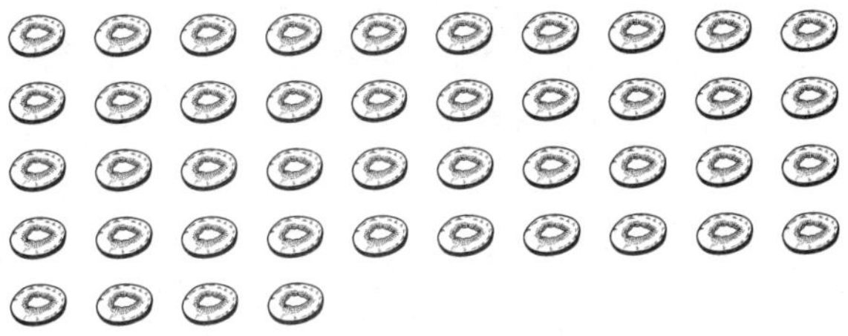

Circle the number that would give Rosa a greater number of pieces.

35 18 49

3 Mary has 119 dolls.

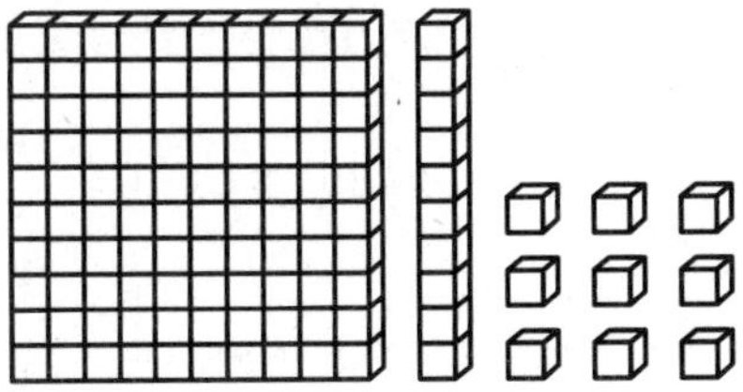

What are two numbers that are less than 119?

Answer______________________

4 Xavier has 102 stickers. Bill has more stickers than Xavier.

How many stickers might Bill have?

Answer______________________

5 Which number is less than the number shown?

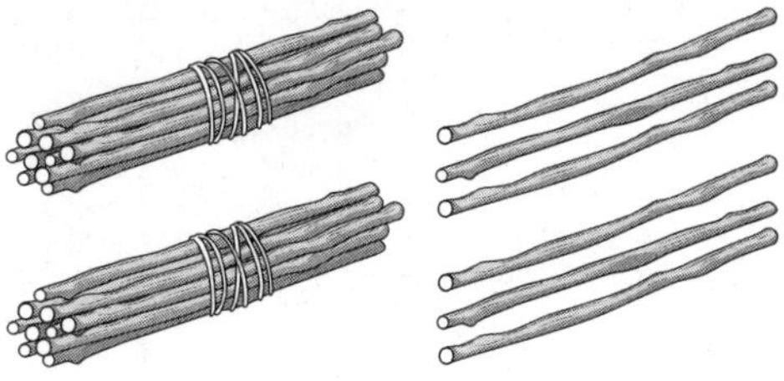

- ⬭ 36
- ⬭ 26
- ⬭ 20

6 Look at Tanner's blocks.

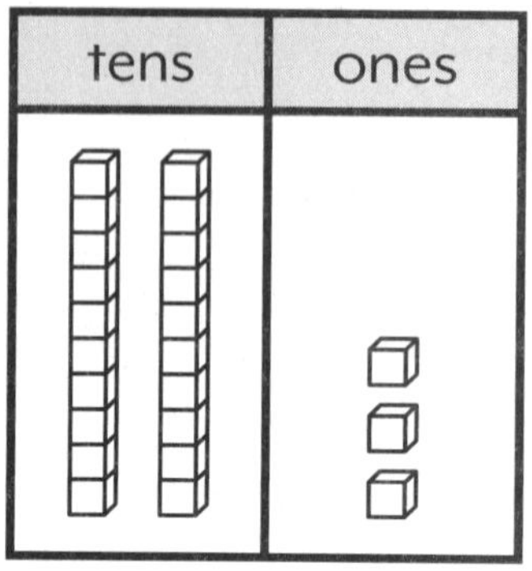

What is a number that is less than Tanner's number of blocks?

Answer______________________

What is a number that is greater than Tanner's number of blocks?

Answer______________________

---

7 Adrian has 24 grapes. Ben has 18 grapes. Leo has a greater number of grapes than Adrian.

Circle the number of grapes Leo might have.

17 21 27

How do you know?

____

Name: ______________________________

Unit 5 – Standard 1.2(E)

Getting Started

Unit 5: Compare Numbers to 120

TEKS LEARNING TARGETS

- I can use place value to tell if a number is greater than a given number up to 120.
- I can use comparative language including *greater than*, *less than*, and *equal to*.
- I can use place value to tell if a number is less than a given number up to 120.

Focus for 9 Traits of Critical Thinking™

Strive: *I use effort and determination to focus on challenging tasks.*

What clues do you use to decide if a number is greater than another number? Do you use the same strategy to decide if a number is less?

____

____

Reflect: *I review my thoughts and experiences to guide my actions.*

What are some key points to remember about place value? Do those points help you compare numbers?

____

____

Instruction

Name: ______________________

Concept Exploration

Standard 1.2(E) – **Unit 5**

What is a good strategy to use when counting large numbers of objects?

____

____

When comparing numbers, what do you find most challenging?

____

____

compare	**greater than**	**less than**	**place value**
equal	**hundreds**	**ones**	**tens**

When you compare numbers, you think about how they are alike and how they are different. In the space below, create a word web of words that are used to compare numbers.

Comparing Numbers

What strategy do you use to help you learn the different words that have the same meaning?

____

____

What strategy do you use to make sure that you are using the correct words to compare numbers?

____

____

Instruction

Name: ______________________________

Concept Development

Standard 1.2(E) – **Unit 5**

See the example.

101 is more than 98.

Circle the correct answer.

is more than

73 is equal to 78

is less than

62 is less than 99.

62 is fewer than 99.

47 is greater than 38.

47 is more than 38.

Circle the words that make the comparison true.

109 ______________ 120

is less than is equal to is fewer than

When you are comparing numbers, you are trying to decide if they are alike or different.

When comparing numbers, there are words that have similar meanings.

Try It!

1) Draw a model that is equal to 35.

Try It!

2) Circle all the numbers that are less than 57.

49 63

23 58 120

18 55

Illegal to Copy

Name: ______________________________

Instruction

Unit 5 – Standard 1.2(E)

Concept Application

1 Look at the number of stars in set A and set B.

Circle the statement that tells about the pictures.

Set A is greater than set B.

Set A is less than set B.

Set A is equal to set B.

2 Tony has 35 football cards.
Clay has 49.

Finish the sentence to make the statement true.

________________ has more

cards than ________________.

3 Use cubes to build each number.
Circle the words to make the sentence true.

35 ________________ 42

is greater than   is less than

4 Look at the numbers.

119   118

Write a true sentence to compare the numbers.

____

____

5 Don counts his pennies.
He puts his pennies in stacks of 10.
He has some left over.

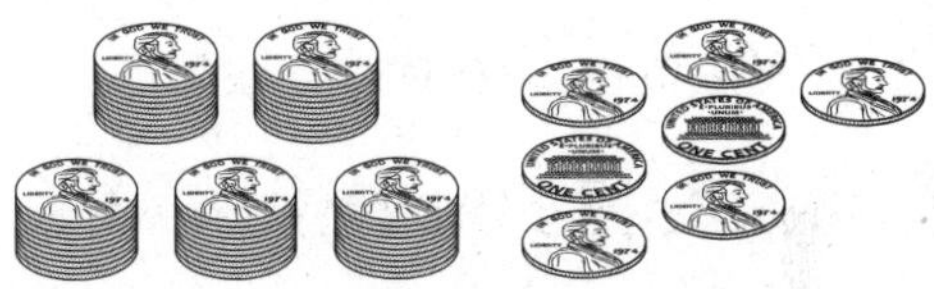

How many pennies does Don have?

____

Darla has 57 pennies.

Compare the amounts and circle the correct answer.

Darla has more pennies than Don.

Darla has less pennies than Don.

Darla and Don have the same number of pennies.

Instruction

Name: ____________________

Concept Practice

Standard 1.2(E) – **Unit 5**

1 Ric has 57 dimes.
Daisy has 63 dimes.
Ric has less money than Daisy.

Circle all the words that mean the same as less money.

fewer dimes

a smaller amount

more money

2 Frieda has 44 toy cars.
Desiree has 54 toy cars.

Fill in the blank to make the sentence true.

Desiree has ____________________ toy cars than Frieda.

3 Compare the numbers and circle the correct answer.

34 34

34 is greater than 34.

34 is less than 34.

34 is equal to 34.

4 Circle the true statements.

33 is less than 97.

97 is greater than 33.

109 is less than 108.

39 is less than 59.

79 is equal to 97.

67 is less than 76.

5 Each bundle has 10 sticks.
Compare the bundles of sticks.

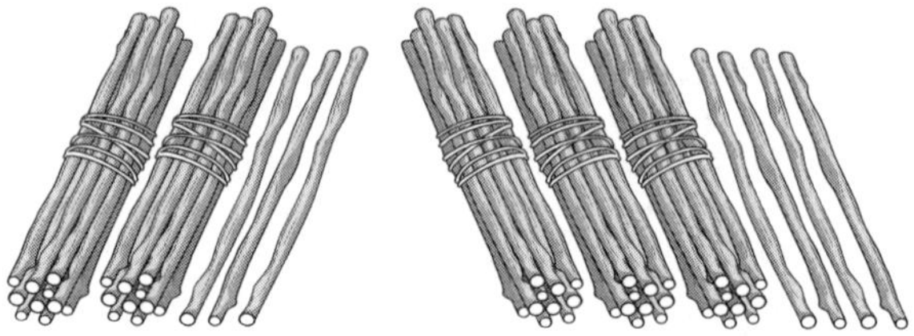

Who has more tens?

Answer ____________________

Who has the greater number of sticks?

Answer ____________________

Eggs in One Basket

Play *Eggs in One Basket* with a partner. In each round, take turns rolling two number cubes. Arrange the number cubes to make the greatest possible two-digit number. The player who makes the greater number in each round colors an egg in the basket. The first player to color all 10 eggs wins. Repeat with new partners for round 2.

Round 1

Player 1 ____________________

Player 2 ____________________

Round 2

Player 1 ____________________

Player 2 ____________________

Extension

Name: ______________________________

Standard 1.2(E) – **Unit 5**

Math Challenge

Liane thinks that 6 tens and 0 ones is less than 5 tens and 9 ones. Rose thinks that 6 tens and 0 ones is greater than 5 tens and 9 ones.

Which student is right? ______________________________
Use pictures and words to explain your thinking.

Reflection on My Learning

Compare the two numbers.

110 **101**

Write a sentence to explain how they compare.

____

Reflection on Critical Thinking

Circle the traits you used most often in this unit.

I show ______________________________ when I ______________________________ .

Illegal to Copy

Name: ______________________________

Assessment

Unit 5 – Standard 1.2(E)

Concept Check

1 Circle the sentences that are true.

18 is less than 19.

100 is more than 99.

17 is equal to 71.

50 is greater than 20.

2 Tamia and Mae picked apples from a tree.

Circle each sentence that is true.

Tamia has a greater number of apples than Mae.

Mae has fewer apples than Tamia.

Mae and Tamia have the same number of apples.

3 How do you know 27 is greater than 22?

- ⬭ There are the same number of tens, but 27 has more ones.
- ⬭ There are the same number of tens, but 27 has fewer ones.
- ⬭ There are the same number of ones, but 27 has more tens.

4 Which number is greater than 46?

- ⬭ 64
- ⬭ 46
- ⬭ 39

5 Write the numbers.

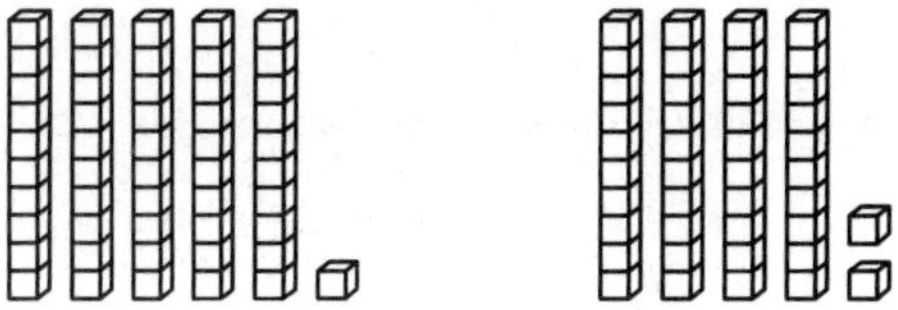

________ ________

Which sentence is true?

- ⬭ A is less than B.
- ⬭ B is less than A.
- ⬭ A is equal to B.

6 Draw base 10 blocks to show each number.

81	38

Write a sentence to compare the numbers.

____

7 Look at the numbers.

45 54 67 110 99

Draw a line under the number that is greater than 100.

Draw a circle around the number that is less than 50.

Place an X on the number that is equal to 67.

8 Kip writes the following sentence.

27 is equal to 72 because they have the same digits.

Is Kip correct? ____________________

Explain your answer.

____

____

Illegal to Copy

Name: ____________________

Unit 6 – Standard 1.2(F)

Getting Started

Unit 6: Order Whole Numbers

TEKS LEARNING TARGETS

- I can identify numbers up to 120.
- I can identify a number that is greater than another number.
- I can identify a number that is less than another number.
- I can order a group of numbers from least to greatest or greatest to least.

Focus for 9 Traits of Critical Thinking™

***Adapt:** I adjust my actions and strategies to accomplish tasks.*

How would you explain the idea of less? How might you change your thinking to explain the idea of more?

____

____

***Reflect:** I review my thoughts and experiences to guide my actions.*

How might you use a number line in math?

____

____

Instruction

Name: ______________________

Concept Exploration

Standard 1.2(F) – **Unit 6**

1	2	3	4	5	6	7	8	9	10
11	12	13	14	15	16	17	18	19	20
21	22	23	24	25	26	27	28	29	30
31	32	33	34	35	36	37	38	39	40
41	42	43	44	45	46	47	48	49	50
51	52	53	54	55	56	57	58	59	60
61	62	63	64	65	66	67	68	69	70
71	72	73	74	75	76	77	78	79	80
81	82	83	84	85	86	87	88	89	90
91	92	93	94	95	96	97	98	99	100
101	102	103	104	105	106	107	108	109	110
111	112	113	114	115	116	117	118	119	120

How are the ideas of greater than and less than related? How are they different?

____

____

Do you find it harder to organize numbers from greatest to least or least to greatest? Why?

____

____

Illegal to Copy

between	**greater than**	**least**	**ones**
compare	**greatest**	**less than**	**place value**
digit	**hundreds**	**number line**	**tens**
equal			

Match the concepts.

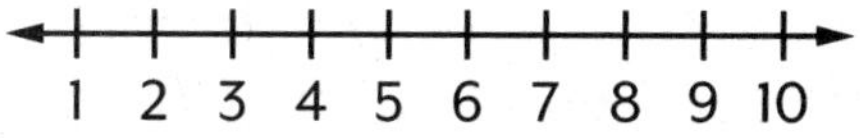

119

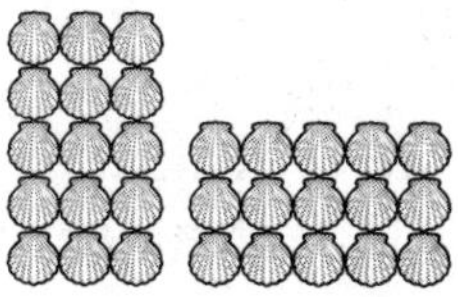

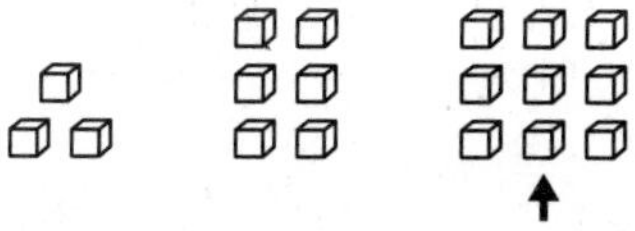

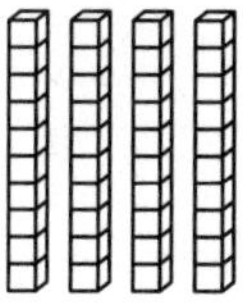

tens

least

greatest

equal

hundreds

number line

How did you have to ***adapt*** your thinking when matching the picture with the vocabulary word?

____

____

Instruction

Name: ____________________

Concept Development

Standard 1.2(F) – **Unit 6**

81	82	83
91	92	93
101	102	103

Place an X on the hundreds place in each number.

Underline the tens place in each number.

Circle the ones place in each number.

Select 3 numbers on the chart.

Use the open number line to order the numbers you selected from least to greatest.

Turn and tell an elbow partner one thing you notice about the numbers on the number line.

When ordering numbers, look at the place value.

Compare the hundreds, then the tens, and then the ones places.

If place values are the same when you compare them, move to the next place value in each number.

When using a hundred chart, notice the numbers are greater by 1 as you move to the right.

When using a hundred chart, notice the numbers are greater by 10 as you move down a column.

The numbers on a number line are greater as you move to the right.

Try It!

1) Kayla says that 87 and 78 are equal since they have the same digits.

Explain why Kayla is right or wrong.

____

____

Try It!

2) Look at the numbers on the number line.

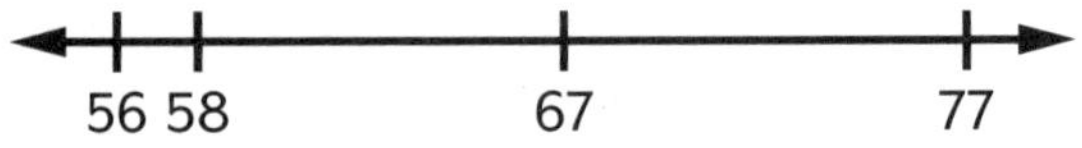

Write the numbers in order from greatest to least.

____

Illegal to Copy

Name: ____________________

Unit 6 – Standard 1.2(F)

Instruction

Concept Application

1 Which number line does NOT show the numbers in correct order?

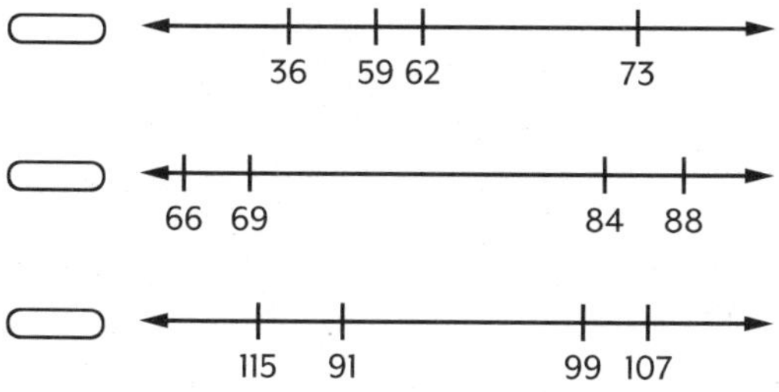

2 Stefan sees these cars at the store.

Write the prices of the cars from least to greatest.

________, ________, ________

3 Use the open number line to correctly place the numbers.

101, 109, 120, 118

Write the numbers in order from least to greatest.

____

4 Draw base 10 blocks to show each number.

45	54

Place the numbers on the open number line.

Locate and label one number that is less than 45 and one number that is greater than 54.

5 Write the number shown beneath each picture.

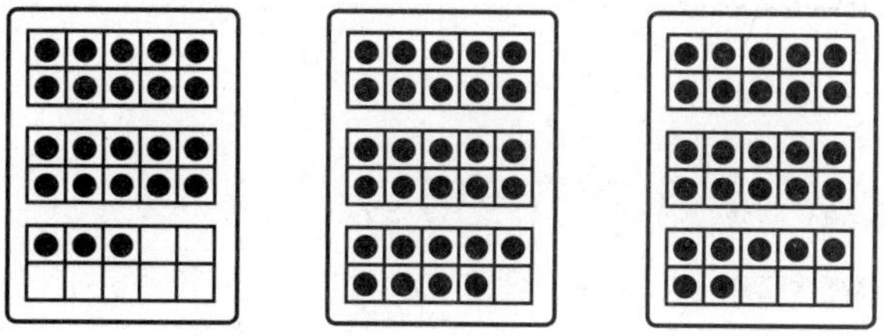

________ ________ ________

Write the numbers in order from greatest to least.

________, ________, ________

Instruction

Name: ______________________

Concept Practice

1 Circle the correct sentence.

The number with the star is less than the number with the circle.

The number with the star has 2 tens and 5 ones.

The number with the circle has 4 tens and 4 ones.

2 Write a true sentence about the number line.

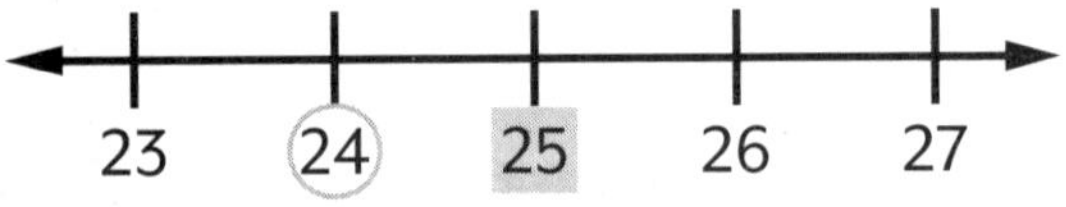

____

____

3 Which group of numbers is in order from greatest to least?

- ⬭ 101, 100, 99, 98
- ⬭ 98, 99, 100, 110
- ⬭ 88, 99, 77, 100

4 Look at the number line.

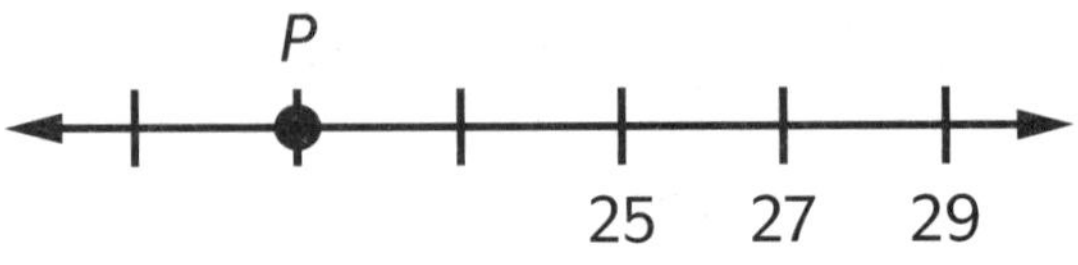

Which sentence is correct?

- ⬭ *P* is less than 25.
- ⬭ *P* is equal to 25.

5 Look at the numbers.

97 100 103

Circle the true statements.

97 is less than 103.

103 is greater than 97.

100 is between 97 and 103.

Illegal to Copy

Balloon Pop

Play *Balloon Pop* with a friend. Each player needs a set of 0 to 9 tiles. The game begins with tiles facedown. Each player turns over one tile and places it on the game board. Players repeat this step one more time and then compare the numbers formed. The player with the larger number scores a point. Clear the game board, shuffle the tiles, and play again. The winner is the first person with ten points.

Player 1

Player 2

Extension

Name: ______________________________

Standard 1.2(F) – **Unit 6**

Math Challenge

Find the mystery numbers.

The number of days in October ____________________

The number of days in one week ____________________

The number of students in your class ________________

Locate the mystery numbers on the open number line.

Reflection on My Learning

Explain the steps you would use to compare 27 and 32.

____

____

____

Reflection on Critical Thinking

Circle the traits you used most often in this unit.

I show ________________________ when I ________________________.

Illegal to Copy

Name: ______________________________

Assessment

Unit 6 – Standard 1.2(F)

Concept Check

1 Fill each oval with a number. The numbers in each row should be in order from least to greatest.

46 ( ) **67**

( ) **87** **110**

99 ( ) **119**

2 Al sees these shoes at the store.

Write the prices in order from greatest to least.

____

3 Use the open number line to correctly place the numbers.

45, 73, 99, 67

Circle the greatest number.

4 The table shows Taylor's toy cars.

Taylor's Cars

Color	Number
Purple	39
Green	29
Blue	34

Which shows the colors in order from least to greatest?

- Green, Blue, Purple
- Purple, Blue, Green
- Green, Purple, Blue

5 Look at the number line.

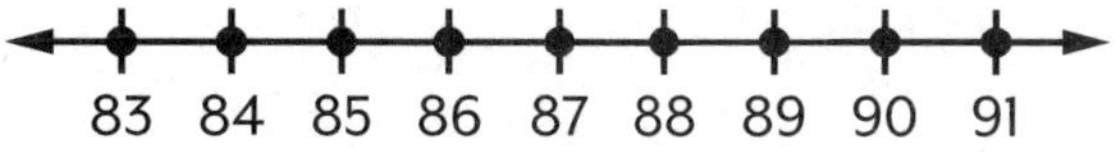

Which set of numbers is in order from least to greatest?

- 87, 85, 83
- 88, 89, 81
- 84, 87, 89

Illegal to Copy

Assessment

Name: ____________________

Concept Check

Standard 1.2(F) – **Unit 6**

6 Draw base 10 blocks to show each number. Then, write the numbers in order from least to greatest.

104	81	38

____

7 Locate and label 59, 42, 33, and 29 on the open number line.

Then, locate and label one number greater than 59 and one number less than 42.

8 The numbers on this number line are NOT in order.

Use the open number line to place the numbers in correct order.

Illegal to Copy

Name: ____________________

Unit 7 – Standard 1.2(G)

Getting Started

Unit 7: Compare Whole Numbers

TEKS LEARNING TARGETS

- I can use the symbols >, <, and =.
- I can compare two numbers using symbols for *greater than*, *less than*, or *equal*.

Focus for 9 Traits of Critical Thinking™

Communicate: *I use clear language to express my ideas and to share information.*

Think about a time you used the wrong word when explaining something. How did it change the idea you were trying to share?

____

____

Inquire: *I seek information that excites my curiosity and inspires my learning.*

What approach do you take if you are unsure about how to solve a problem?

____

____

Instruction

Name: ____________________

Concept Exploration

Standard 1.2(G) – **Unit 7**

How did the group members ***communicate*** the same information as the number sentence you wrote?

What questions came up when you were using the *greater than* and *less than* symbols?

Illegal to Copy

Instruction

Vocabulary Mastery

compare	**greater than (>)**	**number**	**place value**
digit	**least**	**order**	**symbol**
equal (=)	**less than (<)**		

Use the Word Bank to fill in the blanks.

Word Bank	
>	ones
<	tens
=	

Molly thinks of a number that has 9 ____________ and 7 _______________.

Her number is ____________ 96 and _______________ 98.

Label the open number line. Show the three numbers on the number line.

How were you able to determine which word or symbol went in each blank?

____

____

How might it change your answer if 97 is switched to 79?

____

____

Instruction

Name: ____________________

Concept Development

Standard 1.2(G) – **Unit 7**

Greater than > 85 > 76

Less than < 76 < 85

Equal to = 85 = 85

Write the symbol in the circle that makes the sentence true.

43 ◯ 47   100 ◯ 100

Look at the comparisons and circle the symbols that mean *is greater than*.

10 < 39   55 > 23   62 > 96

Look at the comparisons and underline the symbols that mean *is less than*.

6 < 15   34 < 43   76 > 67

When comparing numbers, we sometimes use symbols in place of words.

Always read the number sentence aloud to check your answer. *43 is less than 47.*

If you get confused when using the greater than and less than symbols, remember that the *BIG* opening is next to the *BIGGER* number.

Remember the *SMALLER* side of the symbol points to the *SMALLER* number.

Try It!

1) Write >, <, or = in the circle.

47 ◯ 61   100 ◯ 99

Try It!

2) 29 is less than 32.

Rewrite the sentence using the correct symbol.

____

Name: ______________________________

Unit 7 – Standard 1.2(G)

Instruction

Concept Application

1 Cindy and Saj collected shells at the beach.

Write >, <, or = in the box to compare the number of shells.

Cindy's Shells   Saj's Shells

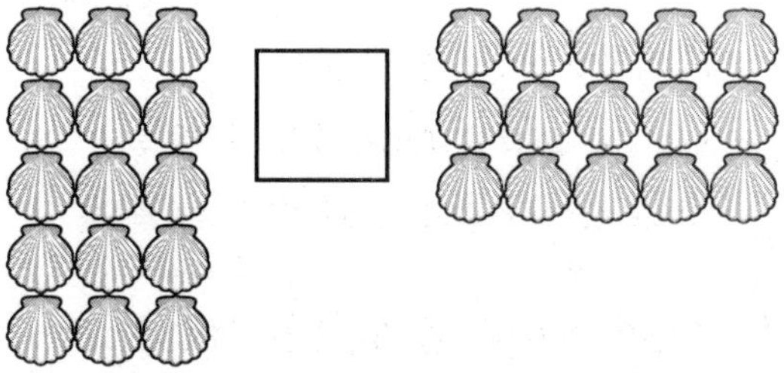

2 Which of the following is NOT true?

- ⬭ 93 < 100
- ⬭ 89 = 89
- ⬭ 97 < 79

3 Farmer Green has 87 pigs.
Farmer Gray has 87 pigs.

Use numbers and >, <, or = to compare the pigs.

________ ◯ ________

4 Write a number in each empty circle.
The number should make the number sentence true.

◯ > 64

99 = ◯

◯ < 33

5 Write the numbers under the pictures.

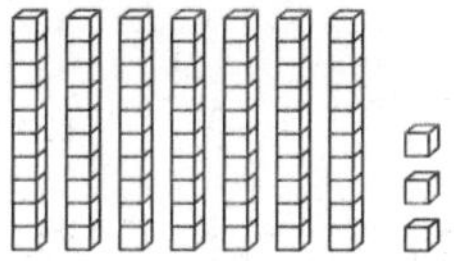

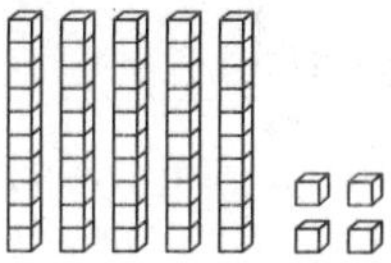

________   ________

Compare the numbers and write a number sentence to show the comparison.

________ ◯ ________

1 Which symbol makes this comparison true?

74 ◯ 47

- ⬭ >
- ⬭ <
- ⬭ =

2 Jen saved 63 pennies.
Mark saved 63 pennies.
Which is true?

- ⬭ 63 > 63
- ⬭ 63 < 63
- ⬭ 63 = 63

3 Compare the sticks.

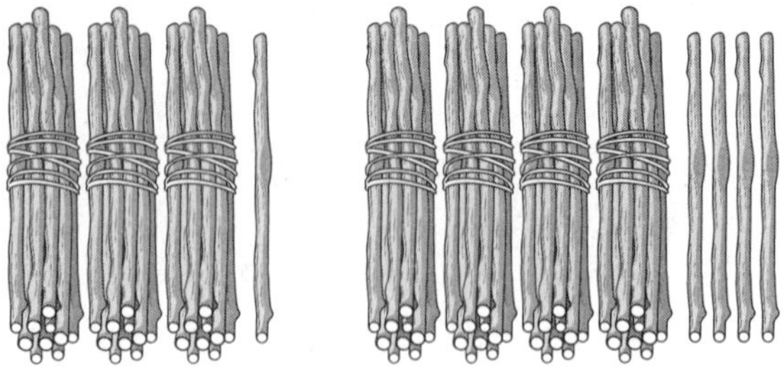

Which comparison is NOT true?

- ⬭ 31 < 44
- ⬭ 44 > 31
- ⬭ 31 = 44

4 Compare the blocks.

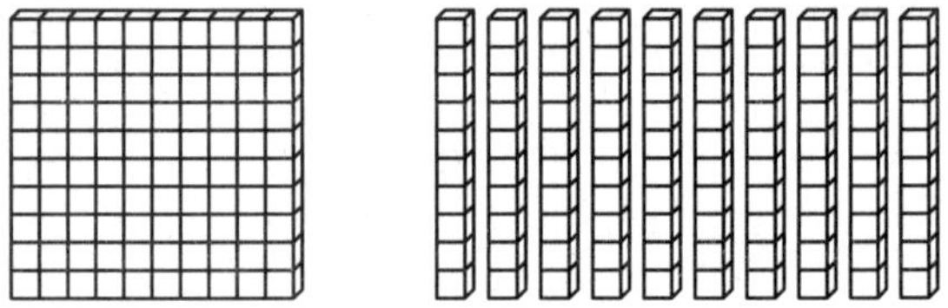

Write a comparison that is true.

Answer ______________________________

5 Write a number in the blank to make a true number sentence.

23 < ________

97 < ________

89 > ________

63 = ________

6 Compare the two sets.

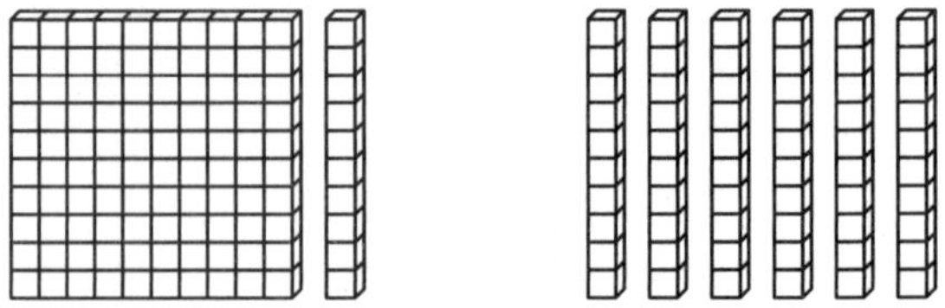

Write a comparison that is true.

Answer ______________________________

Name: ______________________________

And the Winner Is...

Play *And the Winner Is...* with a partner. Partners need one set of 0–9 number tiles and a game board. Place tiles facedown. Players each select two tiles and turn the tiles over. Players make the largest possible two-digit number and record the numbers on the game board. After recording the numbers, players write > or < to compare the two numbers. The player with the greater number records his or her name in the Winner column. Play continues for 9 rounds. The player with more wins is the winner.

Player 1	> or <	Player 2	Winner
1.		1.	
2.		2.	
3.		3.	
4.		4.	
5.		5.	
6.		6.	
7.		7.	
8.		8.	
9.		9.	

And the Winner Is... ______________________________

(Winner's name)

Illegal to Copy

Extension

Name: ______________________

Standard 1.2(G) – **Unit 7**

Math Challenge

Bo modeled a number with these base 10 blocks.

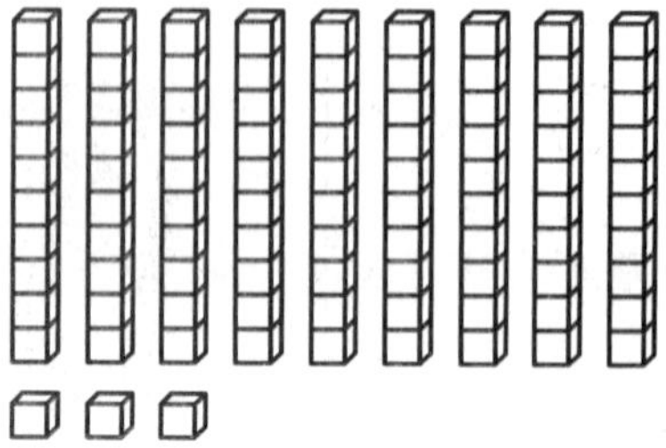

Tan modeled a different number that is less than Bo's number. Draw a picture that could model Tan's number.

Write the numbers on the lines and >, <, or = in the ◯ to compare.

_______ ◯ _______

Reflection on My Learning

Explain why 10 > 7 and 7 < 10 are both true comparisons.

____

____

Reflection on Critical Thinking

Circle the traits you used most often in this unit.

I show ______________________ when I ______________________ .

Illegal to Copy

Assessment

Concept Check

1 Which symbol makes this comparison true?

96 ◯ 69

- ⬭ >
- ⬭ <
- ⬭ =

2 Circle all the number sentences that are true.

19 < 91

72 > 27

34 = 43

100 > 99

3 The comparison is NOT true.

54 = 45

Which answer makes it true?

- ⬭ 54 equals 45
- ⬭ 54 > 45
- ⬭ 45 > 54

4 Look at the shoes and prices.

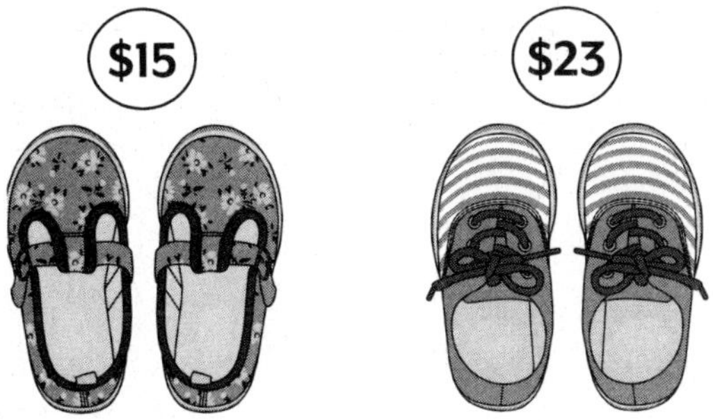

Which is true?

- ⬭ $15 > $23
- ⬭ $23 < $15
- ⬭ $15 < $23

5 Use the numerals to form two numbers that each have two digits.

3 6 9 0 2

________ ________

Compare the numbers you made using a number sentence.

________ ◯ ________

 Name: ______________________

6 Write the number under each set.

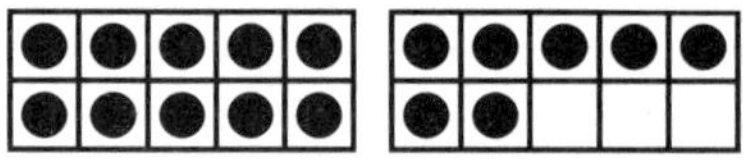

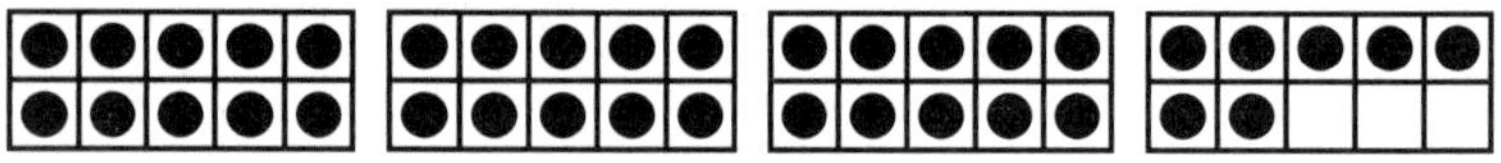

______________ ______________

Compare the numbers using >, <, or =.

______ ◯ ______

---

7 Draw a circle around the numbers that are less than 50.

Make an X on the numbers that are greater than 50.

Pick two numbers and write a comparison. Use > or < in the comparison.

65 89 12 42 40 46 79 51

Answer ______________________

---

8 Darlene collects 19 leaves in the yard. Diane collects 27 leaves.

Who collects more leaves? ______________________

Draw a picture using base 10 models to show the number of leaves each girl collects.

Write a comparison sentence to describe the picture.

______ ◯ ______

 Illegal to Copy

Name: ______________________________

Getting Started

Unit 8 – Standard 1.3(A)

Unit 8: Find Sums of Multiples of 10 and One-Digit Numbers

TEKS LEARNING TARGETS

- I can use objects to find the sum of a multiple of 10 and a one-digit number.
- I can use pictures to find the sum of a multiple of 10 and a one-digit number.

Focus for 9 Traits of Critical Thinking™

Examine: *I use a variety of methods to explore and to analyze.*

How do blocks or counters help you find a sum?

____

____

Link: *I apply knowledge to reach new understandings.*

How is adding using counters the same as adding using numerals?

____

____

Instruction

Name: ______________________________

Concept Exploration

Standard 1.3(A) – **Unit 8**

Groups of Ten	Left Over

Why are the extra counters called left overs?

____

____

How do the counters represent the numerals?

____

____

Illegal to Copy

add	equal (=)	number sentence	sum
addends	multiple of 10	ones	tens

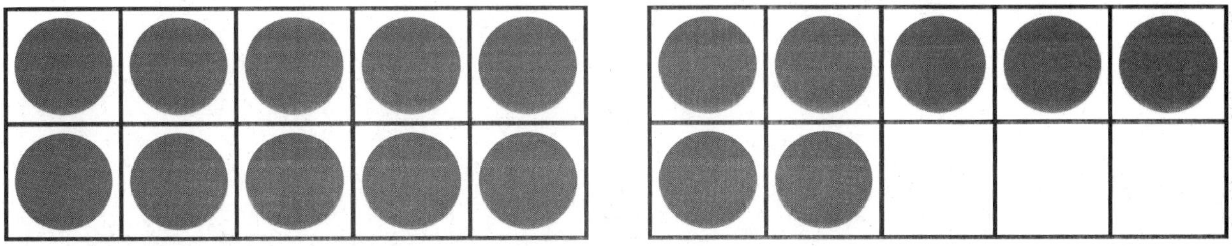

How many tens do you see? ______ ten(s)

How many ones do you see? ________ones

What addition number sentence matches the picture?

____

Circle each addend in your addition problem.

Draw a triangle around the sum.

Draw a box around the equal sign.

How does knowing the vocabulary terms help you solve the problems?

____

____

How is a number sentence similar to a sentence you read in a story?

____

____

□ + ◯ =

Draw 5 tens. **Draw 4 ones.**

______ tens + ______ ones = ______

50 + 4 = 54

Addend plus ***addend*** equals the ***sum***.

You can add *multiples* of ten (10, 20, 30, 40, ...) and ones.

The objects inside the □ show an *addend*. The objects inside the ◯ show an *addend*.

When you join the addends, you get the *sum*. The answer to an addition problem is called the *sum*.

The equal sign means *is the same as*.

Try It!

1) Select the correct equation.

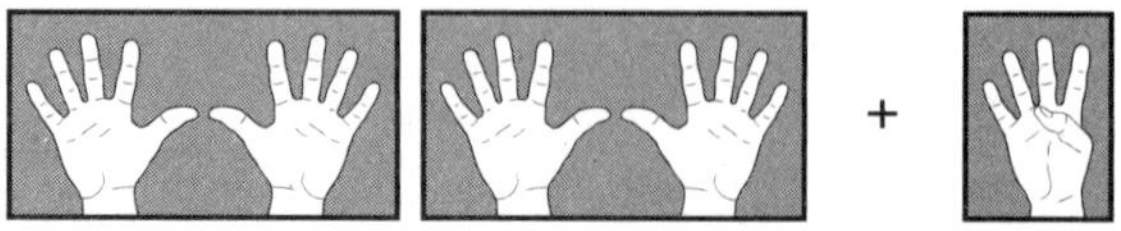

- ⬭ 55 + 4 = 59
- ⬭ 20 + 5 = 25
- ⬭ 20 + 4 = 24

Try It!

2) Write the addition sentence.

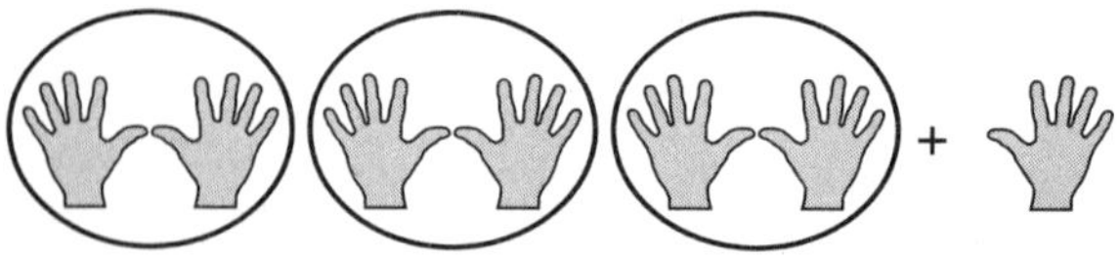

______ + ______ = ______

Name: ______________________________

Unit 8 – Standard 1.3(A)

Instruction

Concept Application

1 Match the set to the number.

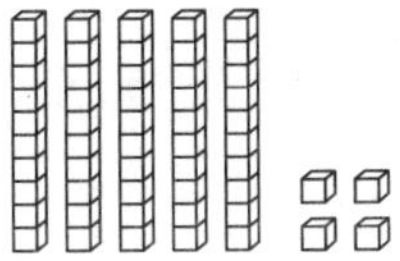

50 + 6 = 56

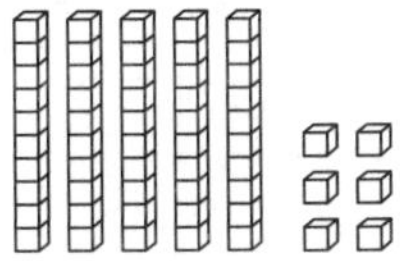

70 + 3 = 73

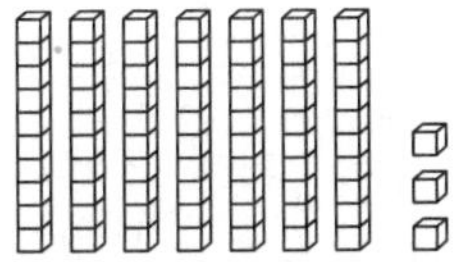

50 + 4 = 54

2 What number sentence is shown with base 10 blocks?

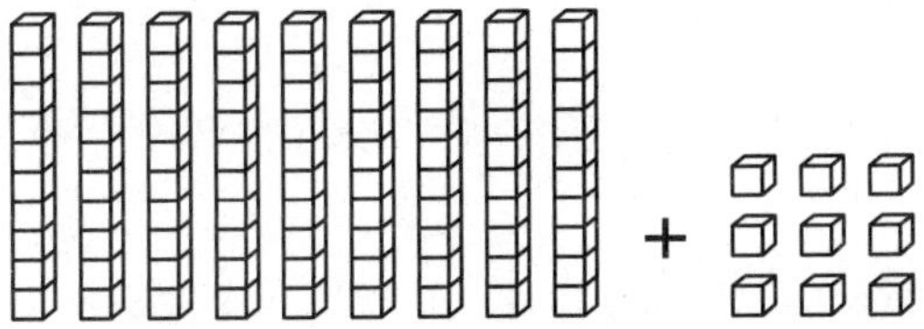

- ⬭ 80 + 9 = 89
- ⬭ 90 + 8 = 98
- ⬭ 90 + 9 = 99

3 David has 40 buttons. He finds more buttons. Now David has 47 buttons. How many buttons did David find?

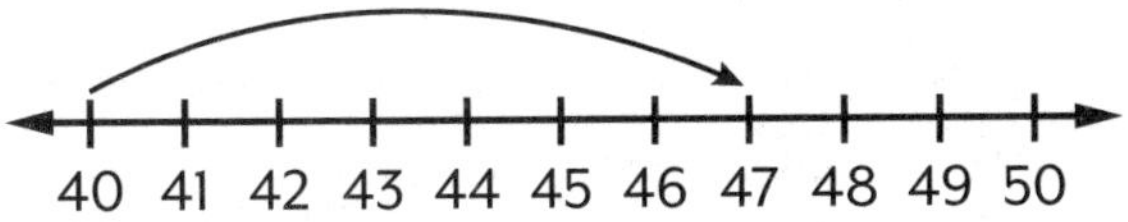

Answer ______________________

4 Meka made trains with Unifix® cubes.

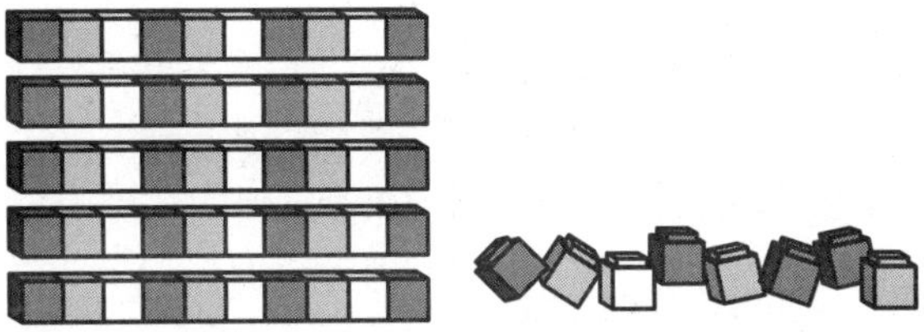

Write the addition sentence that shows how many cubes are in the picture.

_____ + _____ = _____

5 Circle groups of 10 stickers.

How many groups of 10 stickers did you circle?

Answer ______________________

How many stickers are NOT in the groups of 10?

Answer ______________________

What number sentence shows the total number of stickers?

Answer ______________________

1 Write the number sentence shown by the base 10 blocks.

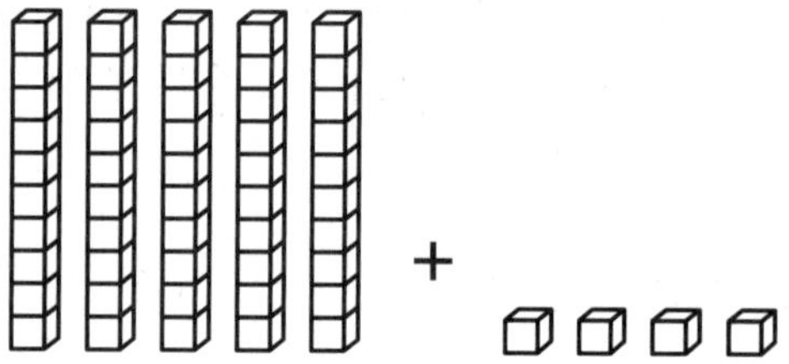

Answer ______________________

2 Kia buys 20 donuts. Katy buys 8 donuts.

What is the total number of donuts?

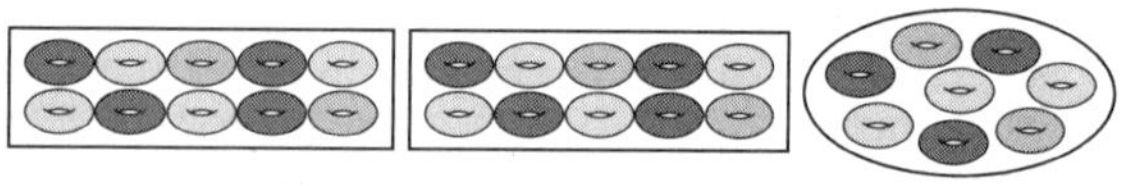

Answer ______________________

3 The class has 90 stickers on the chart. The teacher will add 9 more stickers. How many stickers will the class have then?

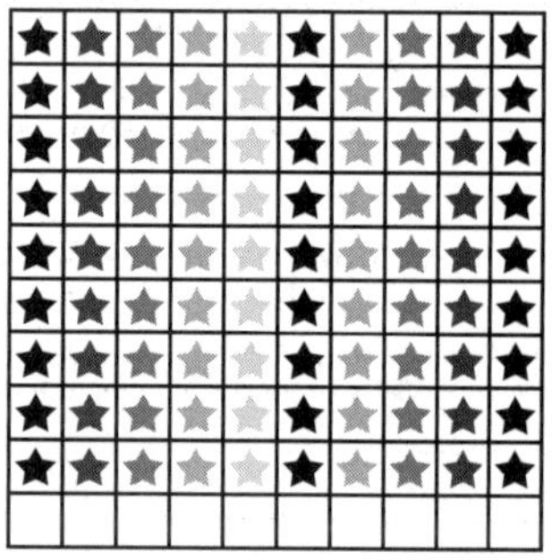

Answer ______________________

4 Mark counts 10 birds in a tree. More birds fly to the tree. Now Mark counts 13 birds. How many birds joined the group?

Answer ______________________

5 Lisa buys 5 packages of pencils. Each package has 10 pencils. She finds 4 more pencils. Which number sentence shows the total number of pencils?

- ⬭ 40 + 5 = 45
- ⬭ 5 + 50 = 55
- ⬭ 50 + 4 = 54

Illegal to Copy

Name: ______________________

Spin-a-Ten

Play *Spin-a-Ten*. Use a paper clip and pencil as a spinner. Spin the spinner. Build the number with Unifix® cubes, counters, blocks, or beans. Write the total value of tens and ones in the chart. Then write the addition number sentence that shows this sum.

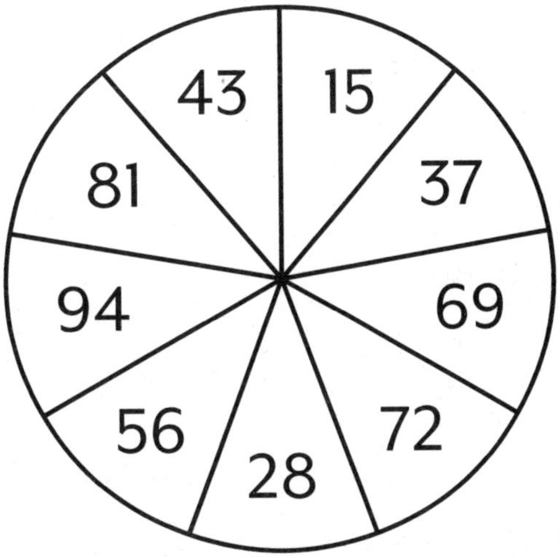

Spin	Total Value of Tens	Total Value of Ones	Addition Number Sentence
1			
2			
3			
4			
5			
6			
7			
8			
9			

Extension

Name: ____________________

Standard 1.3(A) – **Unit 8**

Math Challenge

Karen has 36 toy rings. She wants to share the rings with her friends.

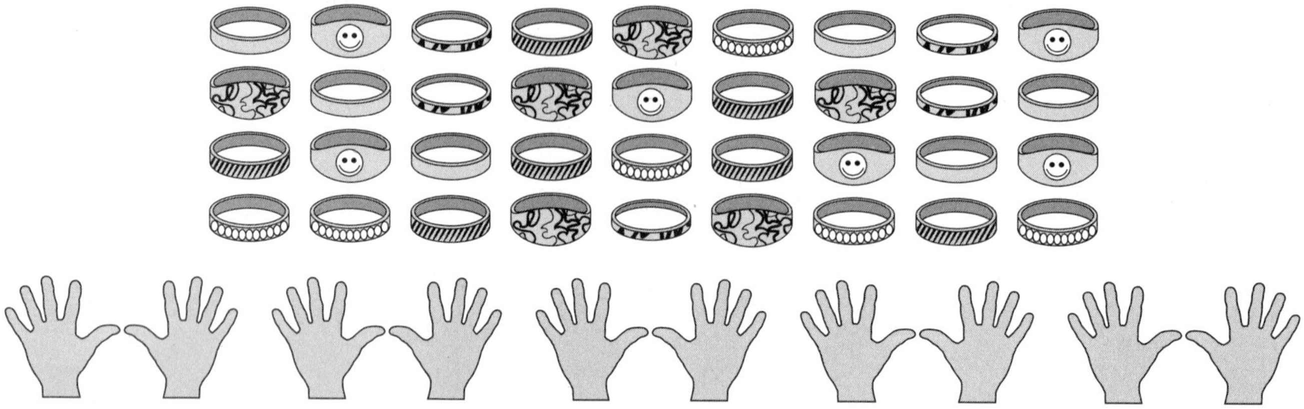

How many friends can have a ring on every finger? ____________

How many rings are left over? ____________

Reflection on My Learning

Tam said, "I can use dimes and pennies to show adding groups of tens and ones." Use words and pictures to explain what Tam means.

Reflection on Critical Thinking

Circle the traits you used most often in this unit.

I show ____________ when I ____________ .

1 Sandra puts 7 beads on a bracelet. She puts 30 beads on a necklace.

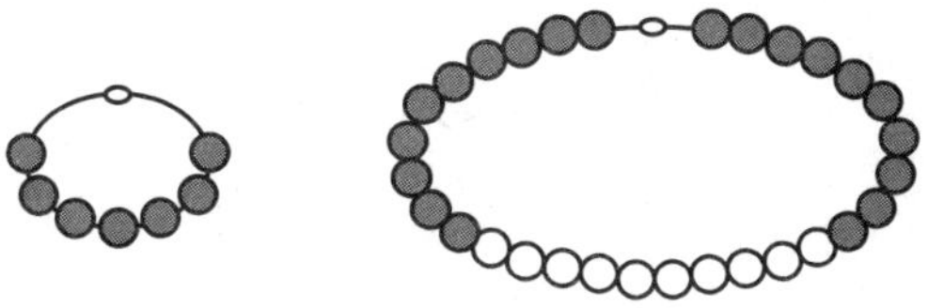

Write a number sentence to show how many beads Sandra used.

Answer ______________________

2 Each box has 10 birthday candles. Mom uses 8 boxes on a cake. Brooke adds 6 more candles.

What is the total number of candles on the cake?

Answer ______________________

3 Draw a picture to show the number sentence.

$30 + 2 = 32$

4 Kathy has 30 flowers in her garden. She plants 9 more flowers.

Which number sentence shows the number of flowers in Kathy's garden?

- ◯ $30 + 0 = 30$
- ◯ $3 + 9 = 39$
- ◯ $30 + 9 = 39$

5 Karla has some jelly beans in jars and one left over.

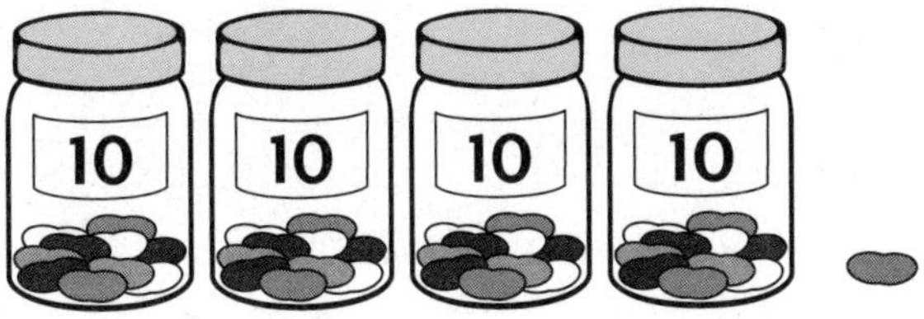

Write a number sentence to show the total.

Answer ______________________

Assessment

Name: ____________________

Concept Check

Standard 1.3(A) – **Unit 8**

6 Fill in the blanks.

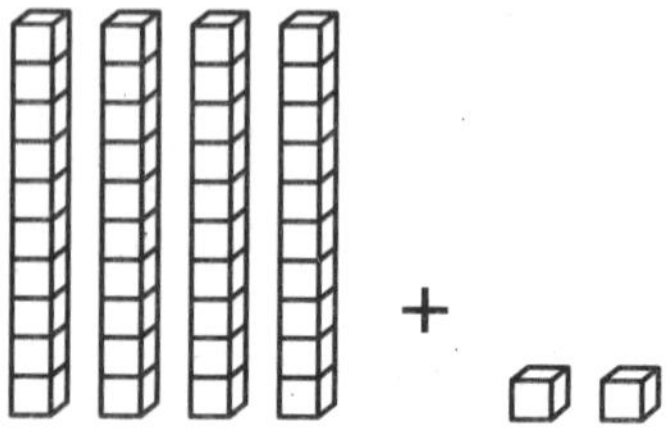

$+ \quad = \underline{\qquad}$

$40 + \underline{\qquad} = 42$

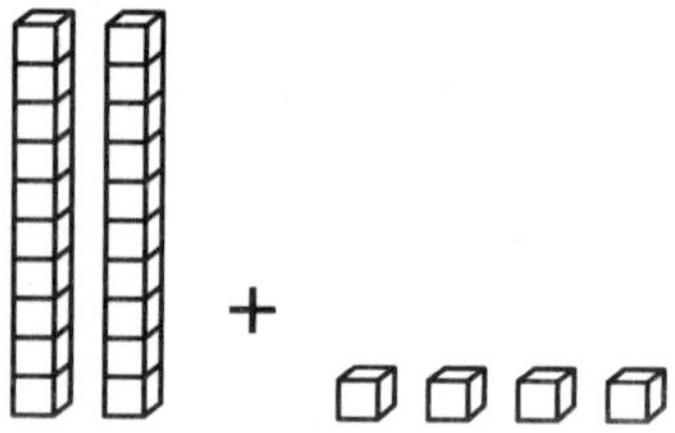

$+ \quad = \underline{\qquad}$

$\underline{\qquad} + 4 = \underline{\qquad}$

7 Marla drew 50 circles in the 10 frames. Mo added 3 more circles.

Draw circles in the 10 frames to show the sum of their circles.

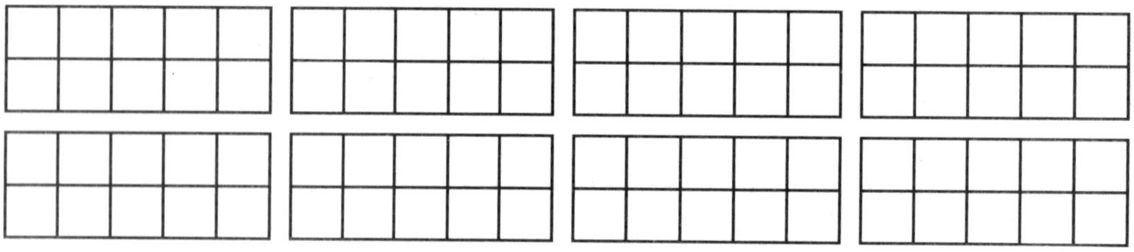

8 Celine picked 30 cherries.

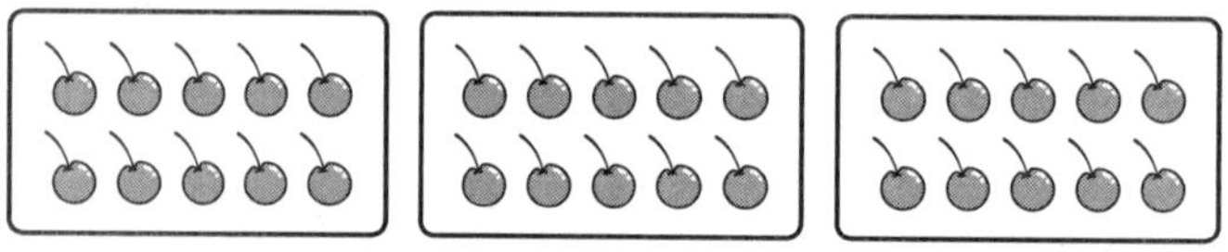

She finds 7 more cherries on the ground and puts them in her tub.
Show this on the drawing.
How many cherries does Celine have now? ____________________

9 There are 50 people in line at the fair. Five more people join the line.

Use the number line to show how many people are in line now.

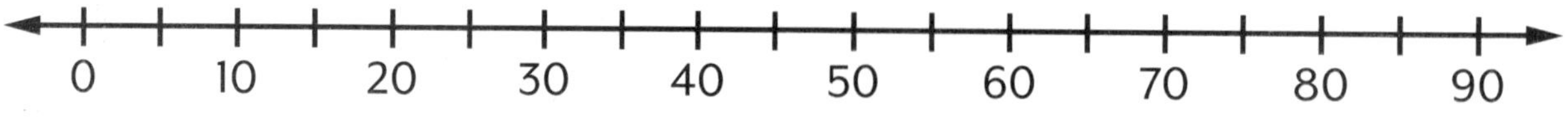

Illegal to Copy

Name: ______________________________

Getting Started

Unit 9 – Standard 1.3(B)

Unit 9: Solve Word Problems: Addition and Subtraction Within 20

TEKS LEARNING TARGETS

- I can identify addition as joining or putting together sets of objects.
- I can identify subtraction as the process of taking away or finding a missing part.
- I can understand subtraction is used in comparing sets of objects to find the difference between the values of the two sets.
- I can use real objects and pictorial models to solve for an unknown in any position.

Focus for 9 Traits of Critical Thinking™

Strive: *I use effort and determination to focus on challenging tasks.*

Would it help to act out the problem or draw a picture? Explain your answer.

____

____

Create: *I use my knowledge and imagination to express new and innovative ideas.*

Do you find it difficult to write addition or subtraction word problems? Why do you feel that way?

____

____

Instruction

Name: ____________________

Concept Exploration

Standard 1.3(B) – **Unit 9**

Do you restate the problem in your own words? How does this help you solve the problem?

____

____

How do you decide whether to ***create*** an addition or a subtraction word problem?

____

____

Illegal to Copy

Name: ____________________

Instruction

Unit 9 – Standard 1.3(B)

Vocabulary Mastery

add	**difference**	**join**	**subtract**
addends	**dozen**	**minus (–)**	**sum**
compare	**equal (=)**	**plus (+)**	**unknown**

Sort the vocabulary words into two groups.

Addition Words	Subtraction Words

Which words did you write in both boxes? ____________________

Why do the words belong in both boxes? ____________________

____

Why is it important to stop and think about the words before you divide them into groups? How does this step help you sort the words?

____

____

Are there any other word banks you might ***create*** to help you with addition and subtraction?

____

____

Savion has 8 black linking cubes and 6 white linking cubes.

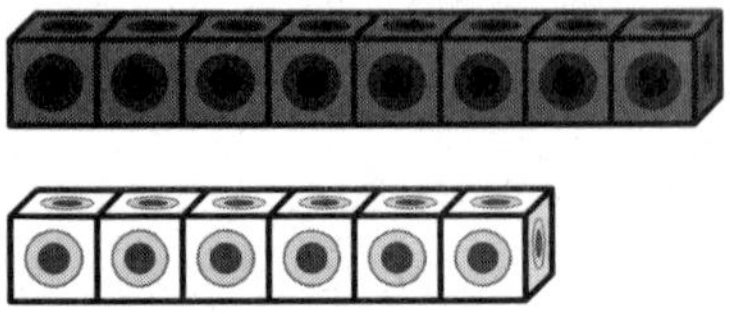

How many cubes does Savion have in all? ________

When joining addends, you may use objects or pictures to create a visual.

Kade saw 4 butterflies. One butterfly flew away.

How many butterflies are left? _____

When separating objects, you may cross out things or remove objects from your work space to help you find the difference.

6
4

There are 6 gray counters and 4 black counters.

How many more gray counters are there? ________

When comparing numbers, you may line up the objects and mark them off to help you see how many more or less.

Zia has 16 pennies. She gives some away. Now she has 10 pennies.

How many did Zia give away?

16 – _____ = 10

Make a problem-solving plan based on the information given and the operation needed to solve the problem.

Try It!

1) Julie saw 8 flowers. She picked 5 flowers. How many flowers are left?

8 – 5 = _____

Try It!

2) Some fish were swimming by the shore. Five more fish swam up. Now there are 10 fish. How many fish were by the shore to start?

_____ + 5 = 10

Illegal to Copy

Name: ______________________

Instruction

Unit 9 – Standard 1.3(B)

Concept Application

1 Nick has 7 dimes.
Valeria has 11 dimes.
How many fewer dimes does Nick have than Valeria?

Choose the operation to solve the problem.

- ⬭ Subtract
- ⬭ Add

2 Penny has 8 gifts with blue bows.
She has 4 gifts with red bows.
How many gifts does Penny have?

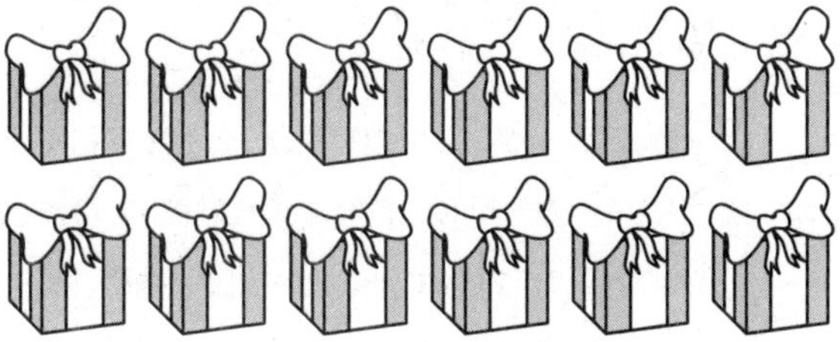

Write a number sentence to find the answer.

_______ ◯ _______ = _______

3 Kevion sees 8 butterflies in the garden. He sees 9 butterflies in a friend's garden. How many butterflies does Kevion see?

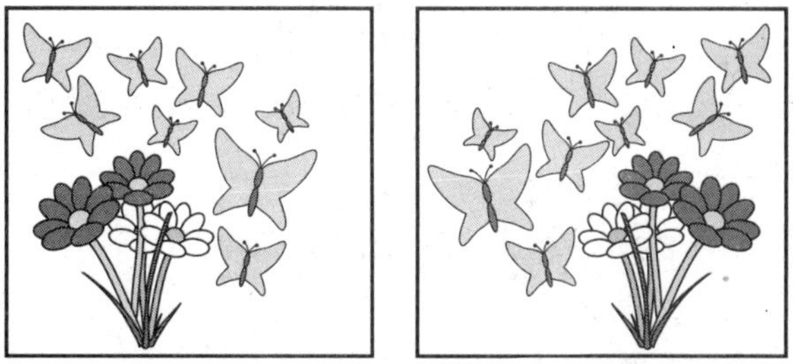

Choose the correct number sentence.

- ⬭ 9 – 8 = _____
- ⬭ _____ = 8 + 9
- ⬭ 8 + _____ = 9

4 The bird watcher saw 12 birds in a tree. Then, 5 birds flew away.

Circle the tree that shows this problem.
Write the number sentence.

_______ ◯ _______ = _______

1 Leo has 11 action figures. Mark has 8 action figures. How many fewer action figures does Mark have than Leo?

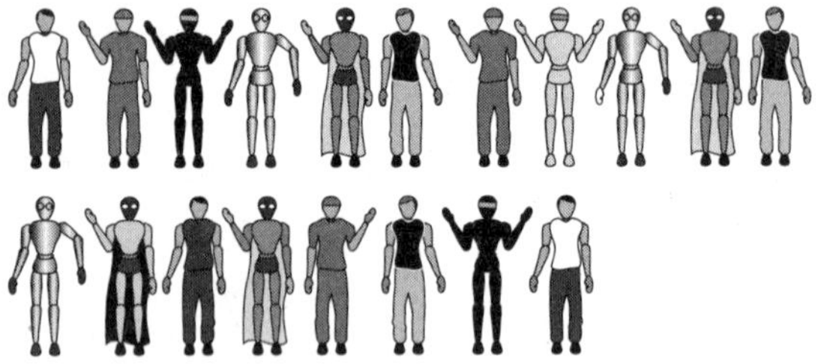

Which number sentence would NOT solve the problem?

- ⬭ 11 + 8 = ____
- ⬭ 11 – 8 = ____
- ⬭ 11 – ____ = 8

2 Leah has a box of 8 crayons. Her brother gives her a box of 10 crayons. How many crayons does Leah have now?

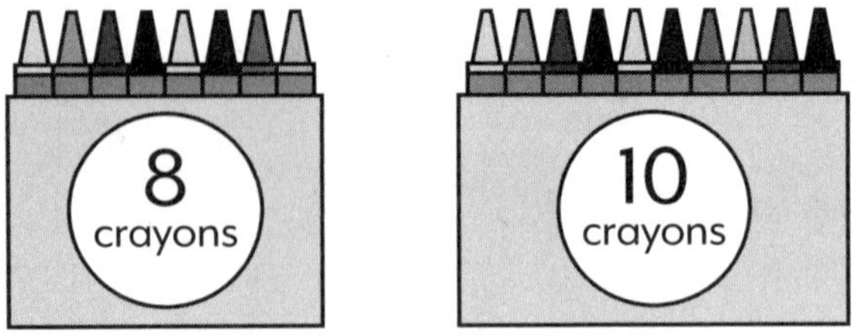

Write the number sentence to solve this problem.

_____ ◯ _____ = _____

3 Tana has 7 video games. Holly gives her 3 more. How many video games does Tana have now?

Choose the operation to solve the problem.

- ⬭ Subtract
- ⬭ Add

4 Mrs. Lin made 16 tacos. Her family ate 9 tacos. How many tacos were NOT eaten?

- ⬭ 25
- ⬭ 8
- ⬭ 7

Illegal to Copy

Colorful Chameleon

Find the missing number in each equation. You may use counters.
Use the key to color the picture.

4 + 2 = ☐

15 – ☐ = 10

7 – ☐ = 7

18 – 17 = ☐

☐ + 1 = 4

11 – ☐ = 7

11 + ☐ = 13

☐ + 9 = 16

Key

If the number in the ☐ is	Color
0	Pink
1	Blue
2	Yellow
3	Orange
4	Red
5	Green
6	Purple
7	Brown

Extension

Name: ______________________________

Standard 1.3(B) – **Unit 9**

Math Challenge

Meg took candy to Ann's party.
She had 16 pieces of candy.
Her brother ate 2 pieces of the candy.
Meg lost some candy on the way to the party.
When Meg got to the party, she had only 8 pieces left.
How many pieces did Meg lose? Draw a picture to show your work.

Reflection on My Learning

Lisa bakes cakes. She needs one dozen eggs. She has 8 eggs.
How can Lisa find out how many more eggs she needs to bake the cakes?
Use words or pictures to explain.

Reflection on Critical Thinking

Circle the traits you used most often in this unit.

I show ______________________ when I ______________________ .

Illegal to Copy

Assessment

Concept Check

1 Ray and Tim rake leaves. The boys fill 15 bags. Tim fills 9 of the bags. Which can be used to find how many bags Ray filled?

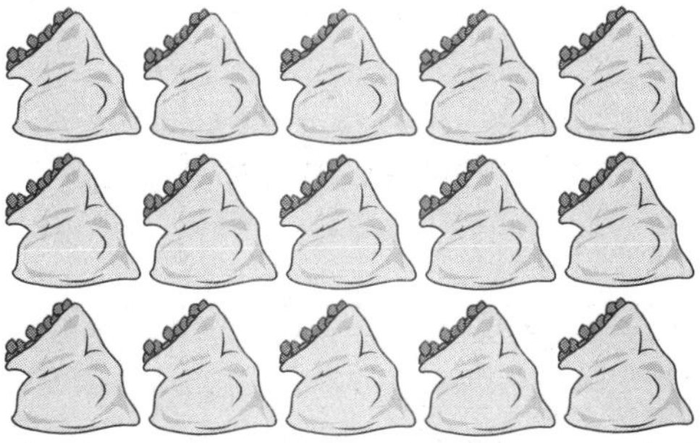

- ⬭ 15 + 9 = ____
- ⬭ ____ – 15 = 9
- ⬭ 9 + ____ = 15

2 Ana ate 9 grapes.
Marcus ate 5 grapes.
How many grapes did Ana and Marcus eat in all?

Answer ____________________

3 There are 5 dogs.
There are 6 bones.

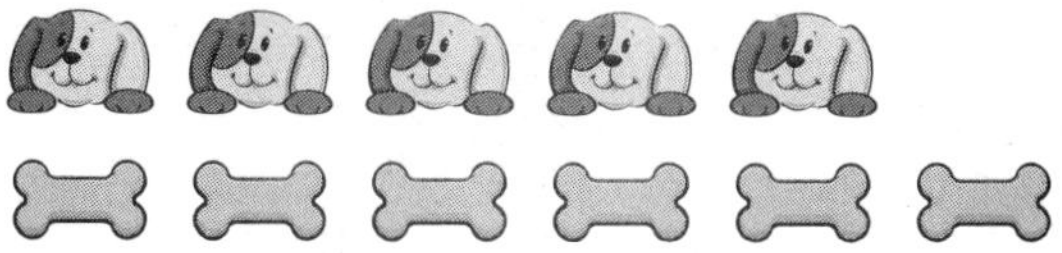

How many more bones are there than dogs?

Answer ____________________

4 Tessa picks 14 flowers.
There are 7 white flowers.
The rest of the flowers are red.

Which can be used to find how many flowers are red?

- ⬭ 14 + 7 = ____
- ⬭ 14 – ____ = 7
- ⬭ 7 – 7 = ____

5 Elena drew 6 gray circles.
Then, Elena drew 7 white circles.

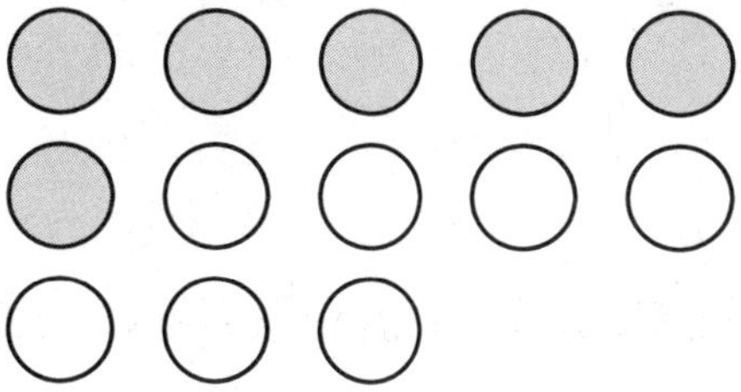

Write a number sentence to show the total of Elena's circles.

____ ◯ ____ = ____

Name: ______________________________

6 Wade has 15 toy cars. He gives 7 cars to his brother.
Wade uses a number line to show how many cars he has left.

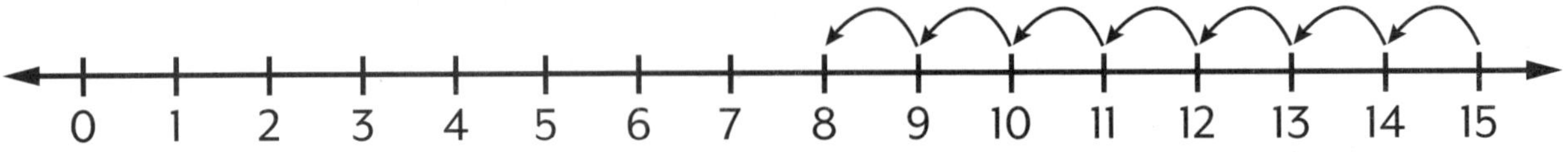

Write a subtraction sentence that shows how many cars Wade has now.

____

7 Circle the number sentence that shows the ten frames.

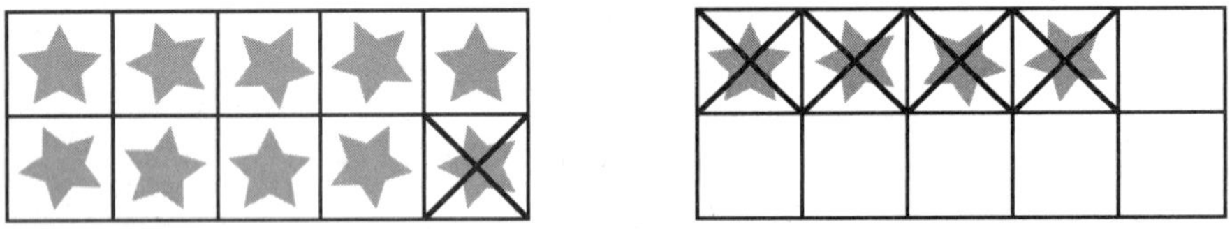

14 – 5 = 9   9 – 5 = 4   10 + 4 = 14

8 Trent has 6 goldfish. Chris has 4 striped clown fish.
Create a visual to show the fish each boy has in his bowl.

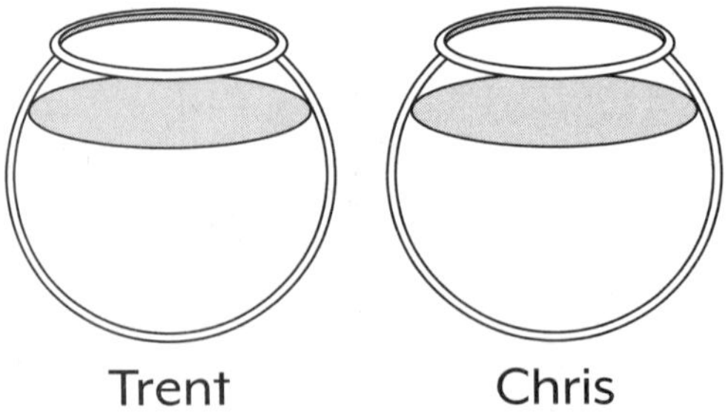

Write a number sentence that shows how many fish Trent and Chris have together.

____

Illegal to Copy

Name: ______________________________

Unit 10 – Standard 1.3(C)

Getting Started

Unit 10: Compose 10 with Two or More Addends

TEKS LEARNING TARGETS

- I can make 10 with two or more addends using objects.
- I can make 10 with two or more addends without using objects.
- I can use strategies to help me solve addition problems.

Focus for 9 Traits of Critical Thinking™

Link: *I apply knowledge to reach new understandings.*

How will you apply your addition skills to help you solve the problems?

____

____

Collaborate: *I work with others to achieve better outcomes.*

How might working with others give you a better understanding of the concept?

____

____

Name: ______________________

How did the story help you see that you can make 10 in many different ways? Give an example.

____

____

How might working with a partner make this activity different?

____

____

Illegal to Copy

Name: ______________________________

Instruction

Unit 10 – Standard 1.3(C)

Vocabulary Mastery

add	**equal (=)**	**sum**	**ten frame**
addends	**plus (+)**	**ten**	**total**
compose			

Use these vocabulary words to label the parts of the problem.
Write your answers on the lines.

total	equals	plus
sum	addend	

$$3 + 5 + 2 = 10$$

How do the words relate to the labeled parts in the number sentence?

____

____

How would you explain the meaning of the word *sum* to a friend?

____

____

Instruction

Name: ______________________________

Concept Development

Standard 1.3(C) – **Unit 10**

Objects
Numbers
Two addends
More than two addends

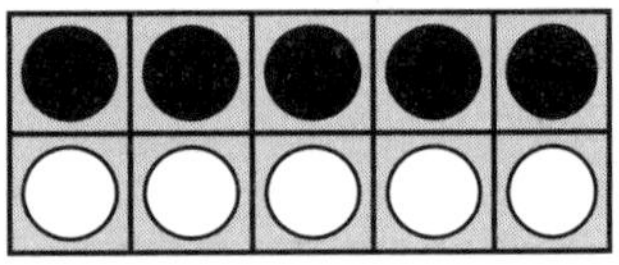

_____ black + _____ white = ______

_____ gray + _____ white + ____ black = ______

$$\begin{array}{r} 2 \\ 3 \\ +\,5 \\ \hline 10 \end{array}$$

2 + 3 + 5 = 10

There are many different ways to compose 10. Another way to say *compose 10* is to say *make 10*.

You can make 10 using ten objects.

You can add more than two addends to make 10.

You can add numbers vertically (up and down) or horizontally (side by side).

Try It!

1)

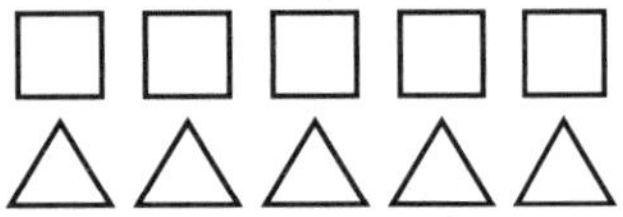

______ squares
\+ ______ triangles
______ shapes

Try It!

2) 1 + 2 + 7 = ______

5 + 4 + 1 = ______

4 + 3 + 3 = ______

Illegal to Copy

1 Maria has 2 white bunnies, 2 black bunnies, and 6 gray bunnies. How many bunnies does Maria have in all?

Answer ____________________

2 Duke buried 5 bones in the front yard. Tiger buried 5 bones in the backyard. How many bones did the dogs bury?

- ⬭ 9
- ⬭ 5
- ⬭ 10

3 Combine the 3 sets of stickers. Write a number sentence to match the picture.

_____ + _____ + _____ = _____

4 Sid draws 3 red flowers. He draws 7 yellow flowers.

Draw Sid's flowers and find the sum.

□
\+ □
―――
□

5 Grandma made 4 apple muffins and 3 banana muffins. She also made 3 pear muffins.

How many muffins did Grandma make? Show your work.

- ⬭ 4
- ⬭ 9
- ⬭ 10

6 Circle three sets of blocks that combine to make 10.

1 Which number sentence matches the 10 frames?

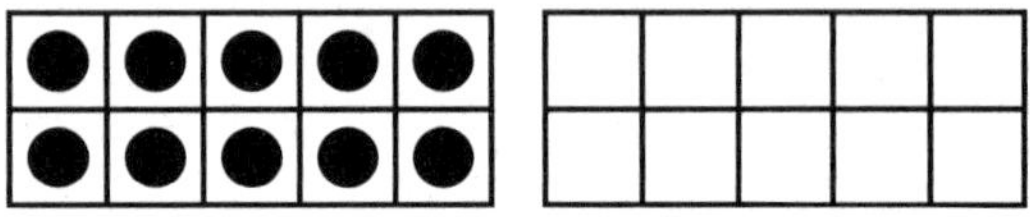

- ⬭ 3 + 5 + 2 = 10
- ⬭ 5 + 5 = 10
- ⬭ 10 + 0 = 10

2 Carl went fishing. He caught 3 red fish. Then he caught 7 blue fish.

Use the open number line to show how many fish Carl caught in all.

3 Collin blew 4 bubbles.
Mark blew 5 bubbles.
Sasha blew 1 bubble.

How many bubbles did they blow altogether?
Choose how to write the problem.

- ⬭ 4 – 5 + 1 = 10
- ⬭ 4 + 5 + 1 = 10
- ⬭ 4 + 5 = 10

4 Kira reads 7 books on Monday. She reads 1 book on Tuesday. By Wednesday, she reads a total of 10 books. How many books does Kira read on Wednesday?

Answer ______________________

5 Mrs. Sharp makes 10 cakes. She makes 4 chocolate cakes. The rest are vanilla cakes.

How many vanilla cakes does Mrs. Sharp make?

- ⬭ 10
- ⬭ 4
- ⬭ 6

6 Trenda makes a bracelet using 10 beads. She uses red, green, and white beads on the bracelet.

Draw a picture of what the bracelet might look like.

Write a number sentence about the bracelet.

____

Tic-Tac-Ten

Play *Tic-Tac-Ten* with a partner. Each player needs a Tic-Tac-Ten board and 9 game markers. Each pair needs either 1–9 digit cards or a 1–9 spinner. Each player writes the digits 1–9 in any order on the Tic-Tac-Ten board. In turn, players spin the spinner (or draw a card). Players cover the numbers on the Tic-Tac-Ten board that make a sum of 10 when added to the player's number. (If a player spins 6, he or she may cover 4 or 3 and 1.) The first player to get 3 in a row wins.

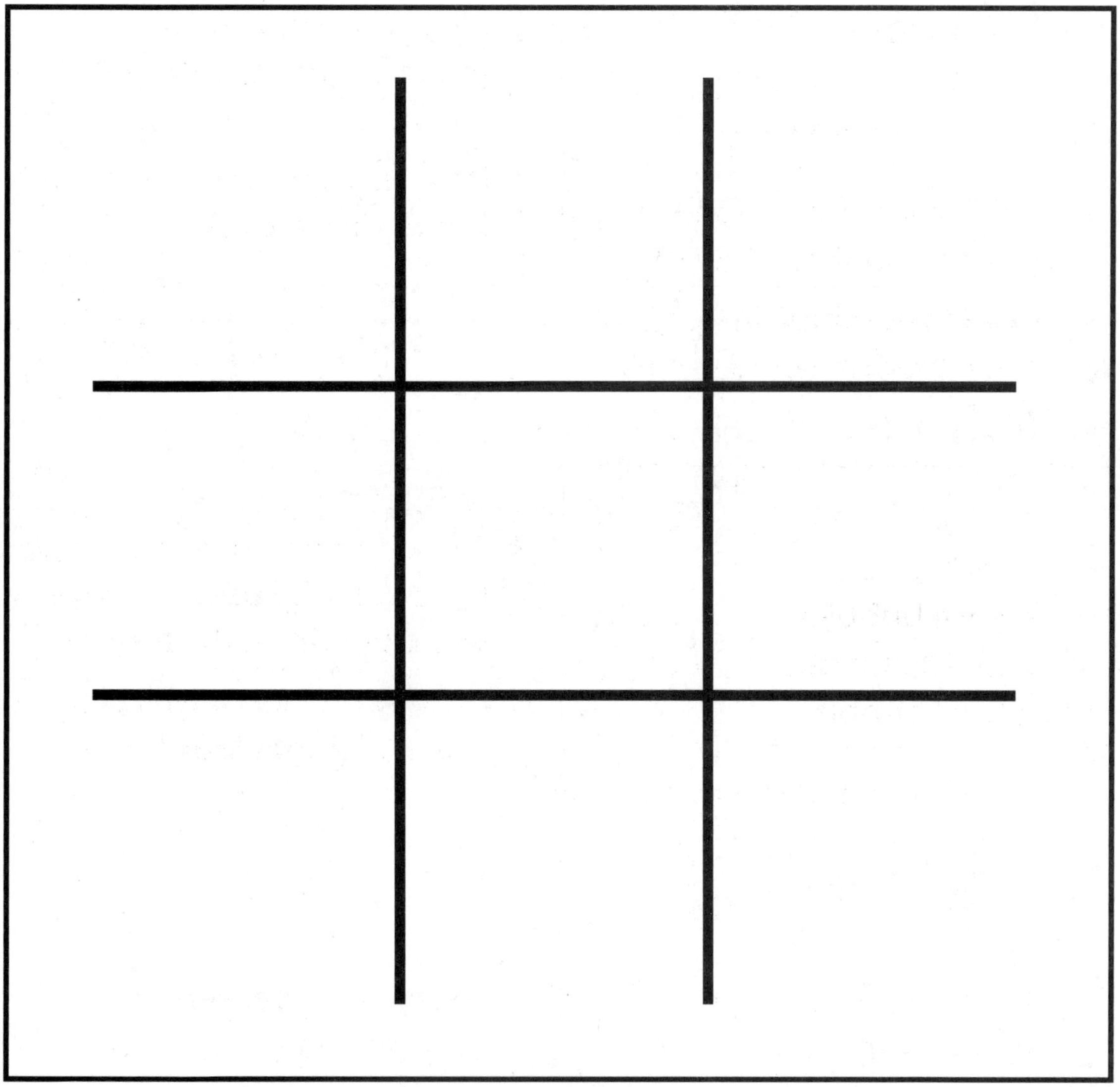

Extension

Name: ______________________________

Standard 1.3(C) – **Unit 10**

Math Challenge

Bobby invites nine friends to a party. He needs a total of 10 napkins, 10 cups, and 10 plates.

He has 4 napkins, 3 cups, and 7 plates.

How many more of each item does Bobby need?

Bobby needs ______ more napkins.

Bobby needs ______ more cups.

Bobby needs ______ more plates.

How many of each item will Bobby need if he invites 5 more friends to his party?

____

Reflection on My Learning

Waldo needs to solve this addition problem.

How can making sums of 10 help him find the answer?

$$\begin{array}{r} 3 \\ 2 \\ 7 \\ +\ 5 \\ \hline \end{array}$$

____

____

____

Reflection on Critical Thinking

Circle the traits you used most often in this unit.

I show ______________________ when I ______________________ .

Illegal to Copy

Name: ____________________

Assessment

Unit 10 – Standard 1.3(C)

Concept Check

1 Write two more addends to make a sum of 10.

____ + 4 + ____ = 10

Draw a picture to match the number sentence.

2 Write the addition fact shown by the crayons.

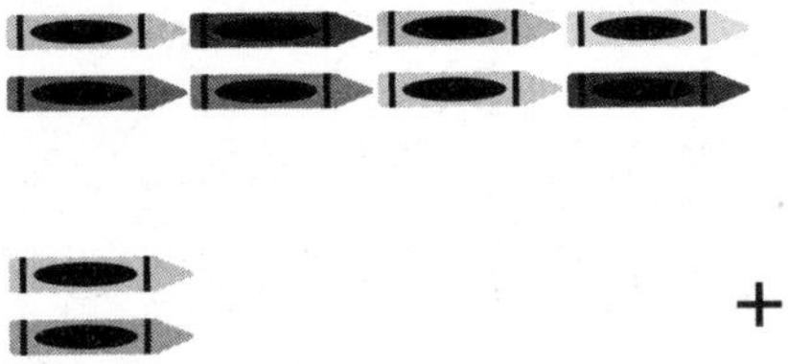

☐
+ ☐
☐

3 Use the open number line to solve this problem. Show each jump. Write the numbers where you land.

4 + 2 + 4 = ____

4 Circle two numbers that equal 10.

6 3 5 4 2 9

Write the number sentence to match.

____

5 Find the total number of toys.

Write a number sentence that matches the picture.

Answer ____________________

6 Zelda has 6 red marbles, 3 blue marbles, and 1 yellow marble.

How many marbles does Zelda have?

- ◯ 4
- ◯ 9
- ◯ 10

Assessment

Name: ____________________

Concept Check

Standard 1.3(C) – **Unit 10**

7 Write the addition fact.

$$\begin{array}{r} \square \\ + \ \square \\ \hline \square \end{array}$$

8 Circle 3 numbers that equal 10 when added.

5	6	7	4	8
9	2	5	3	1

Complete the number sentence.

_______ + _______ + _______ = 10

9 Use counters to solve the problems. Circle the problems with a sum of 10.

$9 + 3 = \square$

$\square + 6 = 10$

$4 + \square + \square = 10$

$$\begin{array}{r} 4 \\ + \ 5 \\ \hline \square \end{array} \qquad \begin{array}{r} \square \\ + \ 3 \\ \hline 10 \end{array} \qquad \begin{array}{r} 4 \\ \square \\ + \ 1 \\ \hline 10 \end{array}$$

Illegal to Copy

Name: ______________________________

Getting Started

Unit 11 – Standards 1.3(D), 1.3(E)

Unit 11: Apply and Explain Fact Strategies: +/– Within 20

TEKS LEARNING TARGETS

- I can use words, objects, pictorial models, and number sentences to solve addition and subtraction problems.
- I can apply strategies to find sums and differences.
- I can explain strategies used to find sums and differences.

Focus for 9 Traits of Critical Thinking™

Reflect: *I review my thoughts and experiences to guide my actions.*

How does using objects or pictures help you solve addition and subtraction problems?

____

____

Adapt: *I adjust my actions and strategies to accomplish tasks.*

How do you change your thinking when you solve an addition problem and then switch to solving a subtraction problem?

____

____

Instruction

Name: ______________________

Concept Exploration

Standards 1.3(D), 1.3(E) – **Unit 11**

Does modeling a story problem with objects help you solve the problem more easily? Explain your answer.

____

____

Do you use the same approach or strategy each time you solve a problem?

____

____

Illegal to Copy

add	**count on**	**fact family**	**subtract**
addends	**difference**	**minus (–)**	**subtraction sentence**
addition sentence	**doubles**	**number sentence**	**sum**
compare	**equal (=)**	**plus (+)**	**unknown**
count back	**equation**		

Use the Word Bank to add the missing letter to the word.

Word Bank

add	addend	difference	fact family
doubles	number sentence	subtract	sum

1 adde ____ d

2 numb ____ r sentence

3 fact f ____ mily

4 subt ____ act

5 ad ____

6 s ____ m

7 dou ____ les

8 diff ____ rence

Write the underlined letters in order to find the math strategy.

Strategy

___ ___ ___ ___   ___ o ___ ___ l ___ s

1 2 3 4   5 6 7 8

How might the near doubles strategy help you solve a problem?

____

____

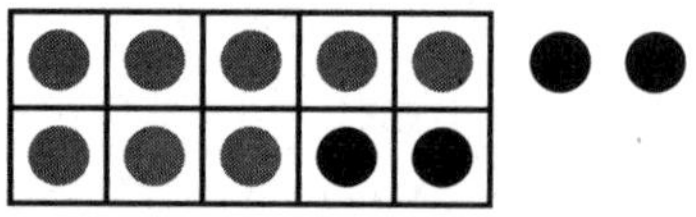

You can make a 10 to help you add. 8 + 4 is the same as 10 + 2.

6 + 6 = 12 6 + 7 = 13

You can use *doubles* or *near doubles* to help you add.

When you add 0 to a number, it stays the same. 3 + 0 = 3
When you add 1, a number is made greater by 1. 3 + 1 = 4

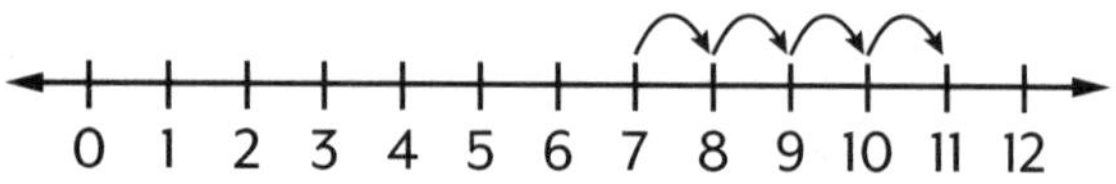

7 + 4 = 11

To add, you can use a number line to *count on.*
To subtract, you can use a number line to *count back.*

15 – 7 =

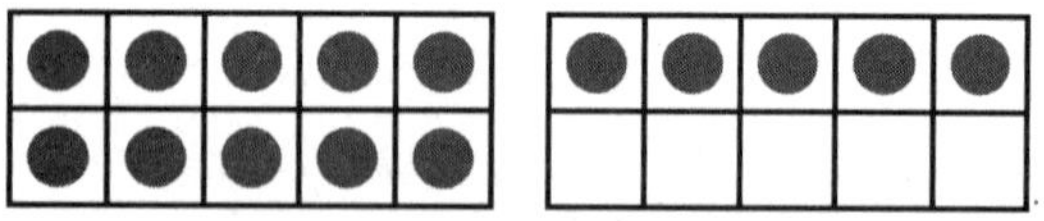

15 – 5 – 2 = ______

10 – 2 = ______

So, 15 – 7 = ______

You can decompose a number to make a 10 and then subtract. In 15 – 7, the 7 is the sum of 5 and 2. One strategy is to subtract 5 from 15 to make 10 and then subtract 2.

Try It!

1) Use the number line to solve.

12 – 5 = ______

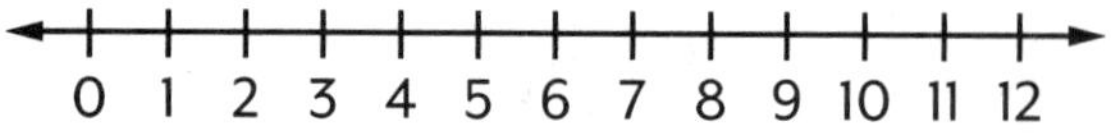

What strategy did you use?

____

Try It!

2) Find the difference of 12 – 5.

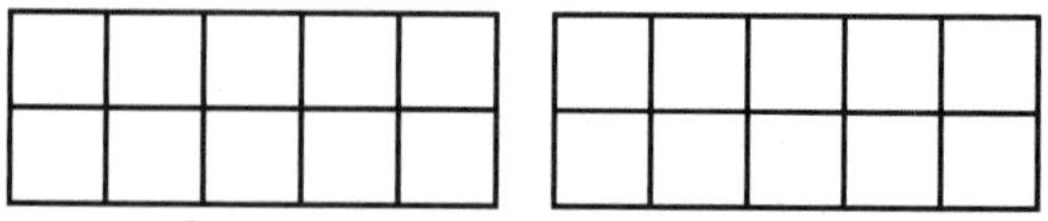

12 – 5 = ______

What strategy did you use?

____

Illegal to Copy

1 Elias eats 9 berries. Carter eats 8 berries. How many berries do the boys eat?

Write a number sentence to show the answer.

Answer ______________________

2 Tausha sees 7 tigers at the zoo. She sees 7 zebras. How many animals does Tausha see?

- ○ 0
- ○ 7
- ○ 14

3 Box two numbers that make a sum of 10.

7 8 4 3 2 6 5

Write a number sentence using the two numbers.

☐ + ☐ = 10

Circle one other number.
Use the 3 numbers to write a new number sentence.

☐ + ☐ + ○ = ____

4 Brandi has 10 cookies. She gives 5 cookies to Lisa. How many cookies does Brandi have left? Show your work.

Answer ______________________

5 Use the number line to solve the problem. Show your work.

14 – 10 = ______

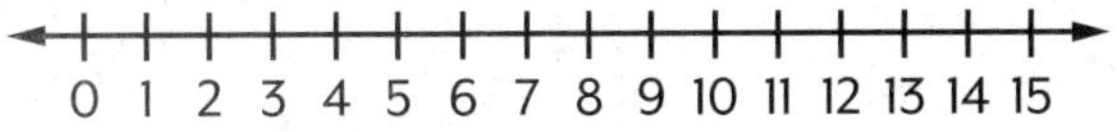

6 Draw a line to match the number to the clue.

☆ 19	1 less than 6 + 6
☆ 15	1 more than 9 + 9
☆ 11	2 more than 10 + 3

Pick a number less than 20. Write a clue like the ones above.

____

____

What is your number? __________

Instruction

Name: ____________________

Concept Practice

Standards 1.3(D), 1.3(E) – **Unit 11**

1 Write the subtraction sentence.

_______ – _______ = _______

What strategy helps solve the problem? ____________________

2 Draw a picture to show this problem.

18 – 8 = _____

Choose the correct answer.

- ⬭ 10
- ⬭ 26
- ⬭ 8

3 Lei had 13 cookies. She ate 6 cookies. How many cookies does Lei have?

Draw a picture and write the subtraction sentence.

_______ – _______ = _______

4 Draw a line to match the picture to the doubles fact.

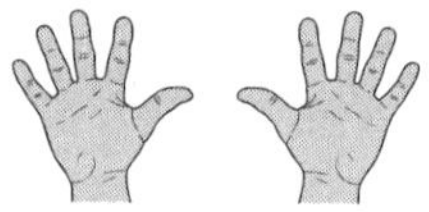

6 + 6 = 12

3 + 3 = 6

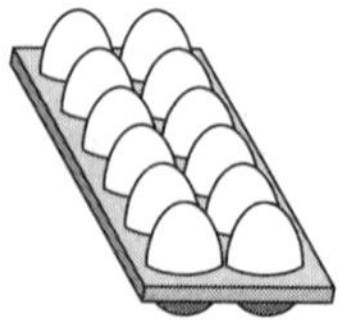

5 + 5 = 10

5 What number sentence best shows the ten frames?

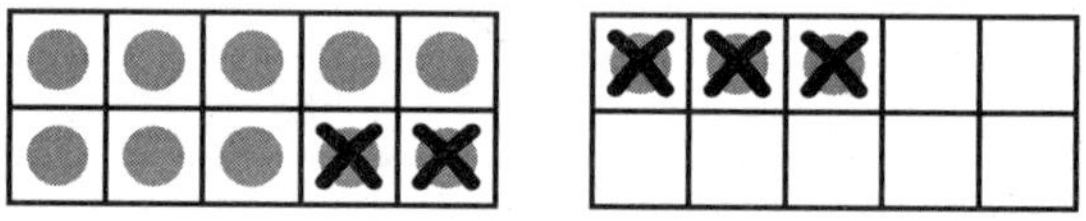

- ⬭ 10 – 5 = 5
- ⬭ 13 – 5 = 8
- ⬭ 5 – 2 = 3

Illegal to Copy

Nim Number Subtraction

Play *Nim Number Subtraction* with a partner. To begin, cover the 20 circles with 20 game markers. Players take turns removing 1, 2, or 3 markers. The winner is the player who removes the last marker. Use tally marks to keep score.

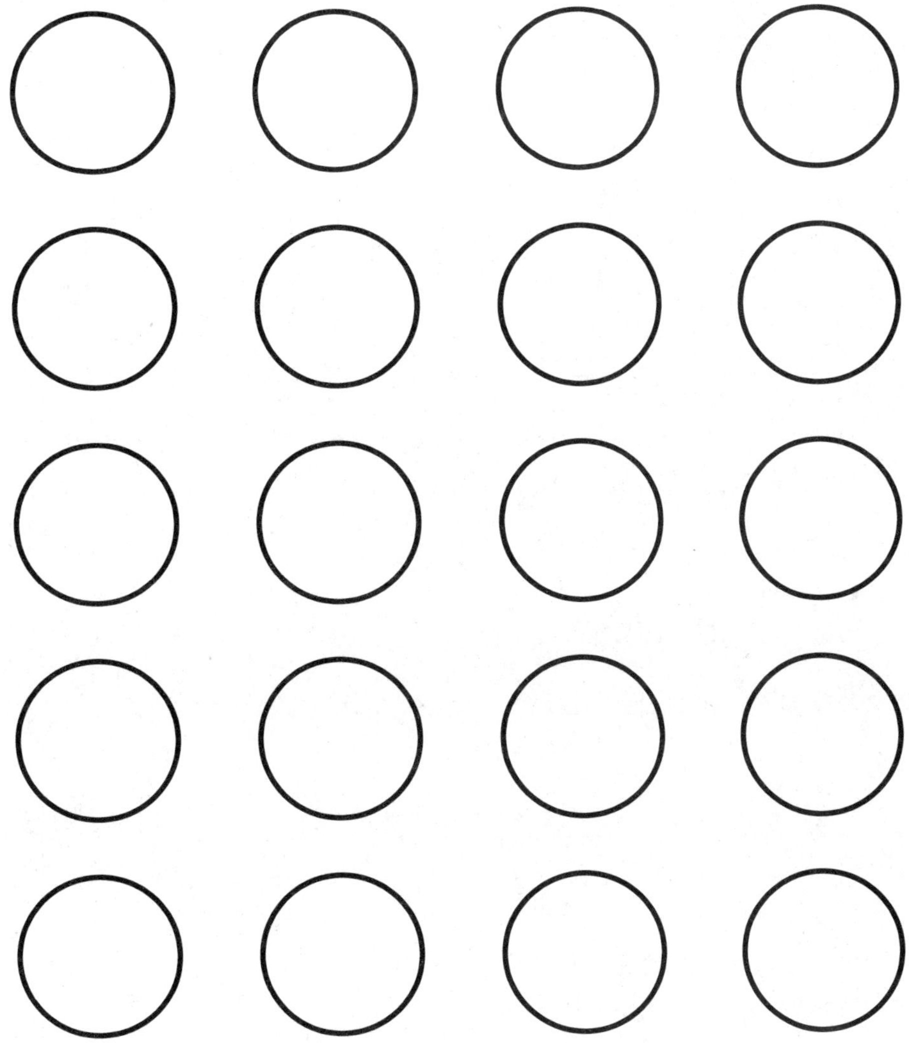

Nim Number Subtraction

Name of Player	Tally of Wins

Extension

Name: ______________________________

Standards 1.3(D), 1.3(E) – **Unit 11**

Math Challenge

Look at this fact family.

3 + 6 = 9 6 + 3 = 9

9 – 3 = 6 9 – 6 = 3

How can knowing fact families help when adding and subtracting?

____

____

Reflection on My Learning

Circle the operation that you understand best.

Addition **Subtraction**

Explain the strategies you use to be successful.

____

____

Reflection on Critical Thinking

Circle the traits you used most often in this unit.

I show ______________________ when I ______________________.

Illegal to Copy

Name: ____________________

Assessment

Unit 11 – Standards 1.3(D), 1.3(E)

Concept Check

1 Kay has 10 lemon cakes and 8 cherry cakes. Match the lemon cakes to the cherry cakes.

How many fewer cherry cakes than lemon does Kay have?

Write the subtraction sentence.

_______ – _______ = _______

Explain how matching the cakes helps solve the problem.

____

____

____

2 Write a clue to match this number using addition or subtraction.

14

____

____

3 Look at the number sentence.

7 – ____ = 7

Which makes the number sentence true?

- ⬭ 10
- ⬭ 0
- ⬭ 7

4 Addy has 5 striped balls and 8 spotted balls. She puts the balls into three groups. Circle two groups that make 10.

Write a number sentence that shows the total number of balls.

____

5 Which number sentence best represents the ten frames?

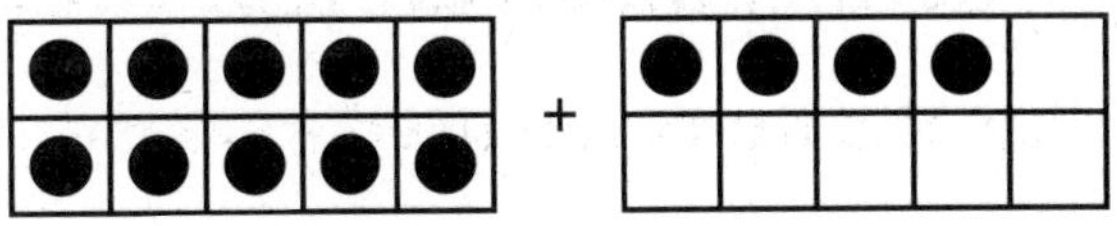

- ⬭ 10 + 4 = 14
- ⬭ 14 – 5 = 19
- ⬭ 10 – 4 = 6

Assessment

Name: ____________________

Concept Check

Standards 1.3(D), 1.3(E) – **Unit 11**

6 Wade uses a number line to solve 13 – 7.
Look at Wade's work to see how he solved the problem.

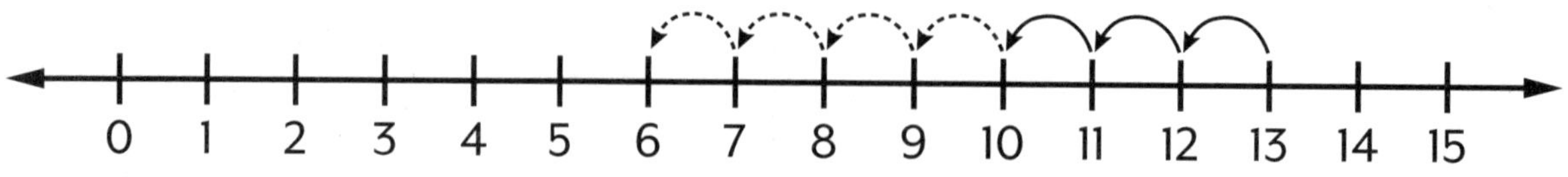

Write a subtraction sentence.

13 – ____ – ____ = ____

---

7 Use words, numbers, or pictures to explain how to find the difference.

15 – 8 = ____

---

8 Tara rode her bike 3 miles. Dana rode her bike 2 more miles than Tara.
How many miles did Dana ride her bike?

Use the open number line to solve the problem.

Write the number sentence.

________ + ________ = ________

Illegal to Copy

Name: ____________________

Unit 12 – Standard 1.3(F)

Getting Started

Unit 12: Generate and Solve Problems Given a Number Sentence

TEKS LEARNING TARGETS

- I can generate addition or subtraction problems when given a number sentence.
- I can solve addition or subtraction problems when given a number sentence.
- I can use strategies to solve addition and subtraction problems within 20.

Focus for 9 Traits of Critical Thinking™

Strive: *I use effort and determination to focus on challenging tasks.*

What type of plan should you use to make sure you are solving addition and subtraction problems correctly?

____

____

Create: *I use my knowledge and imagination to express new and innovative ideas.*

Is there something you might ***create*** to remember the different strategies for solving addition and subtraction problems?

____

____

How do you work to find a solution when you are having a hard time solving a word problem?

____

____

What original word problem did you ***create*** when working with your partner?

____

____

 Illegal to Copy

add	**count on**	**fact family**	**subtraction sentence**
addends	**difference**	**minus (–)**	**sum**
addition sentence	**doubles**	**number sentence**	**take away**
compare	**equal (=)**	**plus (+)**	**unknown**
count back	**equation**	**subtract**	

Draw a picture to represent each word.

Addition	
Subtraction	
Sum	
Difference	

How does your vocabulary demonstrate the ***strive*** trait?

____

____

In the chart, how does the picture you created represent the word?

____

____

Plus +

Minus –

Equal =

There are words and symbols that mean the same thing.

8 + 7 = 15

is the same as

eight plus seven equals fifteen

You can take a number sentence and put it into words.

8 + 7 = 15

Cara has 8 dogs. She also has 7 cats.

How many pets does Cara have in all?

Answer ____________________

You can also use a number sentence to create a word problem.

Try It!

1) Write a number sentence that is the same as these words.

Four plus six equals ten.

____

Try It!

2) Write and solve the number sentence that matches the word problem.

Kale has 2 pigs and 4 hens. How many more hens does Kale have?

____

Instruction

Concept Application

1 Look at this subtraction number sentence.

$11 - \square = 9$

Circle the word problem that can be solved with this number sentence.

I have 11 mints. I give some to my friend. Now I have 9 mints. How many mints did I give to my friend?

I have 11 mints. My friend gives me 9 more. How many mints do I have now?

2 Look at this number sentence.

$10 + \square = 13$

Circle the word problem that can be solved with this number sentence.

Rocco had 10 cars. He found 10 more cars. How many cars does Rocco have now?

Rocco had 10 cars. He found some more cars. Now Rocco has 13 cars. How many cars did Rocco find?

3 Write a subtraction word problem to match the picture.

____

____

____

____

4 Draw a picture and write a word problem for this addition number sentence.

$5 + 9 = \square$

____

____

____

____

____

Instruction

Name: ______________________________

Concept Practice

Standard 1.3(F) – **Unit 12**

1 Look at this addition number sentence.

$12 + 7 = \square$

Circle the word problem that can be solved with this number sentence.

Marlo has 12 dimes and 7 nickels. How many coins does Marlo have?

Tammy has 12 dimes. She loses 7 dimes. How many dimes does Tammy have now?

2 Write a word problem to match the picture. Your word problem should compare the number of bears.

____

____

____

____

3 Look at this subtraction number sentence.

$\square - 9 = 9$

Which problem best matches this number sentence?

Tim had some action figures. He gave 9 to Ben. He has 9 left. How many action figures did Tim have?

Kenya picked 9 flowers. She picked 9 more flowers. How many flowers did Kenya pick?

4 Van made 6 chocolate ice cream cones. Sam made 8 vanilla ice cream cones.

Which equation tells how many ice cream cones the children made?

- ⬭ $8 - 6 = 2$
- ⬭ $14 - 8 = 6$
- ⬭ $8 + 6 = 14$

Illegal to Copy

Name: ______________________________

Addition Wipe-Out

Play *Addition Wipe-Out* with a partner or small group. Each player needs a game board and 16 markers. Each group needs three dice. In turn, each player rolls three dice and adds to find the sum. The player places a marker on the sum of the three numbers. If the number is already covered, the player passes. The winner is the first player to wipe-out (cover) all numbers from 3 to 18.

3	4	5	6
7	8	9	10
11	12	13	14
15	16	17	18

Extension

Name: ____________________

Math Challenge

Three friends found these shells at the beach.

Write an addition or subtraction question using the pictures.
Then, write a number sentence to show the answer.

____

____

Reflection on My Learning

Is it harder to...

- write a word problem when you know the number sentence, or
- solve a word problem when you do NOT know the number sentence?

Explain your answer.

____

____

Reflection on Critical Thinking

Circle the traits you used most often in this unit.

I show ____________________ when I ____________________ .

Illegal to Copy

Name: ______________________________

Assessment

Unit 12 – Standard 1.3(F)

Concept Check

1 Liz has 7 blue eggs and 8 pink eggs. How many eggs does Liz have in all?

Write a number sentence to solve the word problem.

____

2 Write a word problem that matches the picture.

____

____

____

3 Samir checked out 13 books from the library. He read 7 books. How many books does Samir still need to read?

Which number sentence will help solve the problem?

- ⬭ $13 + 7 = \square$
- ⬭ $13 - 7 = \square$
- ⬭ $7 + 13 = \square$

4 Write a subtraction word problem to match the picture. Your word problem should compare the balloons.

Korky Jingles

$9 - 6 = \square$

____

____

5 Use the picture to write a number sentence to compare the number of dogs and bones.

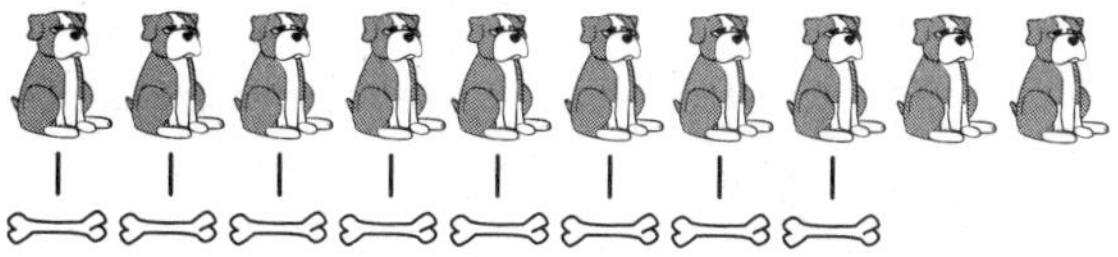

____

____

6 Write a word problem that matches the pictures and number sentence.

10 + 5 = 15

____

____

7 Use the picture and the number sentence to write a subtraction word problem.

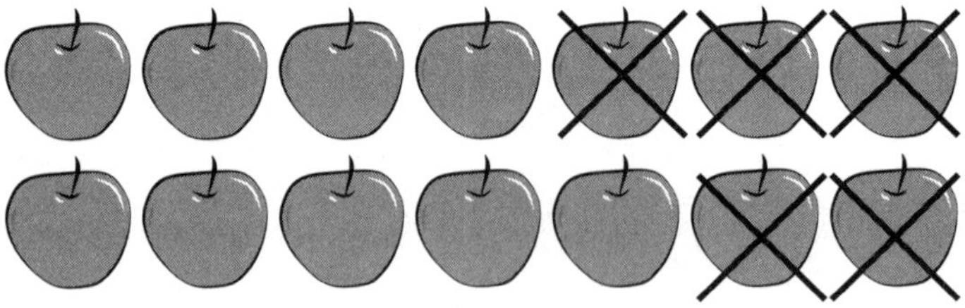

14 – 5 = ☐

____

____

What is the answer to the problem? ______________________

What strategy did you use to solve the problem?

____

____

Name: ______________________________

Unit 13 – Standard 1.4(A)

Getting Started

Unit 13: Identify Coins and Their Values

TEKS LEARNING TARGETS

- I can identify U.S. coins by both heads and tails.
- I can identify the value of U.S. coins.
- I can describe the relationships among U.S. coins.

Focus for 9 Traits of Critical Thinking™

Examine: *I use a variety of methods to explore and to analyze.*

How does taking time to analyze your work help you to be more successful?

____

____

Link: *I apply knowledge to reach new understandings.*

How do you help your learning when you apply math skills in everyday situations?

____

____

How are the various coins similar in appearance?
How are they different?

______

______

Have you ever made a mistake when using money at a store?
Explain what happened.

______

______

Illegal to Copy

Name: ____________________

Unit 13 – Standard 1.4(A)

cent (¢)	**dime**	**penny**	**value**
coins	**nickel**	**quarter**	

dime nickel penny quarter

Order the coins from least value to greatest value.

__________ __________ __________ __________

Order the coins from smallest size to largest size.

__________ __________ __________ __________

Did you put the coins in the same order both times? ____________________

Which coin was in the same place in both lists? ____________________

Why is it important to know the difference between a nickel and a dime?

____

____

Why do you think the sides of each coin are called *heads* and *tails*?

____

____

Quarter

Dime

Nickel

Penny

Put an X on the heads side of each coin. Underline the tails side of each coin.

A quarter is worth 25 cents.
A dime is worth 10 cents.
A nickel is worth 5 cents.
A penny is worth 1 cent.

 is the same as .

 is the same as .

Each coin has a different picture on the front side and back side. The front side is called *heads*. The back is called *tails*.

Each coin has its own value.

Combinations of different coins can have the same value as other coins.

Try It!

1) Draw a triangle around the penny.

Underline the nickel.

Place an X on the quarter.

Try It!

2) One dime has the same value as ________ nickels.

One quarter has the same value as ________ pennies.

One nickel has the same value as ________ pennies.

Illegal to Copy

1 Which coin is worth 10¢?

- ⬭ Quarter
- ⬭ Penny
- ⬭ Dime

2 Match the front and the back of each coin.

3 Pam wants to buy this yo-yo. She pays with one coin.

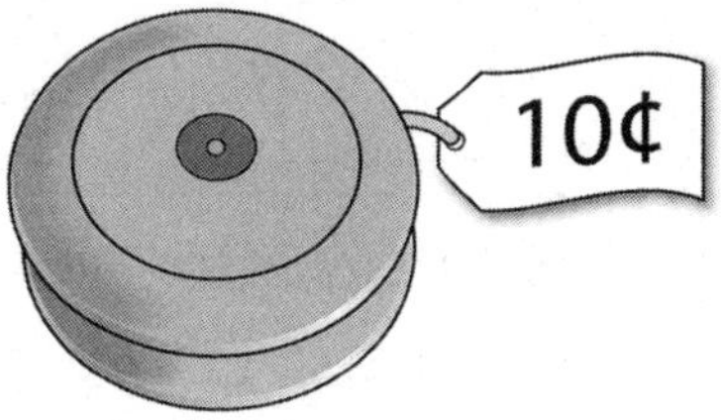

Circle the coin Pam can use to buy the yo-yo.

4 Look at the set of pennies.

Which coin has the same value?

Circle your answer.

5 Beto has 25¢ in his pocket. Circle the coins that equal 25¢.

What other coins could Beto use to make 25¢?

____

____

1 Draw a line to match.

1¢

5¢

10¢

25¢

2 Circle the coin with the greatest value.

3 Circle more than or less than.

 is more than / is less than 

 is more than / is less than 

4 Look at the group of nickels.

Choose the coin that has the same value as the nickels.

- ⬭ 1 dime
- ⬭ 1 penny
- ⬭ 1 quarter

5 Complete each sentence.

One dime has the same value as

__________ pennies.

One nickel has the same value as

__________ pennies.

6 Describe a way you can make 20 cents with coins.

____

____

What coin could you add to make 25 cents?

____

____

Illegal to Copy

Name: ______________________________

Instruction

Coin-O Bingo

Play *Coin-O Bingo* with a partner. Each player needs 20 colored cubes, one game board, and a pencil and paper clip for the spinner. In turn, each player spins the spinner. The player covers a space on the *Coin-O Bingo* board that matches the spin. The first player to cover 5 spaces in a row wins.

C	O	I	N	O
				1¢
dime	nickel		5¢	10¢
25¢	quarter	FREE	1¢	5¢
5¢	penny	dime	quarter	
	10¢		penny	25¢

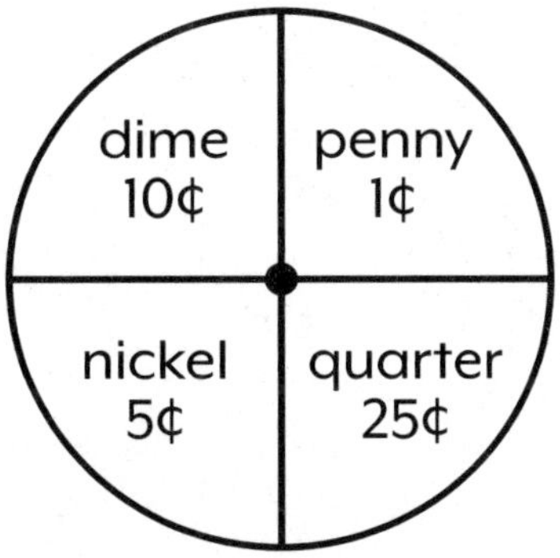

Extension

Name: ______________________________

Math Challenge

Circle the sets of coins that have the same value as 1 quarter.

Explain what coins you could use if you wanted to buy a glass of lemonade for 30 cents.

____

____

Reflection on My Learning

Dad will give you 1 dime or 5 pennies. Which will you choose? Why?

____

____

Reflection on Critical Thinking

Circle the traits you used most often in this unit.

I show ____________________ when I ____________________ .

Name: ________________________________

Assessment

Unit 13 – Standard 1.4(A)

Concept Check

1 Circle the coin in each row with the greater value.

2 Write the value of each coin.

A penny = __________¢

A nickel = __________¢

A dime = __________¢

A quarter = __________¢

3 Draw a box around the coin with the least value.

4 Match the coin to its name.

quarter

penny

dime

nickel

5 What is the value of the coins?

______________________¢

Which coin has the same value? Circle your answer.

6 Carley says she has only nickels in her pocket.

KC says she is wrong because the coins look different.

Circle the name of the person who is right.

Carley KC

7 Circle the coin in each row that matches the amount.

25¢	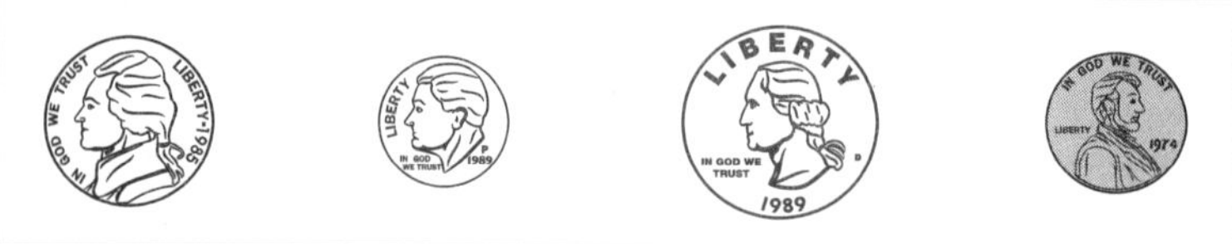
5¢	
10¢	
1¢	

8 Place an X on the pennies. Draw a circle around the nickels. Place a box around the dimes. Use your pencil to shade the quarters.

Illegal to Copy

Name: ______________________________

Getting Started

Unit 14 – Standards 1.4(B), 1.4(C)

Unit 14: Determine the Value of a Set of Coins and Use the Cent Symbol

TEKS LEARNING TARGETS

- I can write a number with the cent symbol to show the value of a coin.
- I can recognize that a number represents an amount of money when the cent symbol follows the number.
- I can skip count by twos, fives, and tens to 100 to count coins.
- I can determine the value of a collection of coins.

Focus for 9 Traits of Critical Thinking™

Collaborate: *I work with others to achieve better outcomes.*

How does your learning improve when you work with others?

____

____

Communicate: *I use clear language to express my ideas and to share information.*

How does your ability to clearly ***communicate*** your ideas and questions allow you to improve as a student?

____

____

Name: ______________________________

Concept Exploration

Dime 10¢ 	Nickel 5¢ 	Penny 1¢ 

What is something you learned about coins today by listening to a classmate?

____

____

How does the cent symbol help others understand the amount of change in a collection?

____

____

Illegal to Copy

Name: ______________________________

Unit 14 – Standards 1.4(B), 1.4(C)

Instruction

Vocabulary Mastery

amount	**dime**	**penny**	**symbol**
cent (¢)	**nickel**	**skip count**	**value**
coins			

Print your first name. ______________________________

Use the key to determine the value of your name.

Key

Vowels = 10¢
Consonants = 5¢

Write the value of your name in cents. ______________________

How does your name's value compare to those of your classmates?

____

____

How does this name activity ***communicate*** your understanding of vowels and consonants?

____

____

Name: ______________________________

Concept Development

5¢

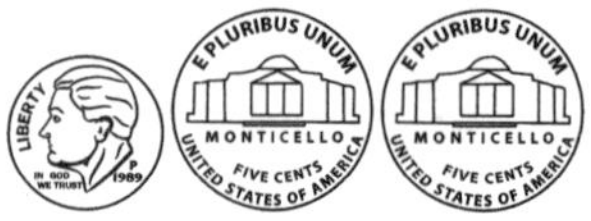

20¢

You need to place a cent symbol (¢) after your number when recording your answer.

A cent symbol (¢) after the number shows that it is an amount of money.

5¢ 10¢ 15¢ 20¢ 25¢

When counting nickels, it helps to count by fives.

10¢ 20¢ 30¢ 40¢ 50¢ 60¢

When counting dimes, it helps to count by tens.

2¢ 4¢ 6¢

When counting pennies, you might count two at a time to skip count by twos.

Try It!

1) Write the numbers as you count.

____ ____ ____ ____ cents

Try It!

2) Write the total value of the coins in cents.

____

Illegal to Copy

1 Dan stacks his coins in twos.

Which shows what Dan says when he counts the coins?

- ⬭ 10, 11, 12, 13, 14
- ⬭ 10, 12, 14, 16, 18
- ⬭ 10, 15, 20, 25, 30

2 Which coin has the value of 10¢?

- ⬭ 
- ⬭ 
- ⬭ 

3 Bess wants to buy a gift for 45¢.

Circle the coins Bess can use.

4 Match the coins to the correct piggy bank.

5 Donna finds these coins. What is the value of the coins?

Answer ______________________

Donna needs two dimes and four pennies to buy some candy. Did Donna find enough money to buy the candy? ______________

Explain your answer.

____

____

1 How much money does Jenny have in her coat pocket?

- ⬭ 38¢
- ⬭ 18¢
- ⬭ 13¢

2 Annalise takes out the trash for 5 days. She earns 5¢ each day.

How much does Annalise earn for taking out the trash?

Answer ______________________

3 What is the value of the coins in cents?

Answer ______________________

4 Kanye has 1 nickel. He trades his nickel to his brother for 3 pennies.

Was this an equal trade? ________
Explain your answer.

____

____

5 Lin has a piggy bank with 56¢ inside.

Circle the coins that might be inside Lin's bank.

Name: ______________________________

Unit 14 – Standards 1.4(B), 1.4(C)

Concept Practice: Motivation Station

Race to a Dollar

Play *Race to a Dollar* with a partner. Each player needs 6 dimes, 7 nickels, and 5 pennies. Partners need one game board and a pencil and paper clip for the spinner. Partners take turns spinning and placing coins on the racetrack. If a player spins a coin that does not have any open spaces, the player passes. The first person to reach one dollar by covering all the coins wins.

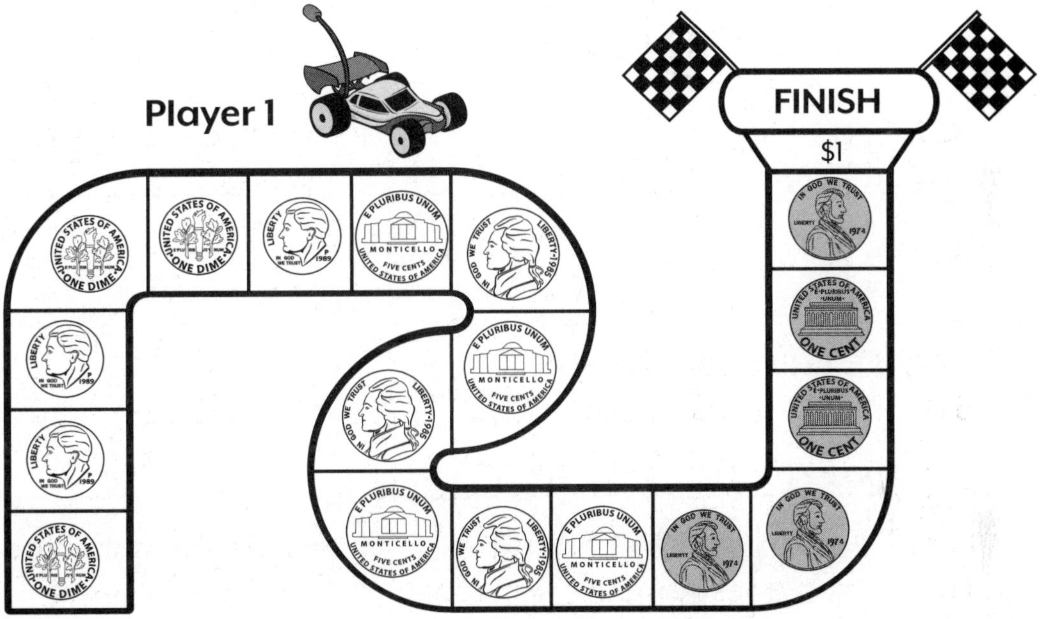

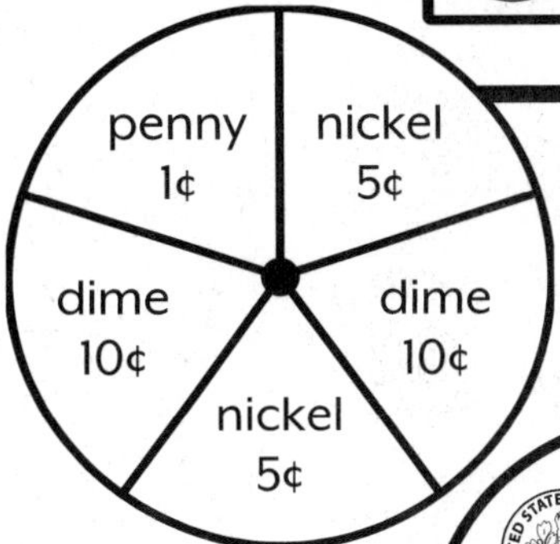

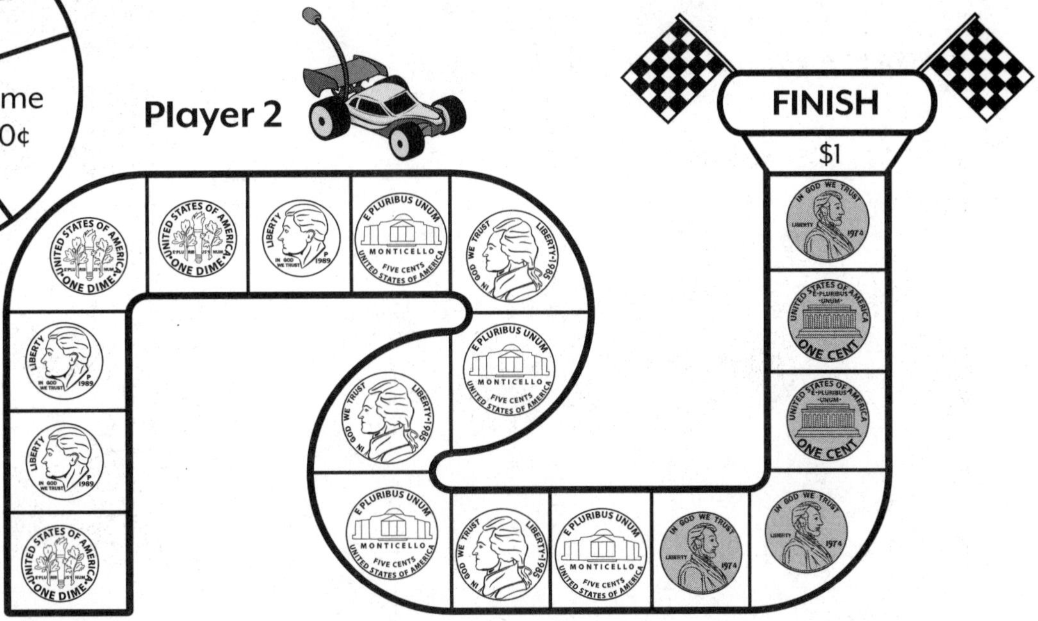

Extension

Name: ______________________________

Standards 1.4(B), 1.4(C) – **Unit 14**

Math Challenge

Write the value of each set of coins in cents.

____

____

Circle the set of coins that has the least value. Then, explain your thinking.

____

____

Reflection on My Learning

How are a nickel and dime alike?

____

How are a nickel and dime different?

____

Reflection on Critical Thinking

Circle the traits you used most often in this unit.

I show ______________________ when I ______________________ .

Name: ____________________________

Assessment

Unit 14 – Standards 1.4(B), 1.4(C)

Concept Check

1 Allie has 10¢.
Her mom gives her 2 dimes.
How much money does Allie have now?

- ⬭ 17¢
- ⬭ 20¢
- ⬭ 30¢

2 What is the value of the quarter in cents?

__________¢

3 A pack of gum costs 35¢. Misty has these coins. Does Misty have enough money to buy the pack of gum?

Answer ____________________

Explain your answer.

____

____

4 Brenda wants to count her money quickly.

Which shows what Brenda says as she counts her coins?

- ⬭ 5, 10, 15, 20, 25, 30
- ⬭ 10, 20, 30, 40, 50, 60
- ⬭ 10, 20, 30, 40, 45, 50

5 Write the value of each coin.

_____ _____ _____ _____

6 Ted's dad offers him 5 dimes or 7 nickels. Which should Ted pick if he wants the greater amount of money? Circle your answer.

Explain your choice.

____

____

Name: ______________________________

7 Martha has 3 nickels. How much money does Martha have?

____

The pictures below show the money Barb and Linda have. Record the amount of money each girl has.

Barb

Linda

__________ __________

Which person has the same amount of money as Martha?

Answer ______________________________

8 Adam has 10 pennies and 1 dime in one pocket. He has 2 dimes in the other pocket. Write the value of the coins in the box beside each pocket.

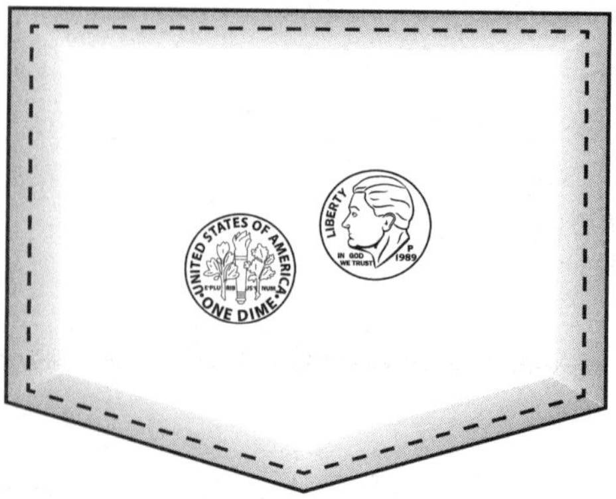

Name: ____________________

Getting Started

Unit 15 – Standard 1.5(A)

Unit 15: Recite Numbers Between 1–120

TEKS LEARNING TARGETS

- I can count forward by ones to 120 from any number.
- I can count backward by ones from any number between 1 and 120.

Focus for 9 Traits of Critical Thinking™

Adapt: *I adjust my actions and strategies to accomplish tasks.*

Do you use the same process for counting backward by ones as you do for counting forward?

____

____

Examine: *I use a variety of methods to explore and to analyze.*

Are there patterns in counting forward that you can apply to counting backward?

____

____

Instruction

Name: ______________________________

Concept Exploration

Standard 1.5(A) – **Unit 15**

1	2	3	4	5	6	7	8	9	10
11	12	13	14	15	16	17	18	19	20
21	22	23	24	25	26	27	28	29	30
31	32	33	34	35	36	37	38	39	40
41	42	43	44	45	46	47	48	49	50
51	52	53	54	55	56	57	58	59	60
61	62	63	64	65	66	67	68	69	70
71	72	73	74	75	76	77	78	79	80
81	82	83	84	85	86	87	88	89	90
91	92	93	94	95	96	97	98	99	100
101	102	103	104	105	106	107	108	109	110
111	112	113	114	115	116	117	118	119	120

How does counting from a number other than 0 require you to think differently?

____

____

How is counting backward like counting forward? How is it different?

____

____

Illegal to Copy

Name: ______________________________

Unit 15 – Standard 1.5(A)

Instruction

Vocabulary Mastery

after	before	between	count	number

Follow the directions to find the mystery number.

1	2	3	4	5	6	7	8	9	10
11	12	13	14	15	16	17	18	19	20
21	22	23	24	25	26	27	28	29	30
31	32	33	34	35	36	37	38	39	40
41	42	43	44	45	46	47	48	49	50
51	52	53	54	55	56	57	58	59	60

1 Start at 57.
2 Count backward 10 spaces. Draw a box around the number.
3 Count backward 5 spaces. Draw a sun around the number.
4 Count forward 1 space. Draw a triangle around the number.
5 Count backward 10 spaces. Draw a circle around the number.
6 Count forward 3 spaces. Draw a cloud around the number.
7 Count backward 20 spaces. Draw a heart around the number.
8 The mystery number has a heart around it.

The mystery number is ______________.

How does counting incorrectly change your answer?

____

____

How did counting help you determine the mystery number?

____

____

1	2	3	4	5	6	7	8	9	10
11	12	13	14	15	16	17	18	19	20
21	22	23	24	25	26	27	28	29	30
31	32	33	34	35	36	37	38	39	40

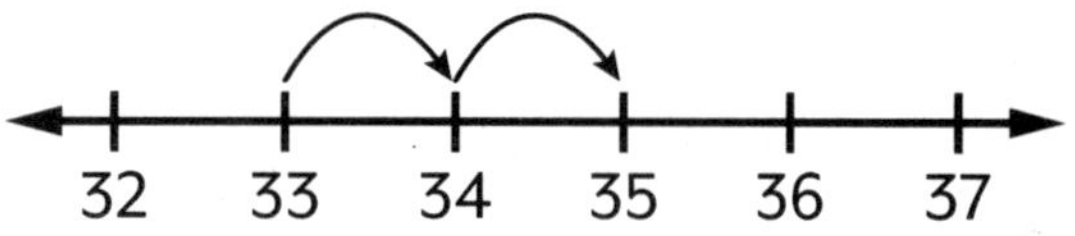

I count on 33, 34, 35.

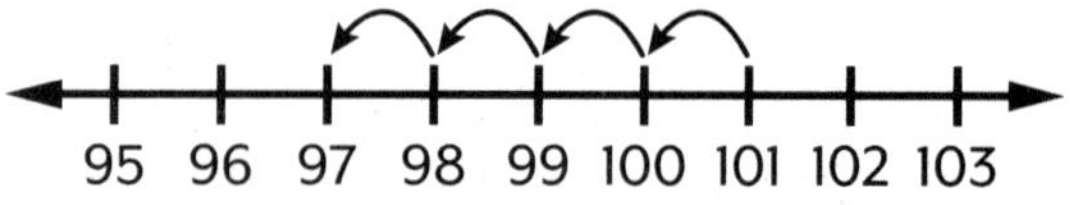

I count back starting at 101. I count 100, 99, 98, 97.

When counting from 1 to 40 on a hundred chart, you will notice patterns in the numbers. For example, the numbers top to bottom have the same digit in the ones place.

You can count forward or *count on* to find the numbers that come after.

You can count backward or *count back* to find numbers that come before.

Try It!

1) Write the missing numbers.

68, 69, ________, 71

88, 89, 90, 91, ________

Try It!

2) Write the missing numbers on the number line.

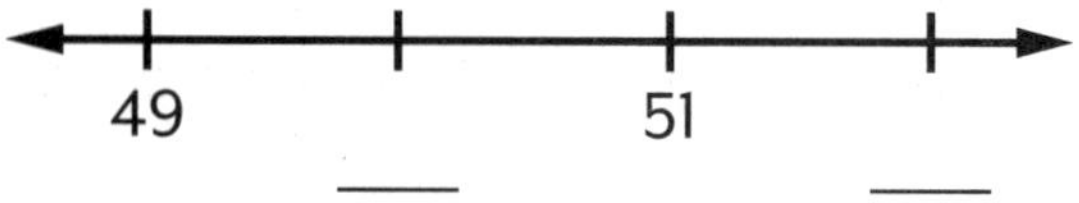

Illegal to Copy

Instruction

Concept Application

1 Reza counted 87 pennies. What 5 numbers will Reza say next as he counts?

- ⬭ 89, 90, 91, 92, 93
- ⬭ 88, 89, 90, 91, 92
- ⬭ 86, 85, 84, 83, 82

2 Lydia counts backward starting at 117. Circle all the numbers Lydia says if she stops counting at 110.

118 110 119 106 98 100 111
115 120 114 112 121 116 113

3 Write the missing numbers.

______, 57, 58, ______, 60, ______

4 Perry is 7 years old. He counts how old he will be in 9 years. What numbers does Perry say as he counts?

____

____

How old will Perry be in 9 years?

____

5 Color the 4 numbers that come before 95 blue. Color the 3 numbers that come after 87 red.

81	82	83	84	85	86	87	88	89	90
91	92	93	94	95	96	97	98	99	100
101	102	103	104	105	106	107	108	109	110

Extend the number chart by filling in the next 5 numbers.

_____ _____ _____ _____ _____

6 The square is cut from a hundred chart. Complete the chart.

		3	4	5	
11	12	13		15	16
21	22		24		26
31					36
41		43	44	45	46
	52		54		

★

What pattern do you see in the column that has a star?

____

Instruction

Name: ____________________

Concept Practice

Standard 1.5(A) – **Unit 15**

1 Rami counts backward. He starts at 83.

What are the next 4 numbers Rami will say?

- ⬭ 82, 81, 79, 78
- ⬭ 84, 85, 86, 87
- ⬭ 82, 81, 80, 79

2 The clock at the football game counts backward from 25 to 15.

25 __ __ __ __ __ __ __ __ __ 15

The count down clock starts at 25. Which list has the other numbers the clock will show as it counts down to 15?

- ⬭ 26, 27, 28, 29, 30, 31, 32, 33
- ⬭ 14, 13, 12, 11, 10, 9, 8, 7, 6
- ⬭ 24, 23, 22, 21, 20, 19, 18, 17, 16

3 Look at the number line.

What number will come next if you continue to count?

Answer ____________________

4 Count backward to fill in the missing numbers.

102, _____, _____, _____

23, _____, _____, _____

120, _____, _____, _____

5 Diandre counts forward from 49. What are the next 4 numbers she will say?

- ⬭ 48, 47, 46, 45
- ⬭ 50, 51, 54, 55
- ⬭ 50, 51, 52, 53

6 Dolan finds 27 acorns on the ground. He collects more and recounts them. He has 33 acorns. What numbers does Dolan count between 27 and 33?

_____, _____, _____, _____, _____

Illegal to Copy

Blackout

Play *Blackout* with a partner. Each player needs a 120 chart, a die, and a crayon. Player 1 rolls the die, chooses any number on the board, and counts forward or backward from the number rolled. After correctly counting, player 1 colors the numbers counted. Players take turns until all numbers are colored. Students count the number of squares colored by each player. The winner is the student with more numbers colored.

1	2	3	4	5	6	7	8	9	10
11	12	13	14	15	16	17	18	19	20
21	22	23	24	25	26	27	28	29	30
31	32	33	34	35	36	37	38	39	40
41	42	43	44	45	46	47	48	49	50
51	52	53	54	55	56	57	58	59	60
61	62	63	64	65	66	67	68	69	70
71	72	73	74	75	76	77	78	79	80
81	82	83	84	85	86	87	88	89	90
91	92	93	94	95	96	97	98	99	100
101	102	103	104	105	106	107	108	109	110
111	112	113	114	115	116	117	118	119	120

Extension

Name: ____________________

Math Challenge

Use the clues to find the mystery number.

The mystery number has 3 digits.

The digit in the hundreds place is 1.

The digit in the tens place is five less than the number 5.

The digit in the ones place is 8 more than the number 1.

What is the mystery number? _____ _____ _____

Count backward from the mystery number. Stop counting when you say a 2-digit number with the same digit in the tens place and the ones place.

At what number did you stop counting? __________

Reflection on My Learning

Ben said, "Counting forward is like adding and counting backward is like subtracting."

Use words, numbers, or pictures to explain what Ben means.

Reflection on Critical Thinking

Circle the traits you used most often in this unit.

I show ____________________ when I ____________________.

Illegal to Copy

1 Tom writes numbers in boxes for a game. He starts at 0 and stops at 68. Write an X in box 68.

0	1	2							

2 Marcus counted 36 marbles. Then he counted these marbles, starting with 37. What was the last number Marcus said?

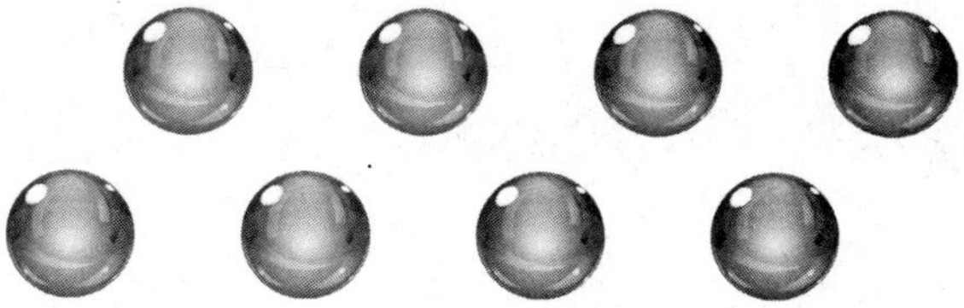

Answer ______________________

3 Sy played a game in which players say numbers in order. The player before Sy said, "18." What number should Sy say?

Answer ______________________

4 Tess counted from 95 to 104. Circle the numbers Tess did NOT say when she counted.

93 102 111 96 89 103

Check your answer.

Write the numbers from 95 to 104.

____, ____, ____, ____, ____,

____, ____, ____, ____, ____

5 Write the number.

Before

____ 18

____ 69

____ 90

6 Count forward to fill in the missing numbers.

32, ____, ____

99, ____, ____

58, ____, ____

Assessment

Name: ____________________

Concept Check

Standard 1.5(A) – **Unit 15**

7 Write the missing numbers in the chart.

	92	93					98		100
101			104		106				

8 Heath has 100 gumballs in a jar. Mom gives him more gumballs.

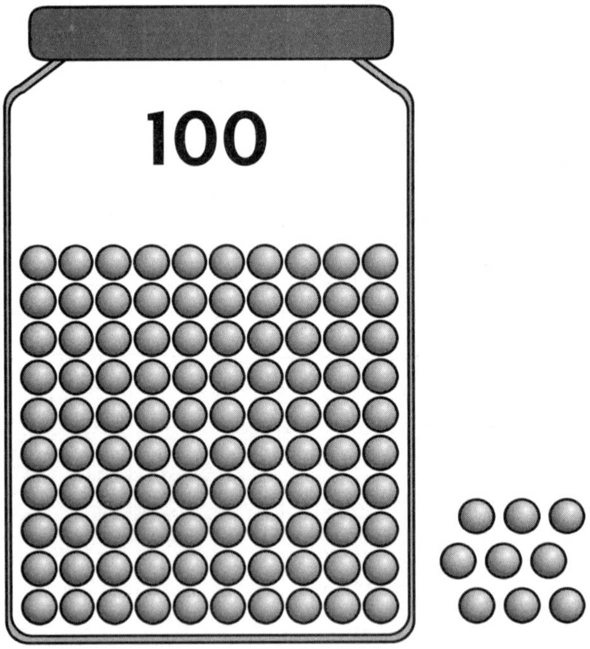

Write the numbers Heath says as he counts the gumballs.

101 ____ ____ ____ ____ ____ ____ ____ ____

Illegal to Copy

Name: ______________________________

Unit 16 – Standard 1.5(B)

Getting Started

Unit 16: Skip Count by Twos, Fives, and Tens

TEKS LEARNING TARGETS

- I can skip count by twos, fives, and tens to 120.
- I can describe the patterns I see when I count by twos, fives, and tens.

Focus for 9 Traits of Critical Thinking™

Communicate: *I use clear language to express my ideas and to share information.*

When you are communicating information with people about how you are counting, why is it important to be very clear?

____

____

Reflect: *I review my thoughts and experiences to guide my actions.*

Are there times when you have seen people use skip counting? Why do you think they chose to do that?

____

____

Name: ____________________

1	2	3	4	5	6	7	8	9	10
11	12	13	14	15	16	17	18	19	20
21	22	23	24	25	26	27	28	29	30
31	32	33	34	35	36	37	38	39	40
41	42	43	44	45	46	47	48	49	50
51	52	53	54	55	56	57	58	59	60
61	62	63	64	65	66	67	68	69	70
71	72	73	74	75	76	77	78	79	80
81	82	83	84	85	86	87	88	89	90
91	92	93	94	95	96	97	98	99	100

How does the hundred chart help you ***communicate*** your understanding of skip counting?

____

____

What is something you learned in kindergarten that you used in this activity?

____

____

Illegal to Copy

Name: ____________________

Instruction

Unit 16 – Standard 1.5(B)

Vocabulary Mastery

pattern	**skip count**

Color the boxes with the numbers that show skip counting by 5. Some boxes have been colored for you.

5	10	2	15	8	20	26	25	29	30	35
40	42	78	45	96	50	82	55	108	60	33
65	70	91	75	42		37		54	80	85
90	94	14	95	22	36		87	99	100	7
	53	12	105	64	83	110	82	66	115	120

The boxes that have color make a mystery word.

Write the mystery word on the line.

Answer ____________________

In this activity you shared information using math. What is another way that information might be shared using math?

____

____

Why do you think some boxes were already shaded for you? Did the shading help you discover the mystery word?

____

____

Name: ____________________

2, 4, 6, 8, 10, 12...

5, 10, 15, 20, 25, 30...

10, 20, 30, 40, 50, 60...

When skip counting, you count only the numbers in the skip-counting pattern.

Fill in the blanks.

2, 4, 6, ____, 10, 12, ____

When skip counting by twos, you are adding 2 each time you count.

5, 10, 15, 20, ____, 30, ____

When skip counting by fives, you count every fifth number. You are adding 5 each time you count.

10, 20, ____, 40, 50, ____

When skip counting by tens, you count every tenth number. You are adding 10 each time you count.

76, 78, 80, 82, 84, 86...

30, 35, 40, 45, 50, 55...

60, 70, 80, 90, 100, 110...

Once you know the patterns, you can skip count beginning with any number in the pattern.

Try It!

1) Complete the pattern.

88, 90, ____, 94, ____, 98, ____

What number are you adding each time you count?

____

Try It!

2) Complete the pattern.

55, 60, 65, ____, ____, ____

Which of these numbers would you say when counting by 10s?

____, ____, ____

Illegal to Copy

Instruction

Concept Application

1 Which set of numbers shows skip counting by twos?

- ⬭ 48, 50, 51, 52
- ⬭ 100, 105, 110, 115
- ⬭ 88, 90, 92, 94

2 Leron marks a pattern on a hundred chart.

21	(22)	23	(24)	25	(26)	27	(28)	29	(30)
31	32	33	34	35	36	37	38	39	40

If Leron continues the pattern, what is the next number he will circle?

- ⬭ 31
- ⬭ 32
- ⬭ 35

3 Ms. Cook's class made a tally chart to show the number of pets they have.

Our Pets

Student Name	Number of Pets
Caroline	卌
Jackson	卌
Preston	卌 卌
Tori	卌

Skip count by fives to find the total number of pets.

Answer ______________________

4 Write the missing numbers for the number line in the spaces.

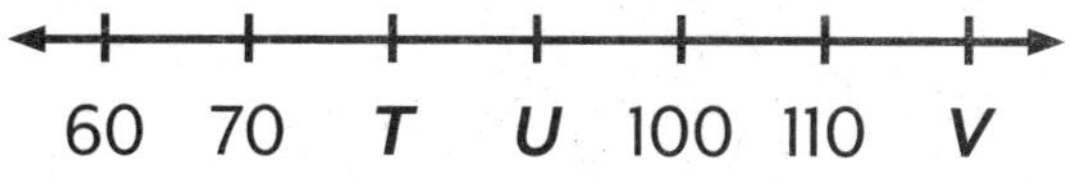

T = ________

U = ________

V = ________

What skip-counting pattern is shown on the number line?

Answer ______________________

5 A group of first graders uses their hand prints to skip count by 10s.

How many fingers did they count?

Answer ______________________

Instruction

Name: ______________________

Concept Practice

Standard 1.5(B) – **Unit 16**

1 Skip count by fives to count the petals on the flowers.

How many petals are on the 5 flowers?

Answer ______________________

2 Shade the boxes to show skip counting by 10.

1	2	3	4	5	6	7	8	9	10
11	12	13	14	15	16	17	18	19	20
21	22	23	24	25	26	27	28	29	30
31	32	33	34	35	36	37	38	39	40
41	42	43	44	45	46	47	48	49	50
51	52	53	54	55	56	57	58	59	60

3 What numbers are missing in the skip-counting pattern?

22, 24, 26, ☐, ☐, ☐

4 Write the missing numbers for the number line in the blanks.

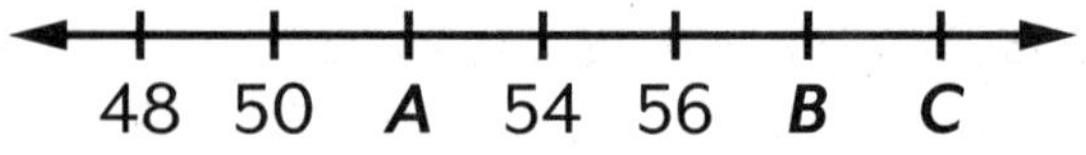

A = ________

B = ________

C = ________

What skip-counting pattern is shown on the number line?

Answer ______________________

5 Which set of numbers shows skip counting by 5?

- ⬭ 25, 30, 35, 45
- ⬭ 95, 100, 105, 110
- ⬭ 50, 60, 70, 80

6 Use the hands to count by 5.

Write the numbers below the hands as you count.

5 ____ ____ 20 ____

Animal Dot-to-Dot

Skip count by 2 from 2–120 to connect the dots. When you finish connecting the dots, color the picture.

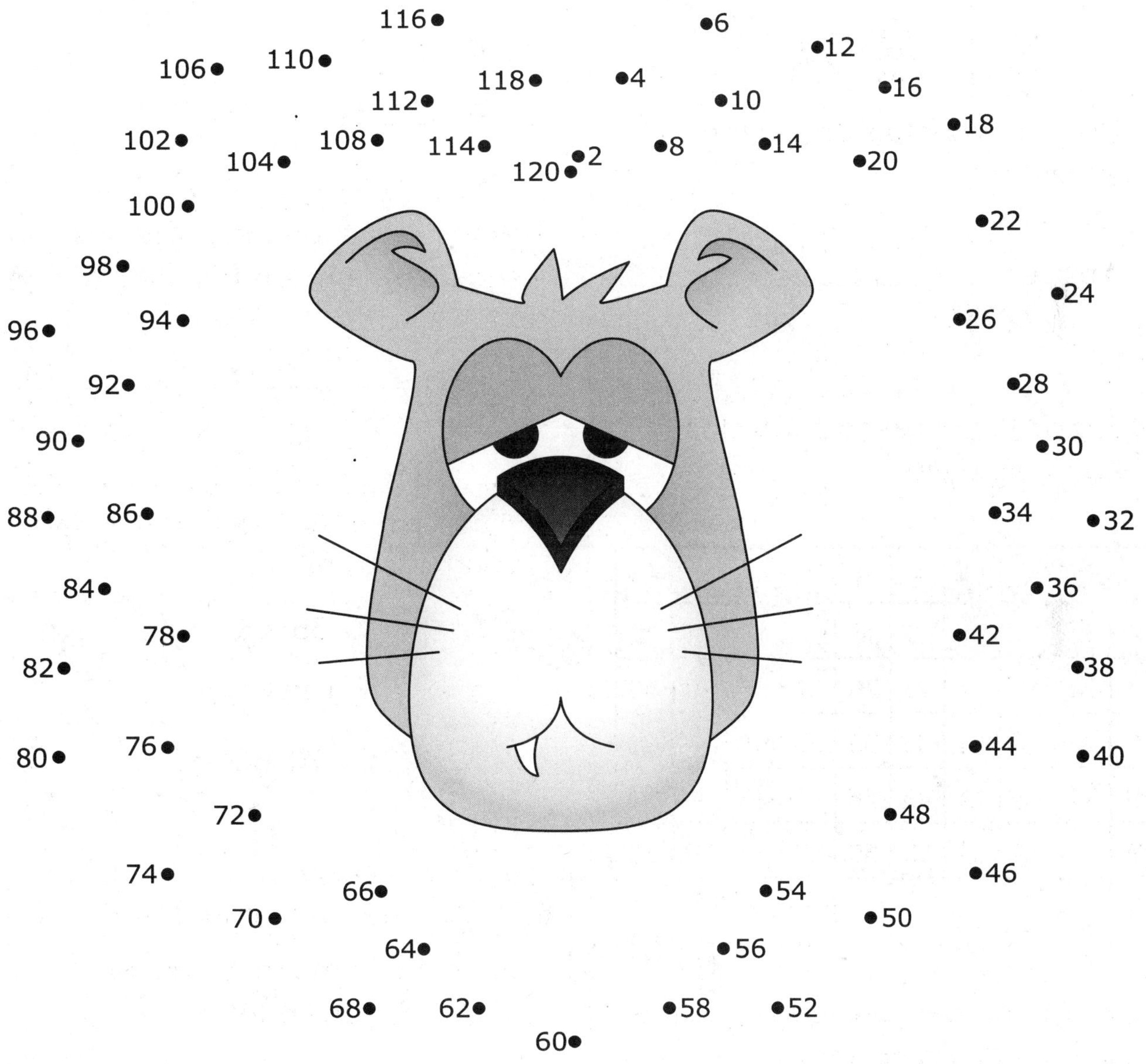

Extension

Name: ____________________

Math Challenge

Complete the graphic organizer to show things you might count by twos.

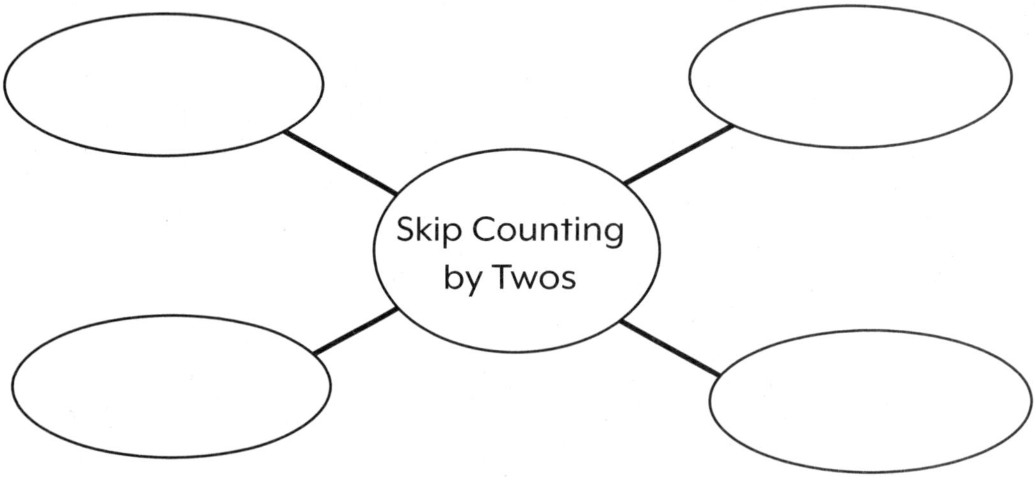

Reflection on My Learning

How can you use skip counting by twos, fives, or tens when you are not at school?

____

____

Reflection on Critical Thinking

Circle the traits you used most often in this unit.

I show ____________________ when I ____________________ .

Illegal to Copy

Name: ______________________________

Assessment

Unit 16 – Standard 1.5(B)

Concept Check

1 Shade the boxes to show skip counting by twos.

1	2	3	4	5	6	7	8	9	10
11	12	13	14	15	16	17	18	19	20
21	22	23	24	25	26	27	28	29	30
31	32	33	34	35	36	37	38	39	40
41	42	43	44	45	46	47	48	49	50
51	52	53	54	55	56	57	58	59	60

2 Look at the picture.

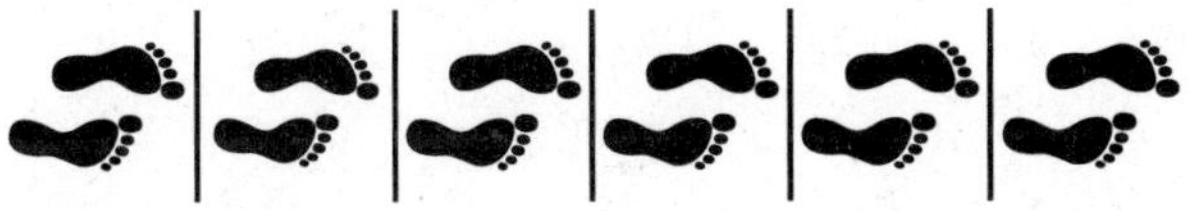

How many toes are in the picture?

Answer ______________________

What skip-counting pattern is shown?

Answer ______________________

3 Heather forms a pattern on a hundred chart with counters.

1	2	3	4	●	6	7	8	9	●
11	12	13	14	●	16	17	18	19	●
21	22	23	24	●	26	27	28	29	●
31	32	33	34	●	36	37	38	39	●
41	42	43	44	45	46	47	48	49	50
51	52	53	54	55	56	57	58	59	60

Heather continues the pattern. Where will she place the next counter?

- ⬭ 41
- ⬭ 45
- ⬭ 50

4 Skip count by 5 to 50. Draw an X on the numbers that do NOT belong.

5 10 15 20 25 26 30 35

39 40 45 48 50 55

5 What numbers are missing in the skip-counting pattern?

80, ☐ , ☐ ,110, 120

What skip-counting pattern is shown?

Answer ______________________

6 Paul uses counters to skip count on a chart.

81	●	83	●	85	●	87	●	89	●
91	●	93	●	95	●	97	●	99	●
101	●	103	●	105	●	107	108	109	110
111	112	113	114	115	116	117	118	119	120

Where should Paul place the next 3 counters?

_______ _______ _______

---

7 Draw 5 circles. Draw 10 marbles in each circle.

Skip count by 10. Write the numbers.

10, 20, _______, _______, 50

---

8 Skip count by 5. Begin with the number 75 and end with the number 105. Write the numbers you say.

75, 80, _______, _______, _______, _______, 105

Illegal to Copy

Name: ______________________________

Unit 17 – Standard 1.5(C)

Getting Started

Unit 17: Determine Numbers 10 More/Less Than a Given Number

TEKS LEARNING TARGETS

- I can use mental math strategies to find 10 more and 10 less than a given number up to 120.
- I can explain my reasoning by using my understanding of place value and patterns on the hundred chart.

Focus for 9 Traits of Critical Thinking™

Inquire: *I seek information that excites my curiosity and inspires my learning.*

Since the goal of this unit is to use your brain to mentally add and subtract 10, what are some things you could do to improve your thinking skills and to focus?

____

____

Link: *I apply knowledge to reach new understandings.*

What are some situations in your life when you might need to add 10 or take away 10?

____

____

Instruction

Name: ____________________

Concept Exploration

Standard 1.5(C) – **Unit 17**

What number is 10 more than 83?

Explain your thinking.

What number is 10 less than 48?

Explain your thinking.

What number is 10 more than

____________________?

Explain your thinking.

What number is 10 less than

____________________?

Explain your thinking.

What was the most challenging part of adding and subtracting 10 in your head?

____

____

Think of a time you had to add or subtract 10 in your head. Share your experience.

____

____

Illegal to Copy

add	**digit**	**subtract**
addends	**ones**	**subtraction**
addition	**place value**	**tens**

Angie has 14 fish. Shay has 10 less fish than Angie.

Draw a picture to show how many fish Shay has in her fish tank.
Write the answer in the box.

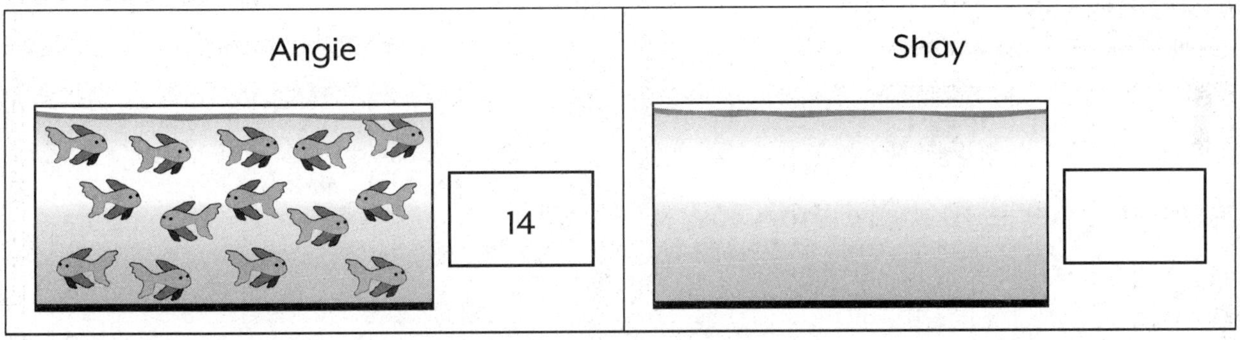

If Shay has 10 more fish than Angie, will the answer be the same? Explain your thinking.

____

____

Is it more important to understand the meaning of *place value* or the meaning of *digit* when determining 10 more or 10 less? Explain your thinking.

____

____

Are there other phrases that mean the same as *10 more* or *10 less*?

____

____

Circle the number that is 10 more.

45	35

Circle the number that is 10 less.

67	57

Circle the digit in the tens place.

Underline the digit in the ones place.

78

What number is 10 more than 78?

Answer ____________________

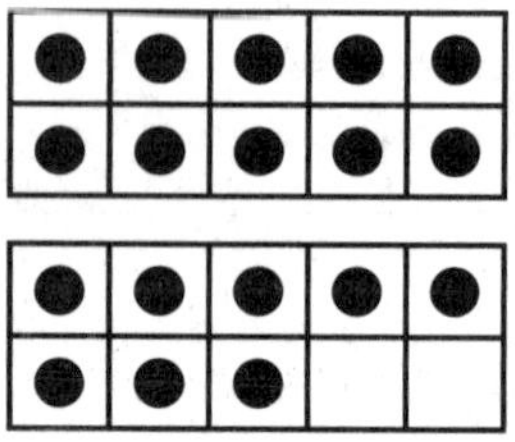

What number is shown? ______

What number is 10 less? ______

The digit in the tens place will change when adding or subtracting 10.

The digit in the ones place does not change when adding or subtracting 10.

Understanding place value is important when determining 10 more or 10 less.

You can use a ten frame, a number line, or a hundred chart to help you find 10 more or 10 less.

Try It!

1) Winnie picked 15 berries. She picked 10 more. How many berries does Winnie have now?

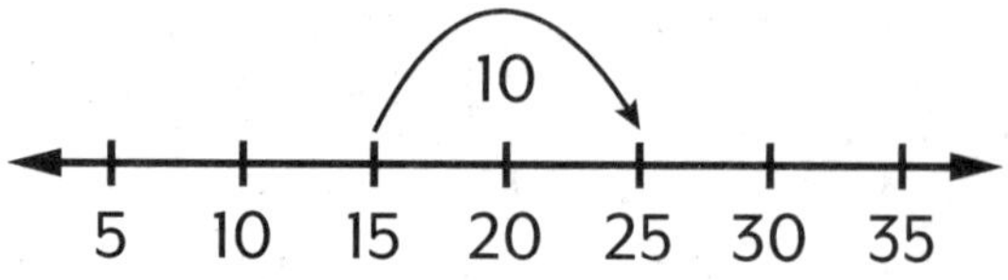

Answer ____________________

Try It!

2) Write the number that is 10 less than 88.

?
88

Answer ____________________

Illegal to Copy

Name: ____________________

Instruction

Unit 17 – Standard 1.5(C)

Concept Application

1 Which does NOT show 86?

- ⬭ 9 tens 6 ones plus 1 ten
- ⬭ 7 tens 6 ones plus 1 ten
- ⬭ 9 tens 6 ones minus 1 ten

2 I have 8 tens and 2 ones. I take away 1 ten. Now I have the number 72.

Is this true or false? Circle the correct answer.

True   False

3 This is part of a 100 chart. Write the missing numbers.

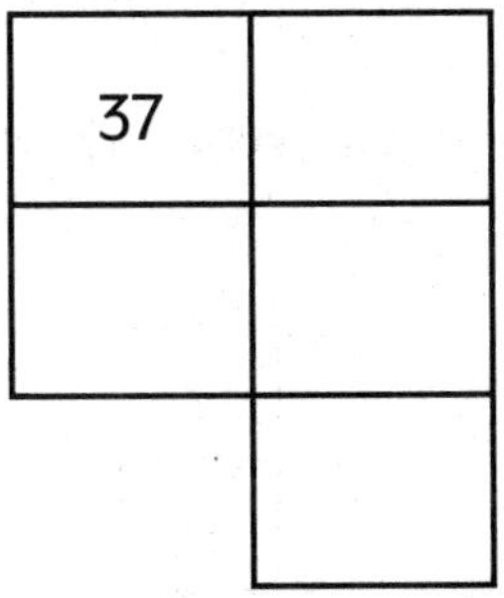

4 Look at the number line.

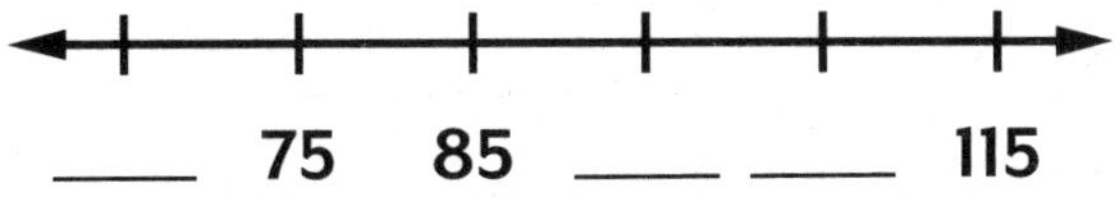

Which numbers complete the number line?

- ⬭ 74, 86, 114
- ⬭ 65, 90, 100
- ⬭ 65, 95, 105

5 Shelly thinks of a number that is 10 more than 40 and 10 less than 60.

What is Shelly's number?

Answer ____________________

Use words or pictures to explain your thinking.

1 Anna picked 30 cherries.

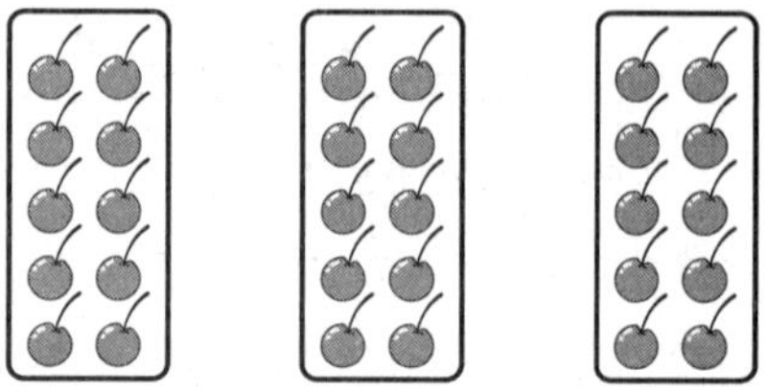

Cindy picked 10 more cherries than Anna.

How many cherries did Cindy pick?

- ⬭ 15 cherries
- ⬭ 20 cherries
- ⬭ 40 cherries

2 Otto thinks of a number.
It is 10 less than 58.
What is Otto's number?

- ⬭ 48
- ⬭ 57
- ⬭ 68

3 What number is 10 more than the number shown?

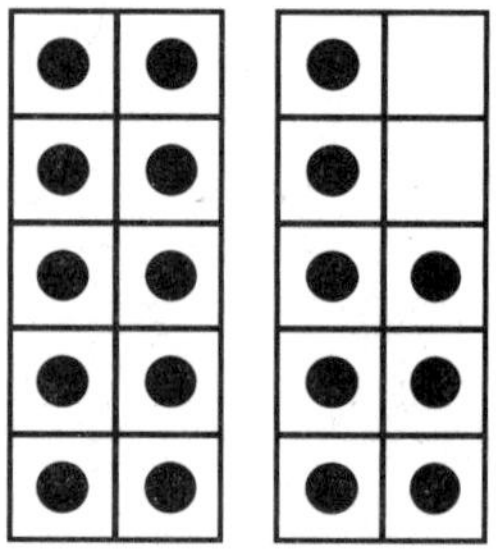

Answer ______________________

4 What numbers are missing? Write the numbers on the lines.

4	
?	______
24	
?	______
44	
?	______
64	

5 What number is 10 less than 37?

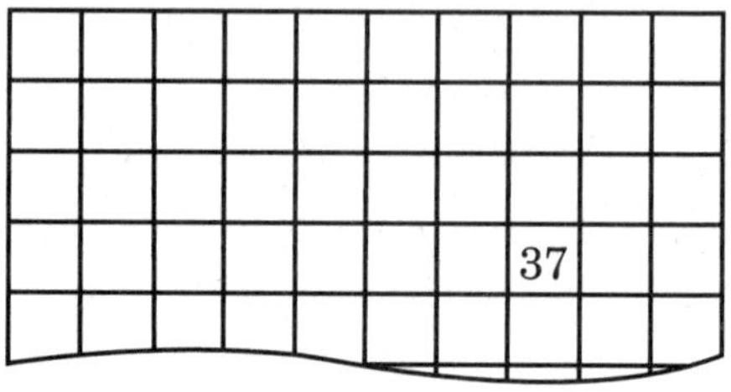

- ⬭ 27
- ⬭ 36
- ⬭ 47

Illegal to Copy

Hickory Dickory Dock

Play *Hickory Dickory Dock* with a partner. Help the mice go up the clock. Each player needs a game piece and a +/– die. Each player places a game piece on 60. Player 1 rolls the die. Player 1 adds ten and moves forward to 70 if a plus sign is rolled. Player 1 subtracts 10 and moves to 50 if a minus sign is rolled. Students take turns. The first player to reach 120 wins.

Extension

Name: ____________________

Standard 1.5(C) – **Unit 17**

Math Challenge

Lucy reads this math problem.

> Matteo and his mom went to the car show. Matteo saw 57 cars. Mom saw 77 cars. How many more cars did Mom see than Matteo?

Lucy draws and shades part of a hundred chart to solve the problem.

51	52	53	54	55	56	57	58	59	60
61	62	63	64	65	66	67	68	69	70
71	72	73	74	75	76	77	78	79	80

How does the chart help Lucy? ____________________

____

Reflection on My Learning

You need to find 10 more than 59. Which tool would you choose? Circle your answer.

hundred chart **base 10 blocks** **number line**

Explain your thinking.

____

____

Reflection on Critical Thinking

Circle the traits you used most often in this unit.

I show ____________________ when I ____________________.

Illegal to Copy

Name: ______________________

Assessment

Unit 17 – Standard 1.5(C)

Concept Check

1 There are 17 snakes in the zoo. There are 10 more monkeys than snakes.

How many monkeys are in the zoo?

__________ monkeys

2 Asia thinks of a number. It is 10 less than 110.

What is Asia's number?

- ⬭ 120
- ⬭ 101
- ⬭ 100

3 Write the number that is 10 less than 31.

?
31

Answer ______________

What number is 10 more than 41?

Answer ______________

4 Lance has 3 baskets of apples. Each basket has 10 apples in it.

Lance gives 1 basket to Merrie.

How many apples does Lance have now?

- ⬭ 20 apples
- ⬭ 29 apples
- ⬭ 40 apples

5 Tavon is 8 years old. Tavon's brother is 10 years older.

How old is Tavon's brother?

- ⬭ 25 years old
- ⬭ 18 years old
- ⬭ 8 years old

6 Which shows 43?

- ⬭ 2 tens 13 ones plus 2 tens
- ⬭ 3 tens 3 ones plus 1 ten
- ⬭ 4 tens 3 ones minus 1 ten

Assessment

Name: ______________________

Concept Check

7 Tyrone reads for 35 minutes every day. Lian reads 10 minutes longer than Tyrone each day. How many minutes does Lian read each day?

Answer ______________________

8 Maddie says that 43 is 10 more than 34.

Do you agree? Circle Yes or No.

Yes No

How do you know? Explain your thinking.

____

____

9 Max is 6 years old. How old will he be in 10 years?

Use the open number line to show your work.

Max will be ______________________ years old.

What other strategy could you use to find the same answer? Use your words or a picture to explain.

Illegal to Copy

Name: ______________________

Getting Started

Unit 18 – Standard 1.5(D)

Unit 18: Represent Word Problems with Addition and Subtraction

TEKS LEARNING TARGETS

- I can describe what is happening in a word problem and what I need to find.
- I can represent word problems using concrete objects or pictorial models.
- I can represent word problems using number sentences.

Focus for 9 Traits of Critical Thinking™

Strive: *I use effort and determination to focus on challenging tasks.*

Has there ever been a time when you struggled to solve a word problem? What did you do to stay on track and not give up? Were you successful in the end?

____

____

Create: *I use my knowledge and imagination to express new and innovative ideas.*

When you ***create*** pictures to help tell a story, is it easier to use characters and objects you are familiar with? Why or why not?

____

____

Name: ____________________

How did you work to stay focused during the firefly story? Did staying focused make it easier to determine what was happening in the word problem?

____

____

What other manipulatives could you ***create*** to model fireflies in the activity?

____

____

Illegal to Copy

add	**equal (=)**	**number**	**subtract**
addends	**equation**	**number sentence**	**sum**
difference	**minus (–)**	**plus (+)**	**total**

Go fishing for vocabulary words. Put the words in ABC order.

1 ____________________

2 ____________________

3 ____________________

4 ____________________

5 ____________________

6 ____________________

7 ____________________

8 ____________________

9 ____________________

10 ____________________

The words *add* and *addend* both begin with the same three letters. How did you decide which word to place first?

____

____

Is there another game you could ***create*** for you and your classmates to practice ABC order?

____

____

Instruction

Name: ______________________________

Krista had 6 cherries and 8 strawberries. How many pieces of fruit did Krista have?

Draw a picture of the problem.

Write the number sentence.

____

Drawing a picture helps you understand a problem.

Jerry had 10 black linking cubes and 7 white linking cubes. How many cubes would Jerry have if he joined them together?

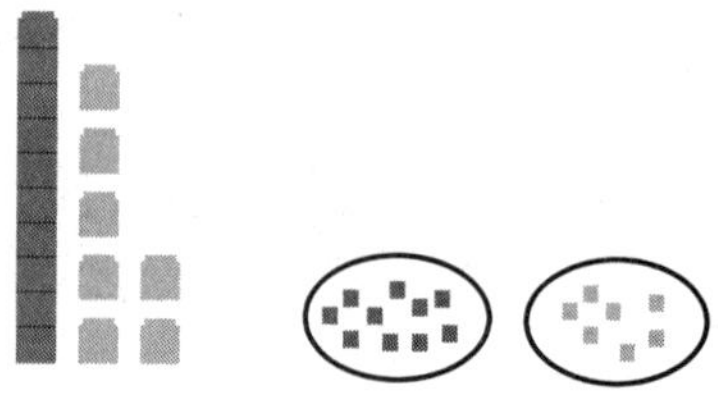

objects models

10 + 7 = 17

number sentence

You can use objects, models, and number sentences to help you solve a problem.

Try It!

1) Kalea has 15 pieces of gum. She gives 8 pieces to her friends.

How many pieces does Kalea have left?

Answer ______________________

Try It!

2) Ben earns 9 pennies. He earns 5 more pennies for making his bed.

How much does Ben have in all?

Answer ______________________

Illegal to Copy

Name: ______________________________

1 Ten ducks swim in the pond. Three more ducks come to swim.

Which equation shows the total number of ducks?

- ◯ $10 + 3 = 13$
- ◯ $10 + 5 = 15$
- ◯ $10 - 3 = 7$

2 There are 14 goats in the barn. Then 6 goats leave.

Which number sentence shows how many goats are still in the barn?

- ◯ $15 - 6 = 9$
- ◯ $14 - 6 = 8$
- ◯ $14 - 10 = 4$

3 Braden has 16 toy trucks. He gives some away. Now Braden has 9 trucks. How many trucks did Braden give away?

Write and solve the number sentence.

____

4 Mr. Monk's class has a fish tank with 5 blue fish and 5 yellow fish. Draw a picture to show Mr. Monk's fish tank.

Write an equation to find the total number of fish in the tank.

____

5 Kesha counts 11 birds on the fence. She counts 3 lizards on the fence. Seven birds fly away.

How many birds are on the fence now?

Answer ______________________________

Which number sentence can be used to find the answer?

- ◯ $11 + 7 = 18$
- ◯ $11 - 7 = 4$
- ◯ $11 + 3 = 14$

1 Ben has 9 stickers. He needs 15 stickers to win a prize.

Draw a picture to show how many more stickers Ben needs.

Use the picture to write a number sentence.

____

2 Tori picked some flowers. Kat picked 8 flowers. Together they picked 14 flowers.

Complete the number sentence.

$\_\_\_ + 8 = 14$

3 Lily makes 12 footprints in the sand. A wave washes away 8 footprints. How many footprints are left?

Use the picture to write a number sentence.

____

4 Fred catches 2 fish on Saturday. On Sunday, he catches 9 fish. Draw a picture to show how many fish Fred catches in all.

Which number sentence matches your picture?

- ⬭ $9 - \square = 7$
- ⬭ $9 + 2 = \square$
- ⬭ $\square + 2 = 4$

5 Max has 16 walnuts. He eats 9 of them. Which can be used to find how many walnuts are left?

- ⬭ $16 + 9 = \_\_\_$
- ⬭ $16 - 9 = \_\_\_$
- ⬭ $\_\_\_ - 16 = 9$

6 There are 9 cows and 8 horses in the field.

Write a number sentence to show the number of animals in the field.

____

Illegal to Copy

Nifty Numbers

Play *Nifty Numbers* with a partner. Each pair of players needs one game board, a 1–6 number cube, and a +/– die. Each player needs 20 counters (different color for each player). Player 1 rolls the number cube and the +/– die. The player adds or subtracts the number rolled from 10. If the sum or difference is shown on the game board, the player covers the square with a counter. If the number is covered, the player passes. The winner is the player with more markers on the board after every number has been covered.

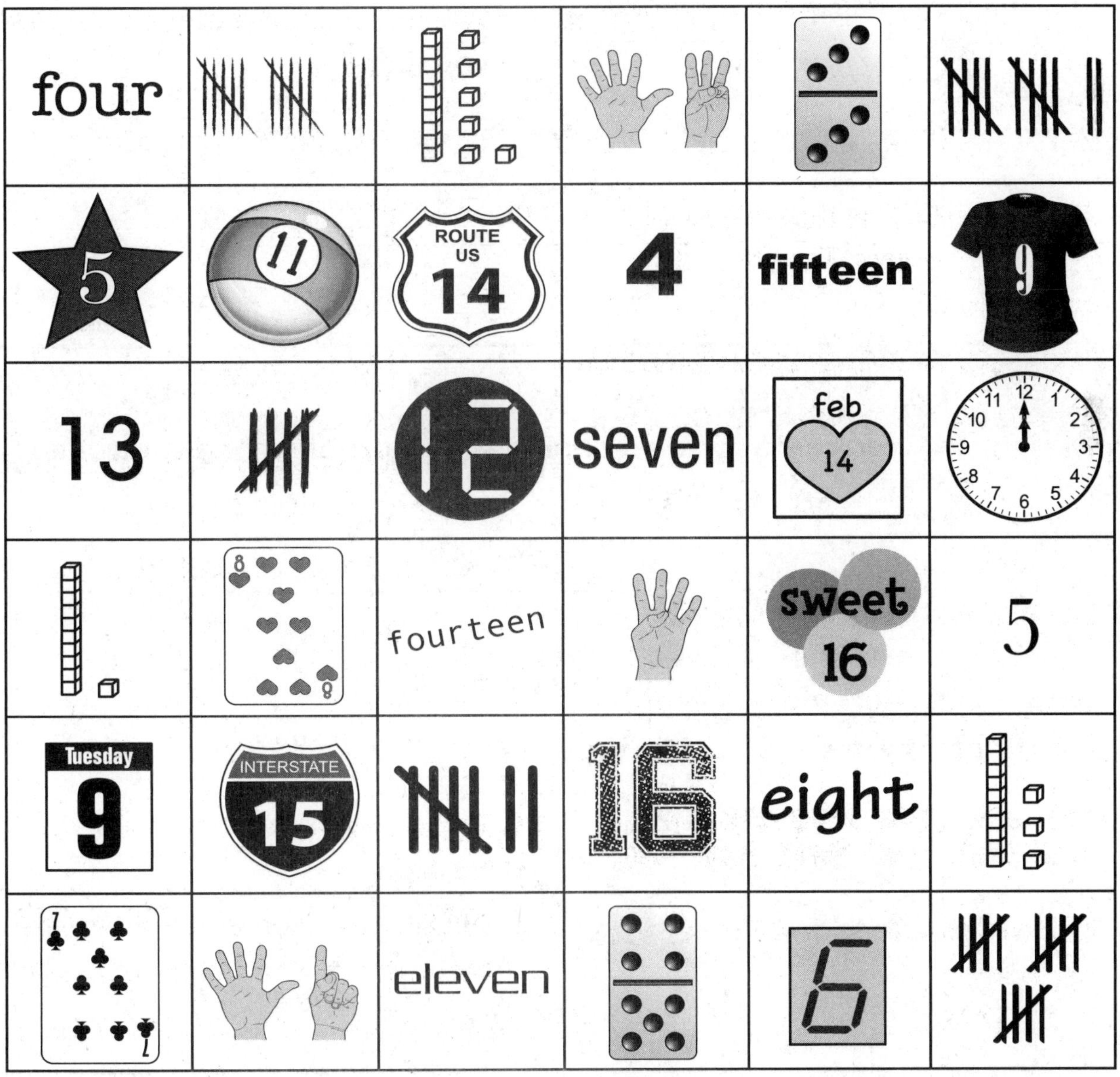

Extension

Name: ______________________________

Math Challenge

Write a word problem about this picture.

____

____

____

____

Now write a number sentence that solves the word problem.

____

Reflection on My Learning

Do you think it is easier to solve an addition word problem or a subtraction word problem? Explain your answer.

____

____

Reflection on Critical Thinking

Circle the traits you used most often in this unit.

I show ______________________ when I ______________________ .

Illegal to Copy

Assessment

Concept Check

1 Use the ten frames to model the problem.

Betty has 6 brown eggs.

She has 7 white eggs.

How many total eggs are there?

Write a number sentence to match your model.

____

2 Duane has 6 acorns.

Duane has 3 more acorns than Pearl.

Use the model to show the number of acorns Pearl has.

Write a number sentence to match the problem.

____

3 Leni has 8 striped bows. She has 5 spotted bows. Draw a picture to show the number of bows Leni has.

Write a number sentence to match the problem.

____

4 There are 20 balloons tied together. Ten of the balloons pop.

Which number sentence shows how many balloons are left?

- ⬭ 20 + 10 = 30
- ⬭ 20 – 10 = 10
- ⬭ 10 – 9 = 1

Assessment

Name: ______________________

Concept Check

Standard 1.5(D) – **Unit 18**

5 Draw a line to match the number sentence to the word problem.

7 + ______ = 12	Ken finds 12 seashells. Lin finds 7 seashells. How many fewer shells does Lin find than Ken?
12 – 7 = ______	Ken finds some seashells. Lin finds 5 seashells. Together Ken and Lin find 12 seashells. How many shells does Ken find?
______ + 5 = 12	Ken finds 7 seashells. Lin also finds seashells. Together they find 12 seashells. How many shells does Lin find?

6 Which number sentence matches the picture? Shade the box.

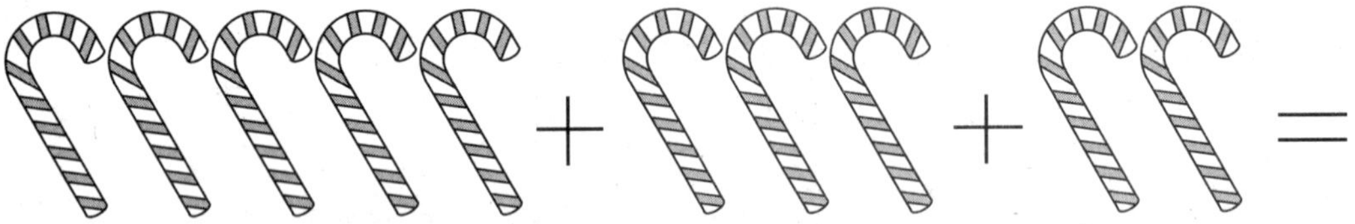

______

5 + 4 + 3 = 12 | 4 + 3 + 2 = 9 | 5 + 3 + 2 = 10

7 Ellie saved 8 dimes. Charlotte saved 9 dimes. How many dimes did Ellie and Charlotte save?

Use the ten frames to model the word problem.

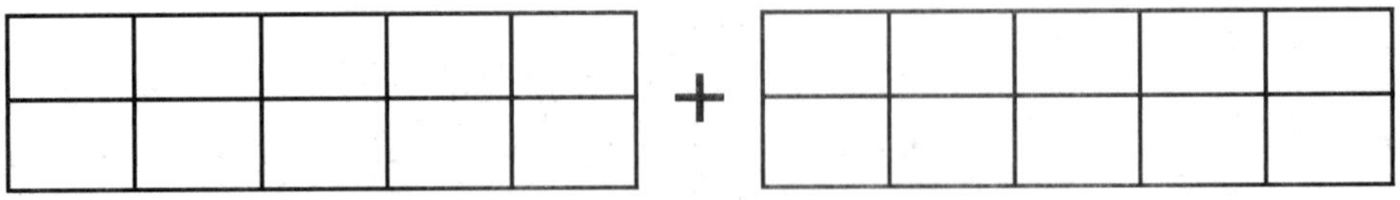

Write a number sentence to solve the problem.

____

Illegal to Copy

Name: ______________________________

Unit 19 – Standard 1.5(E)

Getting Started

Unit 19: Understand the Meaning of the Equal Sign

TEKS LEARNING TARGETS

- I can understand that the equal sign (=) means *is the same as*.
- I can identify expressions on each side of the equal sign (=) as having the same value.

Focus for 9 Traits of Critical Thinking™

Reflect: *I review my thoughts and experiences to guide my actions.*

Based on your understanding, what does this symbol (=) mean? What led you to this understanding?

____

____

Communicate: *I use clear language to express my ideas and to share my information.*

Are there other ways to ***communicate*** besides words? Explain your response.

____

____

Name: ____________________

equals = is the same as

What did you notice about the expression on each side of the equal sign?

____

____

What does = tell you about each side of the equation?

____

____

Illegal to Copy

Name: ______________________________

Instruction

Unit 19 – Standard 1.5(E)

Vocabulary Mastery

add	**equal (=)**	**number sentence**	**symbol**
addends	**equation**	**subtract**	**value**
difference	**expression**	**sum**	

Read and follow the directions.

1 Draw a box around the facts that equal 10.

2 Draw a circle around the facts that equal 8.

3 Color the boxes that show 9 = 9.

3 + 5 = _____	20 – 10 = _____	2 + 7 = 5 + 4	10 + 10 = 20
1 + 1 = 0 + 2	16 – 8 = _____	8 + 2 = _____	4 + 4 = _____
16 – 6 = _____	4 + 3 = 2 + 5	8 + 8 = 16	6 + 3 = 1 + 8

What are the most important ideas to remember about the meaning of the equal sign (=)?

____

____

How might you explain to a friend what the equal sign means?

____

____

Instruction

Name: ______________________________

Concept Development

=

 = 6

7 + 1 = 8 + 0

3 is not equal to 2.

The = symbol means *equal* or *is the same as*.

The = symbol is used in a number sentence to show that both sides of the number sentence have the same value.

You can use pictures or numbers in a number sentence as long as each expression has the same value.

You cannot write an equation with = if the two sides do not have the same value.

Try It!

1) What value can you add to the left side to show an equal number?

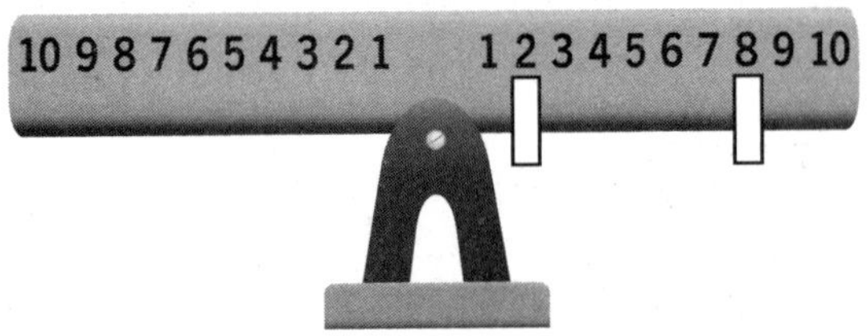

____

Try It!

2) Write a number sentence to match the balance.

____

Illegal to Copy

1 Kate puts blocks on a balance scale.

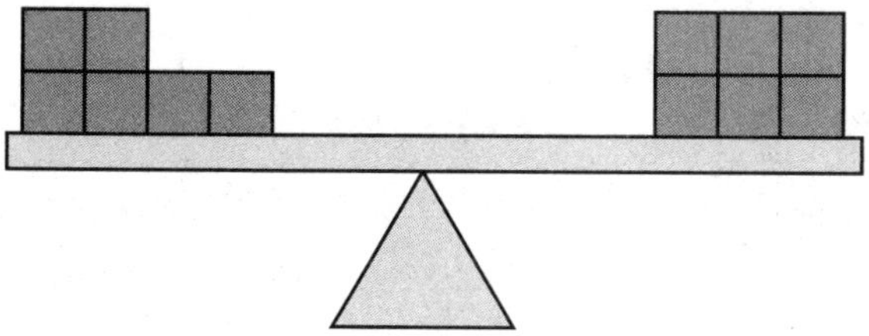

Which best shows Kate's balance scale?

- ⬭ $6 - 6 = 0$
- ⬭ $6 + 0 = 6$
- ⬭ $6 = 6$

2 Circle each equation that is true.

$7 + 2 = 8 + 1$

$5 = 6 + 1$

$4 + 5 = 12 - 3$

3 Is this number sentence true or false?

$10 + 3 = 3 + 10$

Circle the correct answer.

True   False

How do you know? Explain your thinking.

____

____

4 Which equation is true if you write = in the ◯?

- ⬭ 15 – 8 ◯ 7 + 8
- ⬭ 12 – 4 ◯ 7 + 2
- ⬭ 13 – 7 ◯ 4 + 2

5 Write a number in each blank to make the equation true.

4 + 4 = ________ – ________

6 Write a number in the circle to make the equation true.

6 + ◯ = 10 – 3

Can you write a different number in the circle to make the equation true? Explain your answer.

____

____

____

1 Write this word sentence as a number sentence.

One plus five is the same as six.

Answer ______________________

2 Circle True or False.

4 = 14 + 1	True	False
9 = 12 – 3	True	False
7 = 7	True	False
8 + 3 = 9 + 1	True	False

3 Circle the correct answer.

is equal to

13 – 5   4 + 4

is not equal to

How do you know?

____

____

4 Which of the following is NOT correct?

- ⬭ 15 = 16 – 1
- ⬭ 14 + 3 = 17
- ⬭ 15 – 0 = 12 + 2

5 The teacher said, "Six cupcakes and four cupcakes is the same as seven cupcakes and three cupcakes."

Write the teacher's words in numbers and symbols.

____

6 Write a number in the blank to make the number sentence true.

7 + 3 = 9 + ______

What is another way to make this number sentence true?

7 + 3 = ______ + ______

Illegal to Copy

Equal Amounts Make Me Smile

Play *Equal Amounts Make Me Smile* with a friend. Each player needs a game board, one die, and 20 small cubes. The teacher says a number between 6 and 20. Players write the number in each "sum of" box. Player 1 rolls the die. Both players place that number of cubes in oval 1. Player 2 rolls the die. Both players place that number of cubes in oval 3. Players place the number of cubes in ovals 2 and 4 that are needed to make the sum. Players check each other's cubes. The sum of the cubes on one side must equal the sum of the cubes on the other side. Players who correctly balance the number sentence color a smiley face on the chart for each game played.

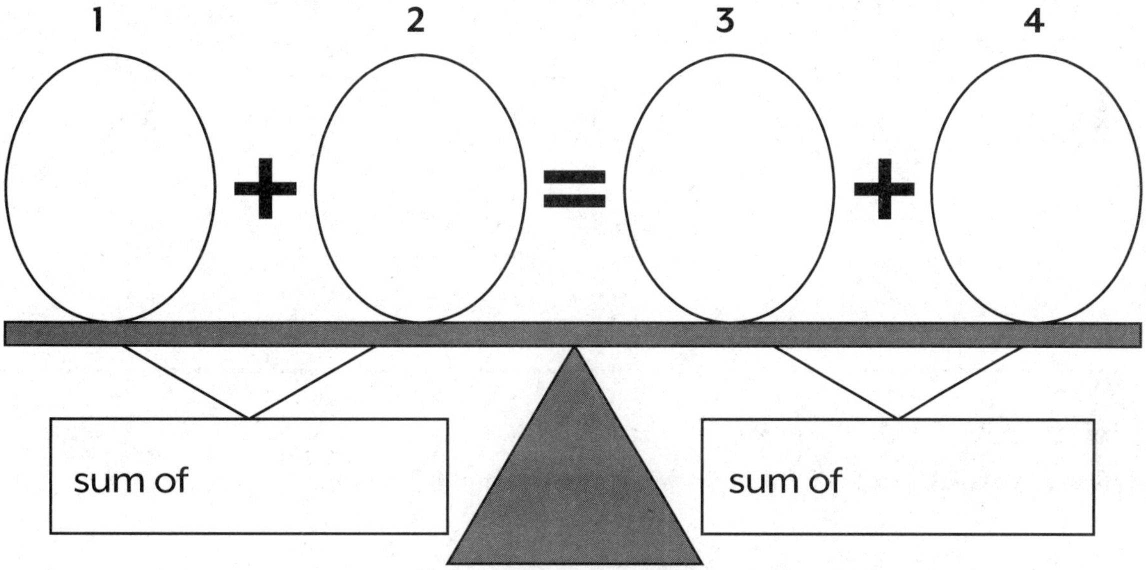

	Player 1	Player 2
Game 1	☺	☺
Game 2	☺	☺
Game 3	☺	☺

Extension

Name: ______________________________

Math Challenge

Circle the number sentences that are true.

$8 = 10 + 2$	$6 + 3 + 5 = 11$	$7 + 0 + 5 = 12$
$13 - 4 = 9$	$14 = 14$	$9 = 6$

Explain why some number sentences are true and some are false.

____

____

____

Reflection on My Learning

Why do you think the equal sign looks like this = ?

____

____

Reflection on Critical Thinking

Circle the traits you used most often in this unit.

I show ______________ when I ______________ .

Illegal to Copy

Name: ______________________________

Assessment

Unit 19 – Standard 1.5(E)

Concept Check

1 Write a number in each blank to make the number sentence true.

3 + 6 = _______ – _______

2 Which number makes both expressions true?

11 – _______ = 8 + 3

- ⬭ 10
- ⬭ 0
- ⬭ 1

3 Make the groups equal.

Draw stars in one of the groups.

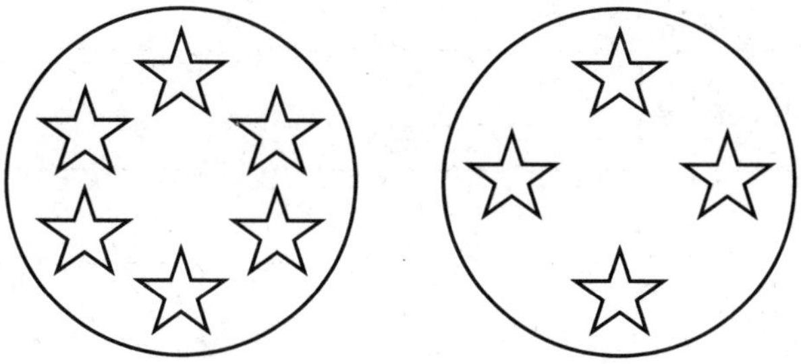

How many stars did you add to make the groups equal?

Answer ______________________

4 Explain how you can make both sides of the balance equal.

____

____

5 Circle all the equations that are true.

9 – 2 = 11

8 = 8

5 + 4 = 4 + 5

4 + 3 = 17 – 10

6 Mark has 4 rocks. He finds 3 more rocks. Susan has 9 rocks and loses 2.
Do Mark and Susan have the same number of rocks? Show your work.

Answer ______________________

Assessment

Name: ____________________

Concept Check

Standard 1.5(E) – **Unit 19**

7 Gina has 3 more rings than Callie.

Callie's rings

How many rings does Gina have?

Gina has __________ rings.

Write a number sentence to show this. ______________________

Ella and Gina have an equal number of rings.

How many rings does Ella have? ______________________

Complete the number sentence. ________ = ________

---

8 Circle the words that make this true.

 + 

is equal to

is not equal to

 + 

---

9 Shade the ovals that show correct number sentences.

(3 = 1 + 2) (5 + 4 = 11 – 3) (8 + 8 = 10 + 6) (12 = 10 + 2)

Illegal to Copy

Name: ______________________________

Getting Started

Unit 20: Determine the Unknown Number in Equations

TEKS LEARNING TARGETS

- I can solve for an unknown value, which may be found in any position in the equation.
- I can use a variety of strategies to find an unknown in an addition or subtraction equation.
- I can explain how to find an unknown value in an equation.

Focus for 9 Traits of Critical Thinking™

Adapt: *I adjust my actions and strategies to accomplish tasks.*

Do all math problems look the same? Do you solve all math problems using the same strategies?

____

____

Strive: *I use effort and determination to focus on challenging tasks.*

When you solve addition and subtraction problems, how do you know if your answer is reasonable?

____

____

Instruction

Name: ____________________

Concept Exploration

Standard 1.5(F) – **Unit 20**

I see 8 birds. Before lunch, I saw 12 birds. How many birds flew away?

8 = 12 – ☐

☐ = ____________

I have 8 rocks. I need 11 rocks for my collection. How many more rocks do I need?

8 + ☆ = 11

☆ = ____________

I have 7 red cars and 7 blue cars. How many cars do I have?

7 + 7 = ?

? = ____________

Give an example of how you used the ***adapt*** trait in this activity.

____

____

How did you break down the problems in order to help you find a solution?

____

____

Illegal to Copy

add	**equal (=)**	**plus (+)**	**symbol**
addends	**minus (–)**	**subtract**	**unknown**
difference	**number sentence**	**sum**	**whole numbers**

Read the clues. Write a word from the Word Bank on each line.

Word Bank

unknown	addition	number sentence
equation	subtraction	equal

1 Joining two groups ____________________

2 Comparing two groups ____________________

3 Another word for a math equation ____________________

4 A number that is not known ____________________

5 A symbol that means "is the same as" ____________________

6 A number sentence with an equal sign ____________________

How do you ***adapt*** your thinking when you realize you have written the same vocabulary word in two blanks? What steps do you take next to find the correct answer?

____

____

Circle the symbol that stands for the unknown in the equation.

11 – ☐ = 7

_____ – 5 = 1

12 + 7 = ?

The unknown is the missing number that solves the equation.

Complete the number sentence by filling in the unknown number.

10 + 6 = _____ + 8

☐ + 7 = 16

13 – 8 = _____

The unknown can be in any position in the equation.

Underline the important numbers in this word problem.

Gia found 15 rocks. She gave some to her sister. Now Gia has 9 rocks. How many rocks did Gia give to her sister?

Write a number sentence to solve.

____

First, decide what you know after reading the problem. Then, decide whether you should add or subtract to solve the problem.

What other equation can be used to solve this problem?

____

Knowing the fact families can help you write a number sentence for a problem.

Try It!

1) Solve.

9 – _____ = 5

Try It!

2) Solve.

6 + 9 = 8 + _____

Illegal to Copy

Name: ______________________

Unit 20 – Standard 1.5(F)

Instruction

Concept Application

1 Raj finds 14 shells. Some are broken. Five shells are NOT broken. How many shells are broken?

Which number sentence does NOT solve the problem?

- ○ 14 – _____ = 5
- ○ _____ + 5 = 14
- ○ 5 + 14 = _____

2 Mack has 7 stars. He needs 10 stars to earn a prize. How many more stars does Mack need?

Which number sentence solves the problem?

- ○ 10 + 3 = 13
- ○ 7 + 10 = 17
- ○ 7 + 3 = 10

3 Circle the problems that can be solved by writing 8 in the blank.

7 + _____ = 15

13 = _____ + 5

18 – 9 = _____

_____ – 7 = 0

4 Use the number line to find the answer to the problem.

11 – ☐ = 9

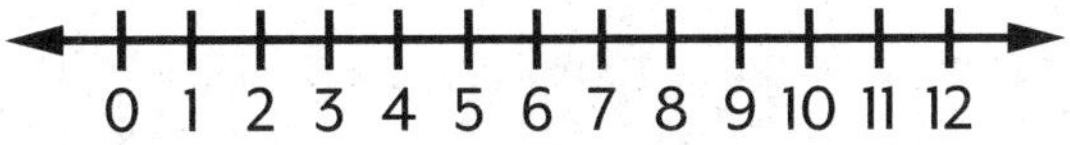

What is the unknown number?

____

5 Montel eats 3 cherry popsicles and 4 orange popsicles. He eats some grape popsicles, too. He eats 11 popsicles in all.

Write a number sentence and solve to find out how many grape popsicles Montel ate.

____

6 Write the numbers in the blanks.

11 = _____ + 5

_____ + 4 = 10

3 + _____ = 1 + 8

Name: ____________________

Concept Practice

1 Len picks 17 flowers. He gives some to Di. Now Len has 8 flowers.

$17 - \_\_\_\_ = 8$

How many flowers did Len give to Di?

Answer ____________________

2 Amy sees 3 stars. Raul sees some stars, too. Together they see 10 stars.

$3 + \_\_\_\_ = 10$

How many stars does Raul see?

Answer ____________________

3 Eli has 6 coins in his pocket. Some coins fall out of his pocket. Now Eli has only 1 coin.

Write a number sentence to solve the problem.

____

How many coins fall out of Eli's pocket?

____

4 There were 11 pencils in the jar. Alex takes some pencils to school. Now there are 3 pencils in the jar. How many pencils did Alex take to school?

Which number sentence solves the problem?

- ⬭ $11 - \_\_\_\_ = 3$
- ⬭ $\_\_\_\_ + 11 = 3$
- ⬭ $11 + 3 = \_\_\_\_$

5 Chiara has 8 books. She has 2 less books than Taz. How many books does Taz have?

Draw a picture of the problem.

Write the answer in the box.

$\square - 2 = 8$

Illegal to Copy

Polka Dot Panda

Play *Polka Dot Panda* with a partner. Partners need one game board, one die, two crayons, and two game pieces. Player 1 rolls the die and moves his or her game piece that many spaces on the game board in either direction. The player colors the polka dot with the number that makes the equation true. Play passes to player 2. Player 2 uses a different color. Players may move in either direction with each roll. The winner is the player with more polka dots after all polka dots are colored.

START HERE	$9 - 2 = ?$	$? + 9 = 11$	$12 - ? = 8$	$3 + 5 = ?$
$10 - ? = 5$				$? + 8 = 13$
$12 - 9 = ?$				$? + 6 = 9$
$10 - 6 = ?$				$? + 2 = 10$
$7 + 2 = ?$				$10 - ? = 1$
$14 + ? = 15$				$11 - 4 = ?$
$4 + 3 = ?$				$? + 8 = 9$
$? + 6 = 12$	$? - 5 = 4$	$4 + 4 = ?$	$12 - 10 = ?$	$15 - ? = 9$

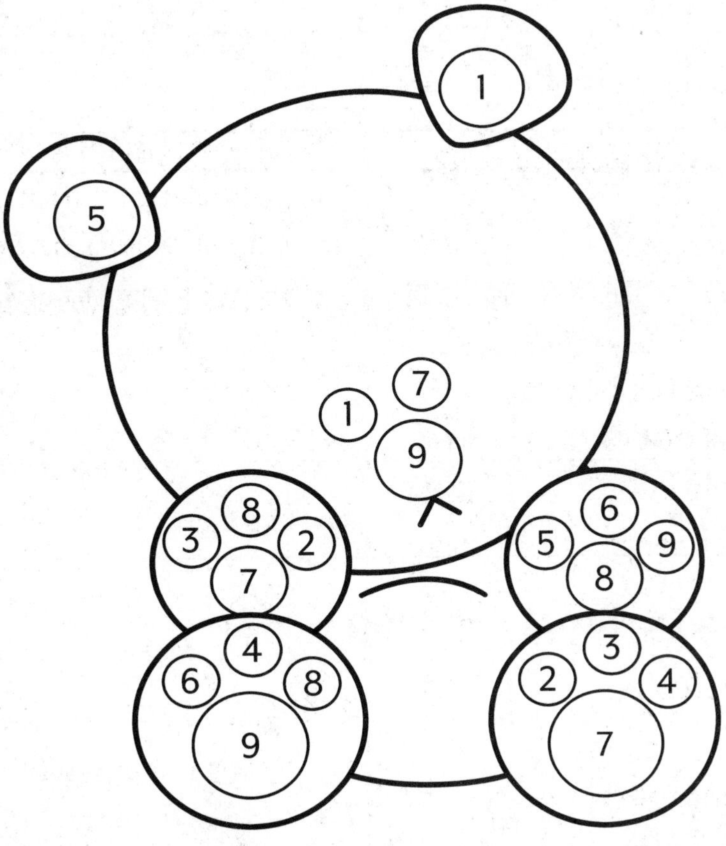

Extension

Name: ______________________________

Standard 1.5(F) – **Unit 20**

Math Challenge

Write number sentences that equal 9.

____ – ____ = 9	____ + ____ = 9
Equal 9	
____ + ____ = 9	____ – ____ = 9

Reflection on My Learning

How can you use addition to solve this problem? Explain your thinking.

14 – ________ = 5

____

____

Reflection on Critical Thinking

Circle the traits you used most often in this unit.

I show ______________________________ when I ______________________________ .

Illegal to Copy

Name: ______________________________

Unit 20 – Standard 1.5(F)

Assessment

Concept Check

1 Karl has some quarters. He spends 8 quarters for a toy. Now he has 6 quarters left.

How many quarters did Karl have before buying the toy?

Answer ____________________

2 Draw a picture to show this subtraction sentence.

11 – ____ = 9

What is the missing number?

____

3 Kate has 7 kittens. There are 3 gray kittens. The rest are black. How many black kittens does Kate have?

Which number sentence solves the problem?

- ⬭ 3 = ____ + 7
- ⬭ ____ = 3 + 7
- ⬭ 7 = 3 + ____

4 Destiny has 10 pennies in her purse. She finds 7 pennies on the floor. How many pennies does Destiny have now?

Write a number sentence to solve the problem.

____

5 Bob had 8 pieces of candy. He ate some of it. He has 2 pieces left.

Draw a picture to show how many pieces of candy Bob ate.

How many pieces did Bob eat?

Answer ____________________

6 Draw a picture to find the unknown number.

____ – 10 = 6

Answer ____________________

Assessment

Name: ____________________

Concept Check

Standard 1.5(F) – **Unit 20**

7 There are 18 socks in the dryer. Nine socks are blue. The rest are white. How many socks are white?

Draw a picture to show your work.

Write a number sentence to find the answer.

Answer ____________________

8 What unknown number makes all the equations true?

$8 + ☆ = 11$ $\quad$ $☆ - 0 = 3$ $\quad$ $4 + 6 = 7 + ☆$

Answer ____________________

Write another number sentence with the same number as the unknown.

Answer ____________________

9 Use the number line to find the unknown number.

$4 + \square = 9$

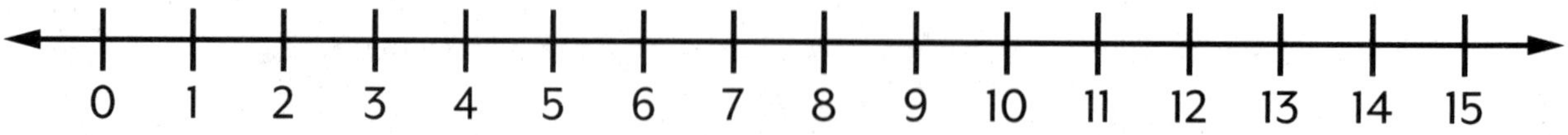

Answer ____________________

Illegal to Copy

Name: ______________________________

Getting Started

Unit 21 – Standard 1.5(G)

Unit 21: Apply Properties of Operations to Add and Subtract Numbers

TEKS LEARNING TARGETS

- I can use the order property (Commutative Property of Addition).
- I can use the grouping property (Associative Property of Addition).
- I can use the Zero Property to add and subtract.
- I can use objects and drawings to represent the properties and recognize patterns in equations where the order and grouping of the addends does not change the sum.

Focus for 9 Traits of Critical Thinking™

Collaborate: *I work with others to achieve better outcomes.*

How does working with a partner or group help you identify more strategies to solve addition and subtraction problems?

____

____

Link: *I apply knowledge to reach new understandings.*

Do you think the addition and subtraction strategies you learned in kindergarten still apply? Do you think they will work for three-digit addition?

____

____

Illegal to Copy

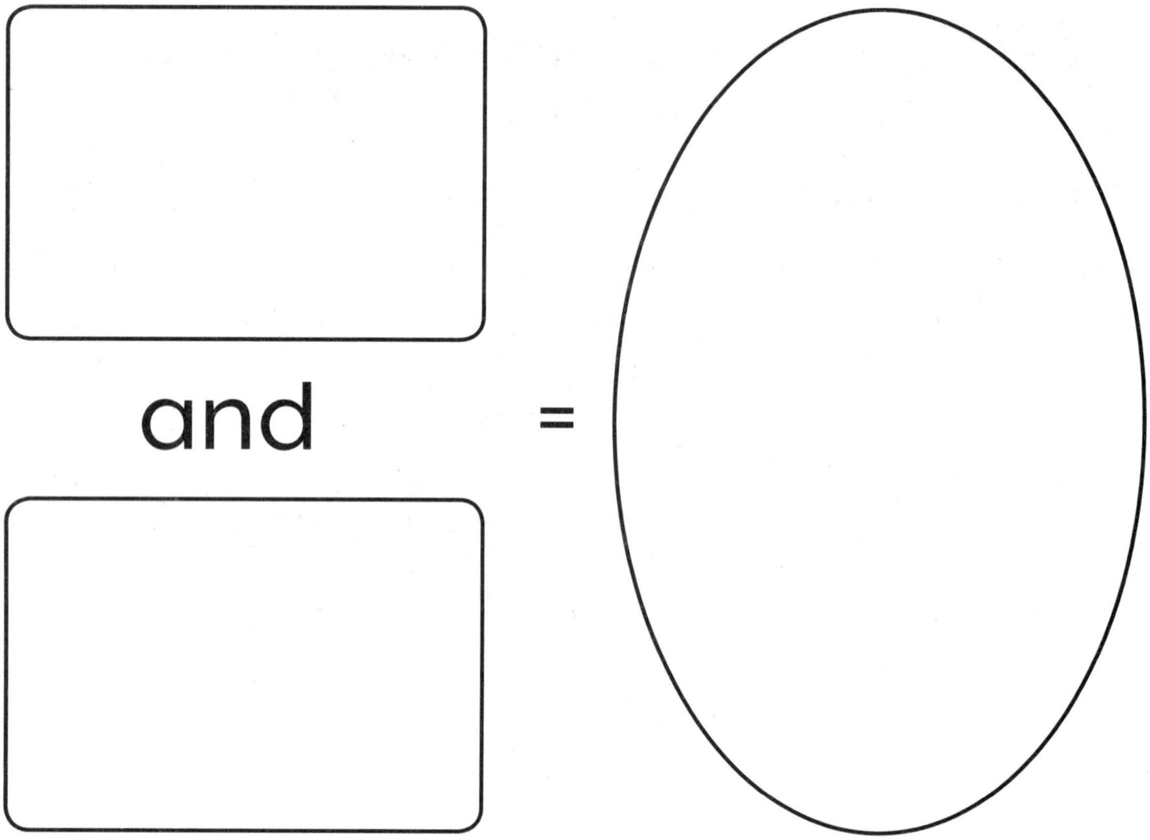

How did your partner help you during this activity? How did you help your partner?

____

____

How are both sides of an equation linked in the Commutative Property of Addition?

____

____

Illegal to Copy

Name: ________________________________

Unit 21 – Standard 1.5(G)

Instruction

Vocabulary Mastery

add	**equation**	**part**	**sum**
addends	**fact family**	**order**	**whole**
difference	**number sentence**	**subtract**	

Find these words hidden in the puzzle.
Words may be written across or down.

Words
add
subtract
first
second
order
sum
difference
addend

s	e	c	o	n	d	d	u	q	g
e	d	n	k	a	k	p	s	w	q
g	e	o	r	d	e	r	e	y	v
f	r	h	s	d	i	v	q	c	q
s	u	b	t	r	a	c	t	q	j
d	i	f	f	e	r	e	n	c	e
a	d	d	e	n	d	e	h	o	s
f	i	r	s	t	g	e	b	l	u
i	i	v	f	l	s	y	a	p	m
x	d	p	o	f	z	m	t	h	i

How might you and a friend make this word search into a game? Do you think your approach would make the word search easier or more challenging?

____

____

How is a word search like playing hide-and-go-seek? How is it different?

____

____

Instruction

Name: ______________________________

Concept Development

Record the sums. Then complete the sentence.

10 + 3 = ______

3 + 10 = ______

The ________________ of the two addends is the same.

The fact family for 10, 3, and 13 is:

10 + 3 = 13	3 + 10 = 13
13 – 3 = 10	13 – 10 = 3

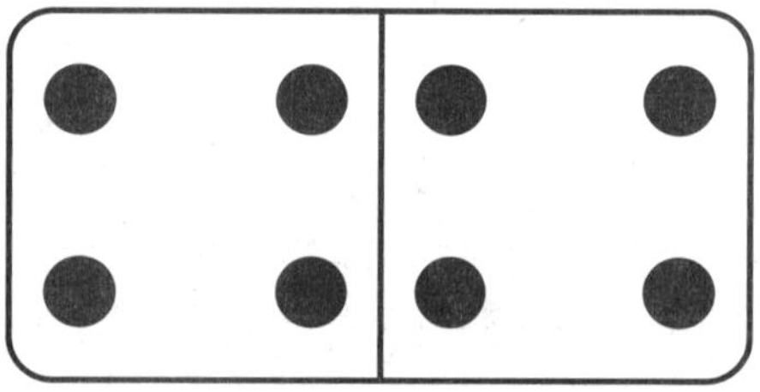

4 + 4 = 8   8 – 4 = 4

You can rearrange the addends in an equation and still get the same sum.

A fact family is a set of related numbers. There are three numbers and four facts in most fact families.

If the fact is a double, there are only two facts in the fact family.

Try It!

1) Circle the numbers you would add to make a 10. Solve the problem.

1 + 9 + 4 =

____

Try It!

2) Write the fact family to represent the picture.

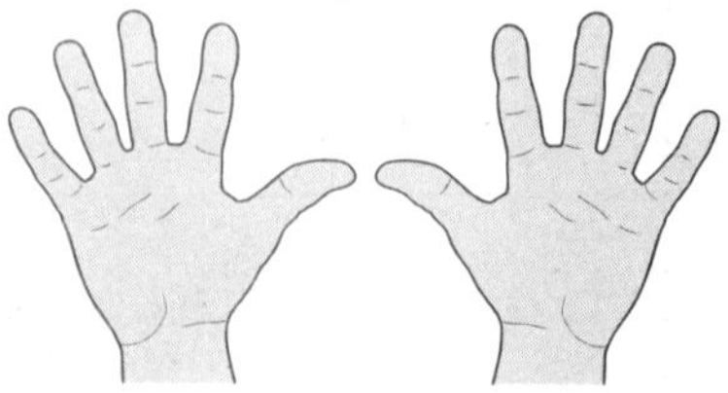

____

1 Tayvion is solving the equation.

8 + 1 + 2 = ____

He adds 8 + 2 first. What is the next step Tayvion should take?

- ⬭ 8 + 2 + 10
- ⬭ 10 – 1
- ⬭ 10 + 1

2 Marta solves the following equation.

11 – 3 = ____

What other equation is related?

- ⬭ 8 + 3 = ____
- ⬭ 11 + 3 = ____
- ⬭ 8 – 3 = ____

3 Use words or pictures to explain how these equations are alike.

9 + 1 + 5 = 15   5 + 10 = 15

4 Kim wants to solve the following problem.

6 + 4 – 1= ____

She makes a 10 and then completes the problem. Which statement describes how Kim solves the problem?

- ⬭ She adds 6 and 4 to make a 10, then adds 1.
- ⬭ She adds 6 and 4 to make a 10, then subtracts 1.
- ⬭ She adds 6 and 4 to make a 10, then subtracts 10.

5 Hunter had 10 marbles.
Travis had 8 marbles.

How many marbles do they have in all?

Answer ____________________

Which number sentence has a sum that is the same as the number of marbles?

- ⬭ 5 + 5 + 10
- ⬭ 6 + 4 + 8
- ⬭ 4 + 7 + 8

1 Sam has 2 pens. Tom has 4 pens, and Sally has 8 pens. How many pens do the children have?

Draw a number line to solve the problem.

Answer ____________________

2 Circle the two addends in each number sentence that equal 10.

8 + 5 + 2 = 15

5 + 5 + 3 = 13

7 + 4 + 3 = 14

4 + 7 + 6 = 17

3 Which number sentence shows the same difference as 10 – 2?

- ⬭ 12 – 2
- ⬭ 8 – 0
- ⬭ 10 + 2

4 Shade the numbers that make a sum of 10. Solve the problem.

| 4 | + | 8 | + | 6 | = ____ |

5 Choose another way to show 6 + 9 = 15.

- ⬭ 15 + 6 = 21
- ⬭ 9 + 6 = 15
- ⬭ 9 – 6 = 3

6 Luz has 10 magnets.
She gives 8 magnets to Darna.
How many magnets does Luz have now?

Draw a number line to show your work.

Answer ____________________

Illegal to Copy

Add 'Em Up

Play *Add 'Em Up* with one or two friends. Each player needs 20 playing cards with numbers 2–10 and a game board. Players turn over their top cards at the same time. Players add the cards and say the sum. The first player to say the correct sum keeps the cards. If there is a tie, players place the cards to the side, and the winner of the next round keeps both sets. At the end of the game, players count their cards and color that many cards on their game boards. The first player with all the cards colored is the winner.

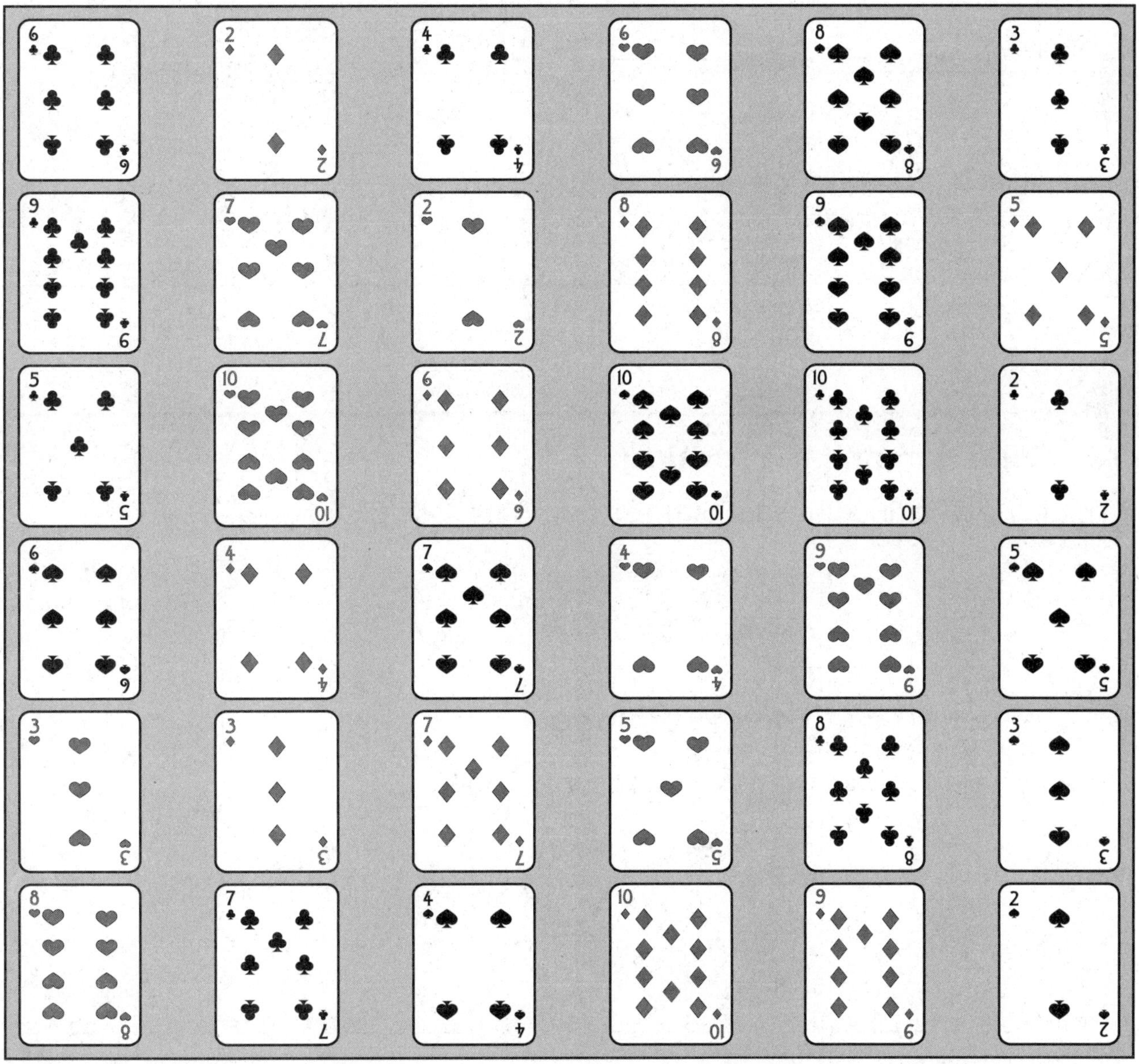

Extension

Name: ______________________________

Standard 1.5(G) – **Unit 21**

Math Challenge

Molly has 5 red crayons and 7 blue crayons. Ewan has 7 red crayons and 5 blue crayons. Color the crayons for each child.

Molly

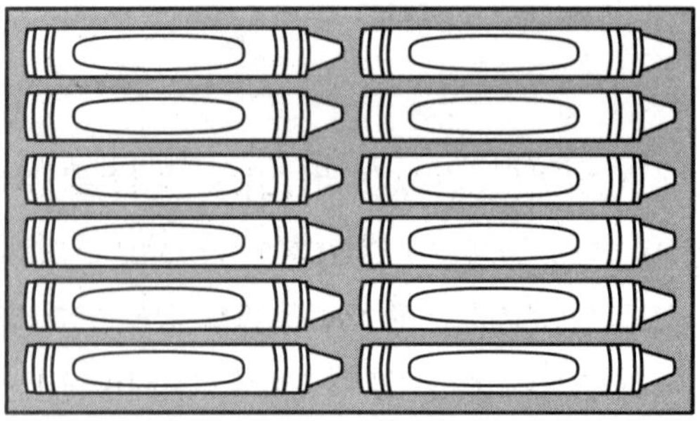

_____ red + _____ blue = _____

Ewan

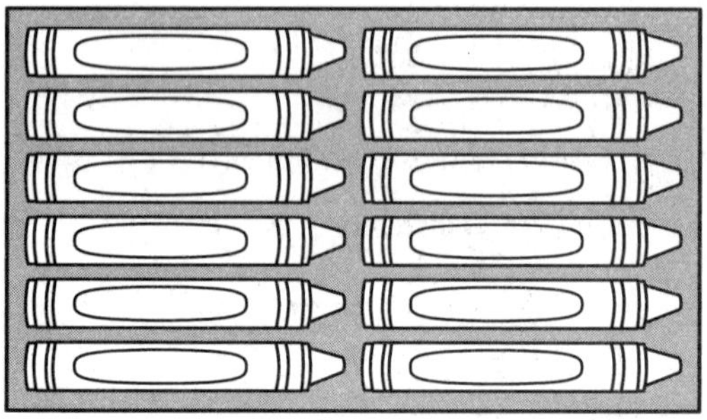

_____ red + _____ blue = _____

How are the number sentences alike? How are they different? Explain.

____

____

Reflection on My Learning

Explain how to find the sum of three numbers. Use pictures or words.

Reflection on Critical Thinking

Circle the traits you used most often in this unit.

I show ______________________ when I ______________________ .

Name: ______________________________

Assessment

Unit 21 – Standard 1.5(G)

Concept Check

1 Alex used an addition fact to subtract 15 – 9.

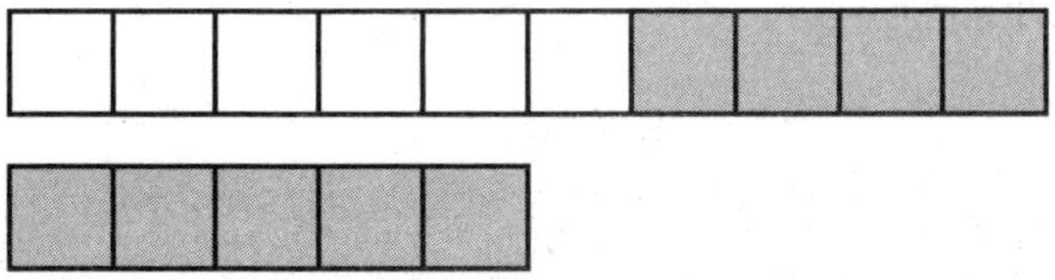

Circle all the addition facts Alex could have used.

9 + ______ = 15

15 + 9 = ______

______ + 9 = 15

2 Write four facts that match the model.

Addition

______ + ______ = ______

______ + ______ = ______

Subtraction

______ – ______ = ______

______ – ______ = ______

3 Write two addition equations using the numbers 8, 5, and 3.

______ + ______ = ______

______ + ______ = ______

4 Olivia saw 3 ducks in the pond. She saw 4 ducks in the grass. Then she saw 6 ducks at the edge of the pond. How many ducks did Olivia see? Use the picture to make a ten and solve.

Answer ______________________

5 Record the sums. Circle all the equations that show a way to add the numbers of dots.

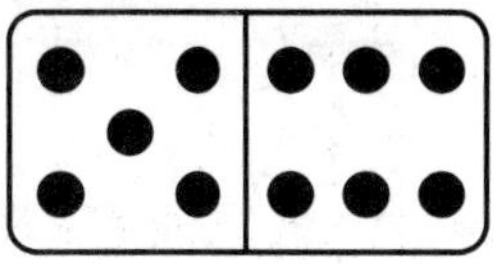

5 + 6 = ______

6 + 5 = ______

5 + 5 + 1 = ______

5 + 5 = ______

Assessment

Name: ____________________

Concept Check

6 Look at the number cards.
Write three different addition sentences with a sum of 17.

4	3	10	17

____

____

____

7 Use words or pictures to explain how these number sentences are alike.

$5 + 5 + 3 = 13$ $\qquad$ $10 + 3 = 13$

8 Terrell made a train with color tiles.

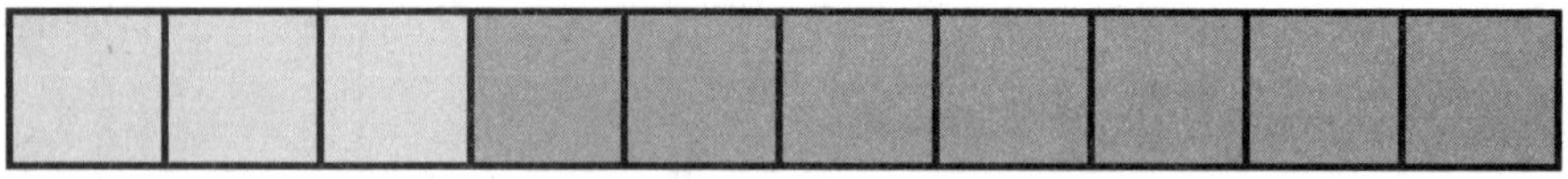

Write two subtraction sentences for Terrell's train.

____________________ ____________________

Illegal to Copy

Name: ______________________________

Unit 22 – Standard 1.6(A)

Getting Started

Unit 22: Classify and Sort Two-Dimensional Shapes

TEKS LEARNING TARGETS

- I can use words to identify two-dimensional shapes.
- I can use attributes to sort and classify two-dimensional shapes.
- I can explain the difference between regular and irregular two-dimensional shapes.

Focus for 9 Traits of Critical Thinking™

Examine: *I use a variety of methods to explore and to analyze.*

Why would it be important to know how squares and rectangles are alike and how they are different?

____

____

Create: *I use my knowledge and imagination to express new and innovative ideas.*

How can I apply my knowledge of shapes when I am creating pictures and models?

____

____

Instruction

Name: ____________________

Concept Exploration

Standard 1.6(A) – **Unit 22**

Same Color	Different Colors
Same Size	**Different Sizes**
Same Shape	**Different Shapes**
Name the Rule–Same	**Name the Rule–Different**

What is an attribute you used to sort the shapes?

____

____

How were the groups you created with your shapes different from your classmates' groupings?

____

____

Illegal to Copy

Name: ____________________

Unit 22 – Standard 1.6(A)

Instruction

Vocabulary Mastery

attribute	hexagon	sides	triangle
circle	rectangle	sort	two-dimensional shape
corner	rhombus	square	

Use the Venn diagram to show how a rhombus and a rectangle are alike and different.

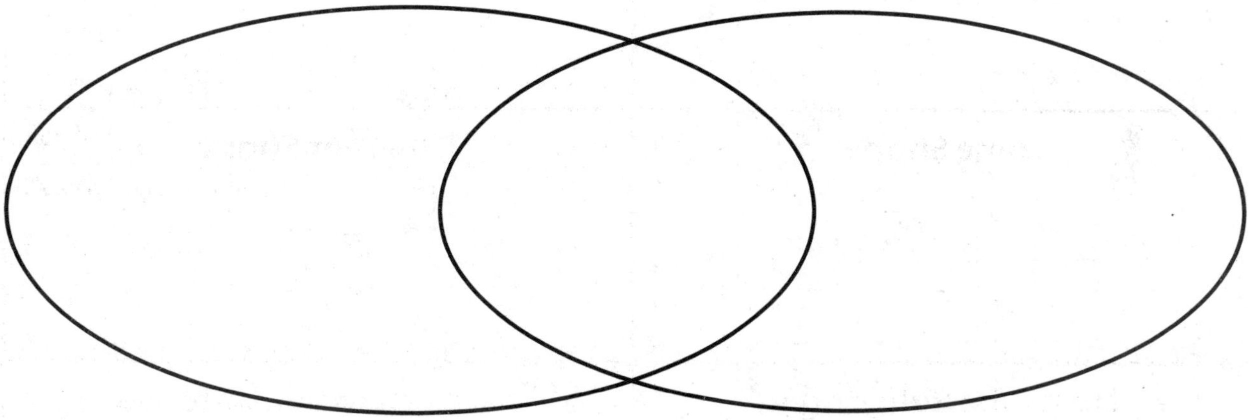

Rhombus Rectangle

Does using a Venn diagram to organize information help you see the similarities and differences of rhombuses and rectangles more easily? Explain your answer.

____

____

How challenging would it be to ***create*** a Venn diagram comparing three shapes? Which shape would you add?

____

____

Instruction

Name: ____________________

Concept Development

Standard 1.6(A) – **Unit 22**

A two-dimensional shape is flat. The shape may have sides, corners, curves, and points. You can describe the shapes using different attributes.

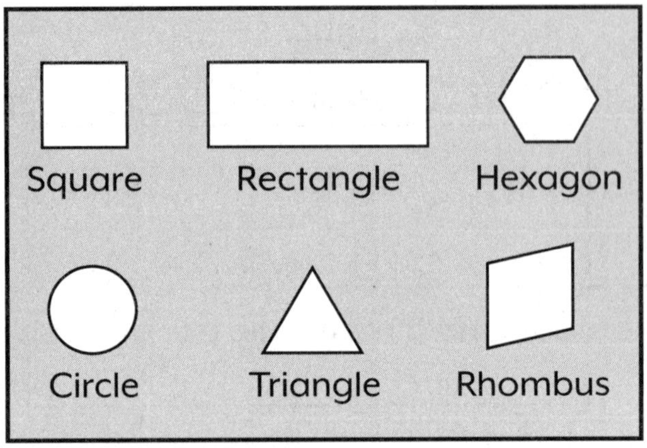

A two-dimensional shape can be classified as regular or irregular. In a regular shape, all sides are equal lengths.

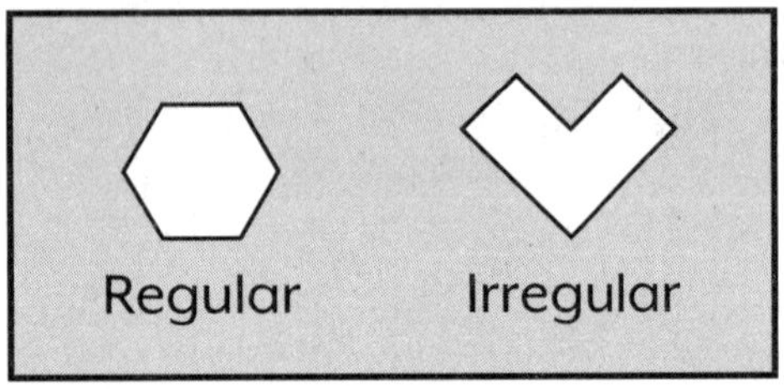

A square is a special rectangle that has four square corners and opposite sides that have equal measures. A square is a special rhombus because it has four equal sides.

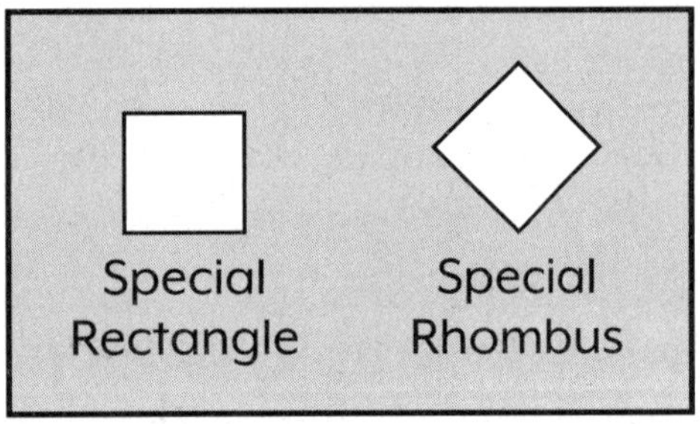

Try It!

1) Draw an X on the regular shape.

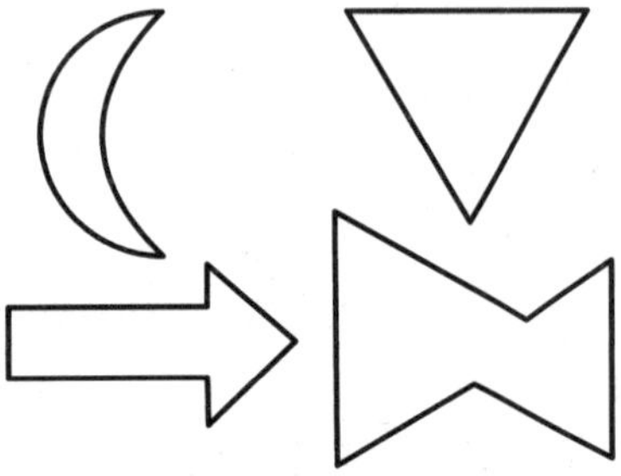

Try It!

2) Explain how the shapes are alike.

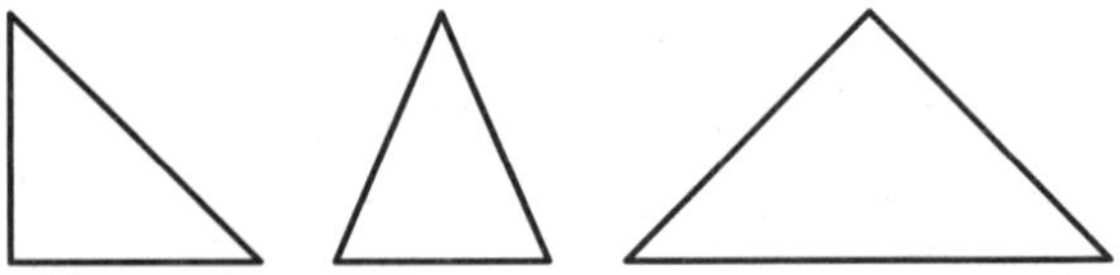

____

____

Illegal to Copy

Name: ______________________________

Unit 22 – Standard 1.6(A)

Instruction

Concept Application

1 Draw a line under the shape with a curve.

2 Place an X on the shape that is different.

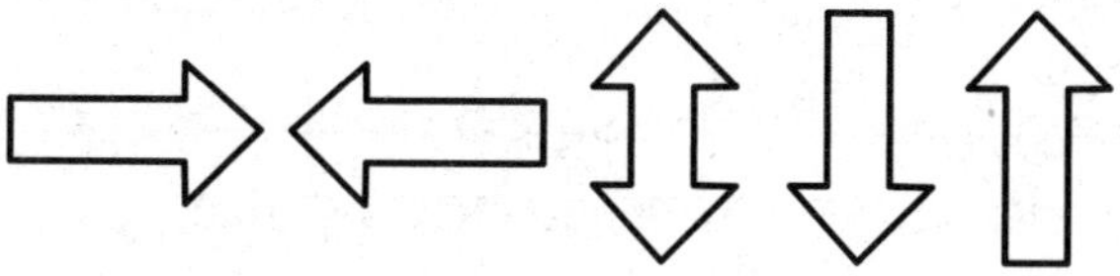

Explain why the shape is not the same.

____

____

3 Draw a shape that has no straight sides and no vertices (corners).

4 Draw three figures in each set.

4 Sides

3 Sides

5 Sort these shapes into two groups by drawing each shape in a box. Label each box.

Illegal to Copy

Instruction

Name: ____________________

Concept Practice

1 Draw a figure with six sides and six vertices (corners).

Write the name of the figure.

Answer ____________________

2 Color the shapes with vertices (corners).

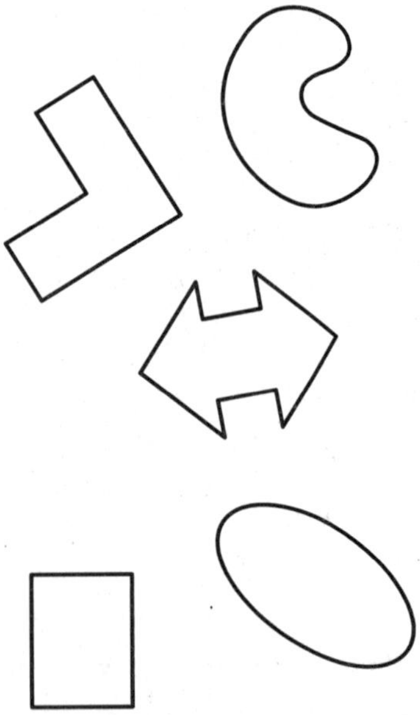

3 Which shape has three sides and three vertices (corners)?

- ⬭ Circle
- ⬭ Square
- ⬭ Triangle

4 Box the shapes that have curves.

5 How are these shapes alike?

- ⬭ All the shapes are round.
- ⬭ All the shapes have six vertices.
- ⬭ All the shapes have straight sides.

6 Draw an X on the shape in each group that does NOT belong.

Group 1	Group 2

Illegal to Copy

Name: ___________________________

Instruction

Unit 22 – Standard 1.6(A)

Concept Practice: Motivation Station

Blast off with Shapes

Use the key to color the space picture.

Key

△	Small – blue
	Medium – red
	Large – green

○	Small – yellow
	Medium – orange
	Large – brown

Extension

Name: ____________________

Standard 1.6(A) – **Unit 22**

Math Challenge

Look at the figures in the boxes.

These are doogles.

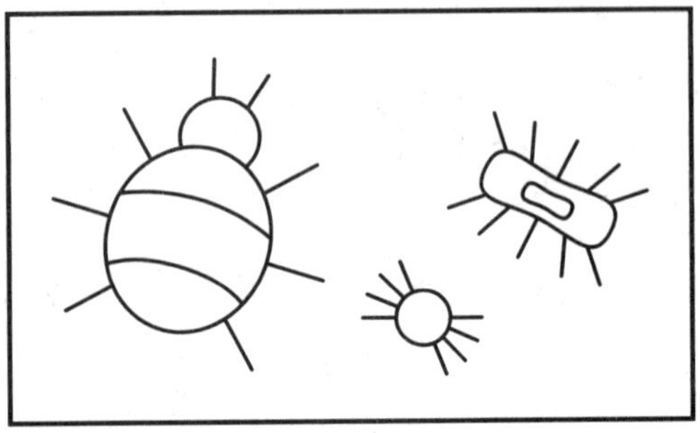

These are NOT doogles.

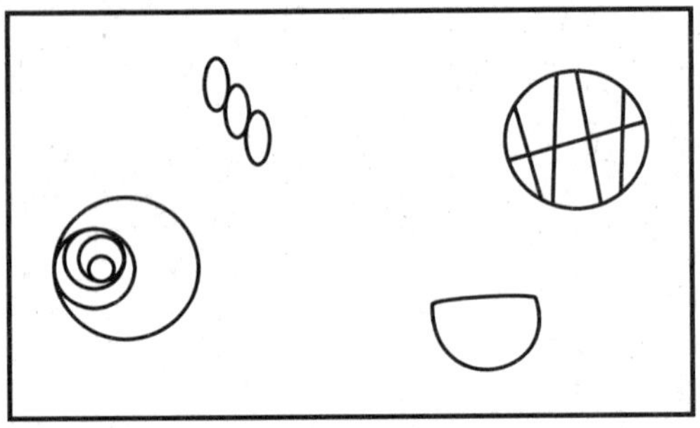

Draw 3 doogles.

Reflection on My Learning

If you draw a house using shapes, would you use circles or rectangles? Use words and pictures to explain.

Reflection on Critical Thinking

Circle the traits you used most often in this unit.

I show ____________________ when I ____________________.

Illegal to Copy

Name: ______________________________

Unit 22 – Standard 1.6(A)

1 Color the shape that does NOT belong.

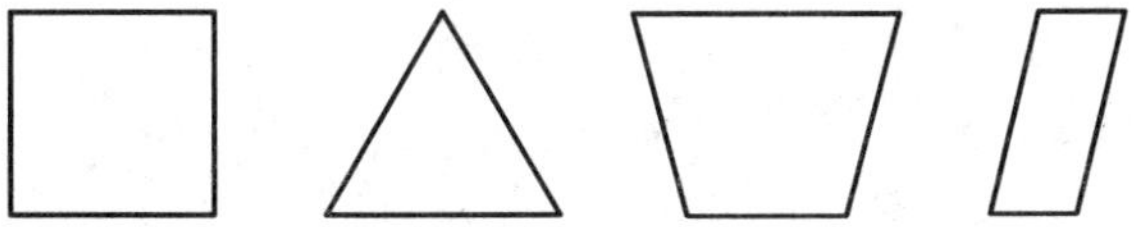

Tell why the shape does not belong.

____

____

2 Circle the shapes that have 4 sides.

3 Which shape does NOT have 4 sides and 4 vertices (corners)?

- ⬭ Rhombus
- ⬭ Hexagon
- ⬭ Rectangle

4 Draw three figures in each set.

Shapes with Curved Lines

Shapes with No Curved Lines

5 How are all these shapes the same?

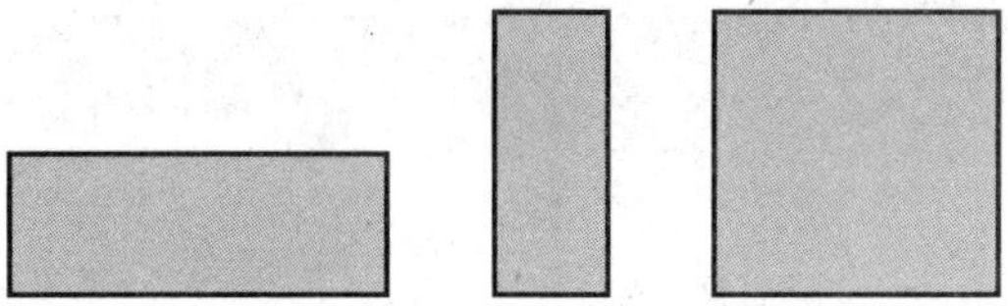

- ⬭ All the shapes have 4 curves.
- ⬭ All the shapes have 3 sides.
- ⬭ All the shapes have 4 vertices (corners).

Illegal to Copy

6 Circle the word that best describes the shapes in the box.

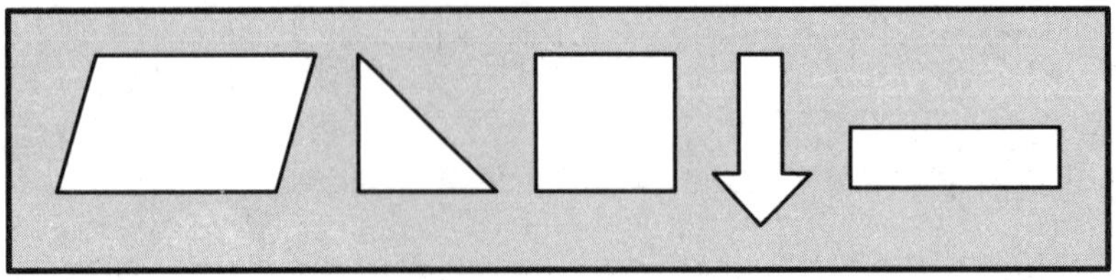

curves   corners   round

---

7 Look at the figures in the boxes.

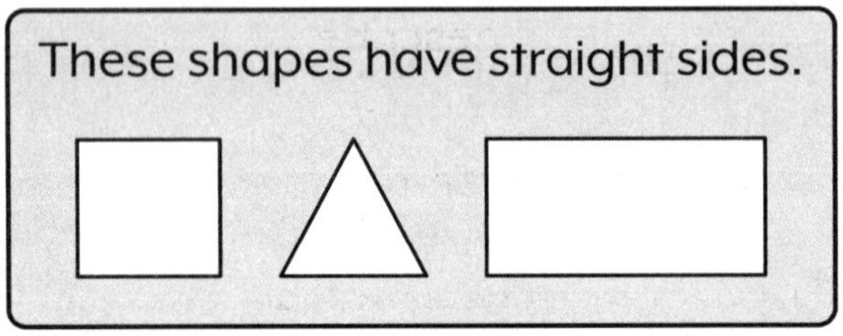

Draw one shape with straight sides and one with curves.

---

8 Complete the chart.

Figure	Number of Straight Sides	Number of Vertices (Corners)

Illegal to Copy

Name: ___________________________

Getting Started

Unit 23 – Standard 1.6(B)

Unit 23: Distinguish Attributes of Two- and Three-Dimensional Shapes

TEKS LEARNING TARGETS

- I can use attributes to identify and describe two- and three-dimensional figures.
- I can compare and contrast two- and three-dimensional figures.
- I can recognize two- and three-dimensional shapes in the real world.
- I can use geometric vocabulary to analyze and describe two- and three-dimensional shapes.
- I can identify defining attributes for two- and three-dimensional shapes.

Focus for 9 Traits of Critical Thinking™

Communicate: *I use clear language to express my ideas and to share information.*

How does good communication help you better understand a concept?

____

____

Inquire: *I seek information that excites my curiosity and inspires my learning.*

When identifying a shape, what attributes are most important?

____

____

Instruction

Name: ______________________

Concept Exploration

Standard 1.6(B) – **Unit 23**

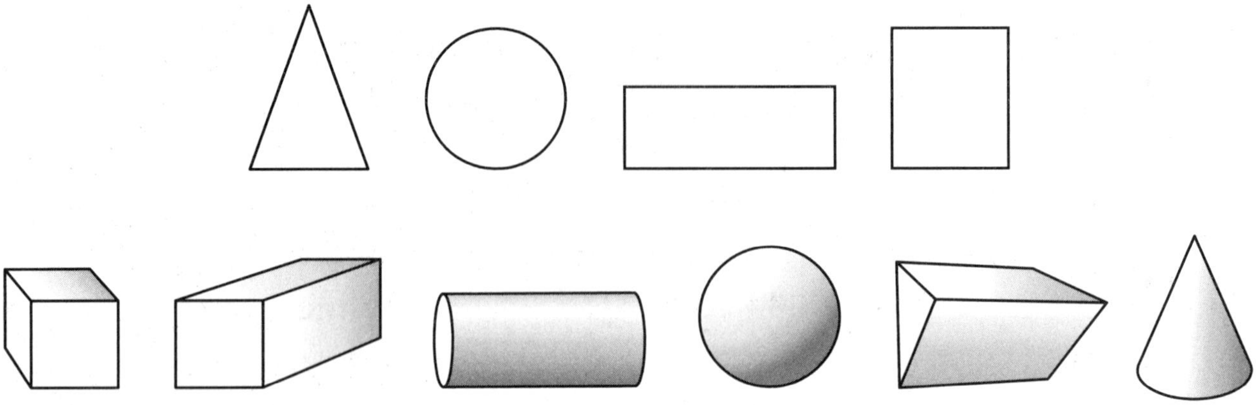

Does the number of sides or the color help determine the shape? Explain your answer.

____

____

What attributes helped you identify the shapes in the activity?

____

____

Illegal to Copy

attribute	**face**	**square**
circle	**open figure**	**three-dimensional solid**
closed figure	**rectangle**	**triangle**
cone	**rectangular prism**	**triangular prism**
cube	**sides**	**two-dimensional shape**
cylinder	**sphere**	**vertex/vertices**

Choose a two-dimensional shape. Write the name of your shape in the middle circle. Use words and pictures to finish the chart.

Name of Shape	2 Attributes
Example	Non-Example

What questions do you have about attributes that define a shape?

____

____

Place an X on the closed figures and a circle around the open figures.

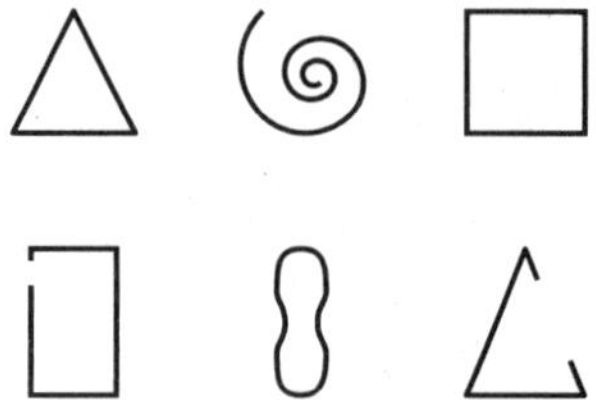

Draw a circle and a rectangle.

Count the faces of the cube.

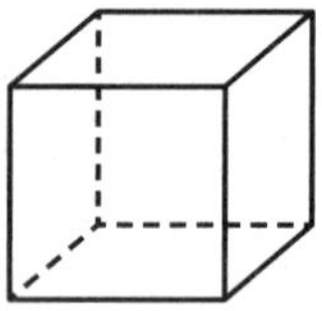

________ faces

Closed figures are two-dimensional figures with ends that touch. Closed figures have no openings.

An open figure is a figure with two ends that do not touch.

Two-dimensional shapes are flat. They are closed figures. You can draw a model of a two-dimensional shape.

Three-dimensional solids are figures that have length, width, and height. Attributes used to describe these solids are faces, edges, and vertices.

Placing an X on each face as you count it can help you get a correct answer.

Try It!

1) Circle the words that define a cone.

cone

One vertex

Circle for a base

Solid figure

Rolls

Try It!

2) Circle the best name for the figure.

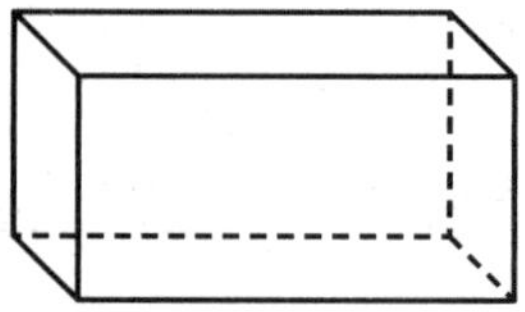

Rectangle

Rectangular prism

Cube

Square

Illegal to Copy

1 Kellen is modeling shapes with different materials. Which material would be best for creating a circle?

- ⬭ Sticks
- ⬭ Yarn
- ⬭ Straws

Explain why your choice is the best to create the circle.

____

____

2 Color the figures that have four equal sides.

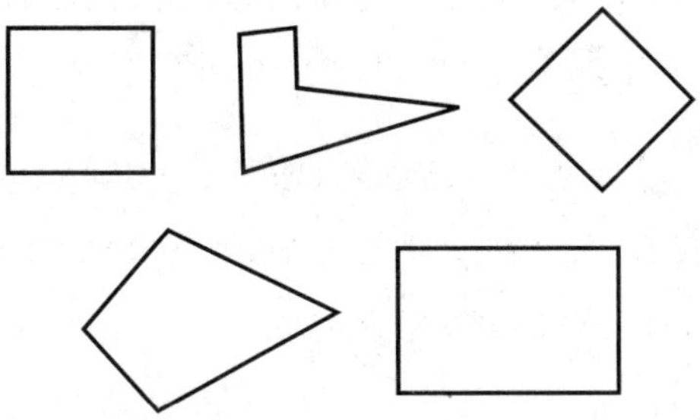

3 Which attribute does NOT describe this figure?

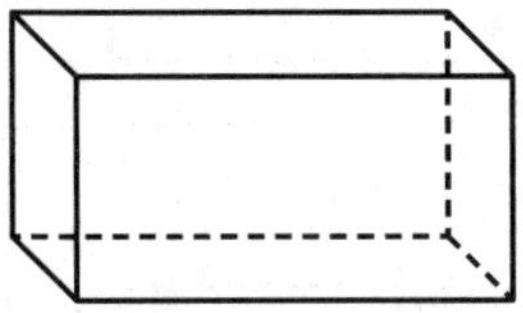

- ⬭ Two-dimensional
- ⬭ Has faces
- ⬭ Has vertices

4 Color the three-dimensional shapes that have edges.

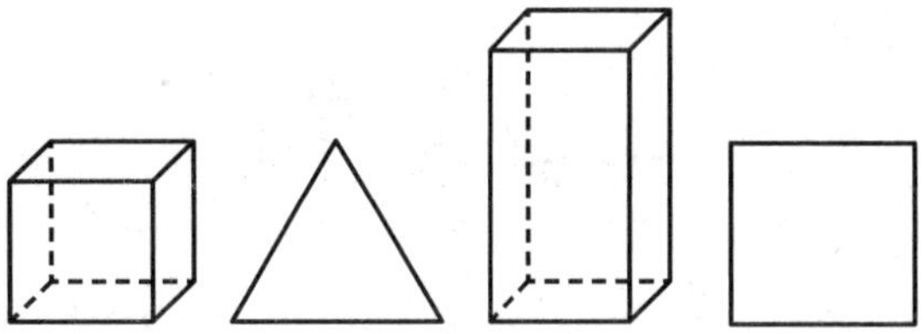

Name another attribute of the figures.

Answer ____________________

5 Two-dimensional figures have vertices.

- ⬭ Always true
- ⬭ Never true
- ⬭ Sometimes true

Explain your answer.

____

____

6 Look at the figures.

How are the figures similar?

____

____

1 Box the figure with four sides.
Circle the three-dimensional figure.
Draw an X on the figure with only three vertices.

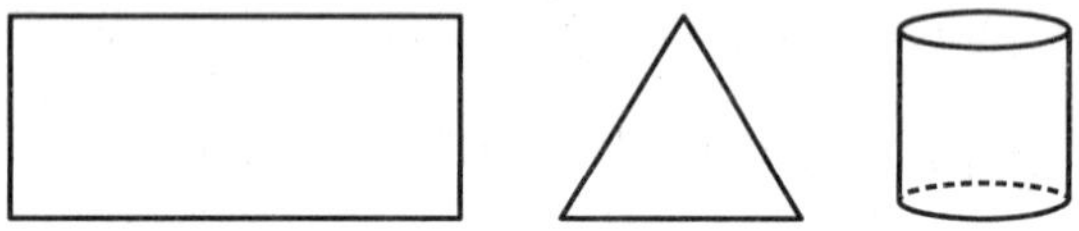

2 Place an X on the figure that does NOT belong.

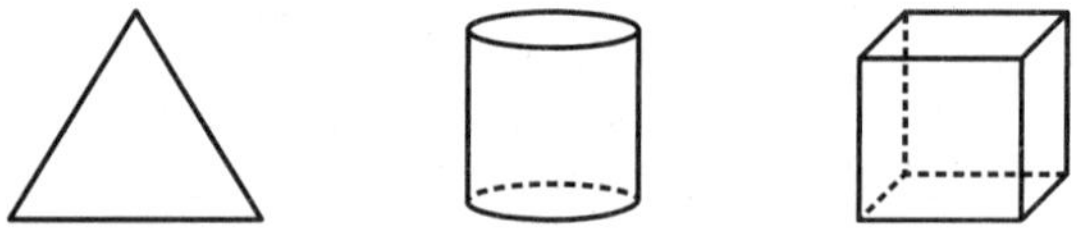

Why did you X this figure?

____

____

3 Underline the words that define a shape.

2-dimensional	small
blue	3 vertices
closed	3 straight sides

4 Look at the words you underlined in question 3.

Which shape is described by the underlined words?
Circle your answer.

5 Circle the items that will roll.

6 Look at the group of figures.

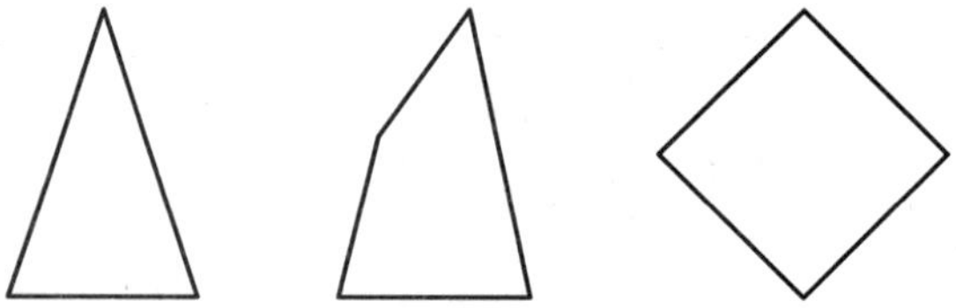

Which is an attribute that does NOT define the figures?

- Straight sides
- Large
- Two-dimensional

Illegal to Copy

Connect Four

Play *Connect Four* with a partner. Each pair needs a paper clip and pencil for the spinner and a game board. Each player needs 10 Unifix® cubes (a different color for each player). In turn, each player spins the spinner to identify a three-dimensional figure. The player places a cube on a space that shows a real-life example of the figure. If no examples are available, the player passes. The winner is the first player to get four Unifix cubes in a straight line.

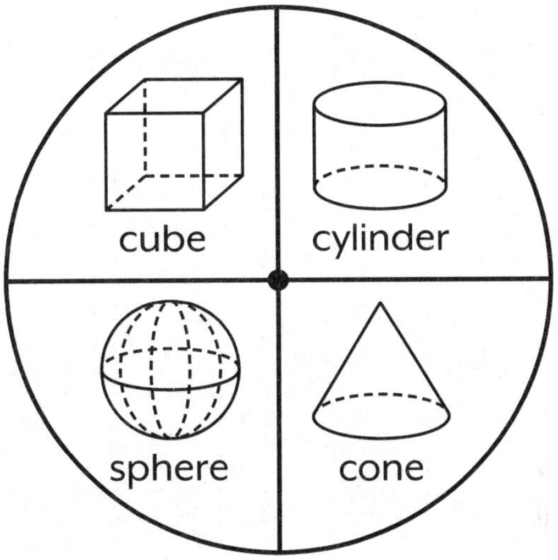

Extension

Name: ____________________

Math Challenge

Look at the cone. Draw the shape you see on the bottom of the cone.

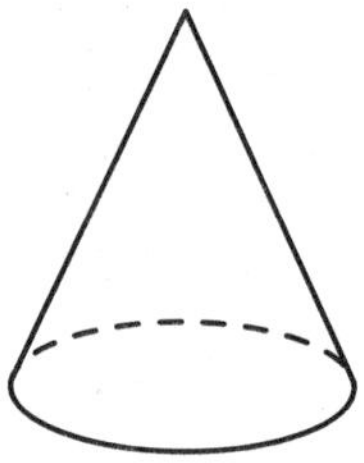

How did you know what shape to draw?

____

____

Reflection on My Learning

How is a sphere different from other three-dimensional figures? Use words or pictures to explain.

Reflection on Critical Thinking

Circle the traits you used most often in this unit.

I show ____________________ when I ____________________ .

Illegal to Copy

Name: ______________________________

Assessment

Unit 23 – Standard 1.6(B)

Concept Check

1 Ali describes a three-dimensional figure. She says, "It has two round bases. It rolls. It has a curved surface."

Which shape does Ali describe?

- ⬭ 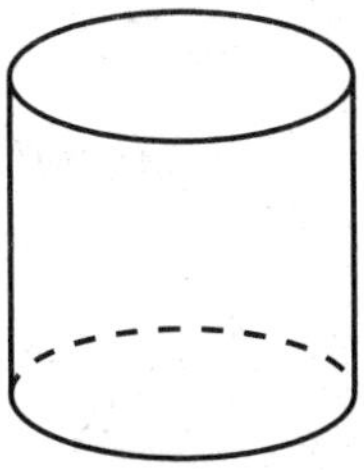
- ⬭ 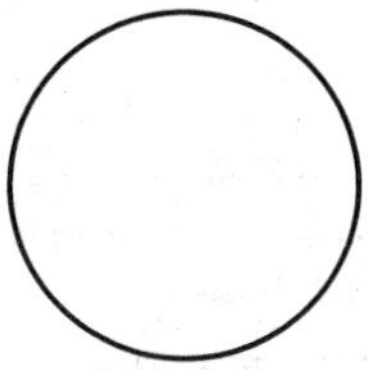
- ⬭ 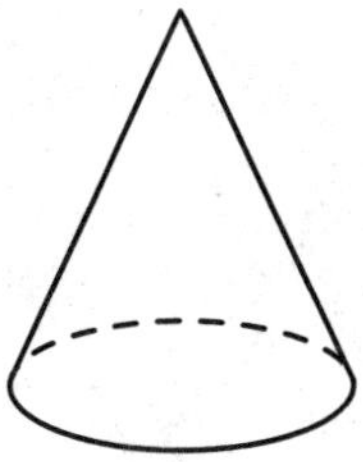

2 Color the figures that have faces.

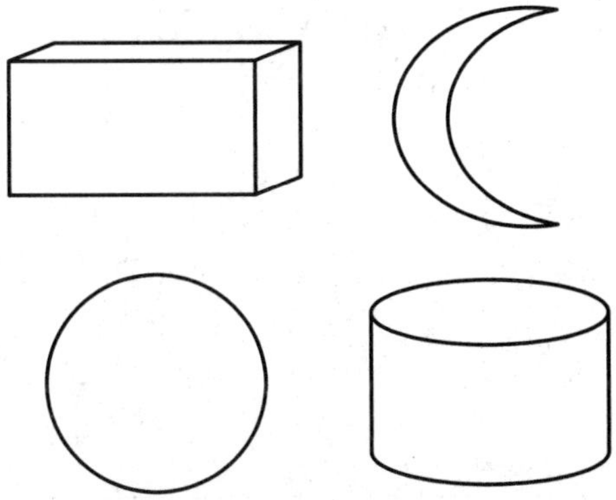

3 Ladarius says that a square is a part of a cube.

Is Ladarius' statement correct?

Answer ______________________________

Explain your answer.

____

____

4 Which of the following attributes does NOT define a cube?

- ⬭ Square faces
- ⬭ Curved figure
- ⬭ Three-dimensional figure

5 First graders brought examples of cones they saw at home.

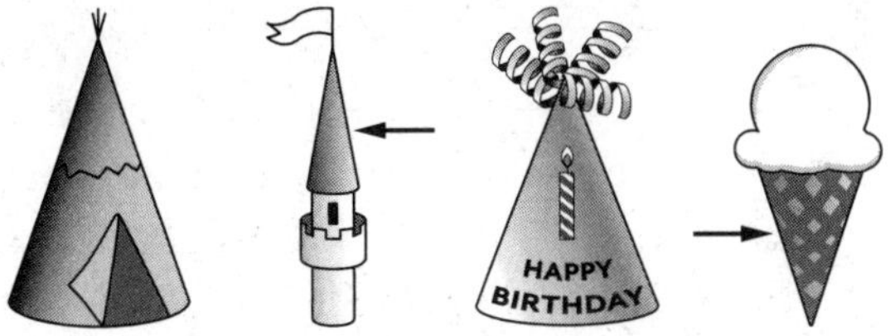

All of the attributes define a cone EXCEPT –

- ⬭ Three-dimensional
- ⬭ One vertex
- ⬭ Red

Assessment

Name: ____________________

Concept Check

Standard 1.6(B) – **Unit 23**

6 Draw a three-dimensional figure for each attribute.

Stacks	Rolls	Has vertices

7 Color the two-dimensional figures blue.
Color the three-dimensional figures red.

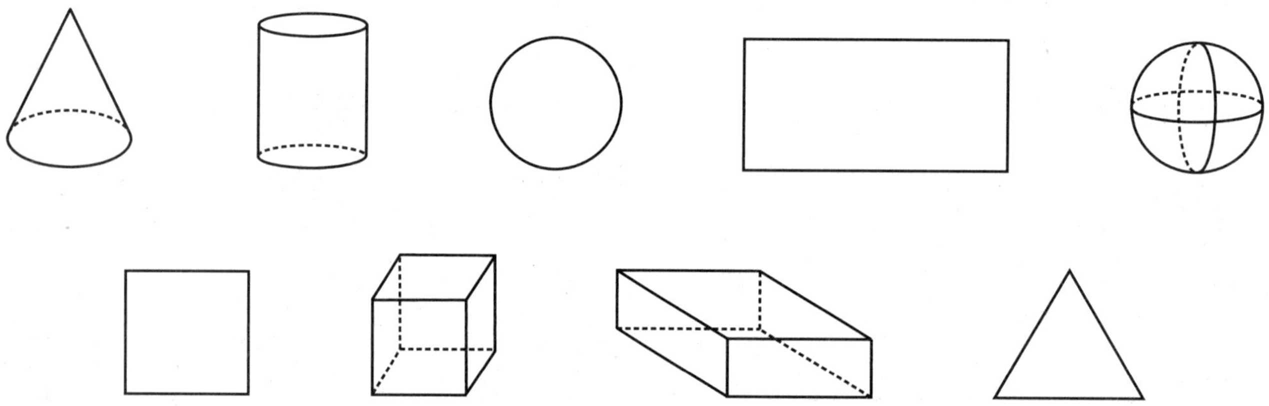

8 Maya drew this shape. Her younger brother said that triangles always have three sides and three vertices and are shaded gray. Is Maya's brother correct? Why or why not?

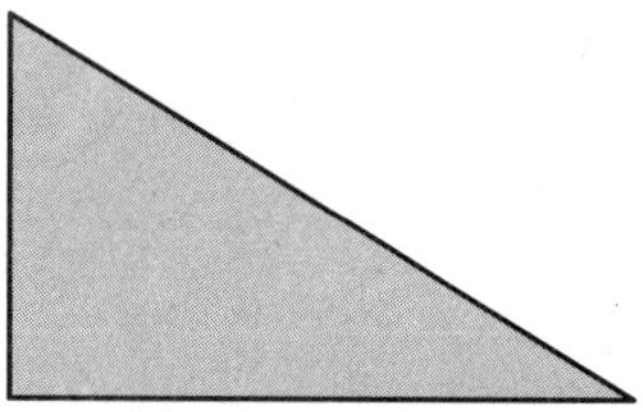

____

____

____

Illegal to Copy

Name: ______________________________

Getting Started

Unit 24 – Standard 1.6(C)

Unit 24: Create Two-Dimensional Shapes

TEKS LEARNING TARGETS

- I can create models of two-dimensional figures including circles, triangles, rectangles, squares, rhombuses, and hexagons.
- I can explain that a square is a special rectangle.
- I can use correct math words for each shape.

Focus for 9 Traits of Critical Thinking™

Collaborate: *I work with others to achieve better outcomes.*

How could you use your arms and hands to make a model of a circle or a square? Would working with a partner or other students make the process easier? Explain your response.

____

____

Reflect: *I review my thoughts and experiences to guide my actions.*

What math words do you know that will help you talk about shapes? How will these words make discussions easier?

____

____

Instruction

Name: ______________________

Concept Exploration

Standard 1.6(C) – **Unit 24**

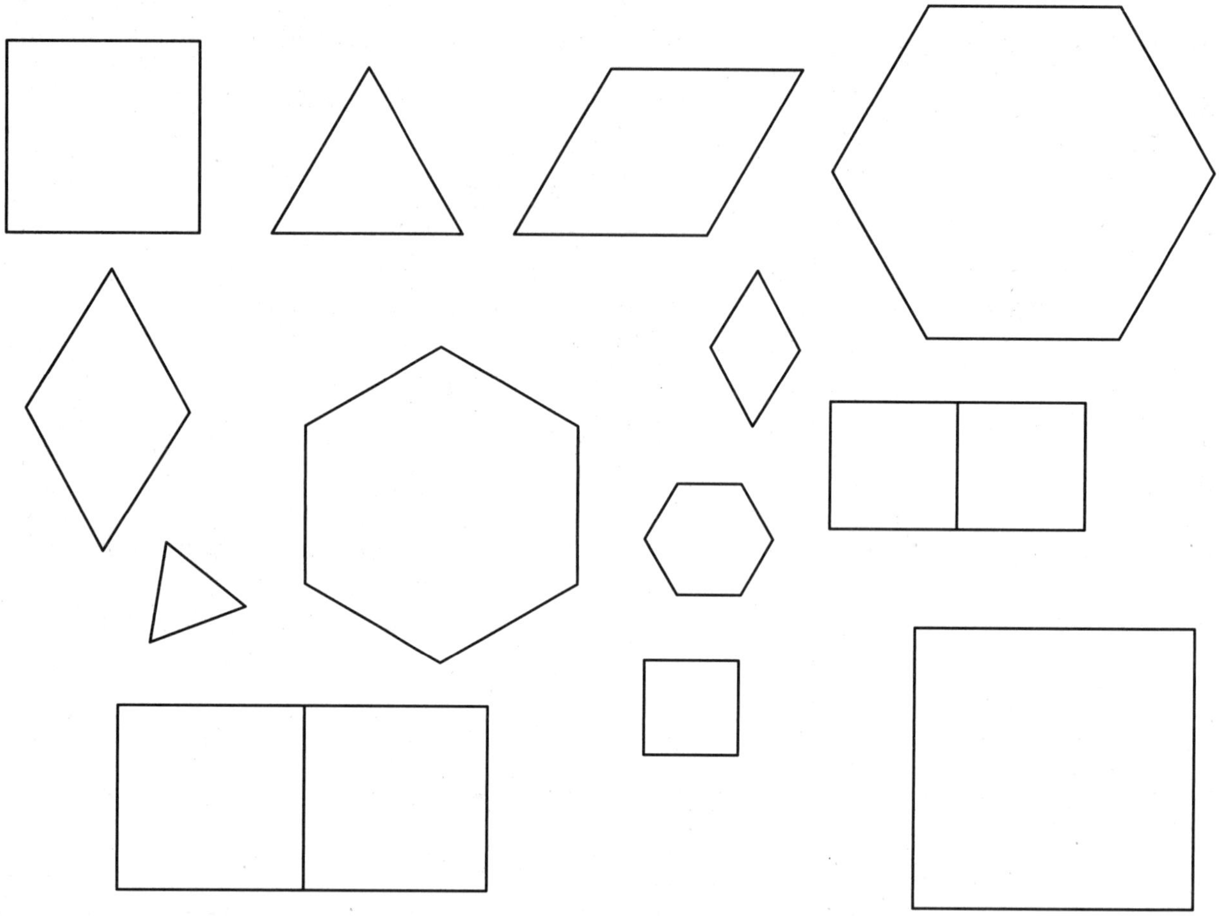

Do you listen carefully when others are speaking during group activities?

____

____

Why does a shape's position not alter what shape it is?

____

____

Illegal to Copy

attribute	**hexagon**	**sides**	**two-dimensional shape**
circle	**rectangle**	**square**	**vertex/vertices**
corner	**rhombus**	**triangle**	

Connect the dots in each box to create two-dimensional shapes.
Write the name of the shape under each picture.

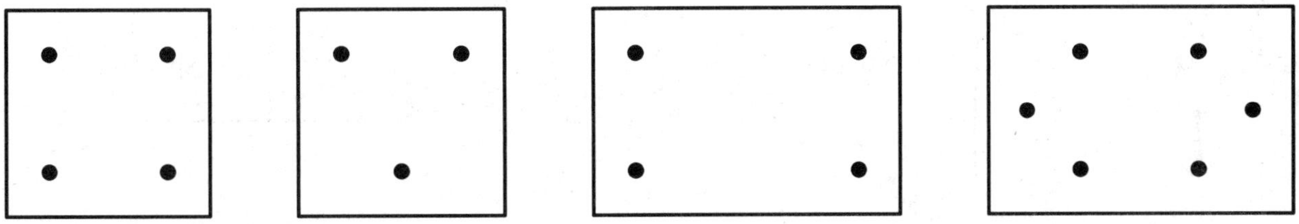

How might you help a friend understand this activity?

____

____

What are some ideas you had about two-dimensional shapes when you were connecting the dots?

____

____

Count the number of sides and vertices.

Then, write the name of the figure.

Sides _____ Vertices _____

Answer ______________________________

Match the shape with its name.

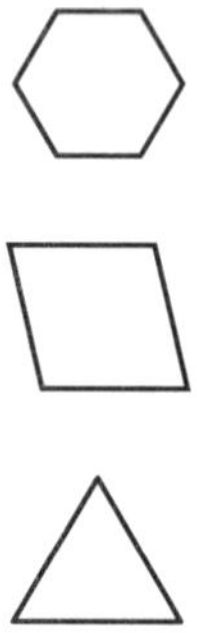

Triangle

Rhombus

Hexagon

Circle all the examples of squares.

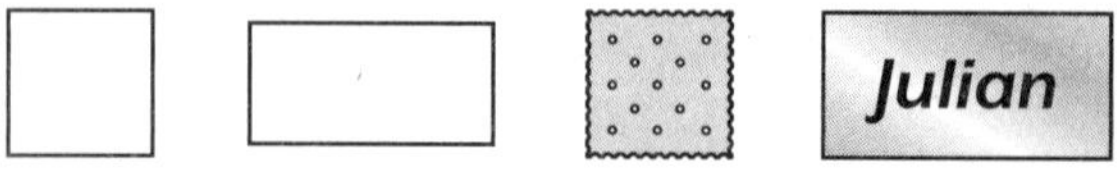

Two-dimensional shapes may be defined by the number of sides and vertices.

When creating shapes, you must include the correct number of sides and vertices.

It is important to call shapes by their names.

A square is known as a special rectangle because it has four sides of equal length and four square corners.

Try It!

1) Draw a figure that has three sides and three vertices.

What is the name of this shape?

____

Try It!

2) Read the definition and place an X on the shapes that apply.

a two-dimensional shape with four sides of equal length

Instruction

Concept Application

1 Mia made a circle out of yarn and a square out of straws.

Explain why those supplies were good to make the shapes.

____

____

2 Bo has two pattern blocks. What new shape can Bo create if he combines the blocks?

- Circle
- Square
- Hexagon

3 Use this curve to create a circle.

4 Read the riddle to find the shape.

I have six sides.

I have six vertices.

My sides are straight.

I am a ____________________.

Draw the shape.

5 Look at the figures.

Draw lines to create a triangle.

Draw lines to create a different shape.

6 Draw one line in the square to create two rectangles.

Instruction

Name: ______________________________

Concept Practice

Standard 1.6(C) – **Unit 24**

1 Use the dot paper to create a triangle and a rectangle.

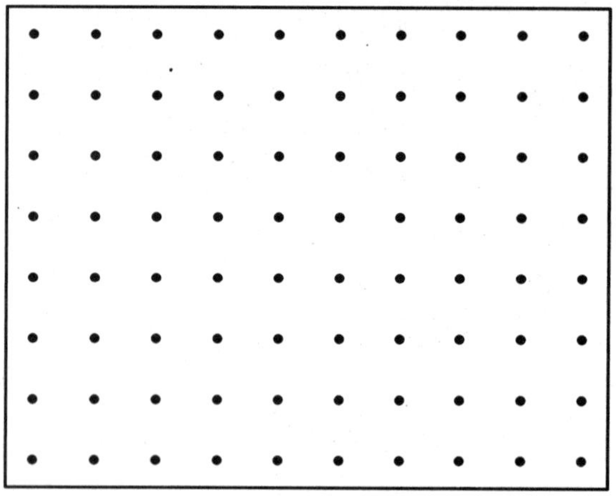

2 Brice sees this symbol on a map.

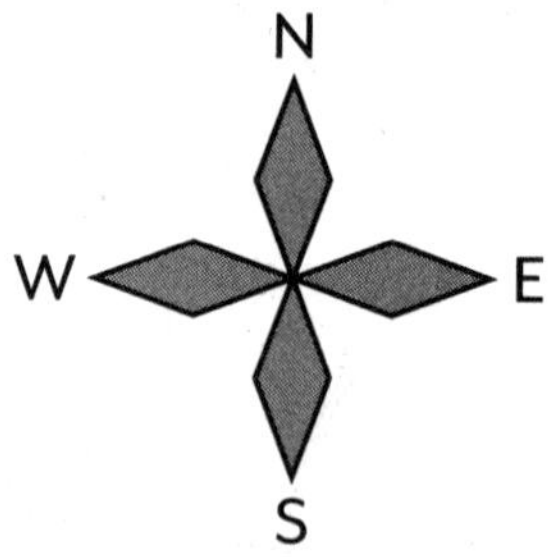

Which shape is used to make the symbol?

- ⬭ Triangle
- ⬭ Square
- ⬭ Rhombus

3 Read the clues.

I am a special rectangle.

I have four equal sides.

What shape am I?

Answer ______________________

4 Draw three things in your home that represent two-dimensional shapes.

5 Connect these lines to create a closed figure with three corners.

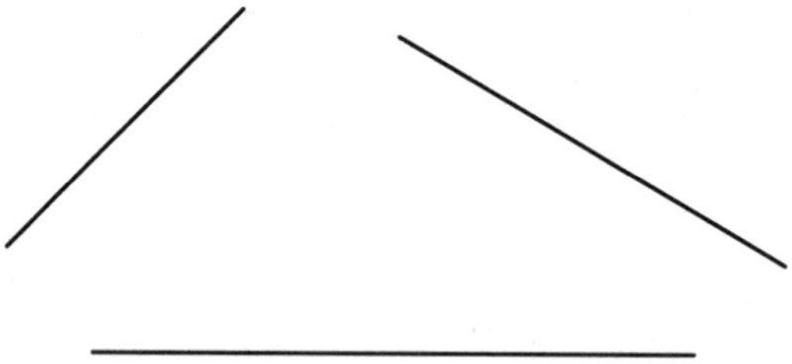

What shape did you create?

Answer ______________________

6 Draw one line in the square to create two triangles.

Illegal to Copy

Count and Cover

Play *Count and Cover* with a friend. Each player needs 16 game markers of the same color. Each player uses a different color. Each pair needs 1 die. Player 1 rolls the die and covers a shape with the same number of sides as the number rolled. Players pass if they roll a 1 or 2 or if the needed shapes are covered. The game is over when all shapes are covered. The winner is the player with more markers on the game board.

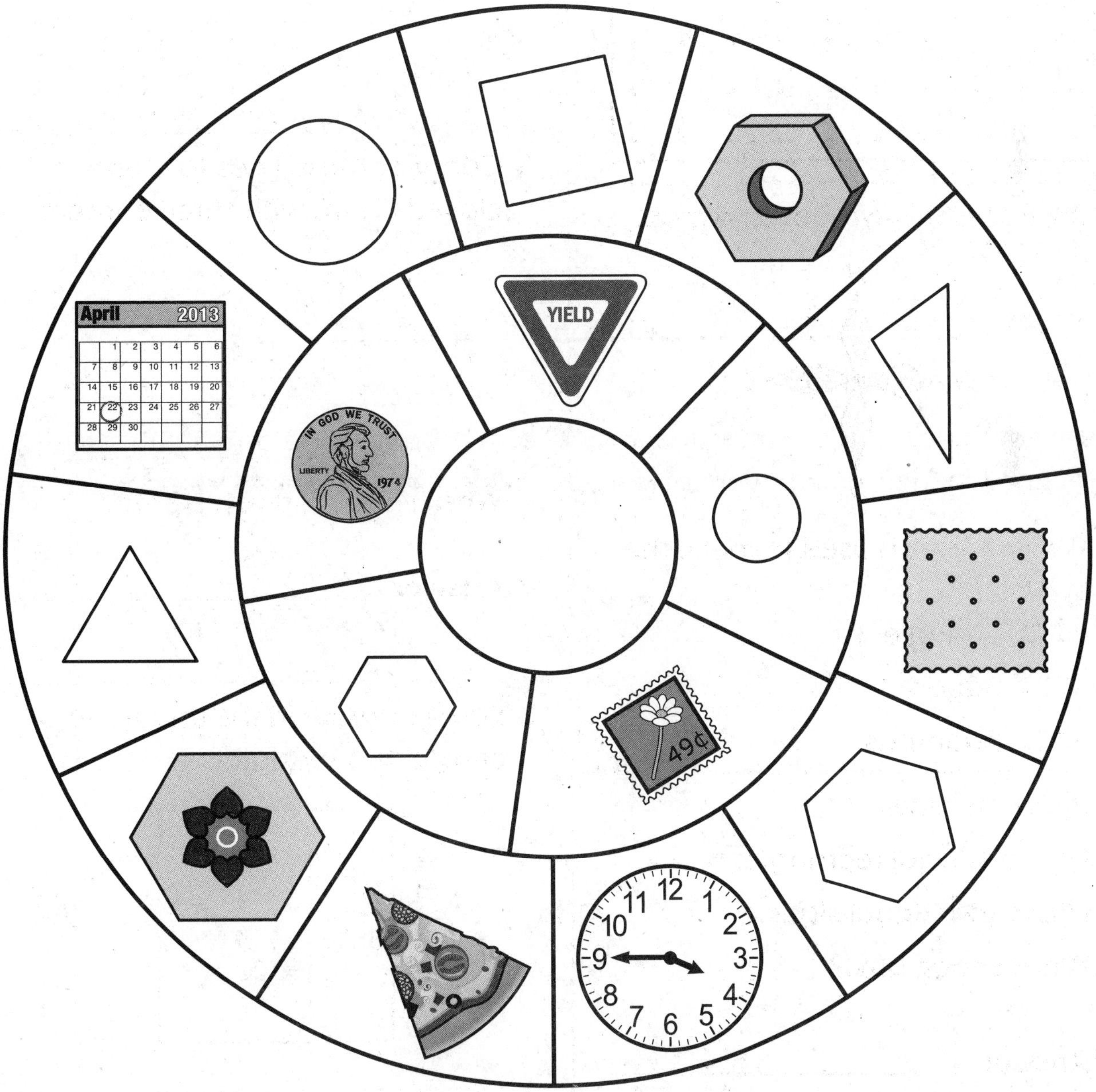

Extension

Name: ______________________________

Standard 1.6(C) – **Unit 24**

Math Challenge

Create an animal using only triangles.

Reflection on My Learning

Your teacher asks you to create a model of a rhombus. He offers you straws, paper and pencil, yarn, or chenille sticks. Which supply would you choose to make your model? Why?

____

____

Reflection on Critical Thinking

Circle the traits you used most often in this unit.

I show ______________________ when I ______________________ .

Illegal to Copy

Name: ______________________________

Assessment

Unit 24 – Standard 1.6(C)

Concept Check

1 Read the clues to find the mystery shape.

I am a curved shape.

I have no straight sides.

I am a ______________________.

Draw the mystery shape.

2 Which shape can you create if you combine the following shapes?

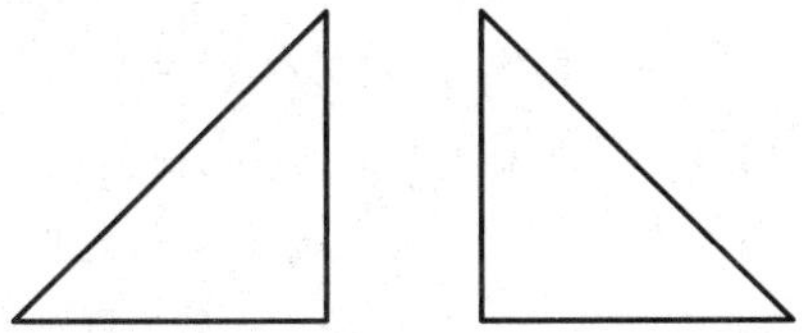

- ⬭ 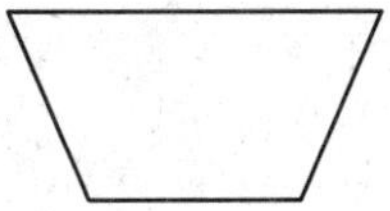
- ⬭ 
- ⬭ 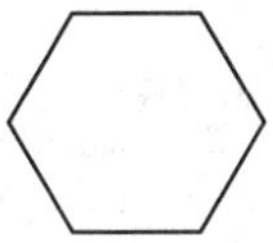

3 Draw lines to create a square.

4 What different shape can you create using two rectangles?

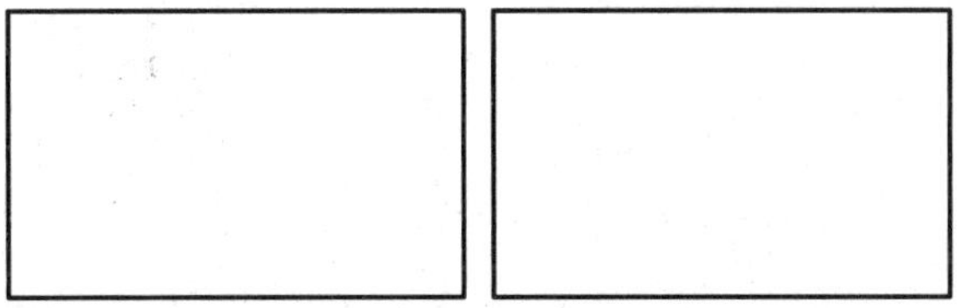

Answer ______________________

Draw the new shape.

5 Draw lines to finish a hexagon.

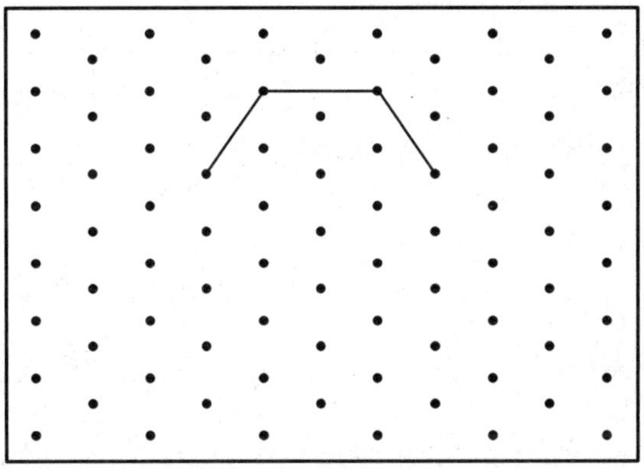

Assessment

Name: ____________________

Concept Check

Standard 1.6(C) – **Unit 24**

6 Pat draws shapes with four straight sides. Circle the shapes Pat draws.

circle	hexagon	rectangle
rhombus	square	triangle

Draw and label the circled shapes.

7 Connect the dots to create a two-dimensional figure.

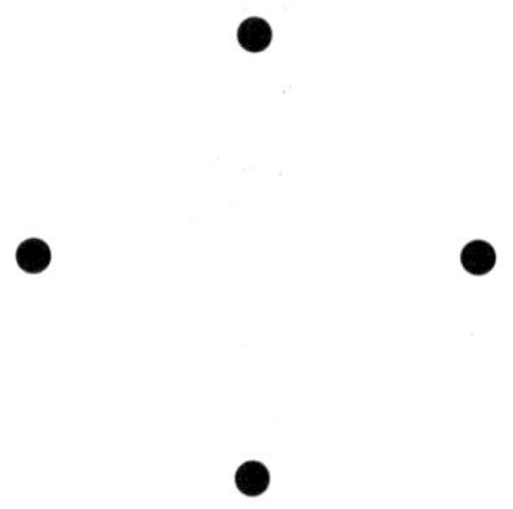

Write the name of the figure. ____________________

Draw two lines to divide the figure into four figures.

What four figures did you create? ____________________

8 Roxanne has two blocks. What new two-dimensional shape can she create with the two blocks?

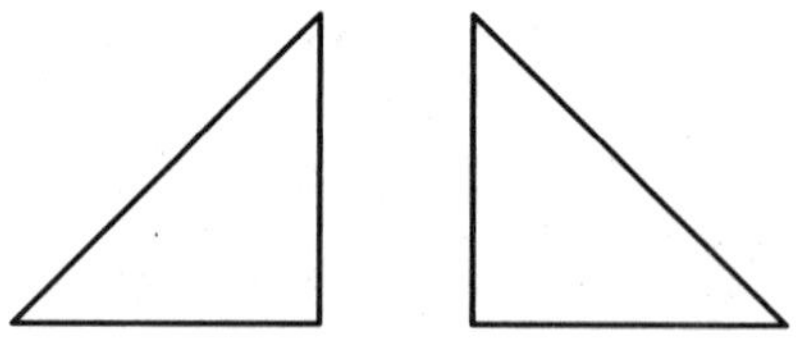

What is the name of the new shape Roxanne can create?

____

Illegal to Copy

Name: ______________________

Getting Started

Unit 25 – Standard 1.6(D)

Unit 25: Use Attributes to Identify Two-Dimensional Shapes

TEKS LEARNING TARGETS

- I can identify two-dimensional shapes using attributes.
- I can describe attributes of two-dimensional shapes using accurate geometric language.

Focus for 9 Traits of Critical Thinking™

Communicate: *I use clear language to express my ideas and to share information.*

What else besides your words can you use to show your understanding of shapes?

____

____

Create: *I use my knowledge and imagination to express new and innovative ideas.*

If you are asked to draw a house, what shapes would you use in your picture? Does looking at an object and identifying its basic shapes help you ***create*** your picture?

____

____

Illegal to Copy

Instruction

Name: ______________________________

Concept Exploration

Standard 1.6(D) – **Unit 25**

Name of Shape	Number of Sides	Number of Vertices	Drawing of Shape	Real-Life Example
Circle				
Triangle				
Rectangle				
Square				
Rhombus				
Hexagon				

How would you explain a rhombus to a kindergarten student?

____

____

What picture can you design that includes triangles, rectangles, rhombuses, and hexagons? Describe your picture.

____

____

Illegal to Copy

Name: ______________________________

Unit 25 – Standard 1.6(D)

Instruction

Vocabulary Mastery

attribute	**equal**	**rhombus**	**triangle**
circle	**hexagon**	**sides**	**two-dimensional shape**
closed figure	**rectangle**	**square**	**vertex/vertices**

Sort the vocabulary words into one of the columns. Use the Word Bank.

Word Bank

circle	curve	equal	hexagon	rectangle
rhombus	side	square	triangle	vertex

Two-Dimensional Shapes	Attributes of Shapes

How do you use math language in your explanations?

____

____

What is another graphic organizer you could ***create*** to share the attributes of the shapes?

____

____

How many sides does a hexagon have?

__________ sides

Draw a hexagon.

Two-dimensional shapes may be defined by the number of sides and vertices.

When creating shapes, you must include the correct number of sides and vertices.

How many vertices does a square have?

__________ vertices

Draw a square.

A square is a special

__________.

A rhombus, a square (a special rectangle), and a rectangle all have four sides and four vertices.

Rectangles and squares have square corners.

Rhombuses and squares have four sides that are the same lengths.

Try It!

1) 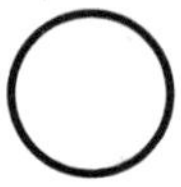

Name this shape. __________

Name one attribute that defines this shape.

____

Try It!

2) 

Name this shape. __________

Where do you see this shape in real life?

____

Illegal to Copy

Instruction

Concept Application

1 What is the name of this shape?

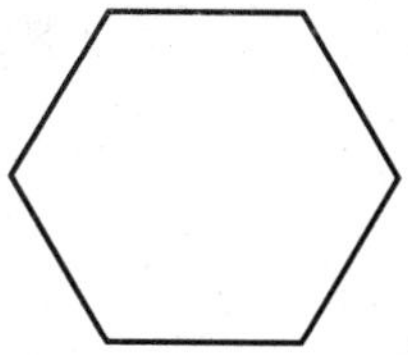

- ◯ Hexagon
- ◯ Rhombus
- ◯ Rectangle

2 Which shape is a triangle?

- ◯ 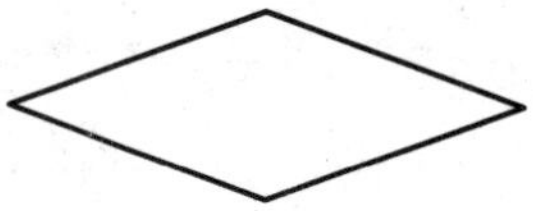
- ◯ 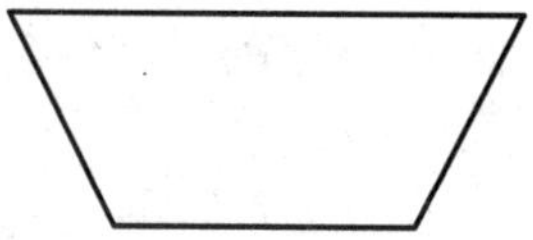
- ◯ 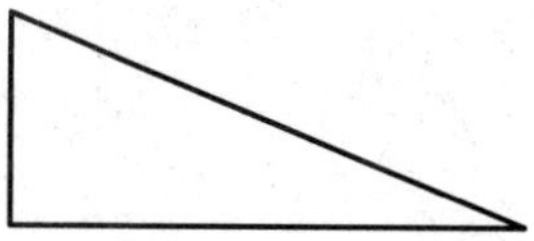

3 Look at the circle.

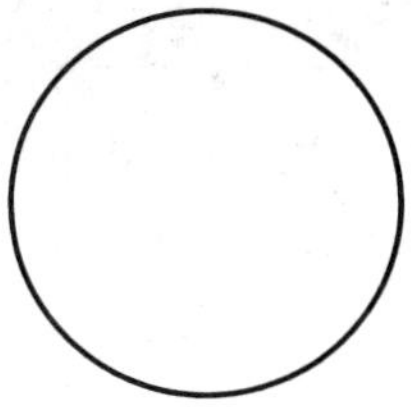

Write numbers to make the sentence true.

A circle has _____ vertices and _____ straight sides.

4 Look at the shapes.

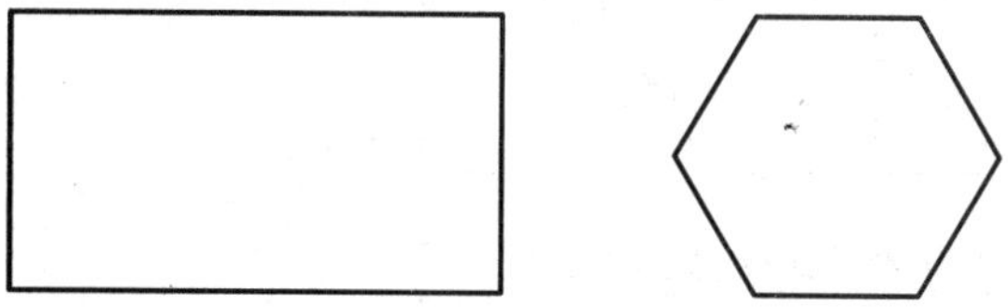

Circle the word that makes this sentence true.

Both shapes have more than three ______________.

vertices   circles

5 Look at the shapes.

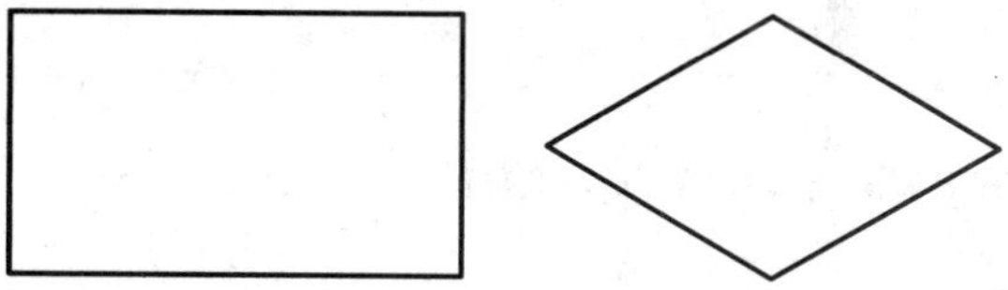

Which attribute does NOT describe the shapes?

Circle the answer.

4 sides   3 vertices   closed figure

What shape does the circled answer describe?

____

Instruction

Name: ______________________________

Concept Practice

Standard 1.6(D) – **Unit 25**

1 What is the name of this shape?

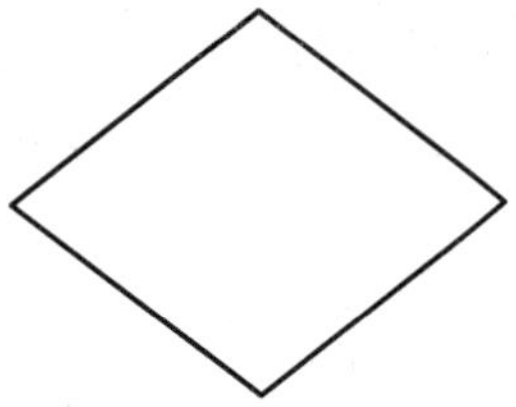

⬭ Square

⬭ Rhombus

⬭ Rectangle

2 Count the shapes you see on the rocket. Write the numbers.

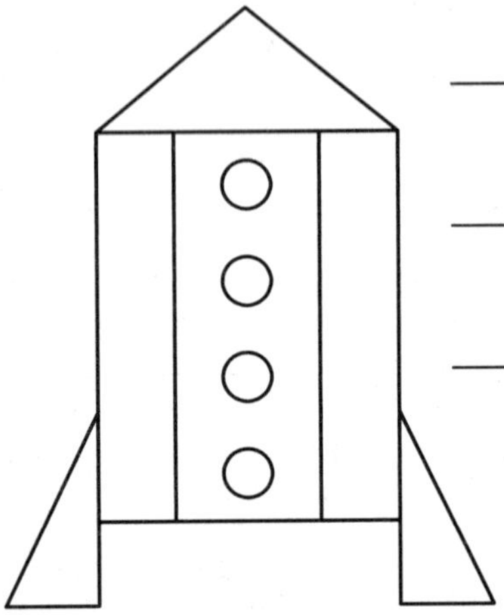

_____ rectangles

_____ circles

_____ triangles

3 Color the shapes that have four vertices and four sides.

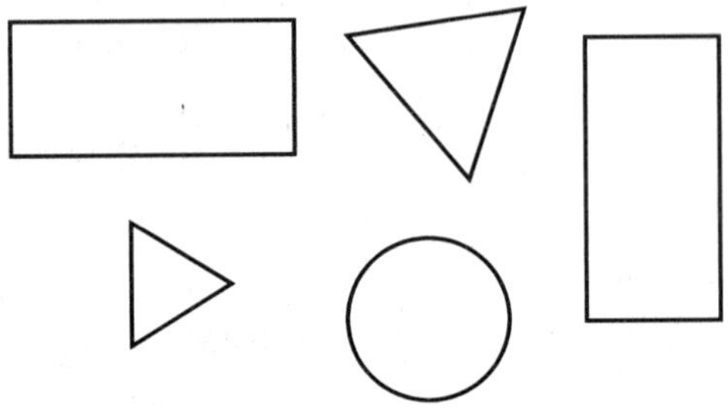

4 Look at the shape.

Circle all the words that describe the shape.

4 vertices	Special rectangle
Square	4 sides
Closed Figure	Hexagon

5 Count the shapes in the cat.

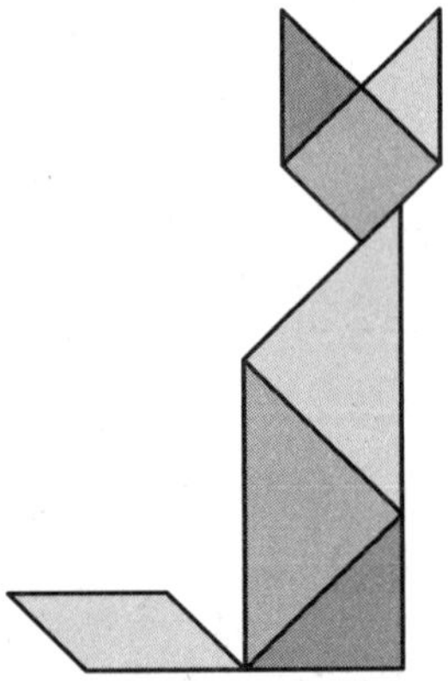

How many shapes have three vertices?

____

How many shapes have four sides?

____

Illegal to Copy

Name: ______________________________

Instruction

Unit 25 – Standard 1.6(D)

Concept Practice: Motivation Station

Roll a Robot

Play *Roll a Robot* with a partner. Partners take turns rolling a die and drawing part of a robot as shown. Draw your robot on a sheet of paper. Players pass if they roll a number for a part that has already been drawn. The winner is the first player to draw the robot with all of its parts. Color your robot.

1	Draw a rectangle for a head.	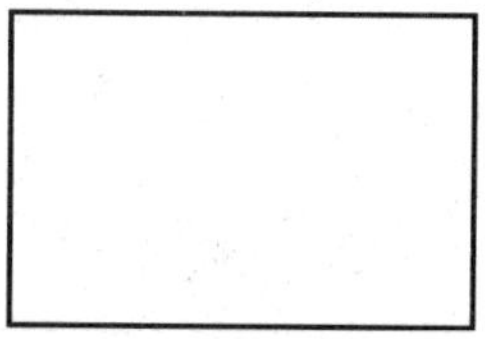
2	Draw a hexagon for the body. Draw rhombuses for the buttons.	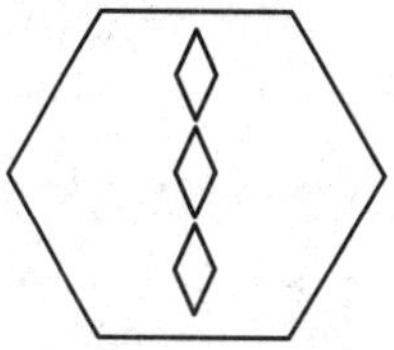
3	Draw rectangles for the legs and feet.	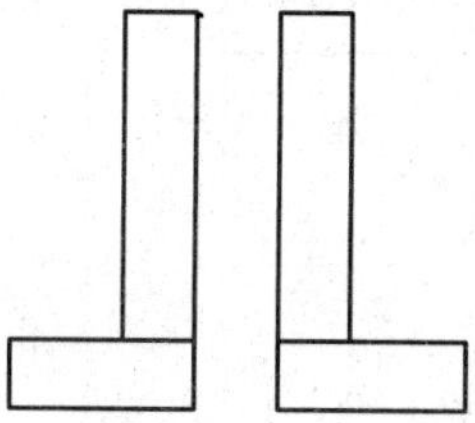
4	Draw rectangles for the arms. Draw triangles for the hands.	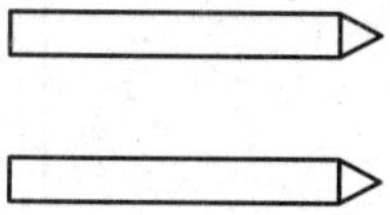
5	Draw circles for the eyes. Draw a rhombus for the nose. Draw a rectangle for the mouth.	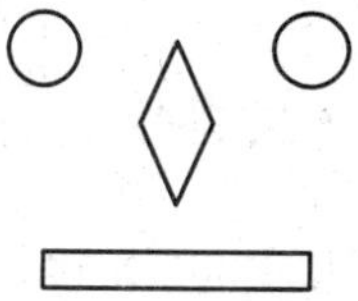
6	Draw squares for the ears.	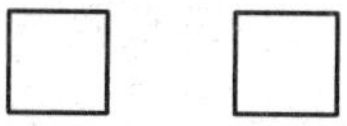

Extension

Name: ______________________________

Math Challenge

Design and draw a picture using only circles, rectangles, rhombuses, and hexagons. Color your picture.

Reflection on My Learning

Why do you think a square is a special rectangle? Use words or pictures to explain.

Reflection on Critical Thinking

Circle the traits you used most often in this unit.

I show ______________________ when I ______________________.

Illegal to Copy

Name: ______________________________

Unit 25 – Standard 1.6(D)

Assessment

Concept Check

1 Color the words that describe a triangle.

straight sides | curved sides | round | 3 vertices

2 Write the correct number of straight sides and vertices in each blank.

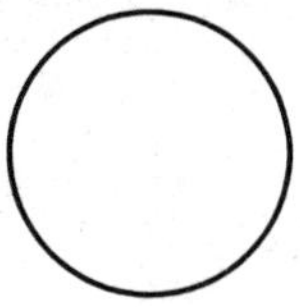

______ sides

______ vertices

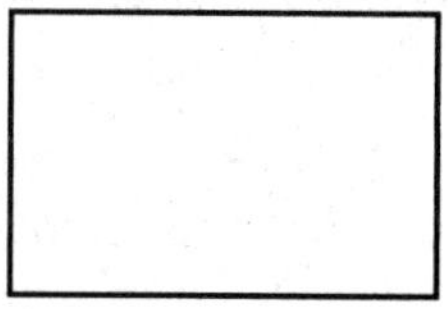

______ sides

______ vertices

3 Look at the hexagon.

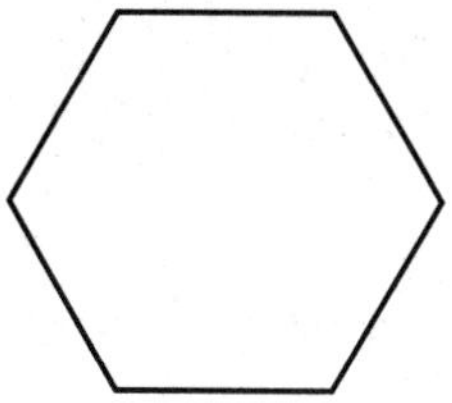

Which sentence about hexagons is true?

- ⬭ All hexagons have exactly 5 vertices.
- ⬭ All hexagons have 6 faces.
- ⬭ All hexagons have 6 sides.

4 The mail carrier looks at stamps while sorting the mail. He sees these stamps.

Which shape of stamp does the mail carrier NOT see?

- ⬭ Square
- ⬭ Hexagon
- ⬭ Rectangle

5 Draw lines to match the shapes to their names.

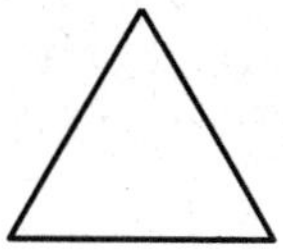

rhombus

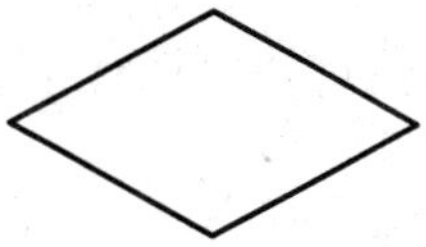

rectangle

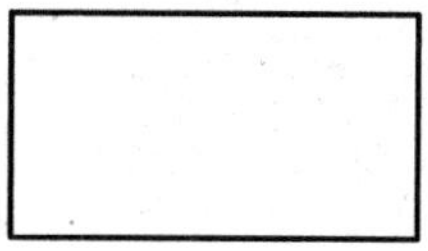

triangle

6 Max drew five shapes. Use the shapes to fill in the blanks.

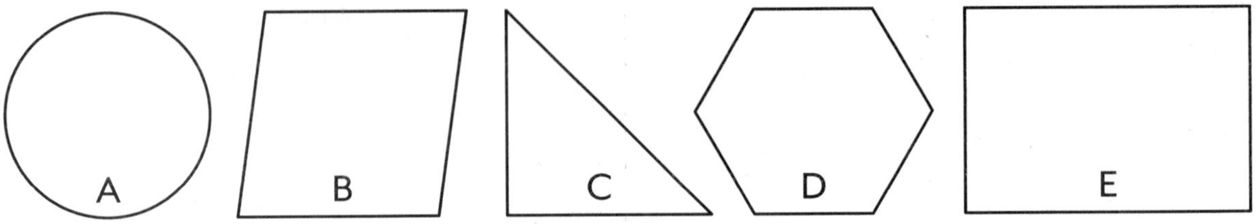

Identify shape D. ____________________

Write the letters of the shapes with four vertices. ____________________

How many sides does shape C have? ____________________

---

7 Write an H on the hexagons in this set of shapes.

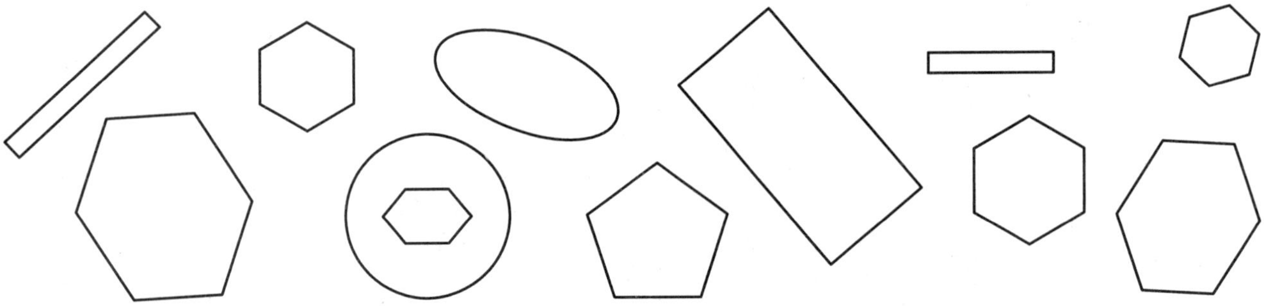

How many hexagons are in the set? ____________________

---

8 Patrice said that a stop sign is shaped like a circle.

Explain to Patrice why her statement is NOT correct.

____

____

Illegal to Copy

Name: ____________________

Getting Started

Unit 26 – Standard 1.6(E)

Unit 26: Identify and Describe Three-Dimensional Solids

TEKS LEARNING TARGETS

- I can identify three-dimensional shapes using math words.
- I can describe attributes of three-dimensional solids using correct math words.
- I can explain the difference between two-dimensional and three-dimensional figures.

Focus for 9 Traits of Critical Thinking™

Communicate: *I use clear language to express my ideas and to share information.*

Why is being able to identify two-dimensional and three-dimensional shapes using math words important?

____

____

Reflect: *I review my thoughts and experiences to guide my actions.*

How might understanding the attributes of two-dimensional shapes help you identify the attributes of three-dimensional solids?

____

____

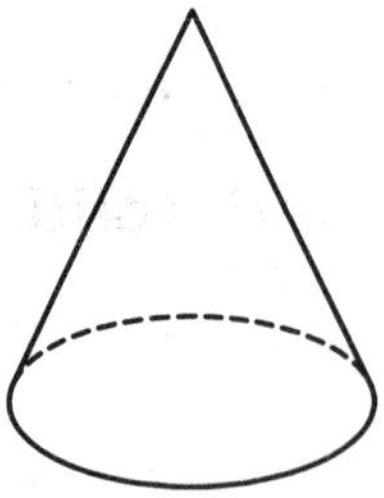

cone

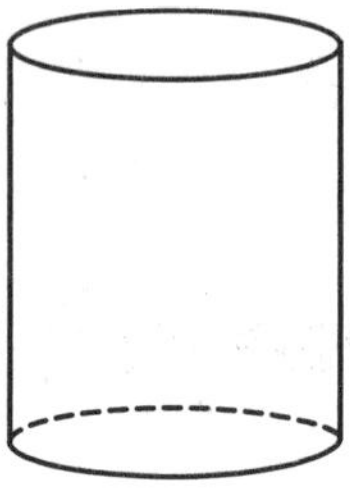

cylinder

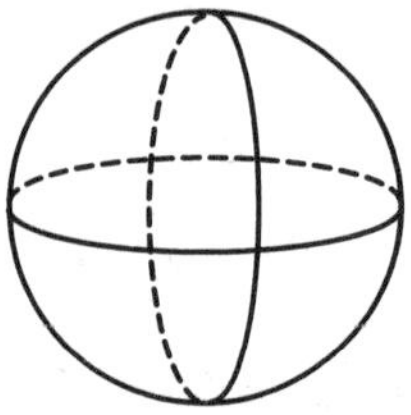

sphere

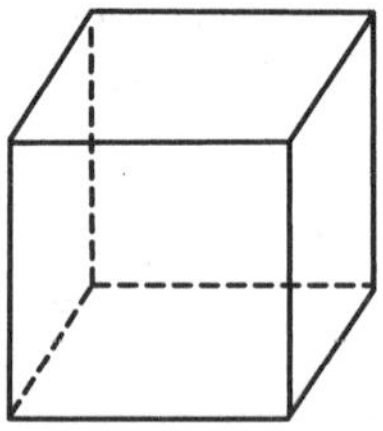

cube

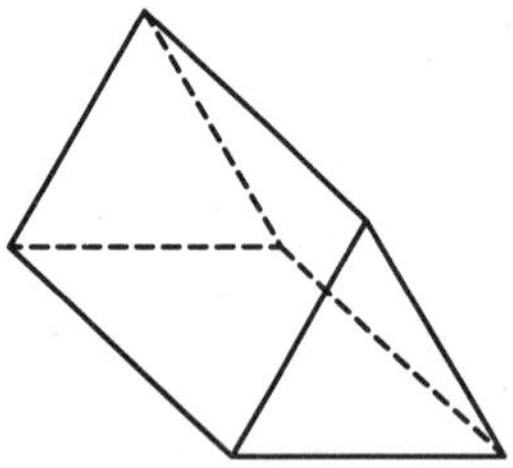

triangular prism

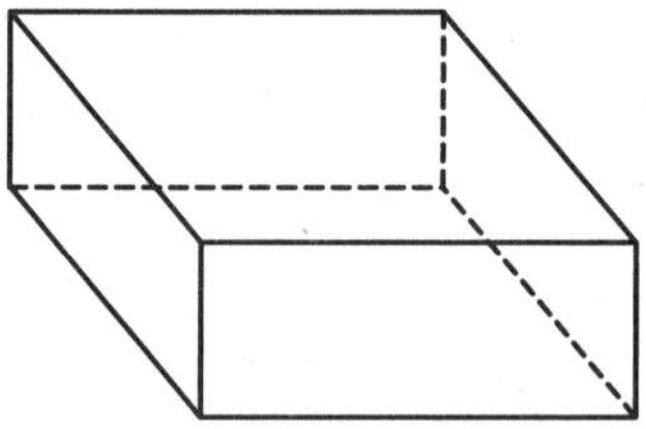

rectangular prism

How did you ***communicate*** with your classmates during this activity? What is something you learned from the discussion?

____

____

What do you find to be most challenging about identifying three-dimensional solids?

____

____

Illegal to Copy

attribute	**cylinder**	**sphere**	**triangular prism**
cone	**face**	**three-dimensional solid**	**vertex/vertices**
cube	**rectangular prism**		

Match the correct name to the three-dimensional solid.

sphere 

rectangular prism 

cube 

cone 

triangular prism 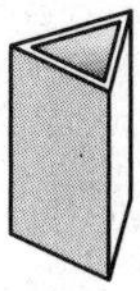

cylinder 

What two-dimensional shapes do you see in rectangular prisms and triangular prisms?

____

____

Instruction

Name: ______________________

Concept Development

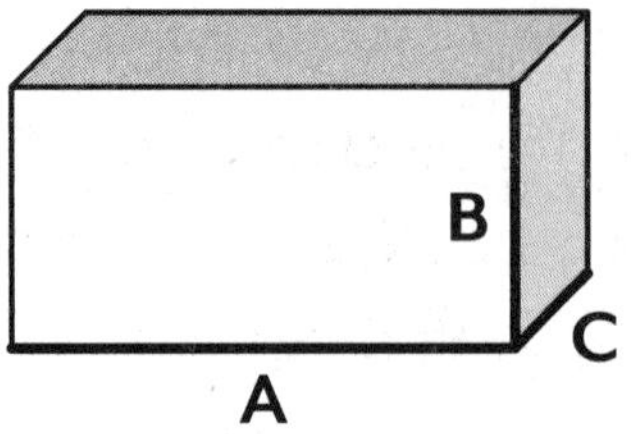

Side A is the **length**.

Side B is the **height**.

Side C is the **width**.

Look at the cube. Mark the length A, the height B, and the width C.

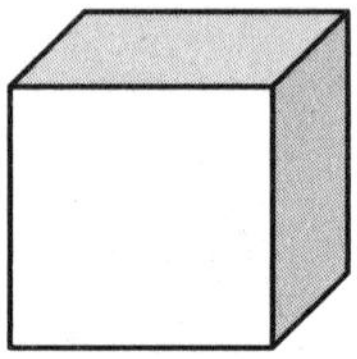

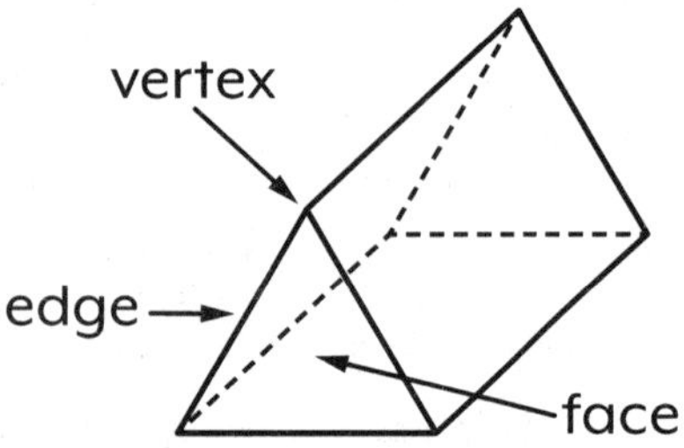

A three-dimensional shape is a solid figure. Three-dimensional solids have length, width, and height.

Three-dimensional solids with straight edges have faces and vertices. These attributes help you name the solid.

Try It!

1) Circle the shape that has one vertex and one flat face.

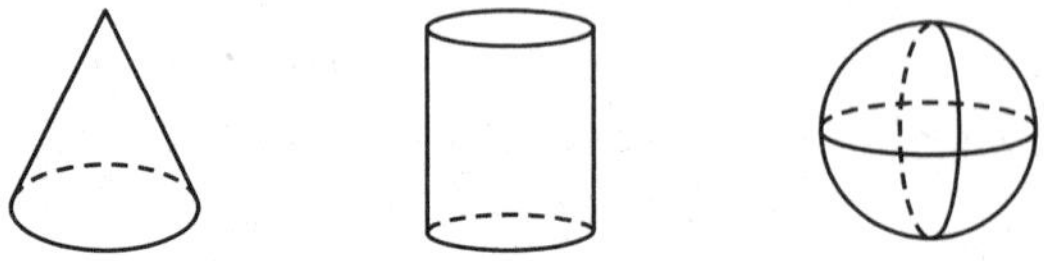

What shape did you circle?

____

Try It!

2) Count the number of edges.

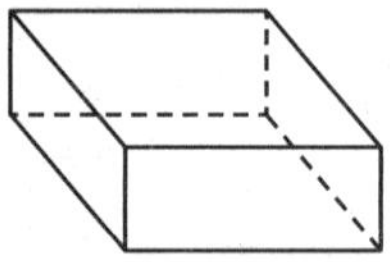

____

What shape do you see?

____

Illegal to Copy

1 Circle the object that is a sphere.

2 Which shape is NOT a cube?

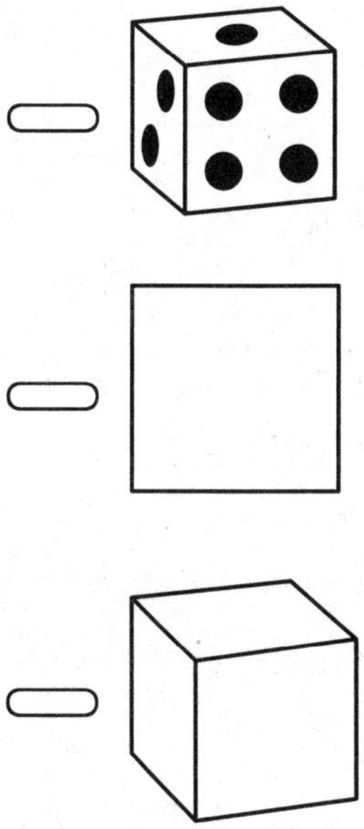

3 Gia opens a can of soda. Circle the three-dimensional figure Gia opens.

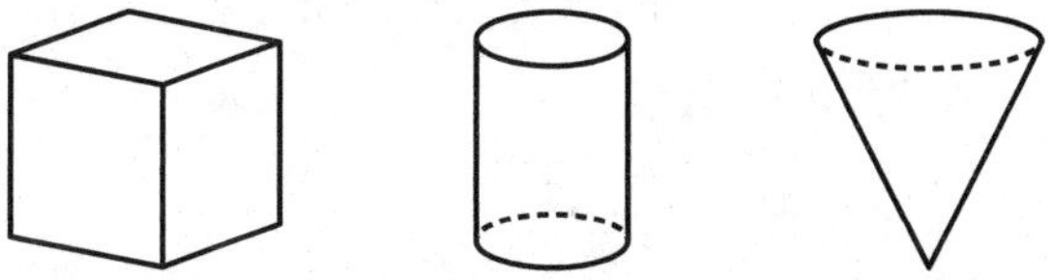

4 Read the clues.

This is a three-dimensional solid.
This solid has 6 square faces.
This solid has 8 vertices.

Circle the picture of this solid.

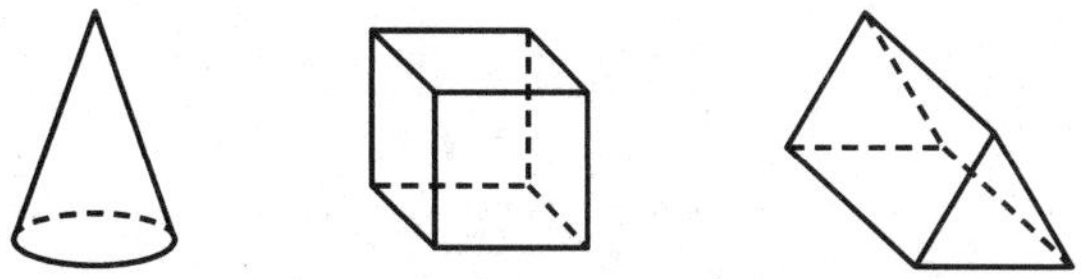

5 Write the correct answers on the blanks.

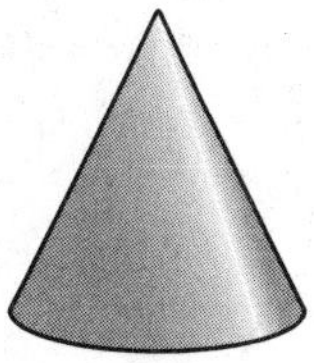

A cone has a base that is a

______________________________.

A cone has ________ vertex.

6 Use words or pictures to show where you see cones in real life.

1 What shape is shown?

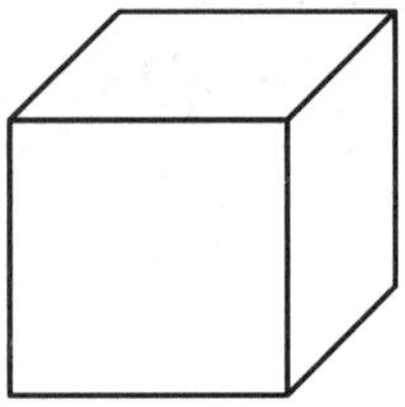

- ⬭ Triangular prism
- ⬭ Cube
- ⬭ Cone

2 Circle the rectangular prisms.

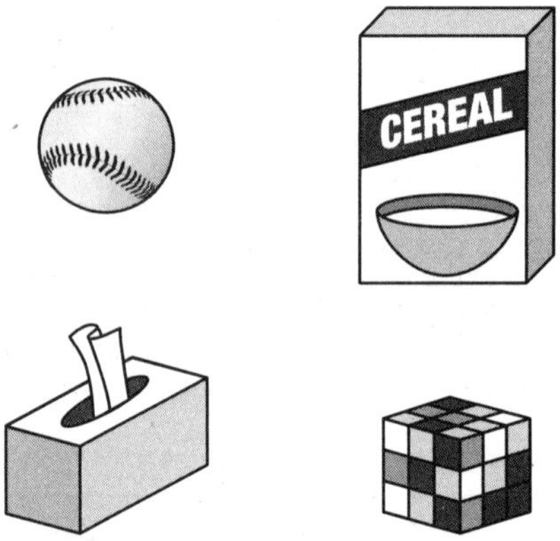

3 Draw a line to match the shape to the number of faces.

cube	2 faces
cylinder	5 faces
triangular prism	6 faces

4 Read the clues.

This is a 3-dimensional solid.
This solid has 0 vertices.
This solid has a curved surface.

Circle the picture of the solid.

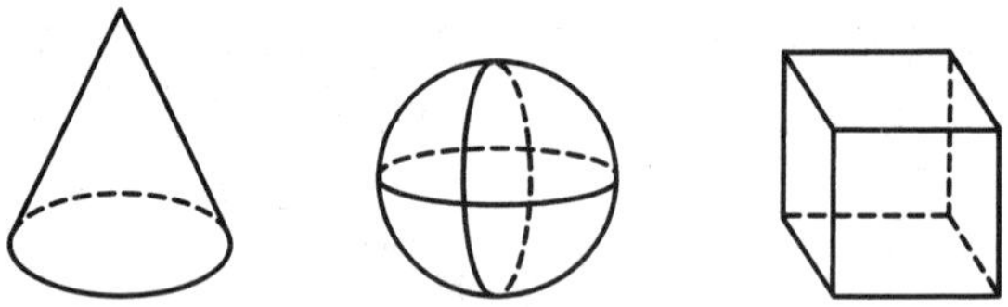

5 Which three-dimensional solid has 6 equal faces?

- ⬭ Triangular prism
- ⬭ Rectangular prism
- ⬭ Cube

6 What shape is shown?

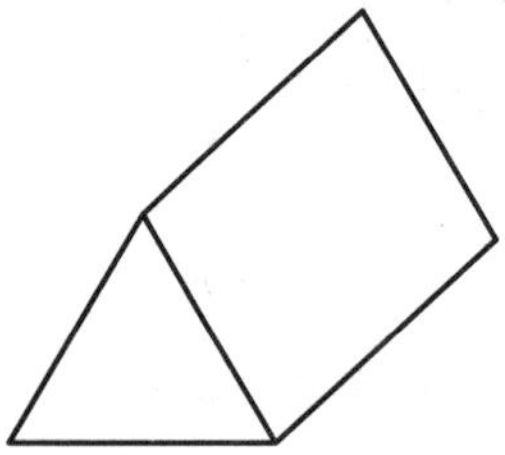

- ⬭ Triangular prism
- ⬭ Sphere
- ⬭ Cylinder

Illegal to Copy

Name That 3-D Shape

Play *Name That 3-D Shape* with a partner. Each player needs a game marker. Each pair needs one game board and one die. Each player places a game marker on START. Players take turns rolling the die and counting that number of spaces on the game board. Players must correctly name the 3-D shape to move to the space. If a player does not correctly name the 3-D shape, the game marker remains in place. Partners check one another's work. The first player to reach the finish is the winner.

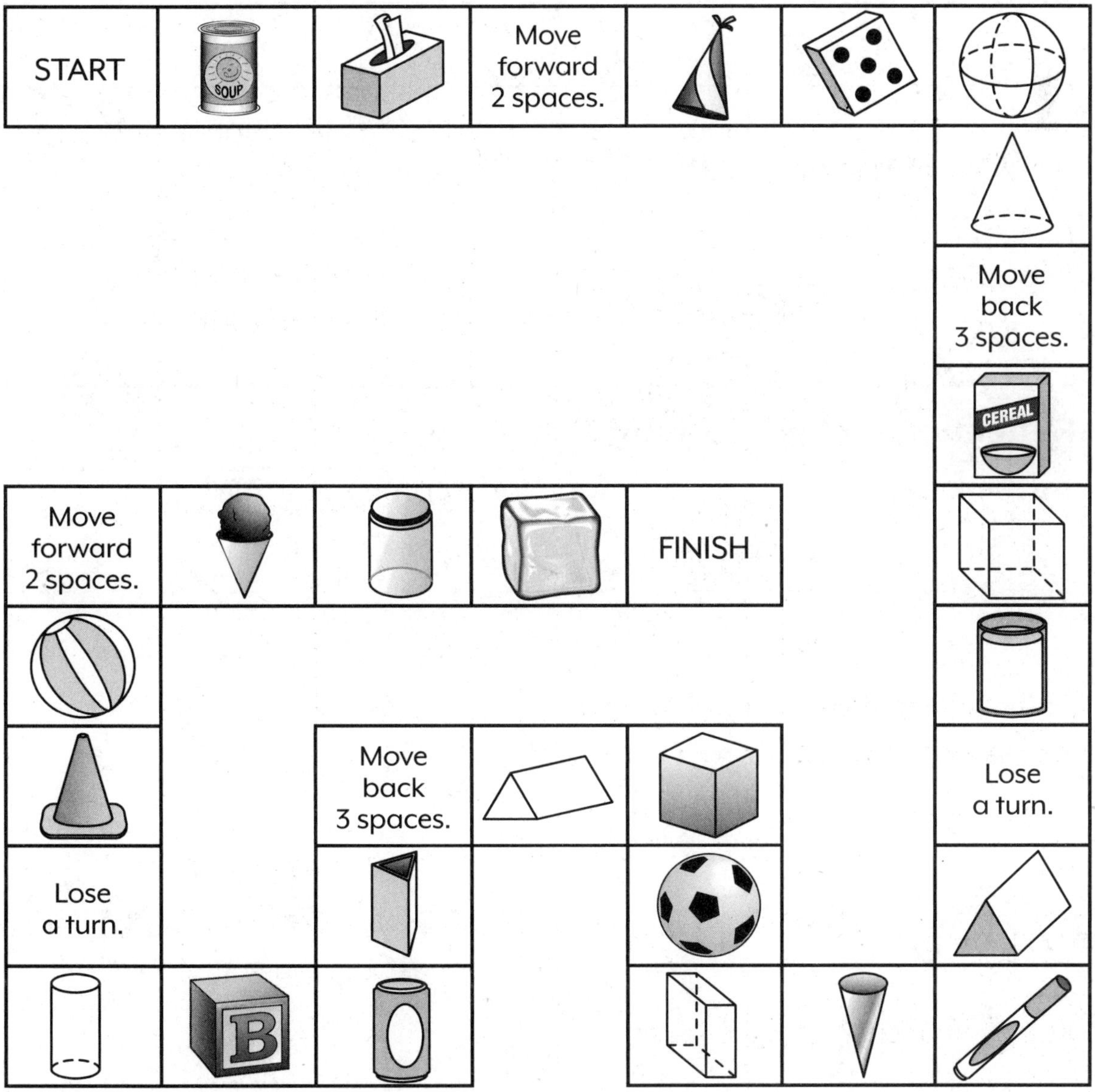

Extension

Name: ______________________

Math Challenge

Look at the cylinder and the cone.

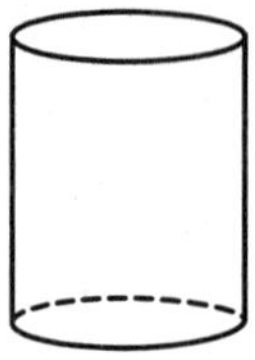

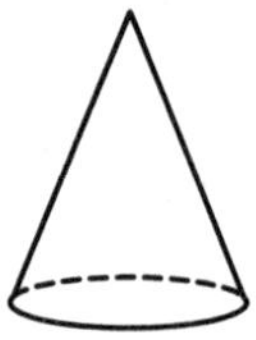

How is the cylinder like the cone?

____

____

How is the cylinder different from the cone?

____

____

Reflection on My Learning

Do you think a cylinder is a good shape for a can of soda? Why?

____

____

Reflection on Critical Thinking

Circle the traits you used most often in this unit.

I show ____________________ when I ____________________ .

Illegal to Copy

1 Which three-dimensional solid has both triangular and rectangular faces?

- ⬭ Cube
- ⬭ Triangular prism
- ⬭ Cylinder

2 Which describes the pizza box?

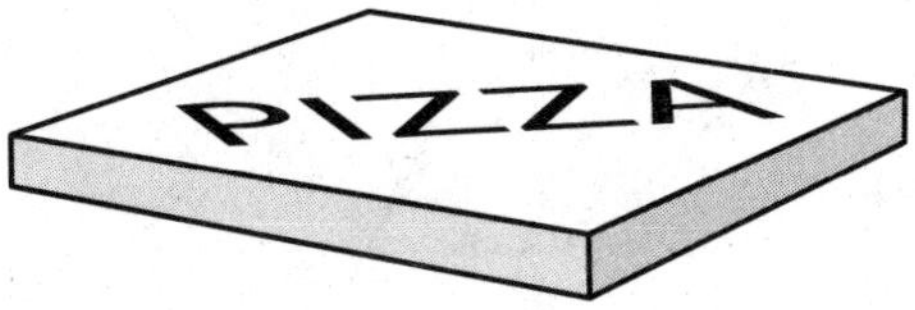

- ⬭ Cube
- ⬭ Rectangle
- ⬭ Rectangular Prism

3 Circle the attribute that does NOT describe the cube.

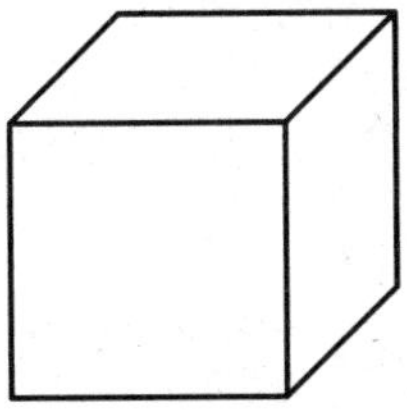

4 edges   8 vertices   6 faces

4 Read the clues.

This is a 3-dimensional solid.
This solid has 1 vertex.
This solid has a curved surface.

Circle the picture of the solid.

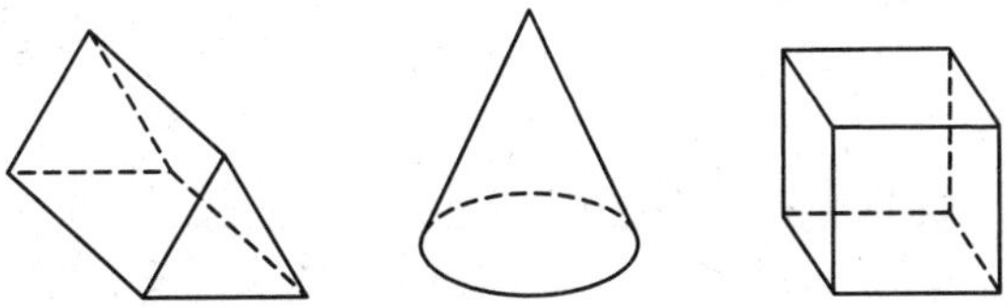

5 Circle the shape that is NOT a sphere.

6 Match the shapes with the number of vertices.

Cube	0 vertices
Cone	8 vertices
Cylinder	1 vertex

Name: ______________________________

Concept Check

7 Circle the solids that are NOT cones.

8 Shade the cylinders.

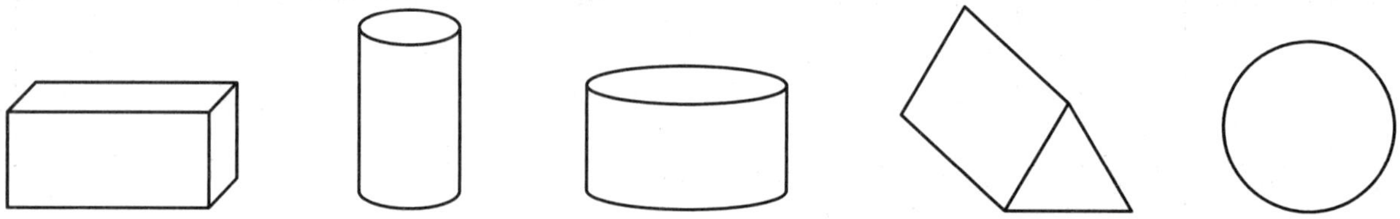

9 Circle the rectangular prisms.

10 What attributes do these solids have in common?

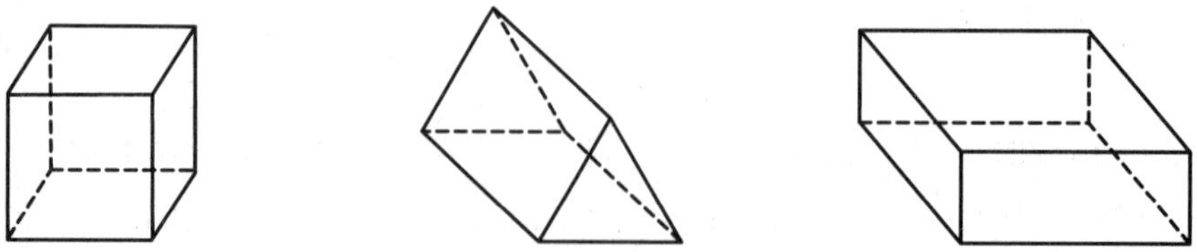

____

____

Illegal to Copy

Name: ______________________________

Getting Started

Unit 27 – Standard 1.6(F)

Unit 27: Compose Two-Dimensional Shapes

TEKS LEARNING TARGETS

- I can create figures using two or more shapes.
- I can compose figures using two or more shapes to model a target shape.
- I can use different figures to compose the same target shape.

Focus for 9 Traits of Critical Thinking™

Adapt: *I adjust my actions and strategies to accomplish tasks.*

Do people always approach problem solving in the same way? Does this idea apply when solving math problems at school?

____

____

Inquire: *I seek information that excites my curiosity and inspires my learning.*

Have you ever thought about how new shapes might be formed by combining a variety of shapes or by combining like shapes? Give an example.

____

____

Name: ____________________

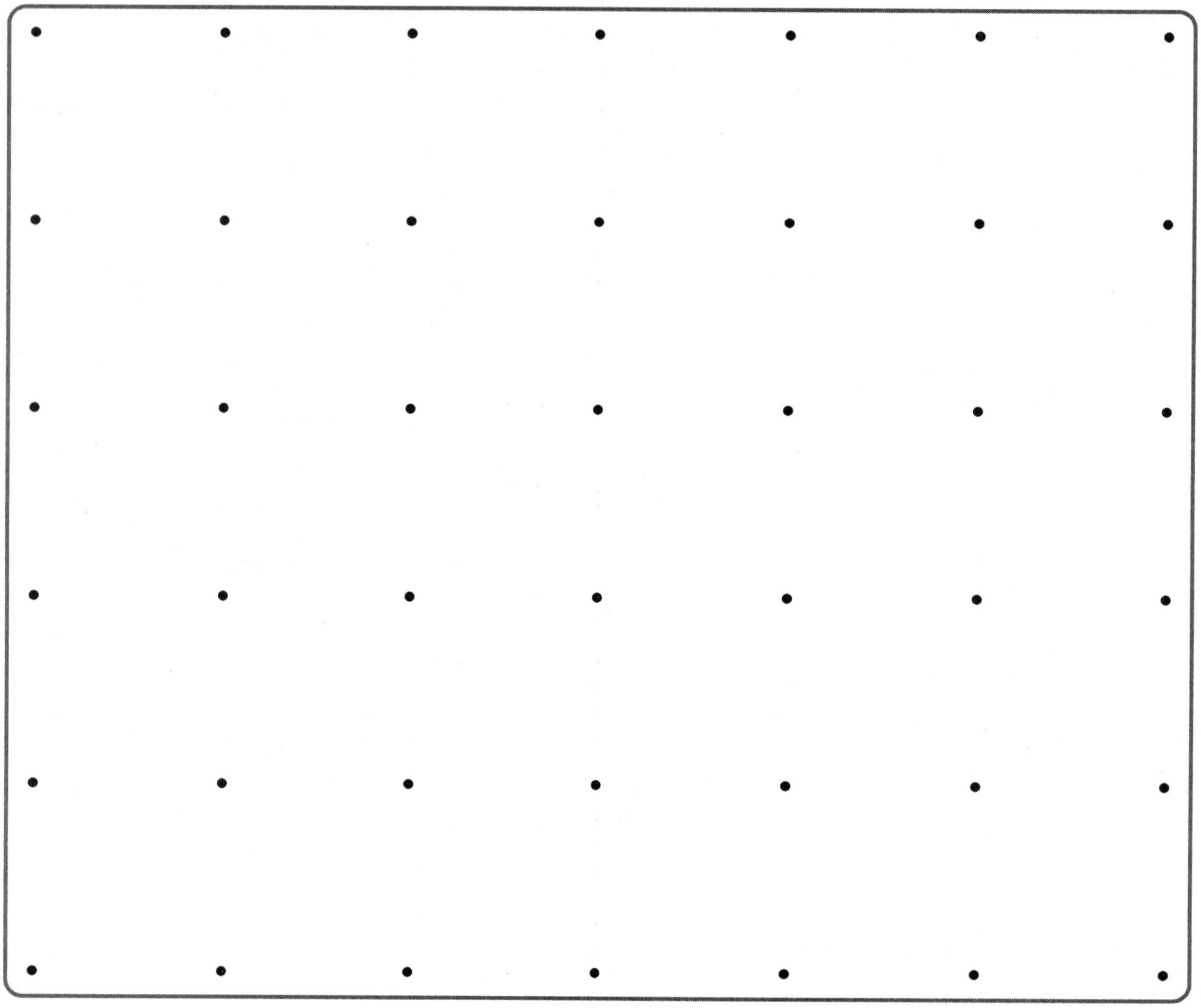

Would you be able to make and combine the same shapes if you were working with geoboards and rubber bands?

____

____

How can you learn more about combining shapes?

____

____

Illegal to Copy

attribute	**corner**	**rhombus**	**triangle**
circle	**hexagon**	**sides**	**two-dimensional shape**
compose	**rectangle**	**square**	**vertex/vertices**

Use the key to color the two-dimensional shapes.

circle	hexagon	rectangle	rhombus	square	trapezoid	triangle
○	⬡	▭	◇	□	⏢	△
red	blue	green	yellow	purple	black	orange

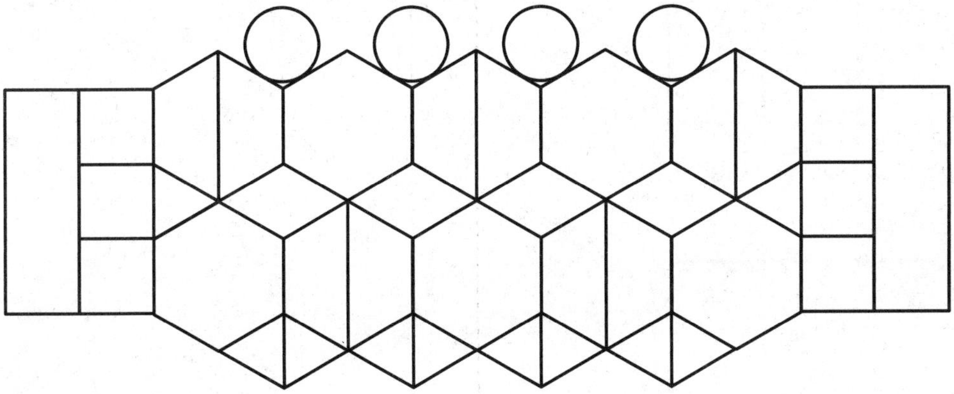

If you used different colors to complete the design, would it change your final product? Why or why not?

____

____

The picture in the activity resembles a tessellation. If you are not familiar with the word, what might you do to find out the meaning?

____

____

Instruction

Name: ____________________

Concept Development

Standard 1.6(F) – **Unit 27**

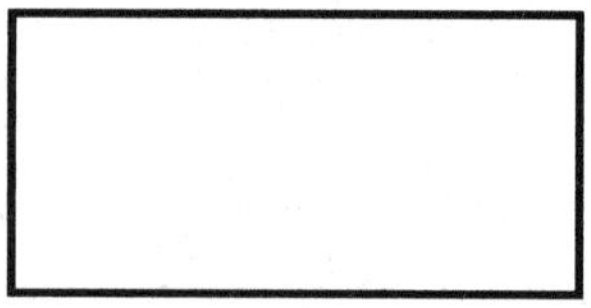

A rectangle can be made from 2 squares or 3 small rectangles.

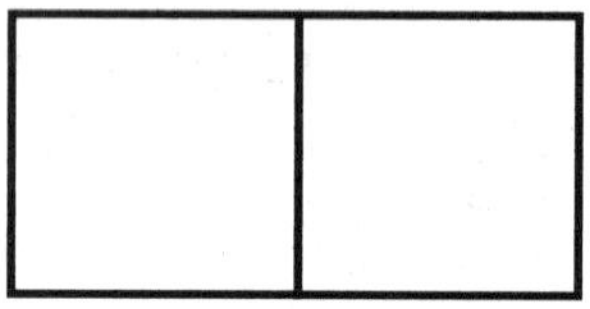

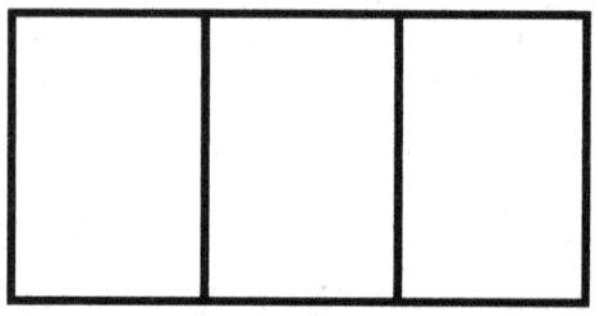

A rectangle can be made from two triangles.

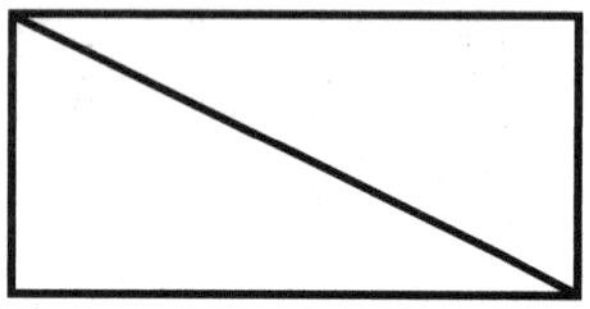

Figures can be made using two or more shapes.

A shape can be composed in many ways. Different shapes can be used.

Try It!

1) This large rectangle is composed of 4 smaller rectangles. Draw lines to show the 4 smaller rectangles.

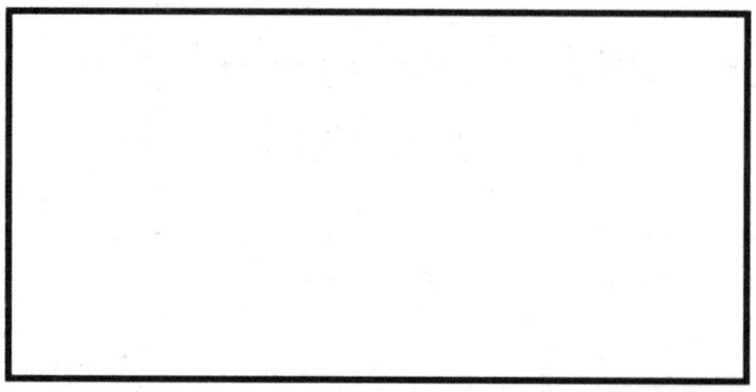

Try It!

2) This square is composed of 2 rectangles. Draw lines to show the rectangles.

Illegal to Copy

Name: ____________________

Unit 27 – Standard 1.6(F)

Instruction

Concept Application

1 Circle the object that can be cut into two triangles.

2 Draw an X on the shape that CANNOT be made by joining squares.

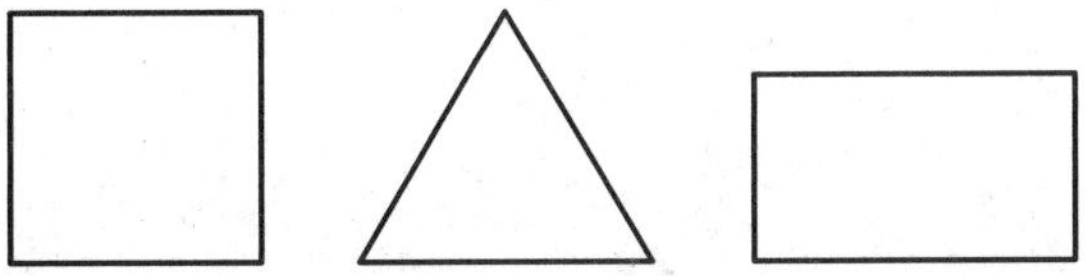

3 Draw one line in the trapezoid to create a triangle and a rhombus.

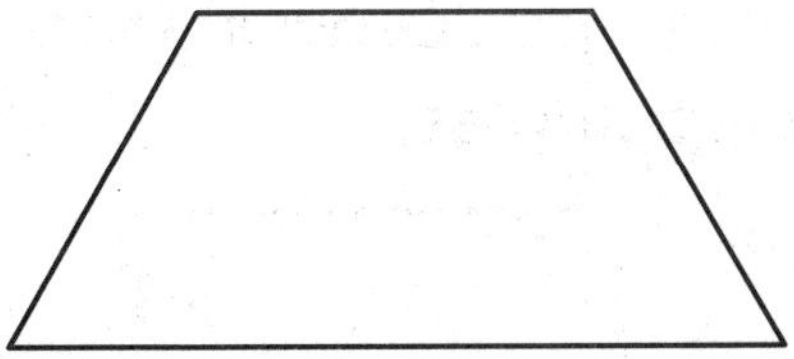

4 Ally uses two shapes to make a hexagon.

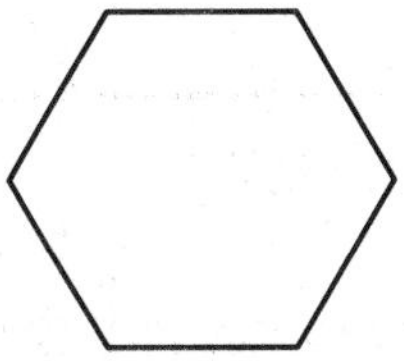

Color the two shapes Ally uses.

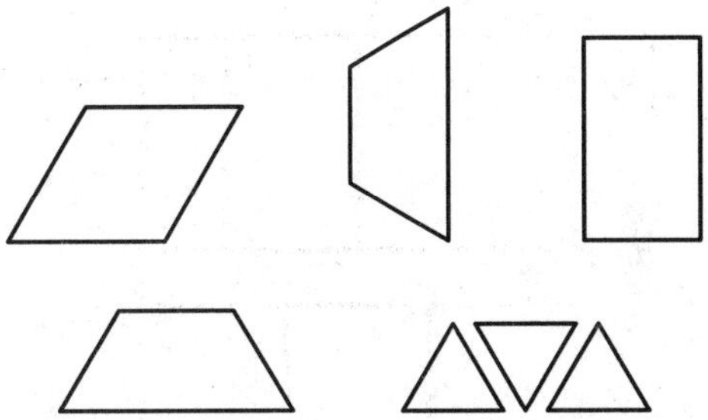

5 Compose a rectangle using two pattern blocks. Draw your rectangle.

6 Draw a square.

Draw a line across the middle of the square. What shapes did you make?

Answer ____________________

Instruction

Name: ______________________________

1 What shapes form this triangle?

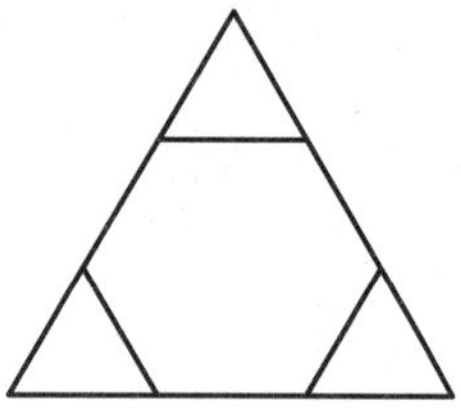

- ⬭ 3 triangles and 1 square
- ⬭ 3 triangles and 1 rectangle
- ⬭ 3 triangles and 1 hexagon

2 Color the 2 shapes Martha can join to make a rhombus.

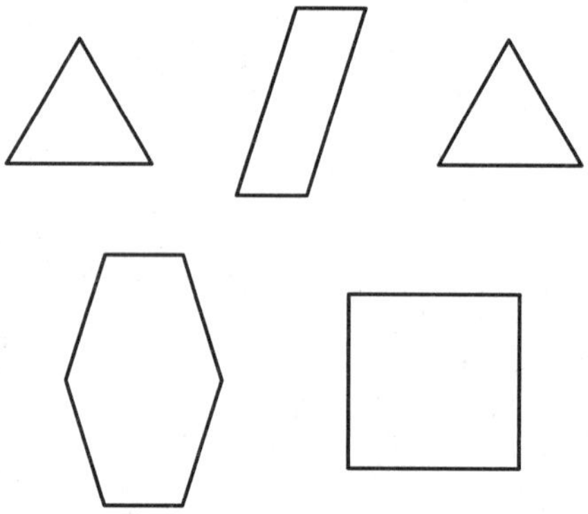

3 What 2 shapes can be joined to make a square?

____

____

4 What is the least number of triangles that can be used to make this rhombus?

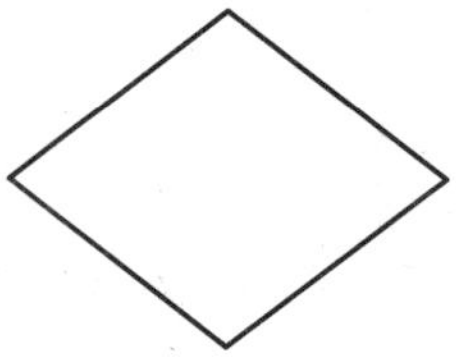

- ⬭ 2
- ⬭ 3
- ⬭ 4

5 Use the dots to help you compose a rectangle using 2 shapes.

Which 2 shapes did you use to compose your rectangle?

____

____

Illegal to Copy

Create a Masterpiece

Use pattern block cutouts to create a picture. Glue the paper pattern blocks on the page. You may draw other details to create your masterpiece.

Extension

Name: ______________________________

Math Challenge

Draw one or more lines inside each rectangle to make different shapes.

What shapes did you make?

____

____

Reflection on My Learning

Why do you think you can create a rectangle from squares, but you cannot create a circle from squares? Explain using pictures and words.

Reflection on Critical Thinking

Circle the traits you used most often in this unit.

I show ____________________ when I ____________________.

Illegal to Copy

Name: ______________________________

Assessment

Unit 27 – Standard 1.6(F)

Concept Check

1 Zack joins these 2 triangles.

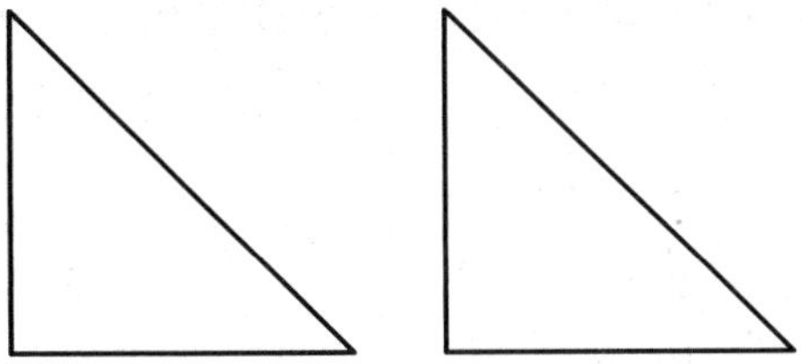

What shape can Zack make?

- ⬭ Circle
- ⬭ Square
- ⬭ Hexagon

2 Lisa has 6 green triangle blocks.

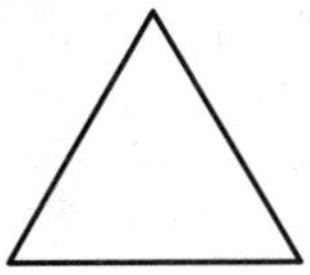

Which of the following shapes can she make using all 6 blocks?

- ⬭ 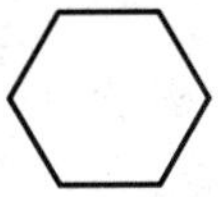
- ⬭ 
- ⬭ 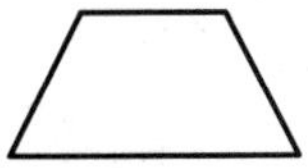

3 Draw 2 lines in the figure to show 1 rectangle and 2 triangles.

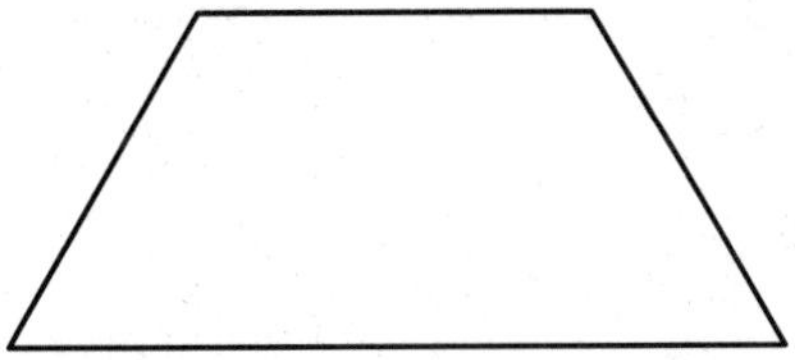

4 Use the dots to compose a rhombus using 2 triangles.

5 Look at the picture.

Write a sentence to describe the shapes that make up the window.

____

____

Assessment

Name: ____________________

Concept Check

Standard 1.6(F) – **Unit 27**

6 Shade the hexagons that can be made with pattern blocks.

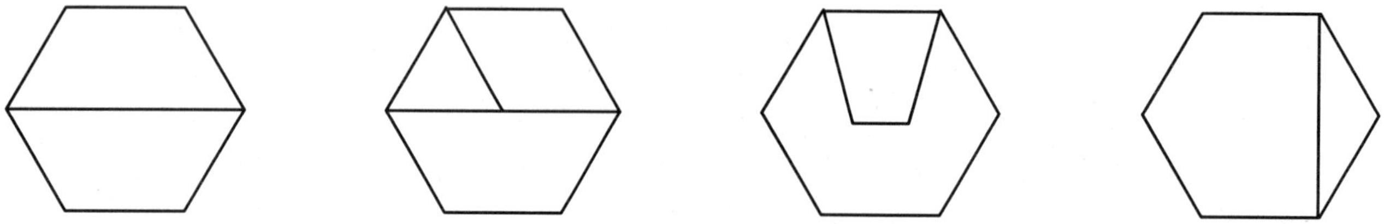

7 Color the shape that can be made by joining three squares.

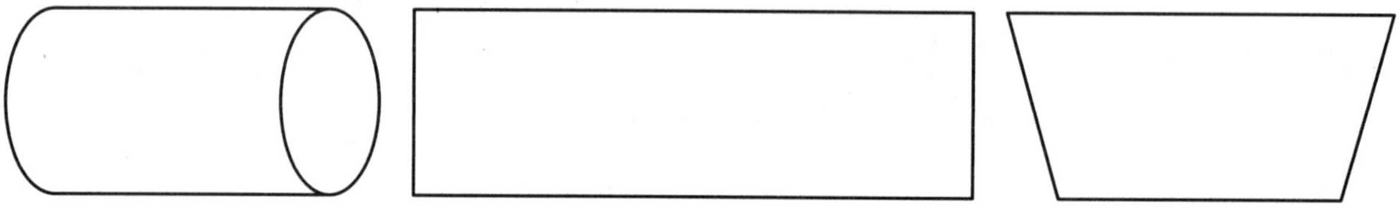

8 Ed uses one blue and six green pattern blocks to make two large triangles.

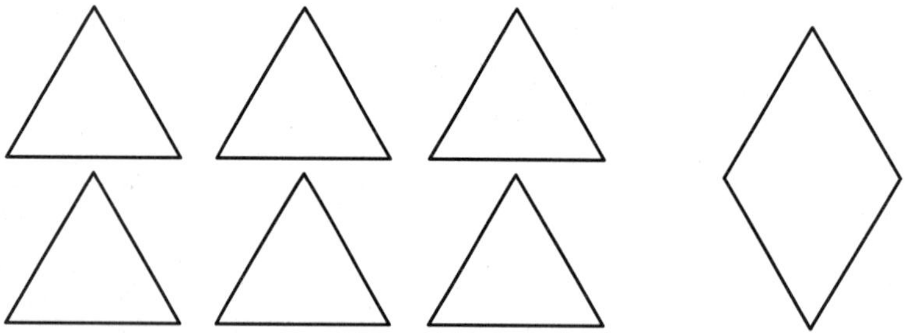

Use pattern blocks to make Ed's triangles.
Draw a picture to show Ed's triangles.

Illegal to Copy

Name: ______________________________

Unit 28 – Standards 1.6(G), 1.6(H)

Getting Started

Unit 28: Identify Halves and Fourths in Two-Dimensional Shapes

TEKS LEARNING TARGETS

- I can partition two-dimensional figures into two and four equal parts.
- I can describe the divided figures using math words.
- I can identify halves and fourths.

Focus for 9 Traits of Critical Thinking™

Collaborate: *I work with others to achieve better outcomes.*

When you are working with others, how important is it to share supplies equally? Why do you believe that way?

____

____

Link: *I apply knowledge to reach new understandings.*

When sharing with a family member or friend, have you ever had a time when another person did not give you your fair share of a treat? How did you feel?

____

____

Illegal to Copy

Name: ______________________________

3 Pizzas

whole	half	fourth

3 Candy Bars

whole	half	fourth

3 Sandwiches

whole	half	fourth

Write a sentence about a time when you had to share your candy, your pizza, or a sandwich with someone. Did each person receive an equal amount?

____

____

Illegal to Copy

Instruction

Vocabulary Mastery

decompose	**fourth**	**part**	**quarter**
equal parts	**half/halves**	**partition**	**whole**

Complete the analogy.

Half is to 2 equal pieces the same way that fourth is to __________ equal pieces.

Use words or pictures to explain the analogy.

In the previous analogy, you compared half to 2 and fourth to 4. Complete the following analogy.

Group work is to talking the same way individual work is to

____.

How did the comparison of a half to 2 help you determine the answer of what fourth is related to?

____

____

Shade one half of the triangle.

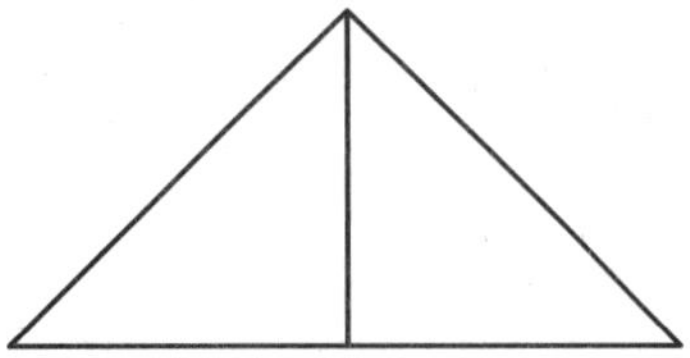

Shade one fourth of the rectangle.

The picture shows 2 pieces, but they are not equal.

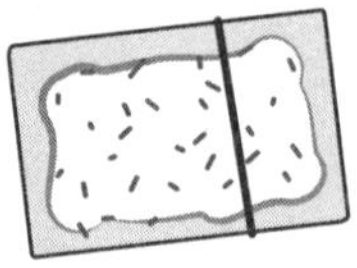

The picture shows 4 pieces, but they are not equal.

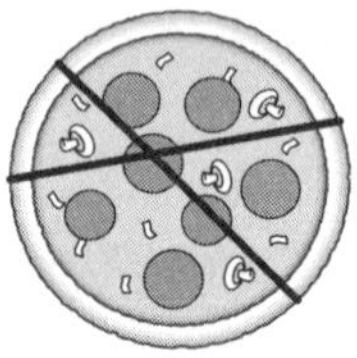

A shape that is divided into two equal shares can be described as *half*, *halves*, or *a half of*.

A shape that is divided into four equal shares can be described as *fourths* or *quarters*.

The term *fair share* means the same as *equal parts*.

A shape that is divided into unequal parts is known as a non-example of halves or fourths.

Try It!

1) Circle the word(s) that describe the picture.

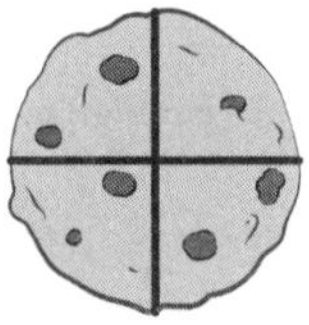

quarters   equal parts   half of

Try It!

2) Put a box around the picture that shows halves. Place an X on the picture that shows fourths. Circle the *non-example* of halves.

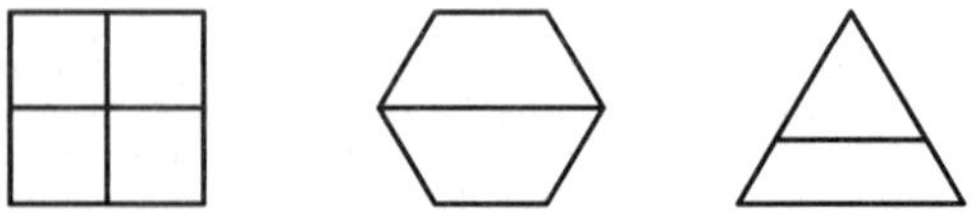

Illegal to Copy

1 Cut the sandwich so you can share it equally with one friend.

Which sentence tells how you share the sandwich?

◯ I give my friend one half of the sandwich.

◯ I give my friend one fourth of the sandwich.

2 Mom, Dad, Rosa, and Ted share a pizza.
Circle the pizza that shows 4 equal parts.

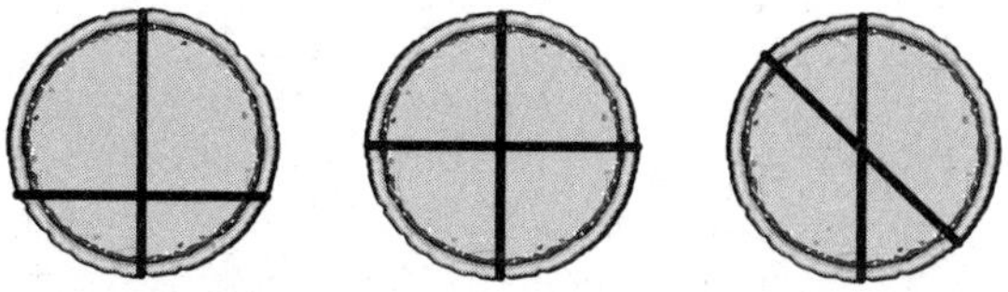

3 Look at this figure.

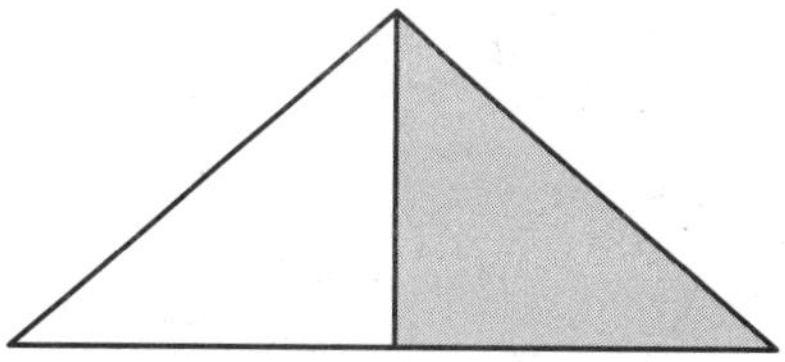

What word names the part of the figure that is shaded? ______________

4 Draw one line in each shape to make two equal parts.

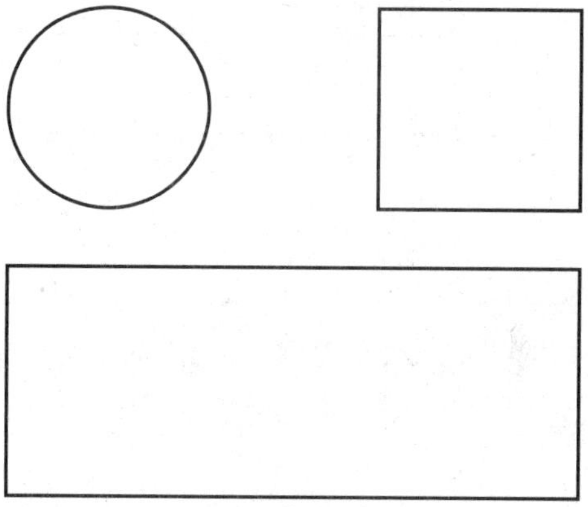

5 Look at the objects.

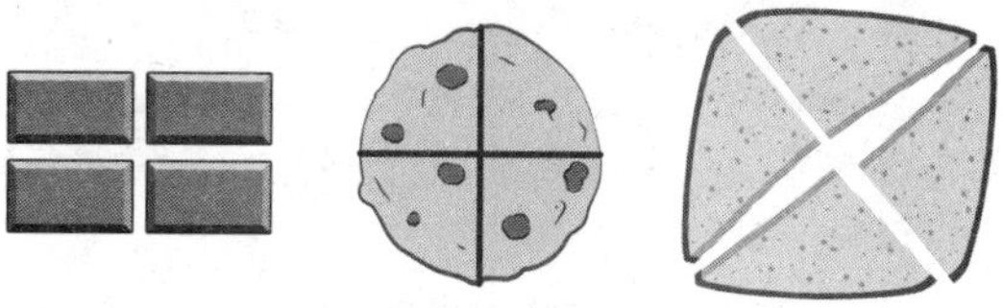

Write a sentence that describes how all of the objects are divided.

____

____

Instruction

Name: ______________________________

Concept Practice

Standards 1.6(G), 1.6(H) – **Unit 28**

1 Which shape is divided into equal shares?

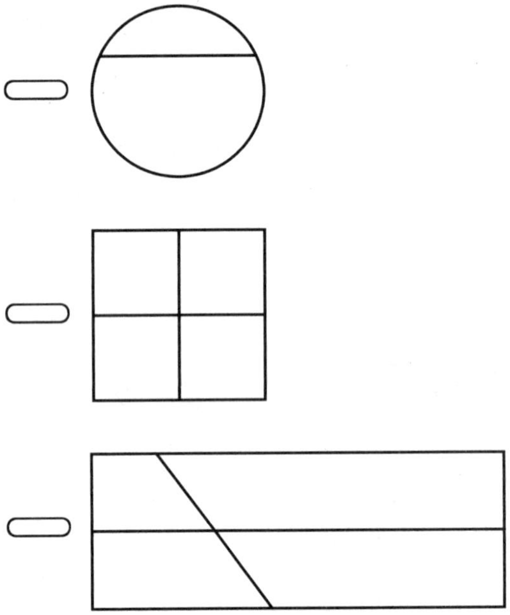

2 Jared cut the cake into halves. Now he needs to cut it into fourths.

Draw one line to show how he should cut it again to make fourths.

3 Look at the pie.

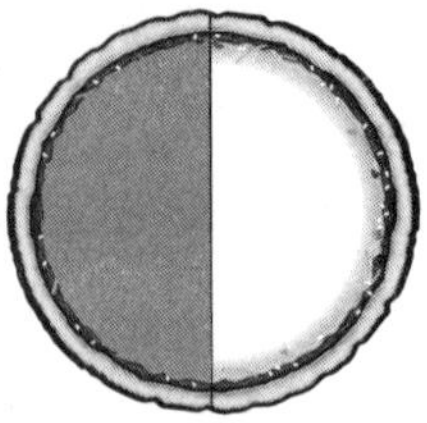

How much of the pie is shaded?

______________ of the pie is shaded.

4 Circle the shapes that show non-examples of equal parts.

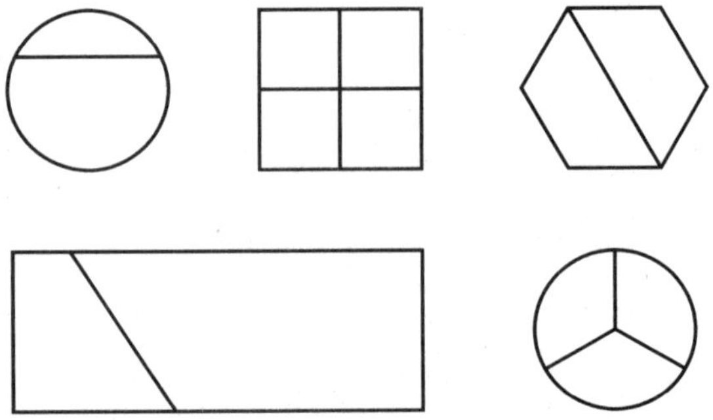

5 Show a way to divide the square into four equal parts.

 Illegal to Copy

Fair Share

Play *Fair Share* with 1 or 2 friends. Each player needs a small game marker. Players share a game board and one die. You and your friends are going to the park. You have snacks to eat along the way. All snacks are divided into 2 or 4 parts. Are the parts equal? Everyone should get a fair share. Take turns rolling the die and moving forward that many spaces. If a player lands on a Fair Share rule, the player reads the rule aloud and stays on the square. If the player lands on a snack that is shared equally, the player stays on the square. If the player lands on a snack that is not shared equally, the player moves backward to the closest Fair Share rule and reads it aloud. The winner is the first person to arrive at the park.

Extension

Name: ____________________

Standards 1.6(G), 1.6(H) – **Unit 28**

Math Challenge

Would you rather have one half of this pie or one fourth of this pie?

Circle your answer.

one half   one fourth

Explain. ____________________

____

Reflection on My Learning

Marla ate half of this candy bar.

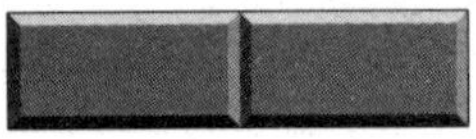

Carla ate half of this candy bar.

Did they each eat the same amount of candy? Explain your thinking.

____

____

Reflection on Critical Thinking

Circle the traits you used most often in this unit.

I show ____________________ when I ____________________ .

Illegal to Copy

1 Liz cuts a pie into fourths.
What words describe one part?

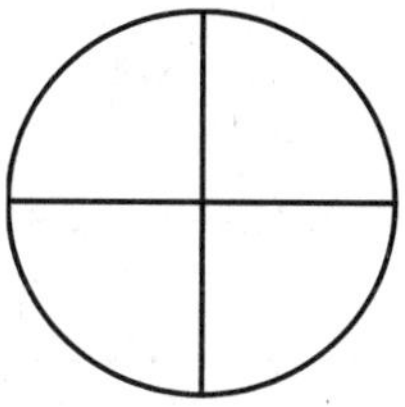

- ⬭ One fourth
- ⬭ One half
- ⬭ One whole

2 Len and his father want to share a pizza equally.
Draw a line to cut the pizza into two fair shares.

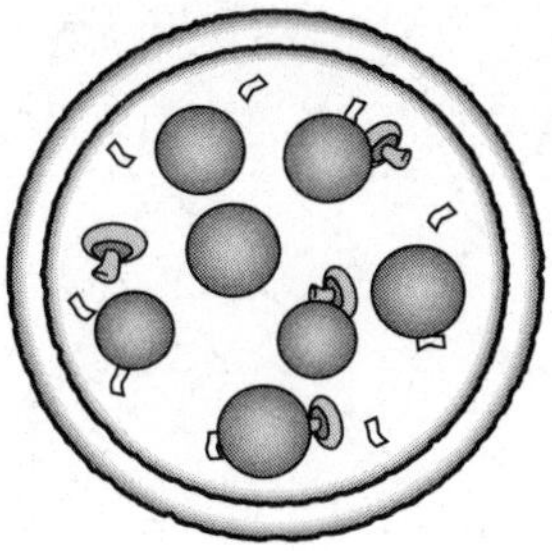

3 Draw lines to divide each shape into 4 equal parts.

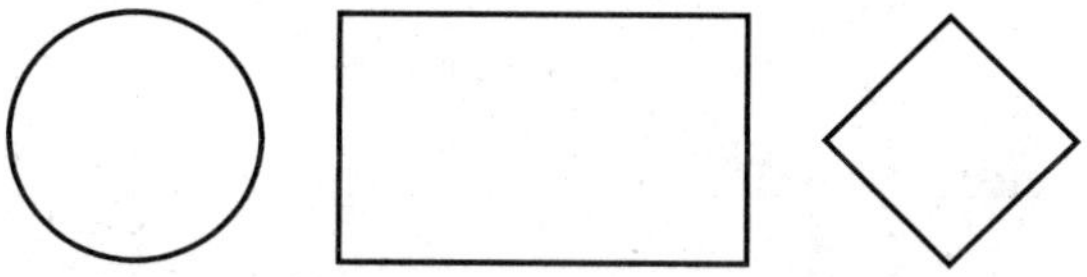

4 Keisha buys a new rug. The rug is half black and half white. Which shows Keisha's new rug? Circle the answer.

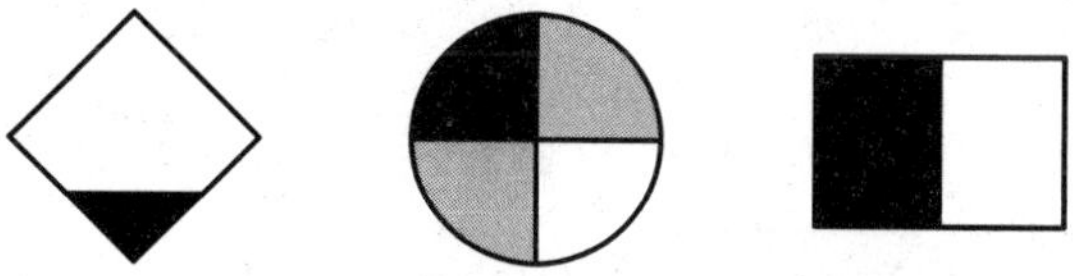

5 The teacher cuts two cookies into equal parts. Match the cookies to their descriptions.

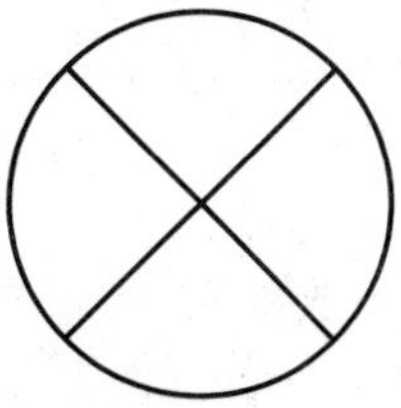

cut in halves

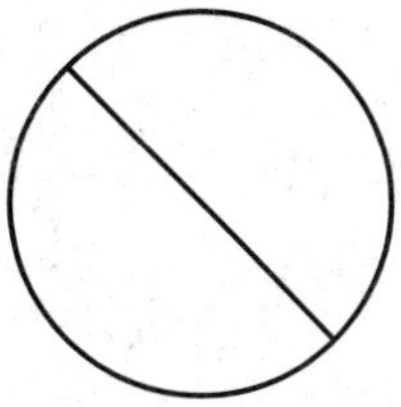

cut in fourths

Circle the word that belongs on the line.

Halves are ______________ than fourths.

larger   smaller

6 Make an X on the shapes that do NOT show equal shares.

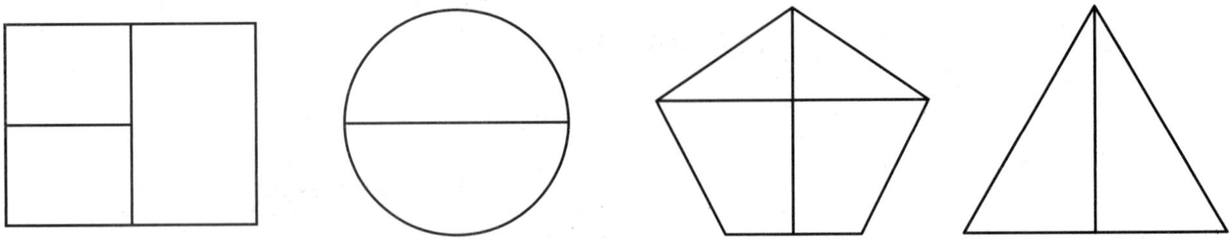

Circle the word(s) that describes the shapes you placed an X on.

examples | non-examples | fair share

---

7 Diego cut his sandwich into halves. Draw a picture to show how Diego cut his sandwich.

---

8 Four friends share a candy bar equally.

Which candy bar is divided correctly?

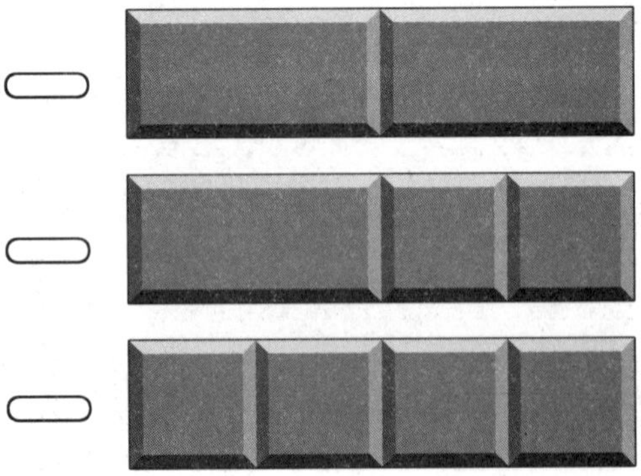

How much of the whole candy bar will each person eat?

Answer ______________________

Illegal to Copy

Name: ______________________________

Getting Started

Unit 29 – Standards 1.7(A), 1.7(B)

Unit 29: Use Tools to Measure and Explain Length

TEKS LEARNING TARGETS

- I can use tools to measure the length of objects.
- I can show that linear measurement is continuous along a line or curve.
- I can show the length of an object using same-size objects.
- I can use same-size objects laid end-to-end without gaps or overlaps to measure the lengths of objects.

Focus for 9 Traits of Critical Thinking™

Examine: *I use a variety of methods to explore and to analyze.*

Have you ever had to measure the length of something? What tool(s) did you use to determine the length?

____

____

Strive: *I use effort and determination to focus on challenging tasks.*

Do you find measuring objects challenging? If so, how do you overcome your challenges? If not, how do you stretch your understanding of measurement?

____

____

Instruction

Name: ____________________

Concept Exploration

Standards 1.7(A), 1.7(B) – **Unit 29**

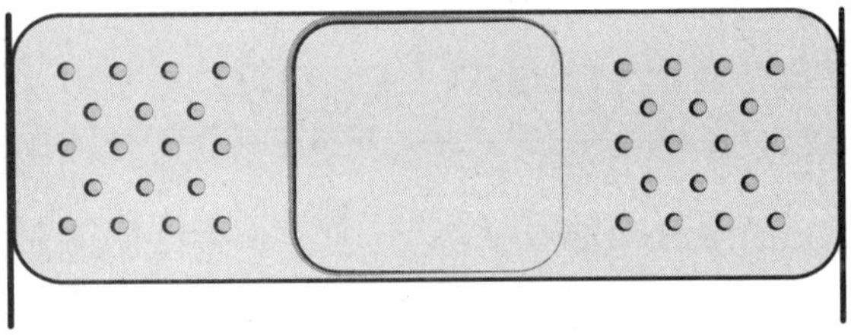

_______ cubes

_______ paper clips

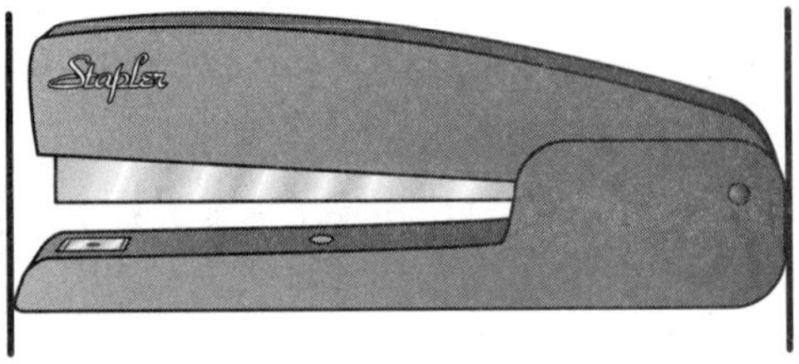

_______ cubes

_______ paper clips

_______ cubes

_______ paper clips

_______ cubes

_______ paper clips

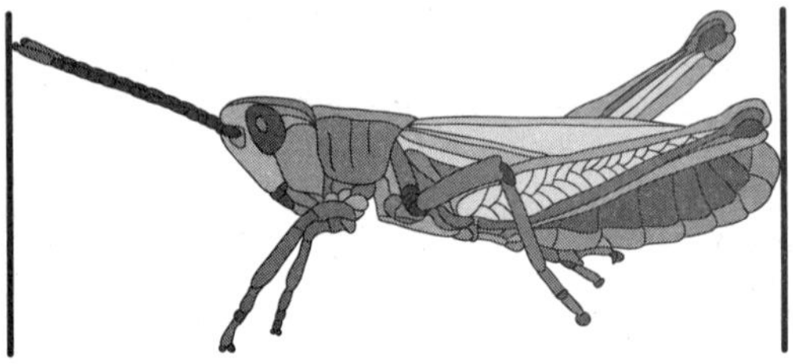

_______ cubes

_______ paper clips

What will happen if you do not place your objects end-to-end when measuring?

____

____

How does using both cubes and paper clips to measure the lengths of objects demonstrate there is more than one way to solve a problem?

____

____

Illegal to Copy

estimate	**longer**	**shorter**
length	**measure**	

Draw three same-size shapes in a row. Make them overlap.

Draw three same-size shapes. Leave gaps between the shapes.

Draw three same-size shapes in a row, end-to-end.

If you don't understand a word that someone is using, what question can you ask to help you fill in the gaps or gain a better understanding?

____

____

If you are unsure of a word, what step can you take before continuing? Do you find this helps you be more successful with an activity?

____

____

Circle the word that makes the sentence true.

Brush A

Brush B

Brush A is __________ than Brush B.

longer shorter

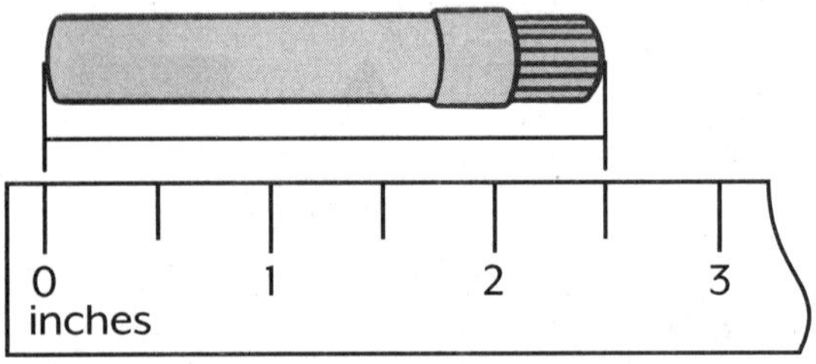

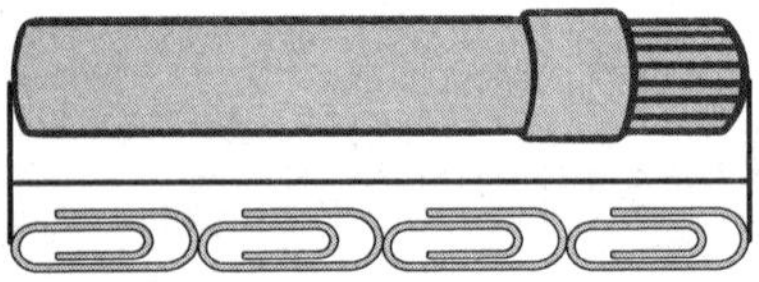

Circle the feather that is being measured correctly.

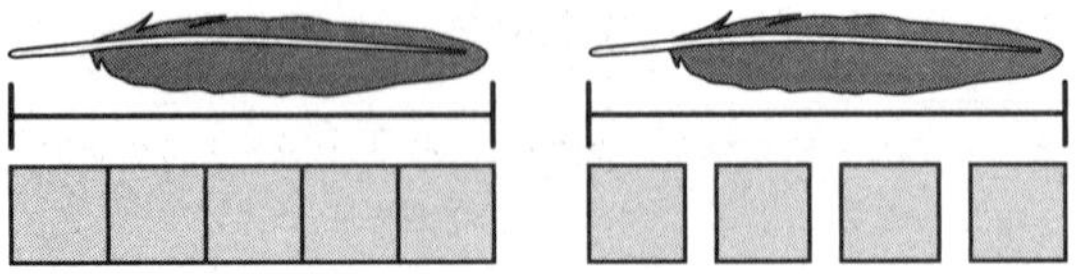

You can compare two objects to determine length.

You can use standard tools or other objects to measure length.

When measuring with objects be sure to line them end-to-end to get an accurate measurement.

Try It!

1) How many squares long is the key?

Answer ____________________

1 What is the length of the pencil?

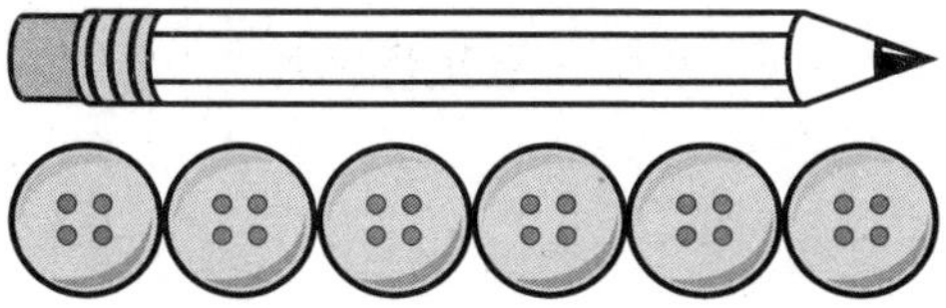

The pencil is ______ buttons long.

2 Kelly measures the toy fish using erasers.

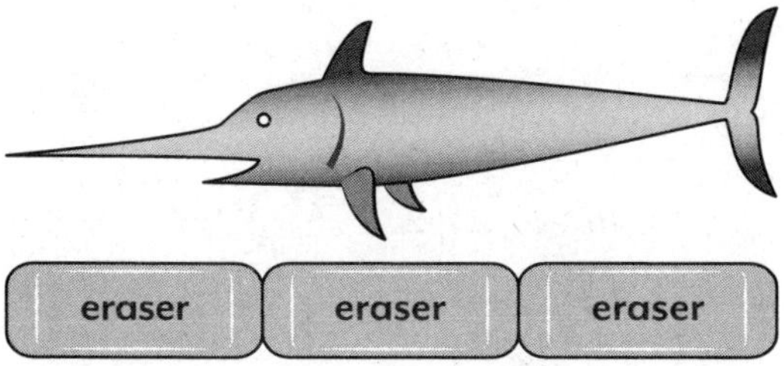

How many erasers long is the toy fish?

Answer ______________________

3 Doug uses keys to measure a picture frame.

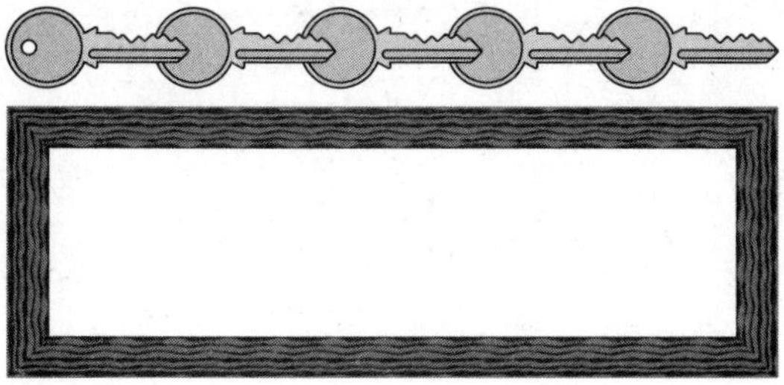

Explain Doug's mistake.

____

____

4 Measure the length of the pen.

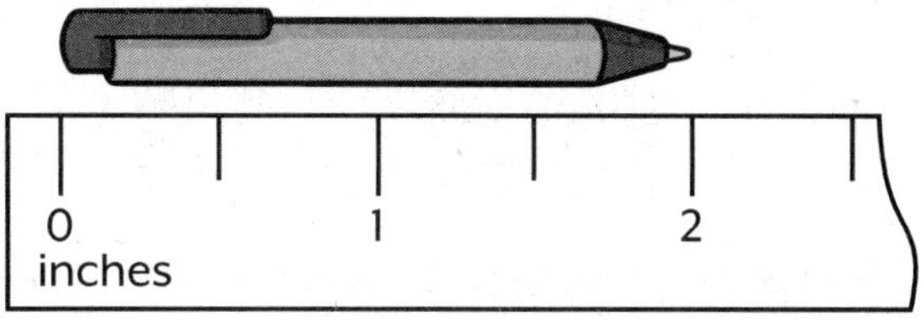

The pen is about __________ inches long.

5 How many paper clips long is the ribbon?

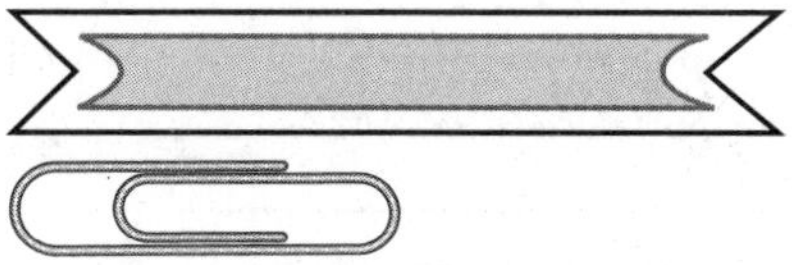

- three paper clips
- two paper clips
- one paper clip

6 Look at the picture.

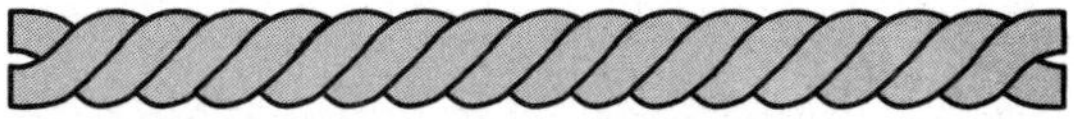

Explain how to use paper clips to measure the length of the rope.

____

____

1 Leah measures her brush with tiles.

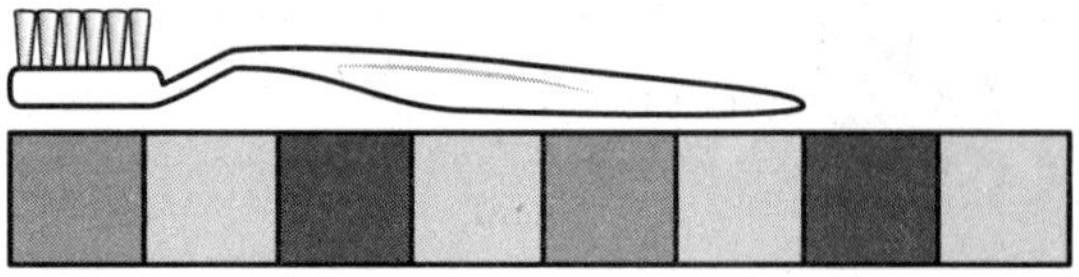

How many tiles long is the brush?

__________________ tiles

2 Mila measures crayons with cubes. Which is longer than 6 cubes?

○ 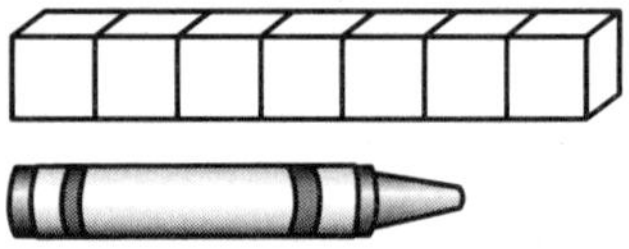

○ 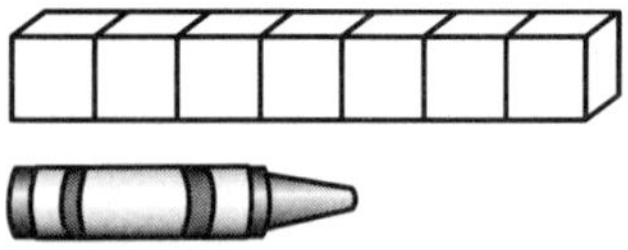

○ 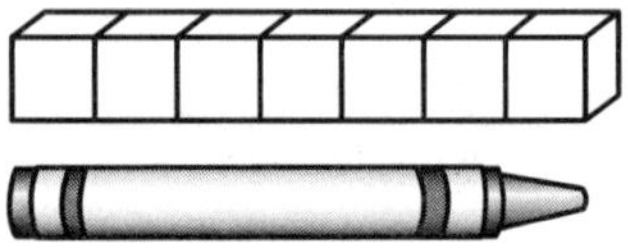

3 Circle the correct way to measure a worm with paper clips.

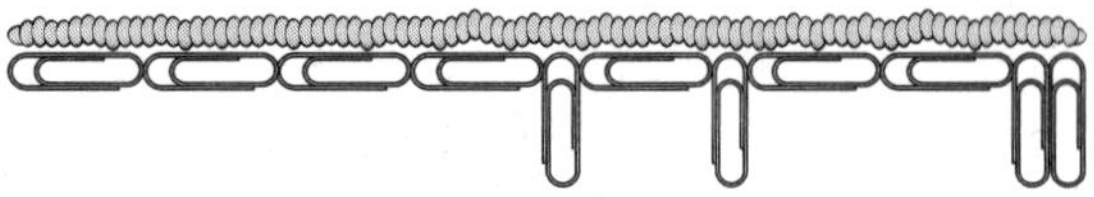

4 Which object is about 4 squares long?

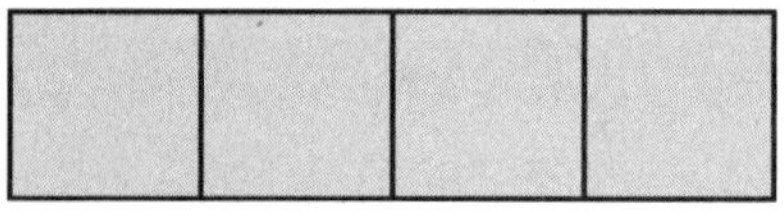

○ 

○ 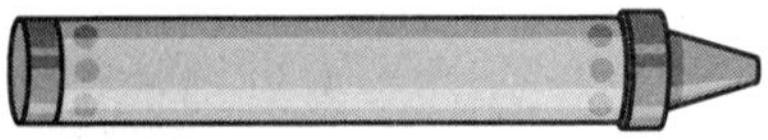

○ 

5 Draw an X on the set of items that is BEST for measuring length.

Explain why.

____

____

Illegal to Copy

Itsy-Bitsy Spider

Play *Itsy-Bitsy Spider* with a partner. Partners need measuring units and one die. Each player needs a game board and a crayon. In turn, each partner rolls the die and places that number of units on the spout on his or her game board. The first player to measure the spout and say how tall it is colors one spider on the game board. Repeat the game using a different measuring unit. Play continues until one player has colored all the spiders on his or her game board.

________ unit cubes

________ Unifix® cubes

________ color tiles

________ small paper clips

________ large paper clips

________ pennies

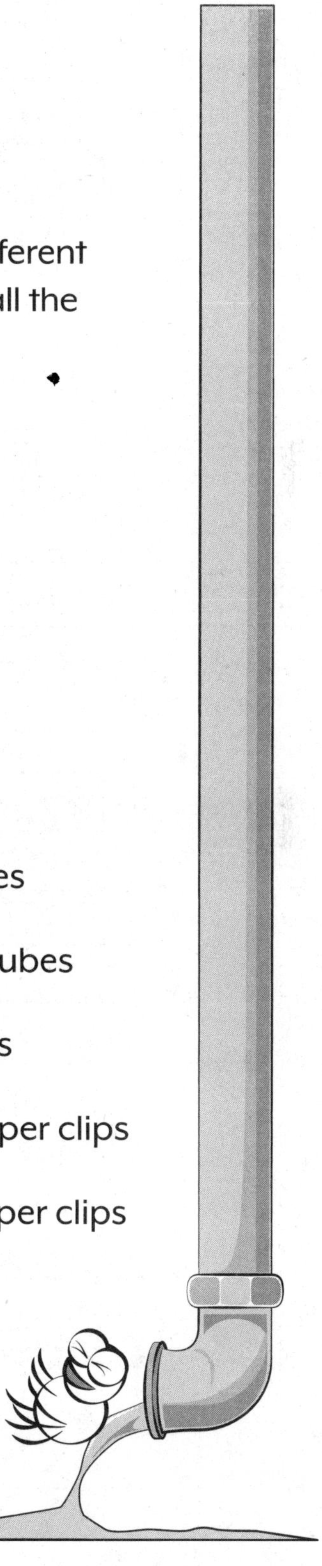

Extension

Name: ______________________

Standards 1.7(A), 1.7(B) – **Unit 29**

Math Challenge

This row of beetles measures 4 cubes long.

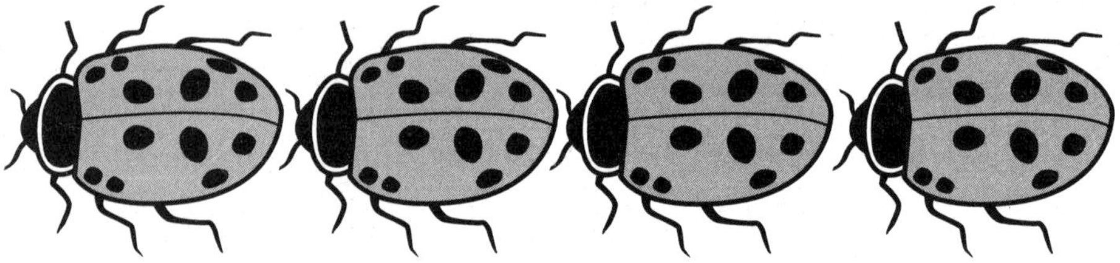

What is the measure of a row of 5 beetles? __________ cubes

How do you know?

____

____

Reflection on My Learning

Why do you think it is important to lay objects end-to-end with no gaps or overlaps when measuring length?

____

____

Reflection on Critical Thinking

Circle the traits you used most often in this unit.

I show ______________ when I ______________ .

Illegal to Copy

Name: ______________________________

Assessment

Unit 29 – Standards 1.7(A), 1.7(B)

Concept Check

1 Measure the length of the stick of gum in inches.

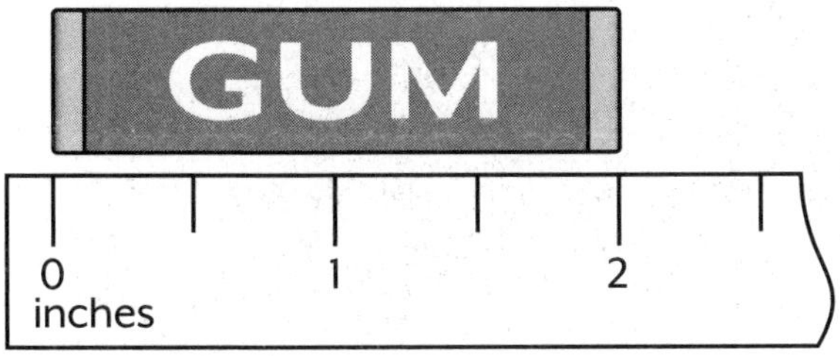

__________ inches

2 What is the length of the key?

- 4 pencil erasers
- 3 pencil erasers
- 2 pencil erasers

3 Tio measures his toy train with cubes. How many cubes long is Tio's train?

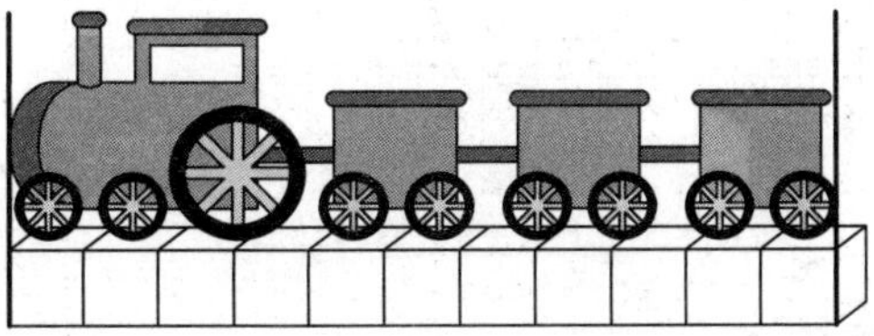

__________ cubes

4 Which shows the BEST way to measure the pen? Circle your answer.

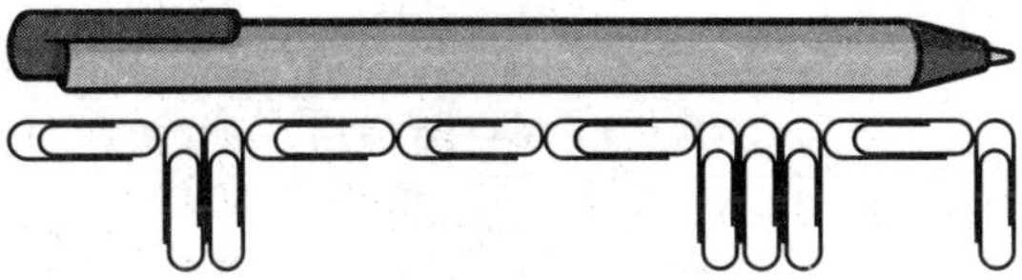

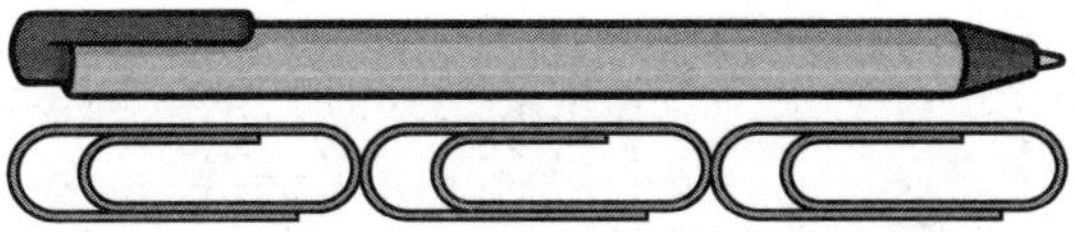

5 Kristen said her straw is 4 shells long.

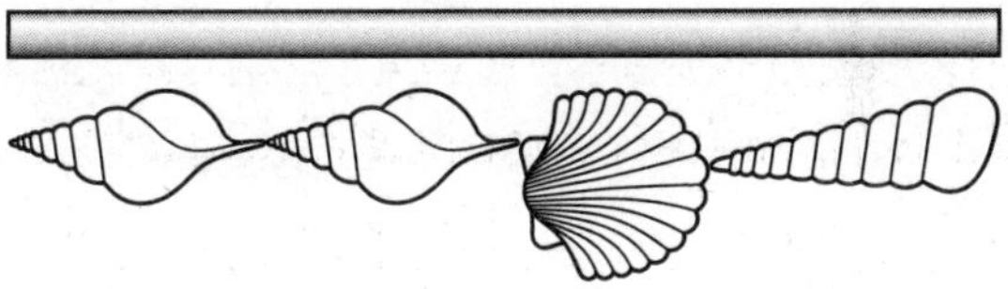

Is she right? __________

Explain your answer.

____

____

Illegal to Copy

Name: ____________________

Concept Check

6 Mike and Ann each measure a book.

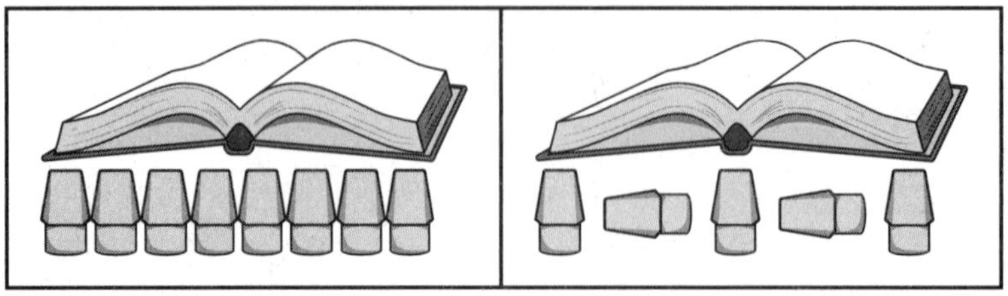

Mike Ann

Who measures the book correctly? ____________________

Why? ____________________

____

7 Dan and Drew both measured a pencil using paper clips.
Who measured correctly?

○ Dan

○ Drew

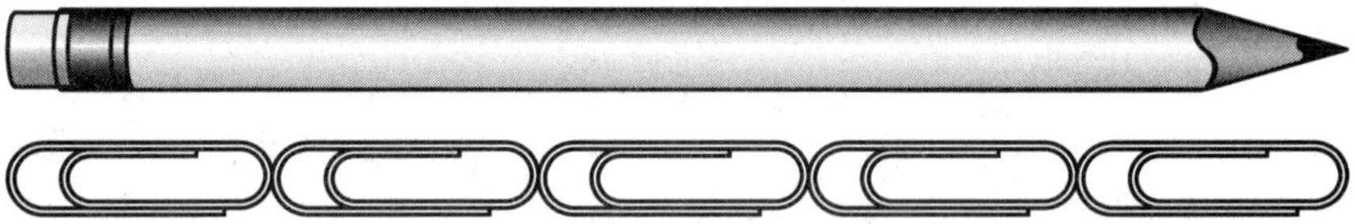

8 How many tiles long is the bookmark? __________ tiles

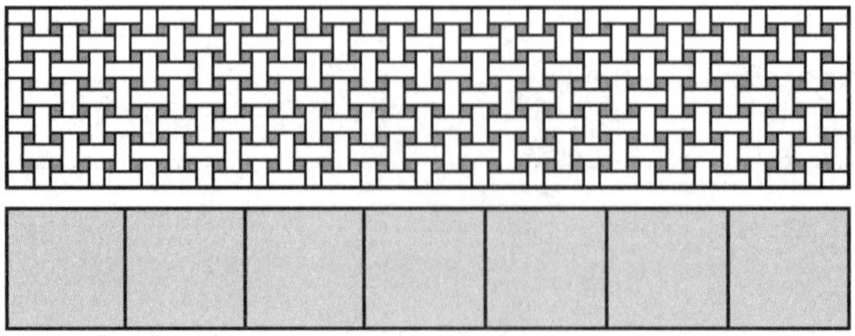

Illegal to Copy

Name: ______________________

Getting Started

Unit 30 – Standards 1.7(C), 1.7(D)

Unit 30: Measure and Report Length with Appropriate Units

TEKS LEARNING TARGETS

- I can measure the same object or distance with units of two different lengths.
- I can describe how and why the length measures of an object will differ when measured with units of two different lengths.
- I can discuss how the size of the measurement unit affects the number of units needed to measure an object.
- I can describe a length using a number and a unit.
- I can measure a length to the nearest whole unit.

Focus for 9 Traits of Critical Thinking™

Adapt: *I adjust my actions and strategies to accomplish tasks.*

Have you ever solved a problem and then had someone work the same problem and get a different answer? Does that always mean one person is wrong? Why or why not?

____

____

Communicate: *I use clear language to express my ideas and to share information.*

When you are sharing information with others, why is it important to have the same understanding of vocabulary?

____

____

Name: ____________________

Concept Exploration

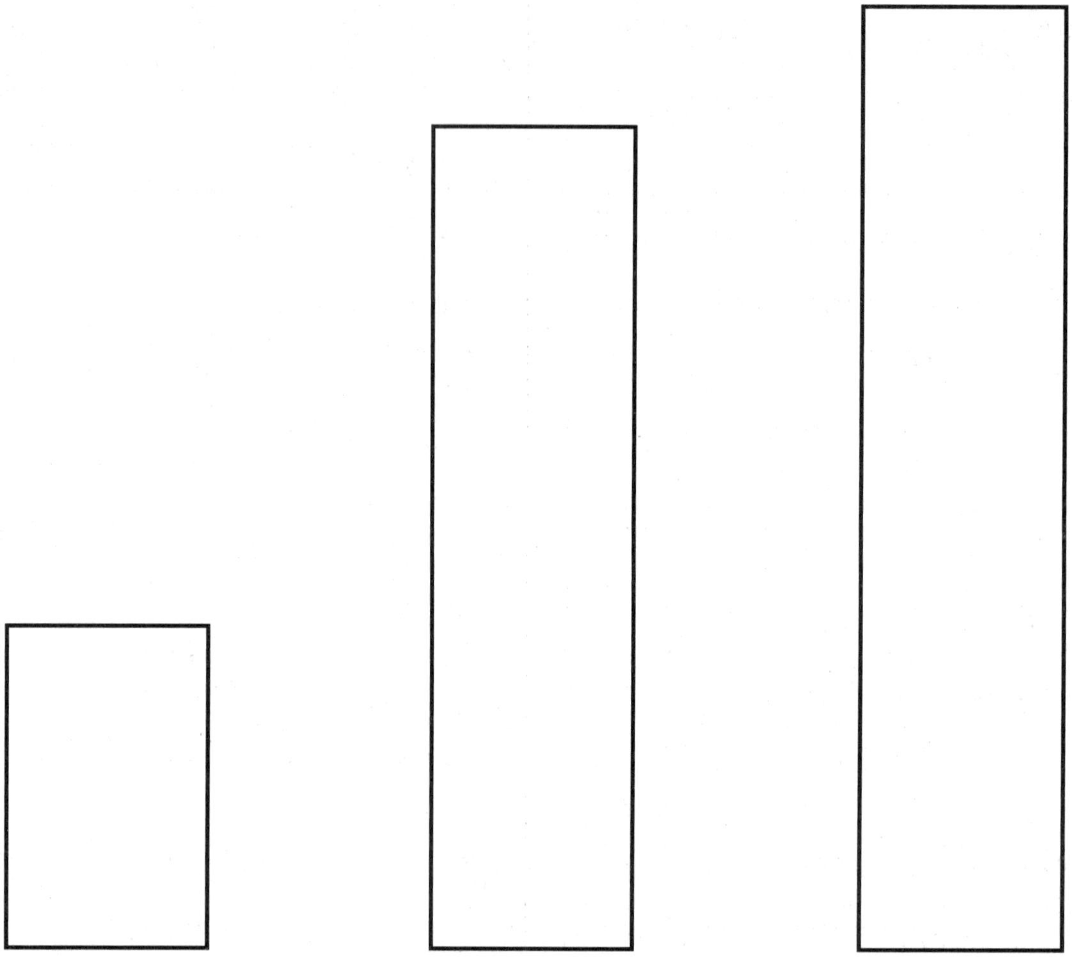

How did the use of different measurement units affect the measure of the object? Did the length really change or just the measurement?

____

____

How might you explain what you noticed about the differences in your measures when you used the different objects to measure length?

____

____

Illegal to Copy

compare	**estimate**	**longer**	**shorter**
equal	**length**	**measure**	

Use blue lines to connect words with the same meanings.

Use red lines to connect words with opposite meanings.

equal	**longer**
more	**less**
distance	**length**
shorter	**same**

What other words could you use that mean the same as *estimate*? Are there words that mean the opposite of *estimate*?

____

____

Is the difference between *longer* and *shorter* more important when you are dealing with measurement? Explain your response.

____

____

Instruction

Name: ____________________

Concept Development

How many paper clips long is the pencil?

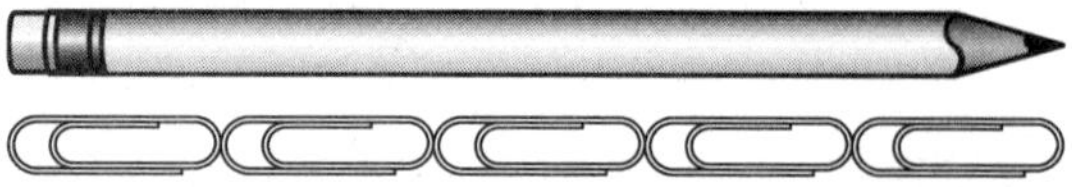

__________ paper clips

How many erasers long is the pencil?

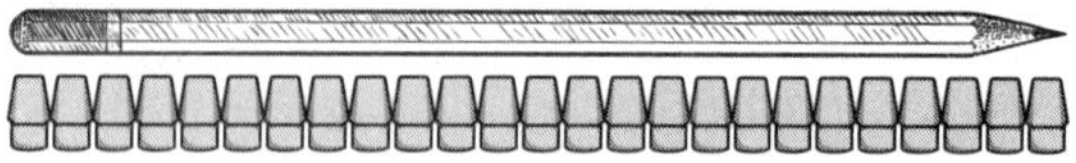

__________ erasers

Circle the picture that shows the correct way to measure with the same-size objects.

How many cans long is the sleeping bag?

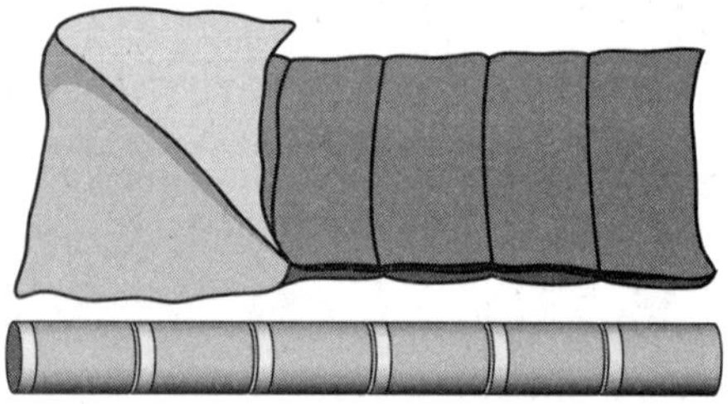

__________ cans

The size of the unit of measure will decide the number of units needed to measure the object.

When you use objects of the same size as a unit of measure, you must place them end-to-end with no gaps or overlaps.

You should always describe a measured length using a number and a unit.

Try It!

1) Fill in the name of the unit.

5 __________

Illegal to Copy

1 About how many cubes long is the Band-Aid®?

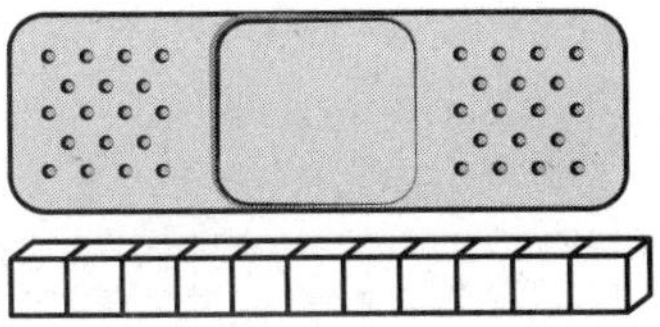

- 20 cubes
- 11 cubes
- 8 cubes

2 A paintbrush measures about 2 crayons long.

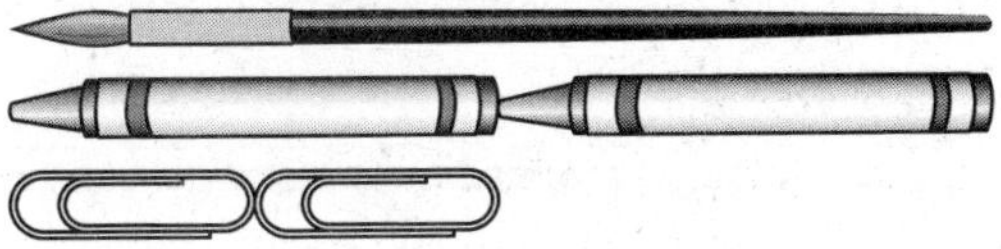

About how many paper clips long is the paintbrush?

- 2 paper clips
- 3 paper clips
- 4 paper clips

3 Amelia and Charlie measure the same flashlight.

Name	Measure of Flashlight
Amelia	4 crayons
Charlie	7 toothpicks

Use the chart to complete the sentence.

The ______________ are longer than the ______________.

4 Sara uses craft sticks to measure the length of her shoe. She measures the shoe again with erasers.

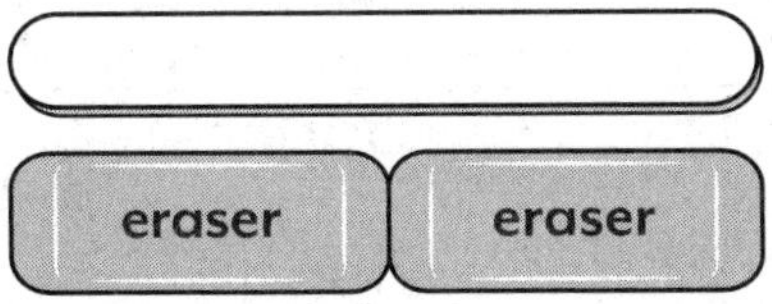

Which statement is true about the measure of Sara's shoe?

- It takes more craft sticks than erasers to measure the shoe.
- It takes more erasers than craft sticks to measure the shoe.
- It takes the same number of craft sticks and erasers to measure the shoe.

5 Su and Mick measure an envelope.

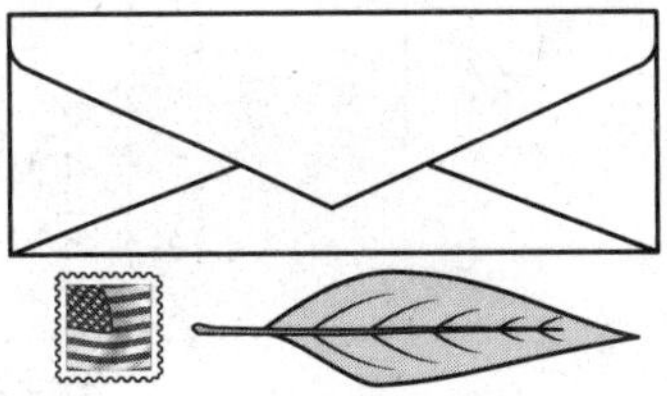

Su measures with stamps.
Mick measures with leaves.
Will Su and Mick get the same measurement? Explain your answer.

____

____

Name: ____________________

1 About how many unit cubes long is the crayon?

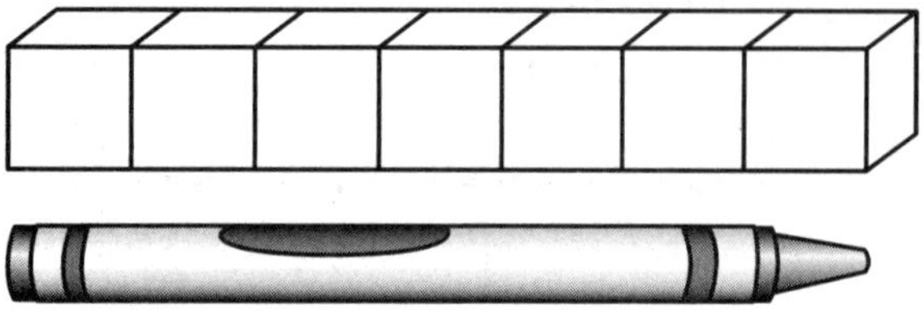

- ⬭ 7 cubes
- ⬭ 9 cubes
- ⬭ 15 cubes

2 Annie and Sid use coins to measure the hamster cage.

Annie says the cage is 34 coins long. Sid says the cage is 15 coins long.

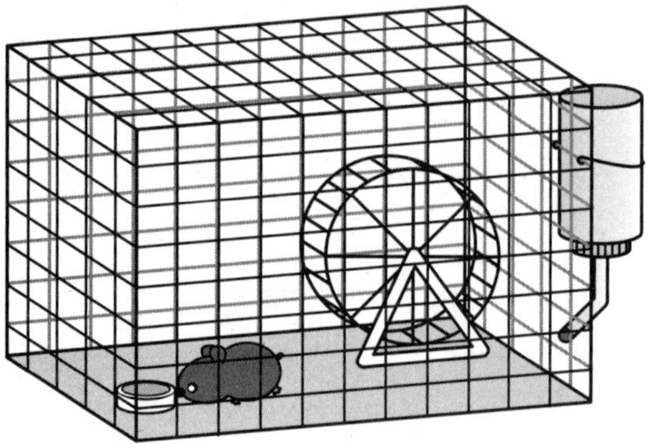

Explain how Annie and Sid can have different answers.

____

____

3 Which object would be best to measure the length of the feather?

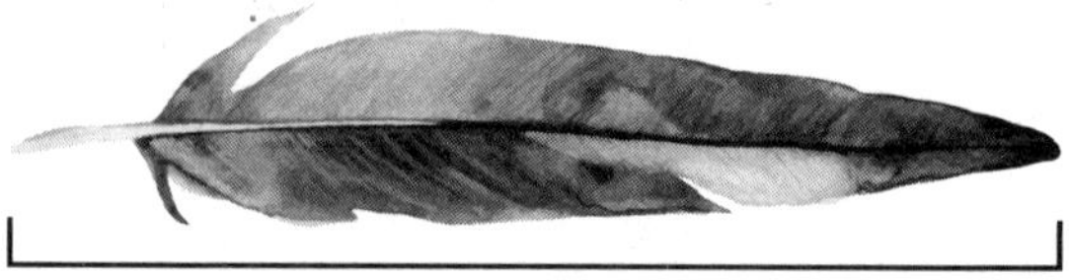

- ⬭ paper clips
- ⬭ pencils

4 Caleb measures the puzzle with paintbrushes and paper clips.

Complete each sentence.
The length of the puzzle is

____________ paper clips.

The length of the puzzle is

____________ paintbrushes.

Why are the measures different?

____

____

Illegal to Copy

Measurement Mania

Choose 10 different objects in your classroom. Measure each object using two different units provided by your teacher. Record each measurement using a number and the name of the unit.

Object to Measure	Measurement with Unit 1	Measurement with Unit 2

Explain why the measurements are different for each object.

____

____

Extension

Name: ______________________________

Standards 1.7(C), 1.7(D) – **Unit 30**

Math Challenge

Would it take more paper clips or more forks to measure the length of a bed?

Circle the answer.

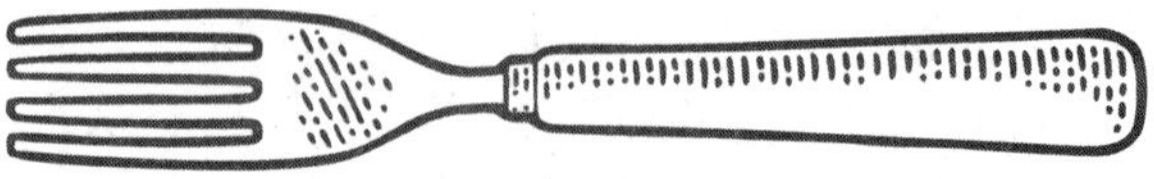

Tell how you know.

____

Reflection on My Learning

Which would be better to use to measure the length of your desk? Circle your choice.

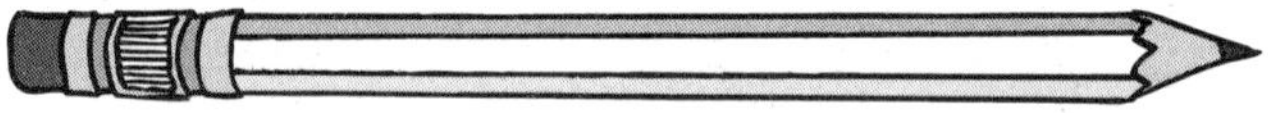

Explain your answer.

____

____

Reflection on Critical Thinking

Circle the traits you used most often in this unit.

I show ____________________ when I ____________________.

Illegal to Copy

Name: ______________________________

Unit 30 – Standards 1.7(C), 1.7(D)

Assessment

Concept Check

1 Brandt measured a dollar bill with cubes and color tiles.

Dollar bill – ______ cubes

Dollar bill – ______ color tiles

Why are the measures different?

____

____

2 Lissa needs to measure the length of the stapler twice. She used paper clips for the first measure and craft sticks for the second measure.

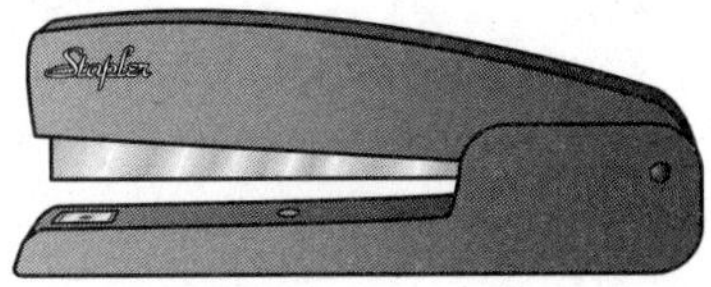

Which measure results in the smallest measure?

- ⬭ paper clips
- ⬭ craft sticks

3 Deonte was measuring objects in the classroom. He measured a book with Unifix® cubes.

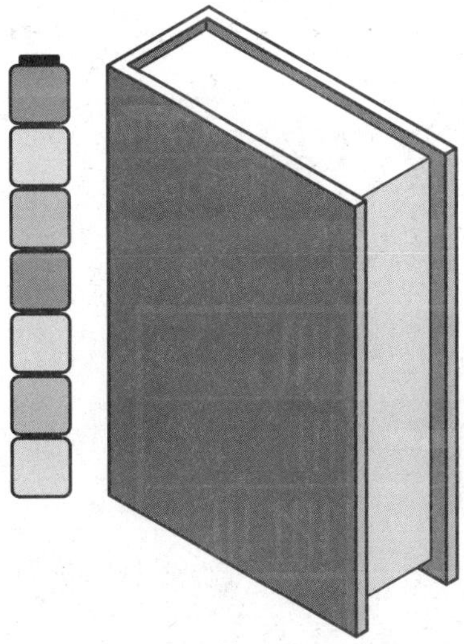

How many cubes long is Deonte's book?

- ⬭ 8 cubes long
- ⬭ 7 cubes long
- ⬭ 9 cubes long

4 Circle the object that would be best to measure the length of the classroom.

toothpicks　　　　straws

Explain why.

____

____

Name: ____________________

5 Mark and Jana are measuring this rope. Mark uses toy cars to measure the rope. Jana uses butterfly stickers to measure the rope.

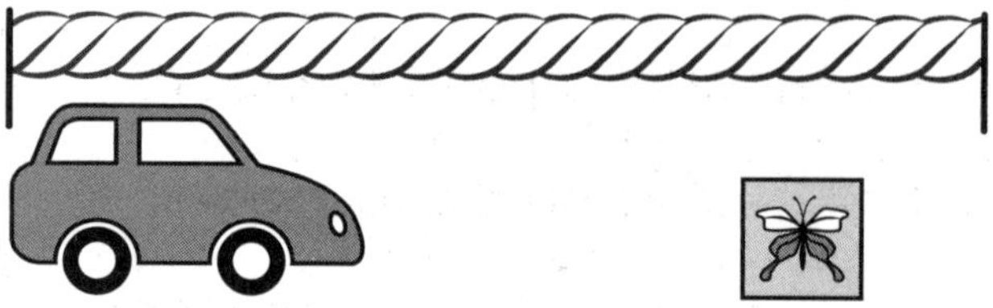

Mark

Jana

Who will use more units to measure the rope?

Mark Jana

____

Why?____________________

____

6 Mya measures a marker using safety pins and paper clips.

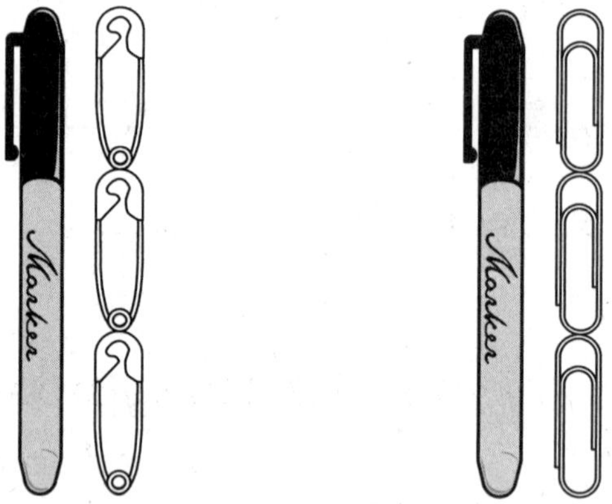

____ pins ____ paper clips

Are the measurements equal? ____________

Why?____________________

____

Illegal to Copy

Name: ______________________________

Unit 31 – Standard 1.7(E)

Getting Started

Unit 31: Tell Time to the Hour and the Half Hour

TEKS LEARNING TARGETS

- I can tell time to the hour and half hour using analog clocks.
- I can tell time to the hour and half hour using digital clocks.
- I can recognize when digital and analog clocks represent the same time.

Focus for 9 Traits of Critical Thinking™

Reflect: *I review my thoughts and experiences to guide my actions.*

Why is it important to be able to read all types of clocks?

____

____

Create: *I use my knowledge and imagination to express new and innovative ideas.*

Have you seen some of the different types of watches made today? Why do you think there are so many different types?

____

____

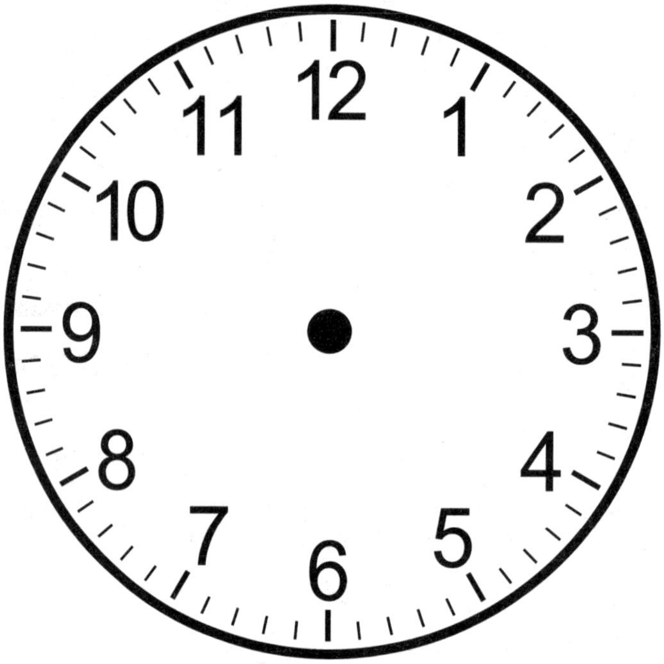

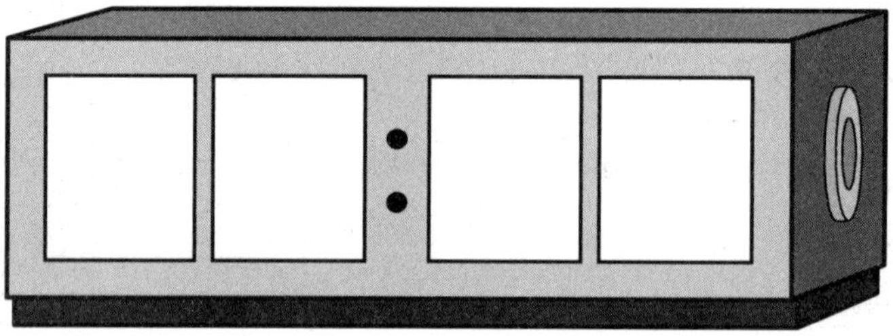

Which type of clock do you find more challenging to read, a digital or an analog? Why do you feel that way?

____

____

What type of chant can you ***create*** to help you remember the difference between an analog and a digital clock?

____

____

Illegal to Copy

analog clock	**half hour**	**hour hand**	**minute hand**
digital clock	**hour**	**minute**	**o'clock**

Draw lines to match the vocabulary word to its picture.

analog clock

digital clock

hour hand

minute hand

Why is it important to be able to identify analog and digital clocks by their names? Can you think of a situation where using the correct word might make a difference?

____

____

Why do you think they created the minute hand longer than the hour hand on an analog clock?

____

____

Analog Clock

Trace over the hour hand in blue.
Trace over the minute hand in red.

Hours Minutes

Digital Clock

What time does the clock say?

____

An analog clock has a minute hand and an hour hand that point to numbers to tell the time.

The hour hand is the shorter hand on an analog clock. It is the hand you read to tell the hour.

The minute hand is the longer hand on an analog clock. It is the hand you read to tell the minute.

A digital clock shows time in numbers.

The colon (shown as :) divides the hours and minutes on a digital clock. The numbers on the left side of the : are hours. The numbers on the right side of the : are minutes.

Half hour and half past the hour are equal to 30 minutes.

Try It!

1) What time does the clock say?

____

Try It!

2) Make the clock read ten o'clock.

____

1 What time does the clock say?

- ⬭ Seventy-three
- ⬭ Seven thirty
- ⬭ Seven

2 The clock shows Bob's bedtime. Choose the time.

- ⬭ 9:00
- ⬭ 8:00
- ⬭ 8:30

3 The time on the clock is

________ : ________.

4 Show nine thirty on the digital clock.

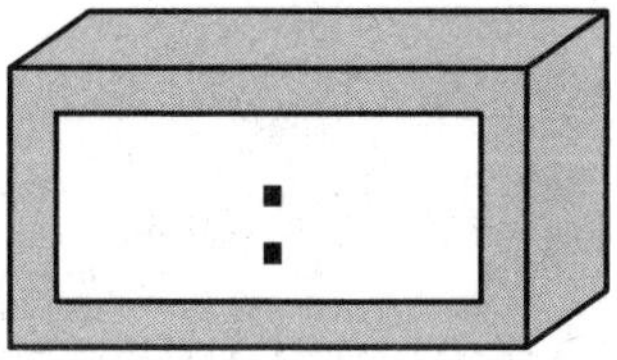

5 Make the analog clock show the same time.

6 Make the digital clock show the same time as the analog clock.

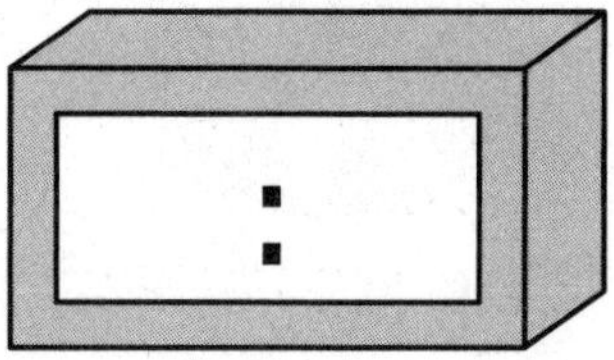

Name: ____________________

Concept Practice

1 Choose the digital clock that shows the same time.

2 Show 4 o'clock on each clock.

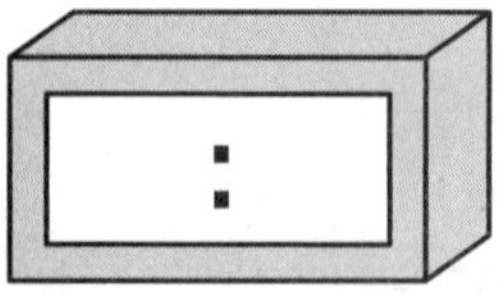

3 Which analog clock shows the same time?

4 Write the time shown on the clock.

______ : ______

Circle all the ways that say the same time as the clock.

half past four   four o'clock

four thirty   past four

Illegal to Copy

Name: ______________________________

Time Match

Play *Time Match* with a partner. Players begin by covering each square on the game board with a color tile. In turn, each player turns over two tiles. If the squares show a matching clock and time, the player keeps the tiles. If the squares do not show a matching clock and time, the player replaces the tiles. The player with more tiles when the board is cleared is the winner.

5:00	**half past two**		**seven thirty**	1:00
	**three o'clock**	7:30	**half past eight**	**half past nine**
five o'clock		**Time Match**	**four o'clock**	
	**one o'clock**	9:30	**twelve thirty**	**six o'clock**
2:30	**ten thirty**	4:00		**eleven o'clock**

Name: ______________________________

Math Challenge

Show a time on the clock. Draw a picture to show what you do at that time.
Write a sentence about your picture.

____

____

____

Reflection on My Learning

Do you think analog clocks or digital clocks are better? Explain your answer.

____

____

Reflection on Critical Thinking

Circle the traits you used most often in this unit.

I show ______________________ when I ______________________.

Illegal to Copy

Name: ______________________________

Assessment

Unit 31 – Standard 1.7(E)

Concept Check

1 Match.

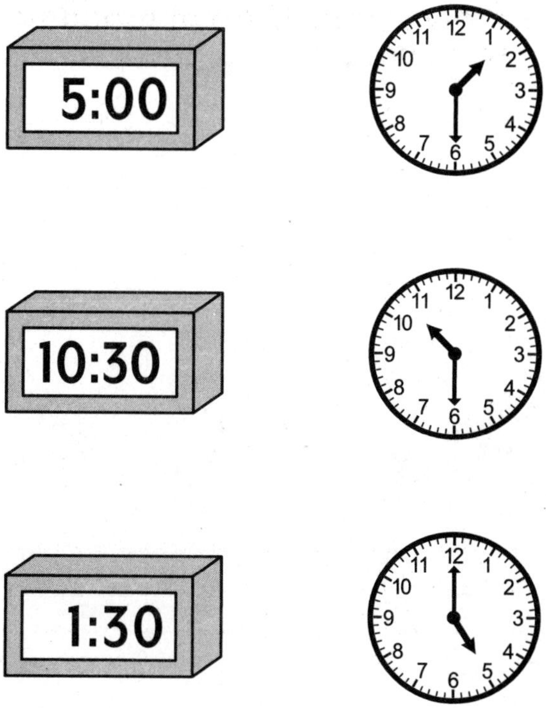

2 Show half past eight on each clock.

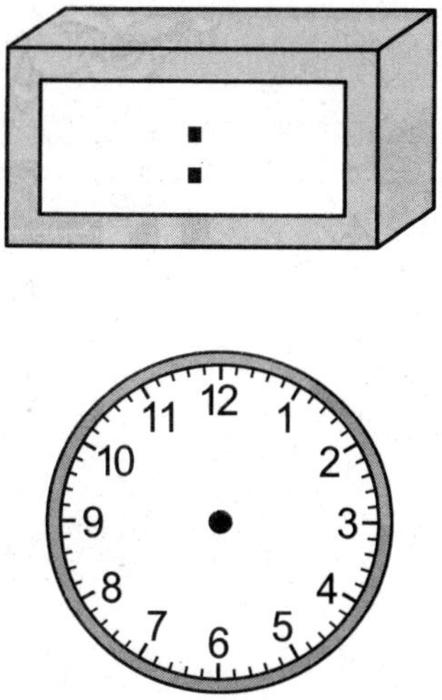

3 The clock shows Dimitri's lunch time. Choose the time.

⬭ 6 o'clock

⬭ 3 o'clock

⬭ 12 o'clock

4 The time on the clock is

________ : ________.

5 Show half past six on the digital clock.

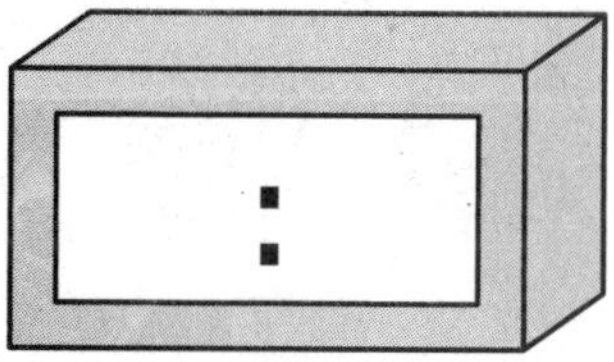

Assessment

Name: ______________________

Concept Check

6 Ted goes to soccer practice at four o'clock. He practices until half past five. On the first clock, show the time Ted goes to practice. On the second clock, show the time practice is over. Write the times beside each clock.

______________  ______________

7 Draw the hour hand between 3 and 4. Draw the minute hand on 6. Show the same time on the digital clock.

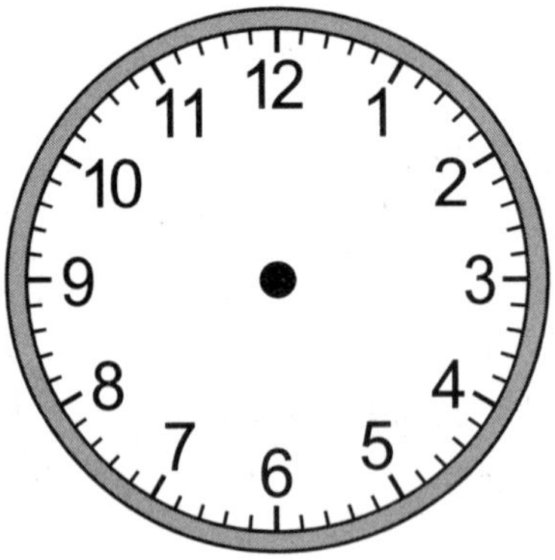

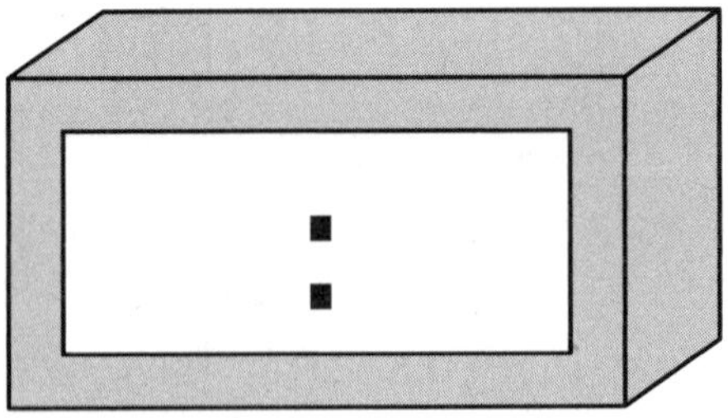

Illegal to Copy

Name: ______________________________

Unit 32 – Standard 1.8(A)

Getting Started

Unit 32: Collect, Sort, and Organize Data

TEKS LEARNING TARGETS

- I can recognize that data can be sorted into multiple categories.
- I can organize data using different types of models or representations.
- I can represent data with appropriate labels and titles.

Focus for 9 Traits of Critical Thinking™

Examine: *I use a variety of methods to explore and to analyze.*

When you are comparing and sorting things, how do you use your senses? Which senses do you use the most?

____

____

Link: *I apply knowledge to reach new understandings.*

Is information always shared in word form? What other ways have you seen information shared in the real world?

____

____

Instruction

Name: ___________________________

Concept Exploration

Standard 1.8(A) – **Unit 32**

Can identical or similar objects be sorted in some way? Explain your response.

____

____

How does knowing how to skip count by 5 help you use tally marks?

____

____

Illegal to Copy

Name: ______________________________

Instruction

Unit 32 – Standard 1.8(A)

Vocabulary Mastery

chart	**sort**	**tally chart**	**T-chart**
data	**table**	**tally marks**	

Draw lines to match vocabulary words to their meanings.

data	**a way to keep count by making marks**
organize	**facts or information**
sort	**to put things in order**
tally chart	**to group things together because they are alike in some way**
T-chart	**a chart used to compare two things**

Why does the question you ask determine the type of information you are able to gather? Give an example.

____

____

How is a tally chart similar to a T-chart?

____

____

Favorite Snack

Food	Tally
Candy	卌 卌 卌
Ice cream	卌
Fruit	|||

What is the favorite snack?

____

Cherry	Not Cherry
卌 ||||	卌 卌

How many candies are NOT cherry?

____

Answer the following questions.

Do you like pizza? __________

What is your favorite kind of pizza?

____

A tally chart is used to keep track of data being counted.

A T-chart can be used to organize data. The lines of a T-chart form the letter T.

You collect data by asking a question. A question that cannot be answered with *yes* or *no* will give you better data.

Try It!

Bedtime	Tally
7:45 P.M.	卌 |||
8:00 P.M.	|||
8:15 P.M.	||||

1) How many people have an 8:00 bedtime? __________

2) What is the bedtime most people have? __________

3) How many go to sleep at 8:15 and 8:00? __________

Illegal to Copy

Name: ______________________________

Unit 32 – Standard 1.8(A)

Instruction

Concept Application

1 How can the apples be sorted?

- ⬭ Small and Large
- ⬭ Cut and Whole
- ⬭ Red and Green

2 Match.

15 

8 

11 

5 

3 How can this candy be sorted?

- ⬭ Candy on sticks and candy not on sticks
- ⬭ Wrapped candy and not wrapped candy

4 Complete the tally chart to show the apples.

Apples	Tally
Leaves	
No Leaves	

5 Tally and total the types of balls.

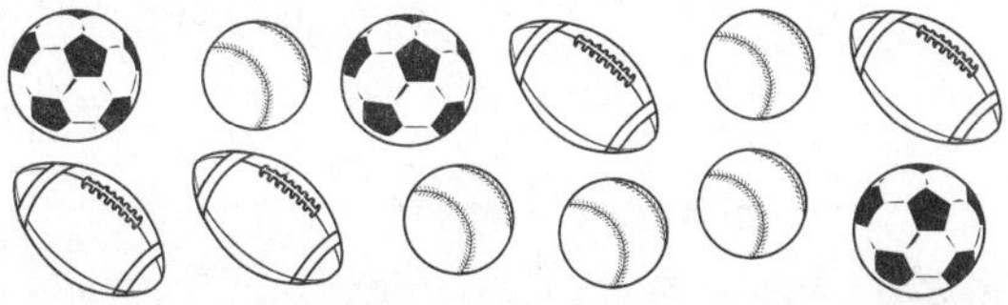

Type of Ball	Tally	Total
 Football		
 Baseball		
 Soccer ball		

Are there more footballs than soccer balls? ______________

Instruction

Name: ____________________

Concept Practice

Standard 1.8(A) – **Unit 32**

1 How can these doors be sorted?

- ⬭ Black and White
- ⬭ Open and Closed
- ⬭ Big and Small

2 Write one way these cookies can be sorted.

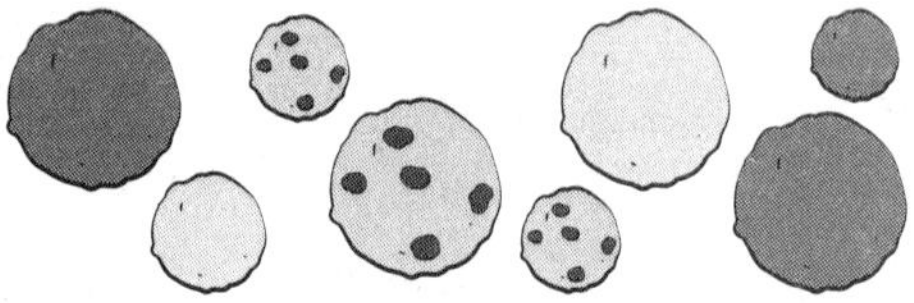

____

____

3 Complete the sentence.

Party Hats

Color	Number of Hats
Red	𝍷𝍷𝍷𝍷
Yellow	𝍸 𝍸
Blue	𝍷𝍷

There are more ____________

hats than ____________

hats.

4 Tally and total the pillows.

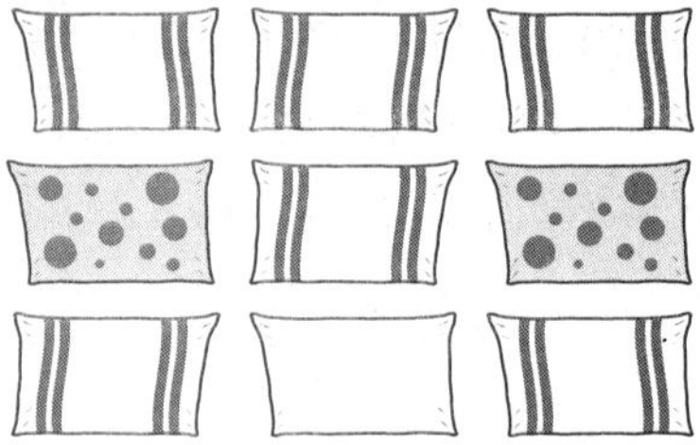

Pillow	Tally	Total
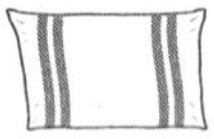		
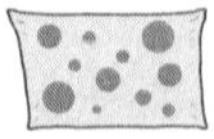		

Which set has the least?

- ⬭ 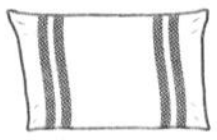
- ⬭ 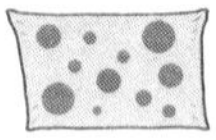
- ⬭ 

5 The tally chart shows the cookies sold at the bake sale.

Bake Sale

Type of Cookie	Number of Cookies
Sugar	𝍸 𝍷𝍷
Chocolate Chip	𝍷𝍷𝍷𝍷
Oatmeal	𝍷𝍷𝍷𝍷

How many cookies were sold in all?

____

Illegal to Copy

Elegant Elephant

Create an *Elegant Elephant*. Use a paper clip for the spinner. Spin the spinner and draw the shape on the elephant. Repeat until you have 15 shapes on the elephant. Color the shapes. When you have created and colored your elegant elephant, complete the T-chart. Make a tally mark for each shape with curves and each shape made from straight lines.

Curves	Straight Lines

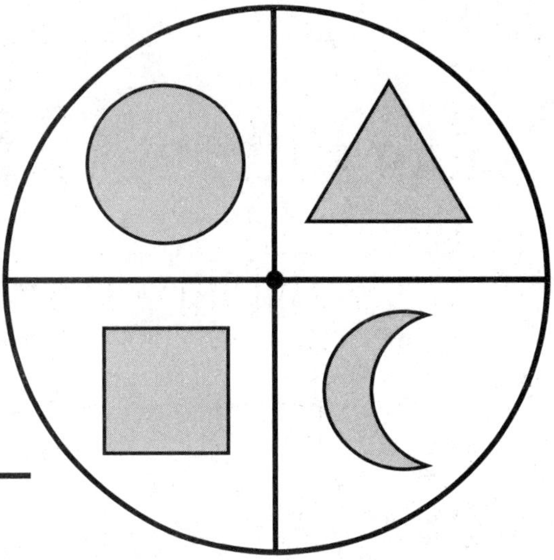

Extension

Name: ______________________________

Standard 1.8(A) – **Unit 32**

Math Challenge

Make a tally chart that shows how many boys and how many girls are in your class. Give your chart a title and labels.

____

Reflection on My Learning

Alexei has a bag of pennies, nickels, dimes, and quarters. He sorts the coins into two groups. How can Alexei sort his coins?

____

____

What is another way Alexei can sort his coins?

____

____

Reflection on Critical Thinking

Circle the traits you used most often in this unit.

I show ______________________ when I ______________________ .

Illegal to Copy

Name: ______________________

Assessment

Unit 32 – Standard 1.8(A)

Concept Check

1 Marty and his friends ate these cupcakes.

Complete the tally chart to show the cupcakes they ate.

Cupcake Type	Tally
Sprinkles	
Chocolate	
Vanilla	

2 Look at the alphabet letters. Sort the letters into two groups. Write the letters in the boxes.

E O a
I C g
e T m z

How did you sort the letters?

____

____

3 Mike sorts his socks. He has white socks and striped socks. He makes a T-chart of his socks.

White Socks	Striped Socks

Use tally marks to show how many white socks Mike has.

____

Use tally marks to show how many striped socks Mike has.

____

4 Sort the shirts into 2 groups. Circle the shirts in group 1. Put an X on each shirt in group 2.

How did you sort the shirts?

____

What is another way you could sort them?

____

5 Draw lines to sort the hats into two groups.

Group 1		Group 2

How did you sort the hats?

____

What is another way to sort the hats?

____

6 Kay counted the colors of leaves on a tree in her yard. She counted 12 red leaves, 8 green leaves, and 10 orange leaves.
Show Kay's information on the tally chart.

Leaves

Color	Tally	Total
Red		
Green		
Orange		

Which color has the greatest number? ____________

Illegal to Copy

Name: ______________________________

Unit 33 – Standard 1.8(B)

Getting Started

Unit 33: Create Picture Graphs and Bar Graphs

TEKS LEARNING TARGETS

- I can use data to create picture graphs.
- I can create vertical and horizontal bar graphs using collected data.

Focus for 9 Traits of Critical Thinking™

Adapt: *I adjust my actions and strategies to accomplish tasks.*

Do you think you can learn as much from a picture as you can from words? Share your thinking.

____

____

Collaborate: *I work with others to achieve better outcomes.*

What are some ways you might let your classmates know you appreciate their ideas?

____

____

What surprises you about the way you can take the same data and present it in three different formats? Can you think of any other way to share the data?

____

____

Did you find it was easy to gather data from your classmates for the graphs? Is there something that you could do to make working together easier?

____

____

Illegal to Copy

Name: ______________________

Instruction

Unit 33 – Standard 1.8(B)

Vocabulary Mastery

bar graph	**data**	**picture graph**	**table**
chart	**key**	**symbol**	

Use the Venn diagram to show how bar graphs and picture graphs are alike and different.

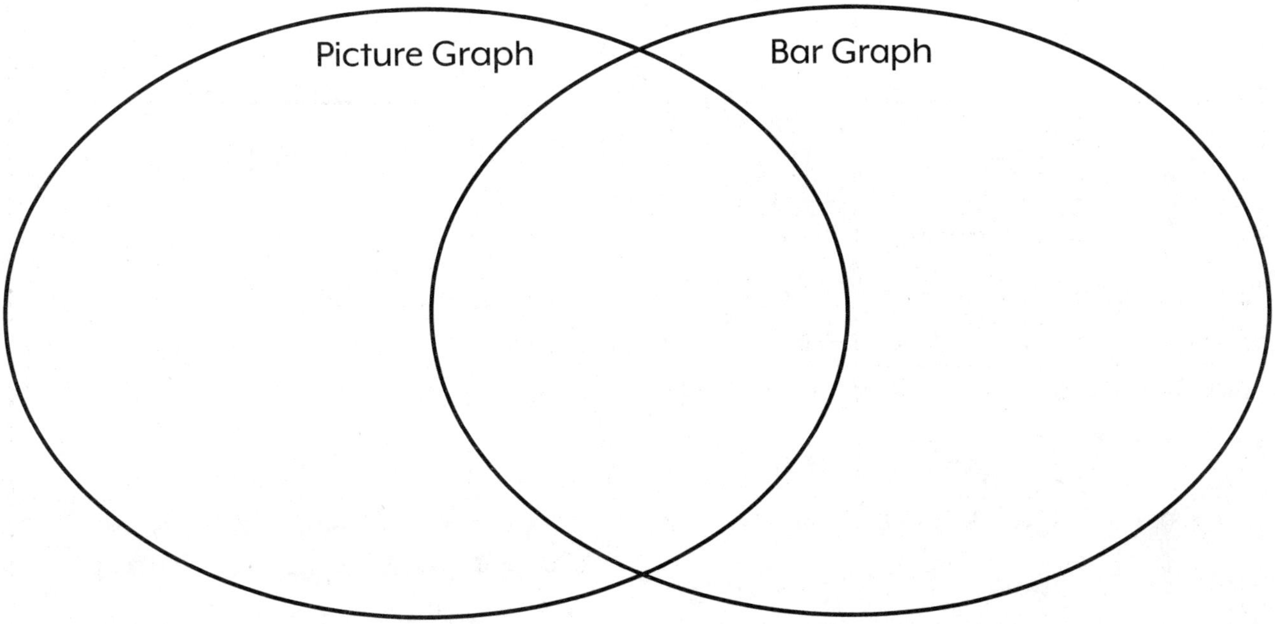

How did you have to change your thinking to represent data in a picture graph and a bar graph?

____

____

How could you and your friends work together to model the picture graph/bar graph Venn diagram?

____

____

Instruction

Name: ______________________________

Concept Development

Standard 1.8(B) – **Unit 33**

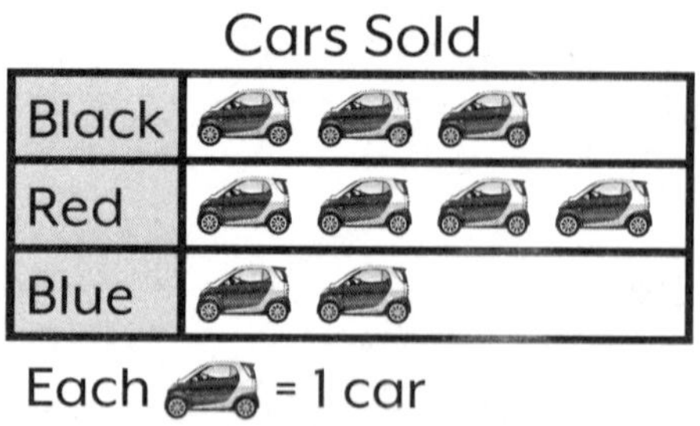

How many red cars were sold?

____

A picture graph uses pictures or symbols to represent data.

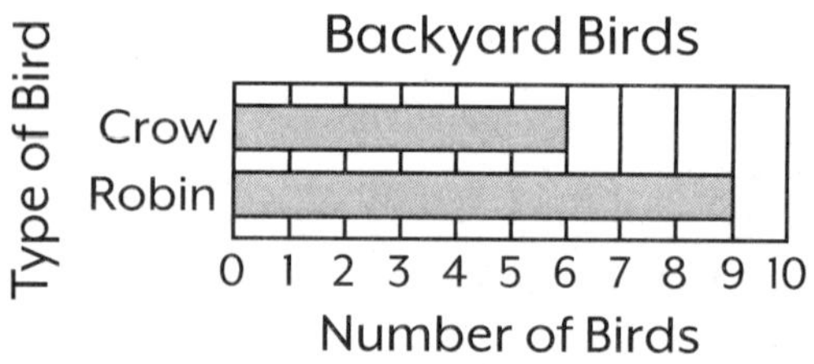

How many crows are in the backyard?

____

A bar graph uses spaces or bars to show data.

Give the graph a title.

____

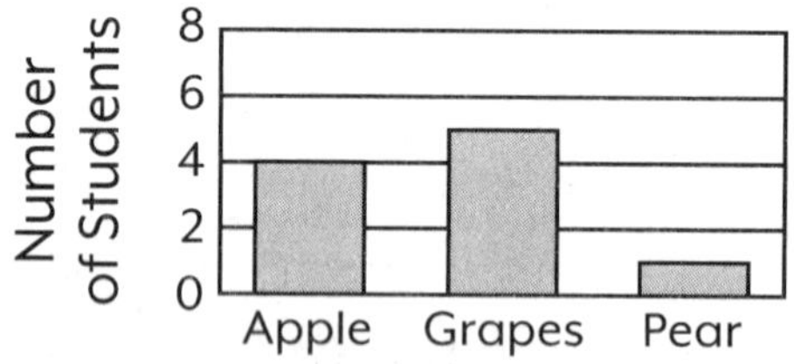

A graph needs a title to help you know what the data is about.

Try It!

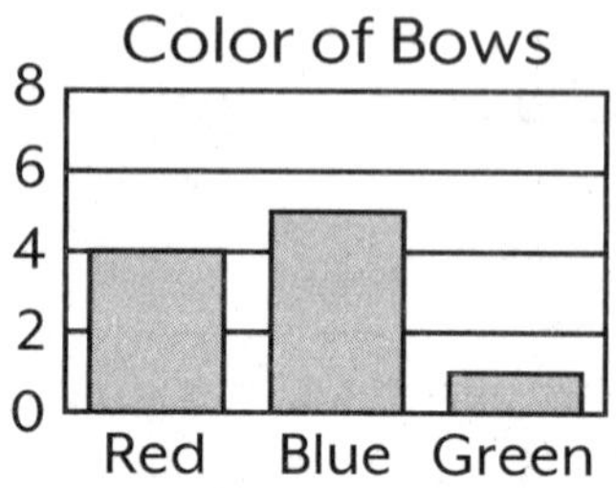

1) How many bows are blue?

____

2) How many bows are green?

____

Try It!

3) Give the graph a title.

____

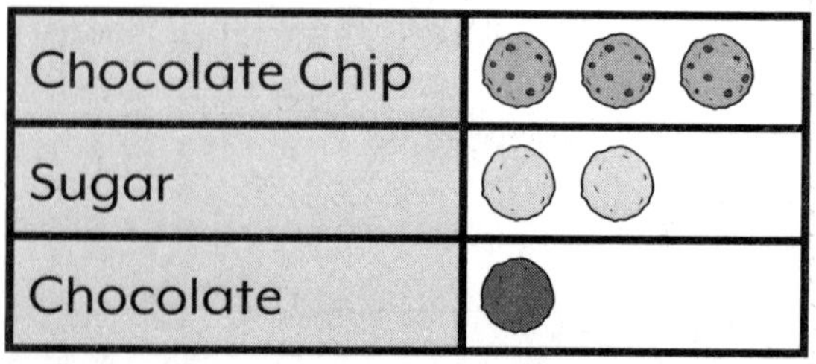

Illegal to Copy

Instruction

Concept Application

Use the chart to answer questions 1–3.

Mr. Starr's students voted for their favorite subjects. The chart shows the results.

Favorite Subjects

Subject	Tally
Reading	𝍸
Math	𝍸 |||
Science	𝍸	

1 Use the chart to create a picture graph. Draw ☺ on the picture graph to show each student's vote.

Favorite Subjects

Reading	
Math	
Science	

Each ☺ = 1 student

2 What subject did most students like best? ______________________

3 Use the information from the chart and picture graph to make a bar graph.

Favorite Subjects

Reading									
Math									
Science									
	0 1	2	3	4	5	6	7	8	9

Use the chart to answer questions 1–6.

1 Ms. Brown asked her students to vote on their favorite foods. Look at the chart. Draw the tally marks.

Favorite Foods

Fast Food	Tally	Total
Hamburger		8
Taco		4
Pizza		12

2 Complete the bar graph to show the information from the chart.

Favorite Foods

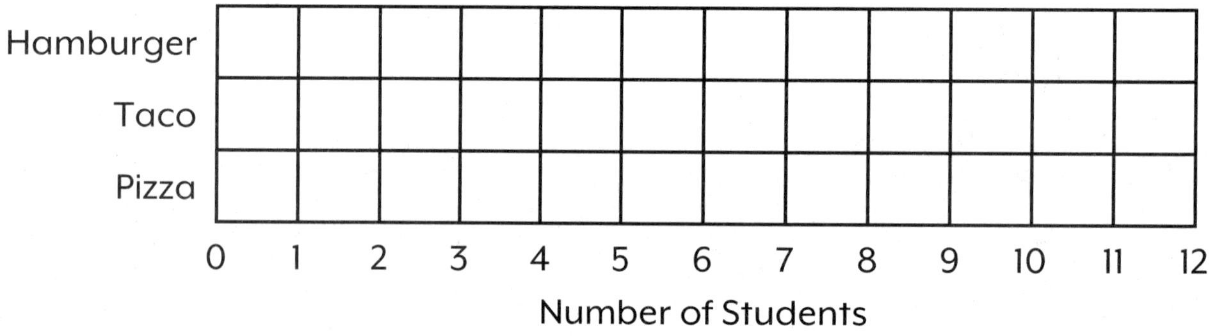

3 What is the favorite food in Ms. Brown's class?

____

4 How many students like tacos? ____________________

5 How many students are in Ms. Brown's class? ____________________

6 How many students like hamburgers or tacos? Explain how you found your answer.

____

____

Illegal to Copy

Shape Find

Find the two-dimensional shapes in the picture. Then complete the tally chart to show how many of each shape are in the picture. Use the information from the tally chart to complete the bar graph. Color the Robo Man.

Robo Man

Shape	Tally	Total Number
Circle		
Triangle		
Square		
Rectangle		
Rhombus		
Hexagon		

Robo Man

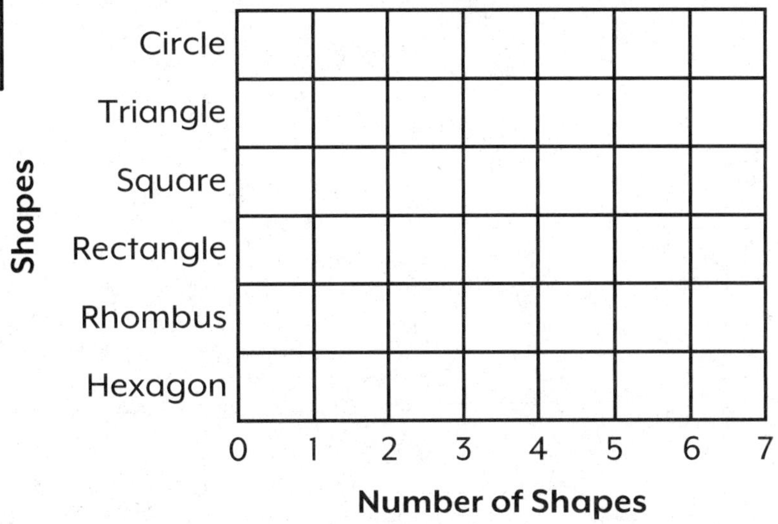

Extension

Name: ____________________

Math Challenge

Dalia asks her friends to name their favorite ice cream flavors. Seven friends choose chocolate. Three friends like strawberry best. Five friends like vanilla. Dalia makes a picture graph to show the data.

Favorite Ice Cream

Each (ice cream cone) = 1 friend

Does Dalia make her picture graph correctly? ____________________

Explain your answer. ____________________

____

Reflection on My Learning

Is it easier to read a picture graph or a bar graph? Explain your answer.

____

____

Reflection on Critical Thinking

Circle the traits you used most often in this unit.

I show ____________________ when I ____________________ .

Illegal to Copy

Look at the graph.

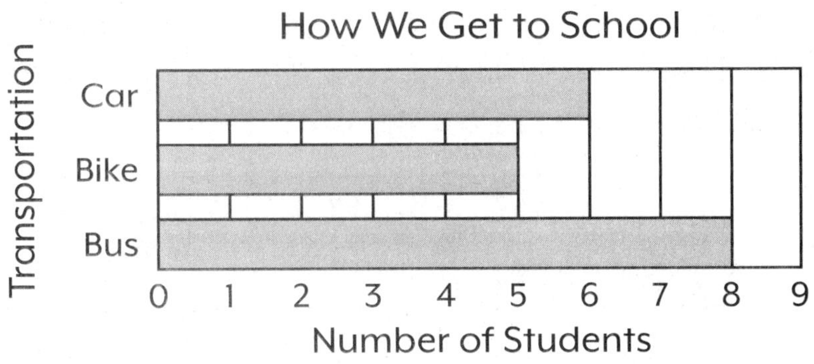

1 Use the bar graph to create a picture graph of the data.

Car	
Bike	
Bus	

Each ☺ = 1 student

Mr. Smith's class went to the zoo. The children ate snow cones. 12 students ate grape, 7 students ate cherry, and 3 students ate lemon.

2 Make the picture graph show the information about the snow cones.

Snow Cones

Grape	
Cherry	
Lemon	

Each (snow cone) = 1 snow cone

3 How many students ate cherry or lemon snow cones?

____

Assessment

Name: ____________________

Concept Check

Standard 1.8(B) – **Unit 33**

4 Look at this chart. Write the totals.

Favorite Days

Day	Tally	Total
Friday	卌	
Saturday	卌 卌 |||	
Sunday	卌 ||||	

5 Complete the bar graph to show information from the chart.

Favorite Days

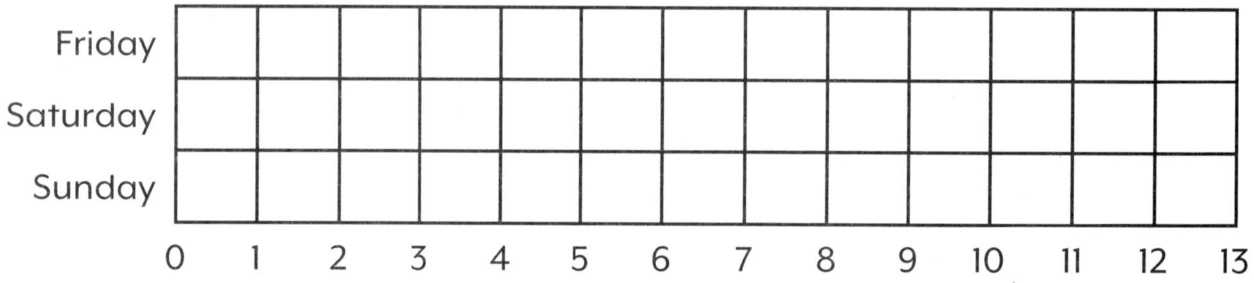

Lade's Candy Shop keeps gumballs in jars. The picture shows the red, blue, and yellow gumballs.

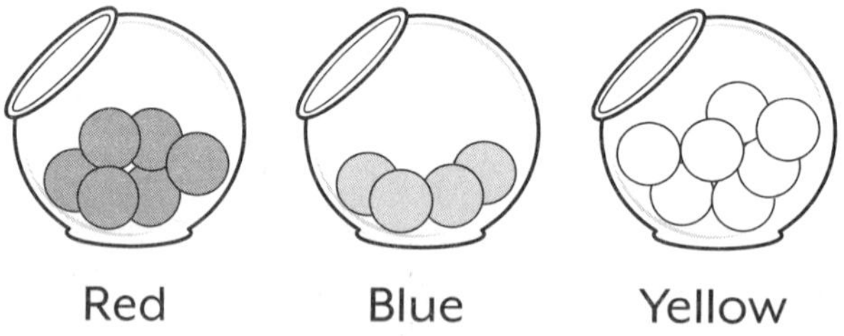

6 Use the picture to create a picture graph of the data. Color the gumballs.

Gumballs

Red	
Blue	
Yellow	

Each ◯ = 1 gumball

Name: ______________________________

Unit 34 – Standard 1.8(C)

Getting Started

Unit 34: Answer Questions Based on Picture Graphs and Bar Graphs

TEKS LEARNING TARGETS

- I can use picture graphs and bar graphs to answer questions.
- I can generate and answer questions related to data found in picture graphs and bar graphs.

Focus for 9 Traits of Critical Thinking™

Inquire: *I seek information that excites my curiosity and inspires my learning.*

When you are communicating information with people about how you are counting, why is it important to be very clear?

____

____

Strive: *I use effort and determination to focus on challenging tasks.*

When you are working to find the answers to your questions, how do you stay focused? Is it easy to stay on task, or do you find your attention wandering?

____

____

Imagine that you are saving money in order to buy something special. How might you use a tally chart or bar graph to show how much money is in your piggy bank?

____

____

How did you know you were on the right track when trading the coins for colored bars on the bar graph? Why is it important to be as accurate as possible?

____

____

Illegal to Copy

Name: ____________________

Unit 34 – Standard 1.8(C)

Instruction

Vocabulary Mastery

bar graph	**data**	**picture graph**
chart	**key**	**symbol**

Look at the picture graph.
Draw lines to match the labels to the parts of the graph.

Categories

Title

Key

Symbol

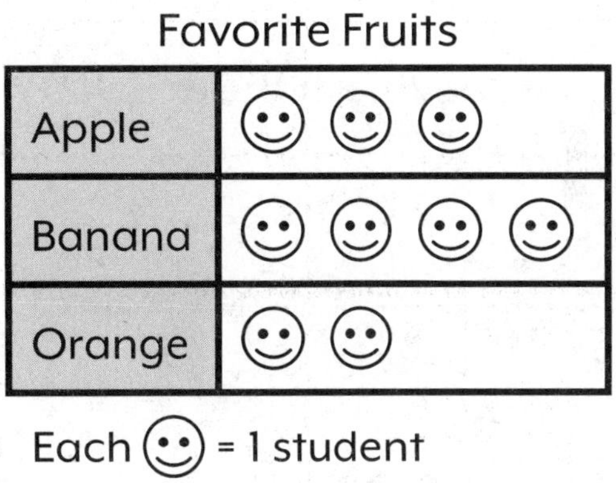

Why do you think each picture graph needs a key? Why do you think that part of the graph is named the key?

____

____

What is your first step when reading a graph? Is this always your first step?

____

____

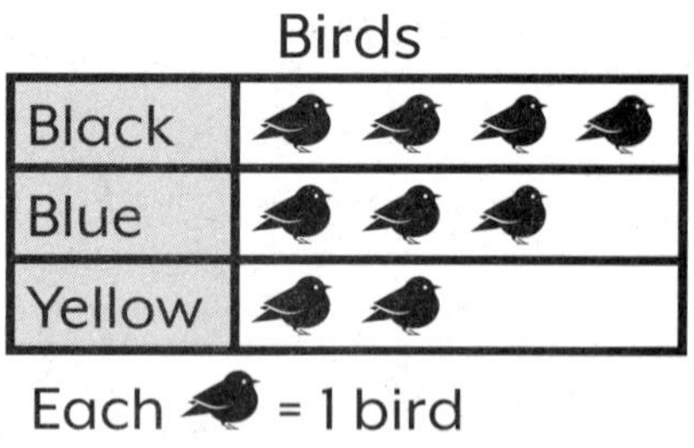

What is the symbol used in this picture graph?

____

What is the title of the graph?

____

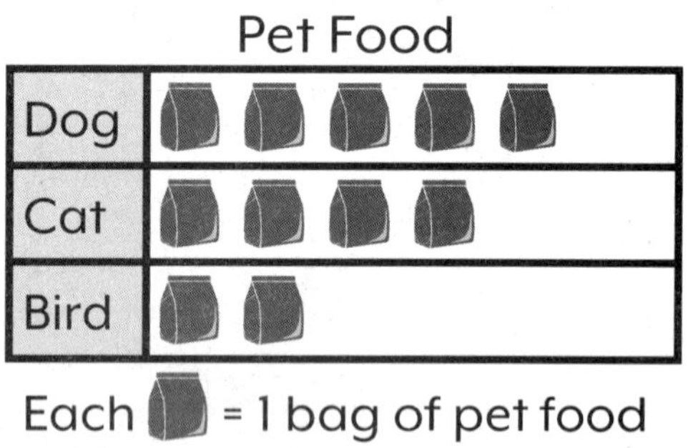

Underline the key in the graph. What is the title of the graph?

____

How many cat food bags were bought?

____

Picture graphs use pictures in place of words. These pictures are called *symbols*.

The *key* in a graph is the part that shows what the symbol means.

The *data* in a graph gives you information on a topic. You can answer questions by analyzing the data in the graph.

Try It!

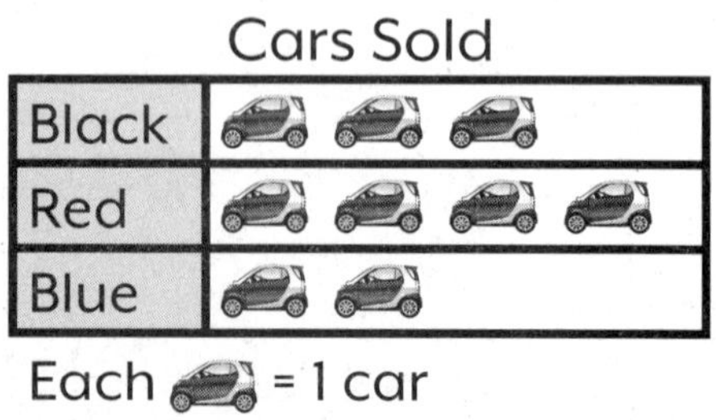

1) How many blue cars sold? ________

2) How many black cars sold? ________

3) How many cars sold in all? ________

Illegal to Copy

Use the picture graph to answer questions 1–3.

1 Look at the picture graph.

Cars in the Parking Lot

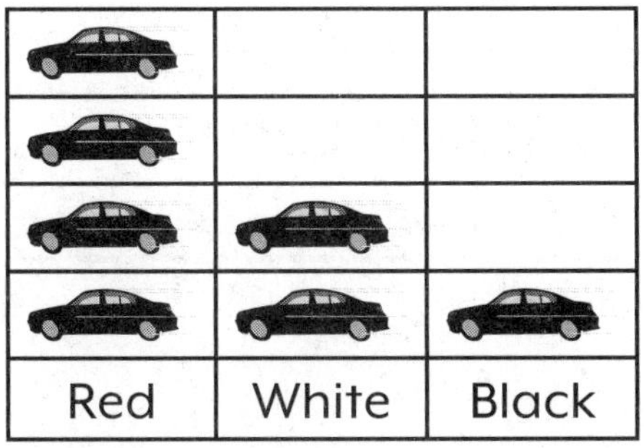

____

What label is missing?

- ⬭ Categories
- ⬭ Title
- ⬭ Symbol

2 How many white and black cars are parked in the lot?

- ⬭ 2
- ⬭ 3
- ⬭ 1

3 How many more red cars are in the lot than black cars?

____

Did you add or subtract to get your answer?

____

Use the bar graph to answer questions 4–6.

4 Fill in the missing labels on the bar graph.

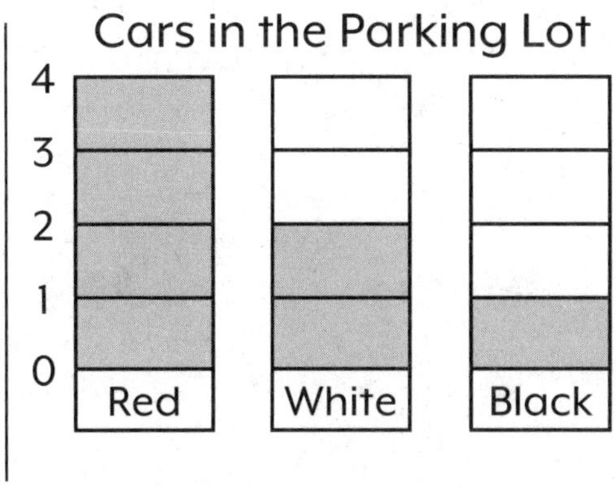

____

5 How many red and white cars are in the lot?

____

Did you add or subtract to find the answer?

____

6 Write a question that can be answered by the graph.

____

____

____

Use the picture graph to answer questions 1–4.

The graph shows the results of a walking contest.

Walking Contest

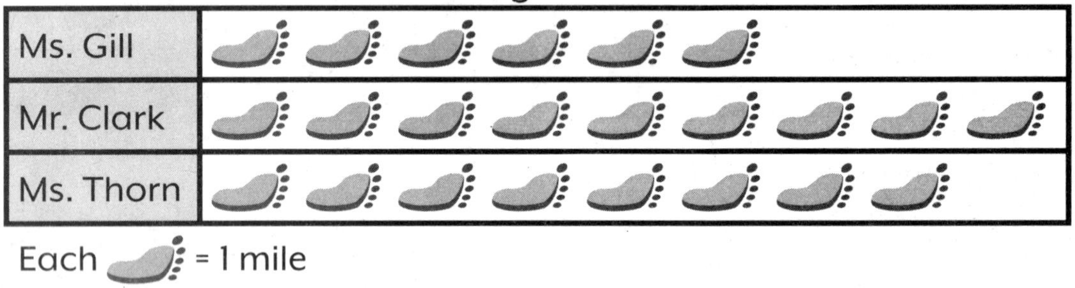

1 How many more miles did Ms. Thorn walk than Ms. Gill?

- ⬭ 14 miles
- ⬭ 8 miles
- ⬭ 2 miles

2 Which teacher walked the most miles? ____________________

3 How many miles did Ms. Gill and Mr. Clark walk in all?

____

4 Who walked more miles, Mr. Clark or Ms. Thorn?

____

How do you know?

____

____

 Illegal to Copy

All About Me Glyph

Use the directions to make a glyph about yourself.

What color are your eyes?

Draw eyes that color.

What does your hair look like?

Draw your hair.

Are you a boy or a girl?

Boy – Draw blue pants.

Girl – Draw a pink skirt.

Do you have a pet?

Yes – Color a yellow shirt.

No – Color a green shirt.

Do you like to sing?

Yes – Draw an open mouth.

No – Draw a closed mouth.

How old are you?

Add that many buttons to your shirt.

Do you have brothers or sisters?

Yes – Add polka dots to your shirt.

No – Add stripes to your shirt.

Extension

Name: ____________________

Math Challenge

Look at the picture graph.

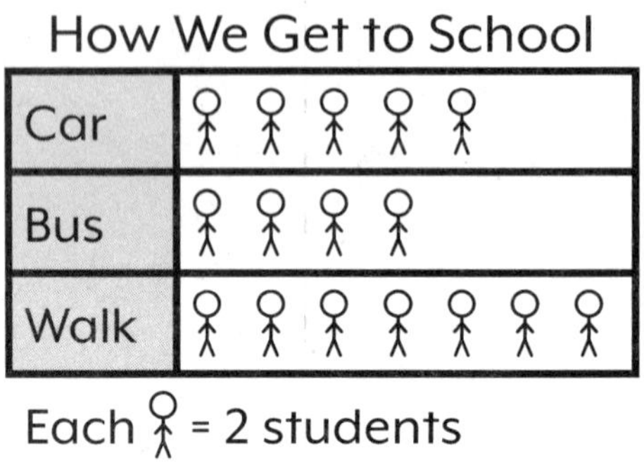

Leslie writes a question about the graph. The answer to Leslie's question is 2. What question did Leslie write?

____

____

Reflection on My Learning

Some people think it is easier to solve a word problem that has a graph. Explain what you think.

____

____

Reflection on Critical Thinking

Circle the traits you used most often in this unit.

I show ____________________ when I ____________________ .

Name: ______________________________

Unit 34 – Standard 1.8(C)

Assessment

Concept Check

Use the bar graph to answer questions 1 and 2.

Mr. Brown's class makes a graph of their favorite days.

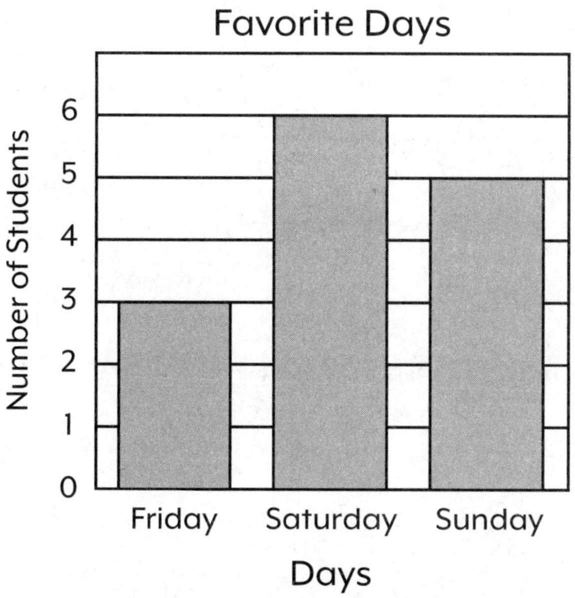

1 How many students like Sunday more than Friday?

Answer ______________________

2 Write a question using the data on the graph.

____

____

____

Use the bar graph to answer questions 3 and 4.

The bar graph shows the drinks Sid's mother buys for a party.

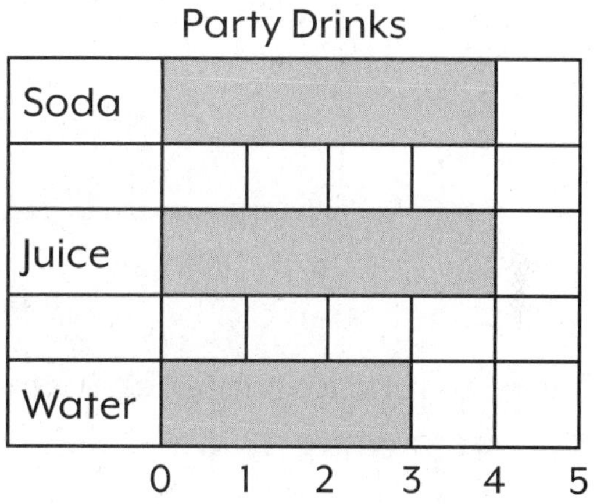

3 Which statement about the graph is true?

- ⬭ Sid's mother buys the same amount of soda and water.
- ⬭ Sid's mother buys the same amount of juice and soda.
- ⬭ Sid's mother buys more soda than juice.

4 Sid's mother bought the least amount of which drink?

Answer ______________________

Assessment

Name: ____________________________

Concept Check

Standard 1.8(C) – **Unit 34**

Use the picture graph to answer questions 5–7.

Ben's class votes on favorite milk flavors. The picture graph shows the vote.

Favorite Milk Flavors

Each  = 1 person

5 Write a number sentence to find how many more students like chocolate milk than white milk.

________ ◯ ________ = ________

6 Write a number sentence to find out how many people like strawberry and white milk.

________ ◯ ________ = ________

7 Write a question using the data on the graph.

____

____

____

Illegal to Copy

Name: ____________________

Getting Started

Unit 35 – Standards 1.9(A), 1.9(B), 1.9(C), 1.9(D)

Unit 35: Manage Financial Resources

TEKS LEARNING TARGETS

- I can understand that people are paid money in exchange for work.
- I can use the word *income* when talking about money earned for work.
- I can recognize that goods and services can be purchased with income.
- I can distinguish between goods and services.
- I can explain the difference between wants and needs.
- I can identify that an exchange of money is spending.
- I can recognize that keeping money and choosing not to spend it is saving.
- I can understand the importance of charitable giving.
- I can identify charitable causes.

Focus for 9 Traits of Critical Thinking™

Reflect: *I review my thoughts and experiences to guide my actions.*

Why do you think it is important to have an understanding of money?

____

____

Link: *I apply knowledge to reach new understandings.*

Have you ever earned money to buy something you really wanted? Have you ever saved money?

____

____

Instruction

Name: ____________________

Concept Exploration

Standards 1.9(A), 1.9(B), 1.9(C), 1.9(D) – **Unit 35**

Job	Pay/Income	Spend	Give to Charity	Save	Money Left

What is something new you learned today? How will you use the new learning?

____

____

What is a real-life purchase that is something you need? What is a real-life purchase that is something you want?

____

____

Illegal to Copy

Name: ______________________________

charity **income** **save** **spend**

earn **needs** **services** **wants**

goods

Label each picture with a word from the Word Bank.

Word Bank

charitable giving	income	need
saving	service	want

____

____

____

____

____

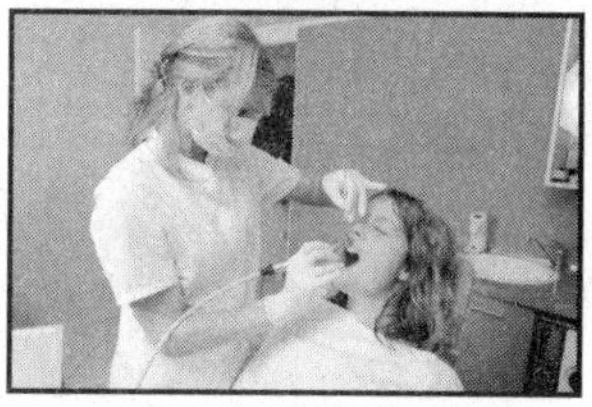

____

What are some new vocabulary words you learned? What do they mean?

____

____

Instruction

Name: ____________________

Concept Development

Standards 1.9(A), 1.9(B), 1.9(C), 1.9(D) – **Unit 35**

Tess *earns* $2 for helping her mother with the laundry.

Income is money earned from working.

Tess *saves* $1 in her piggy bank and *spends* $1 on a hair bow.

It is important to *spend* money wisely and *save* for other items later on.

Tess saves money to buy a new bike. Is the bike a *want* or a *need*?
Circle your answer.

want need

A *need* is something a person must have to live. A *want* is something a person would like to have.

Tess baked cookies to sell. She also watched her friend's dog when her friend was out of town.

**Underline the example of a good.
Circle the example of a service.**

Goods are things that are made to be sold. *Services* are jobs people complete for others. Firefighters and nurses provide important services.

Try It!

1) Look at the grocery list. Put an X on the items that are *wants*.

bread apple pie

milk gum

candy bubbles

eggs toilet paper

Try It!

2) Circle the example of saving.

Buying bubble gum

Going to the video game store

Depositing money in the bank

Illegal to Copy

1 Lucy earns money babysitting. She saves her money to pay for goods. Which of these is NOT an example of goods?

- ⬭ Ice cream
- ⬭ Music lesson
- ⬭ Video game

2 Draw a line to match the word to the picture.

save spend

3 Gordon earns $18. He wants to spend $10 on a game. He will save the rest. How much money will Gordon save?

Answer ____________________

4 Mr. Tate's class wants to save money to give to charity.

new class toys

candy for snack

food for the homeless

Circle the BEST choice for their giving.
Explain your answer.

____

____

5 Max's job is mowing lawns. He earns $15 for each lawn.

Name two items Max might NEED to buy.

____

____

Name two items Max might WANT to buy.

____

____

Instruction

Name: ______________________________

Concept Practice

Standards 1.9(A), 1.9(B), 1.9(C), 1.9(D) – **Unit 35**

1 Draw an X on the things we do NOT need to buy.

food

video games

candy

2 Rita is a dentist. What will she earn for her work?

- A treasure chest full of jewels
- Gold tokens for video games
- Money

3 Rita wants to use some of what she earns to help other people. Which of the choices would be charitable giving?

- Donating clothes to flood victims
- Buying video games for her children
- Filling her pantry with food

4 Which is an example of saving money?

- Putting part of your allowance in a bank
- Giving your brother a dime to do your chores
- Buying a ticket to ride the roller coaster

5 Derek spends part of his allowance to buy milk.

Circle the word that describes what Derek buys.

goods services

Would milk be an example of a want or a need?

Answer ______________________________

Explain your thinking.

____

____

Illegal to Copy

Needs or Wants?

Play *Needs or Wants?* with a friend. Partners need a die and a game board. Each player needs a game marker and 22 counters. Extra counters should be left for the "bank." Players take turns rolling the die and moving that number of spaces. If the player lands on a picture that shows a way to earn income, he or she takes a counter from the "bank." If the player lands on a picture that shows a need or a want, he or she gives a counter to the "bank." Play continues until both players reach the finish. The player with more counters is the winner.

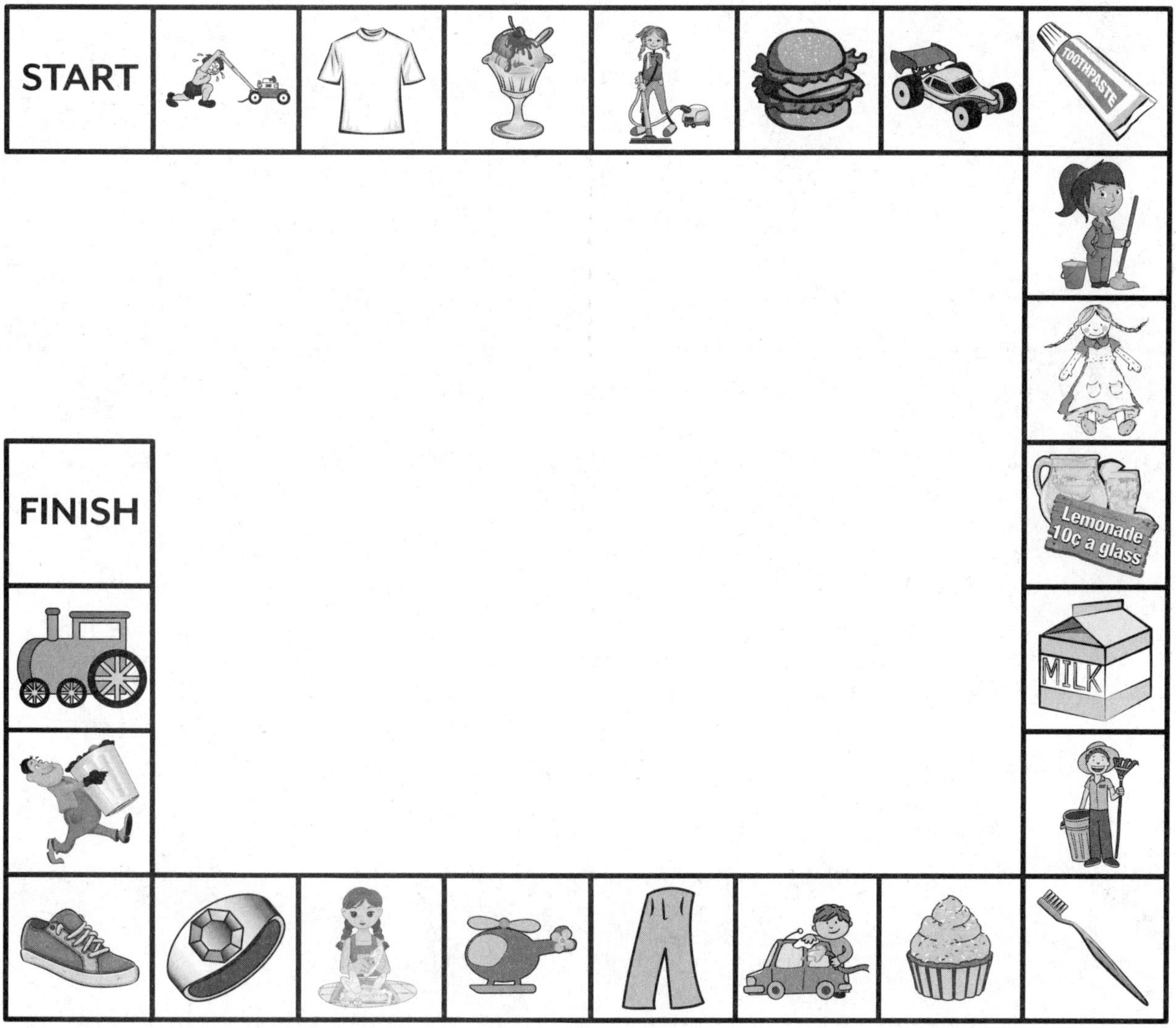

Extension

Name: ______________________

Standards 1.9(A), 1.9(B), 1.9(C), 1.9(D) – **Unit 35**

Math Challenge

Complete the Venn diagram to compare and contrast wants and needs. Use the words from the Word Bank. Add four more words to the Venn diagram.

Word Bank

dentist checkup	clothes	snack
eating out	new backpack	video game

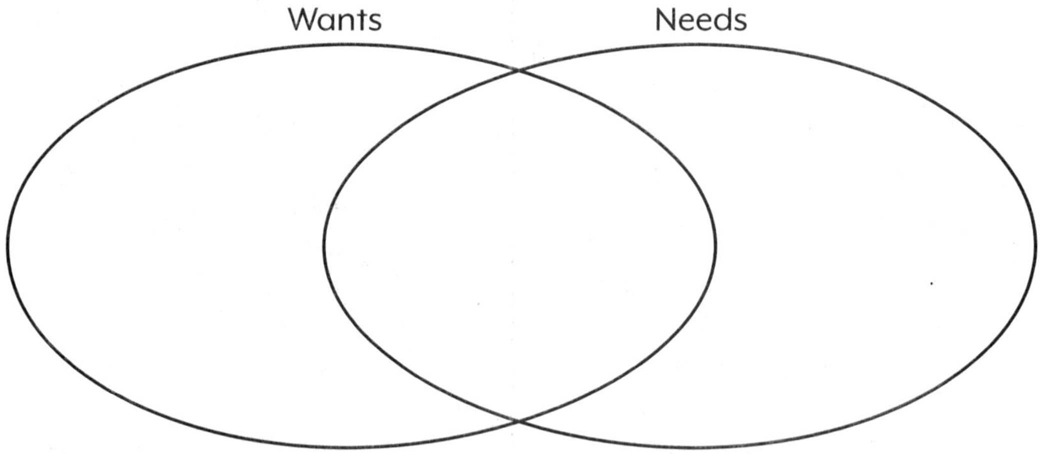

Reflection on My Learning

Write about something you want to buy or do that encourages you to save money.

____

____

Reflection on Critical Thinking

Circle the traits you used most often in this unit.

I show ______________________ when I ______________________ .

Illegal to Copy

Name: ____________________

Assessment

Unit 35 – Standards 1.9(A), 1.9(B), 1.9(C), 1.9(D)

Concept Check

1 It is lunchtime. Hildy wants a cookie. What should she do first?

- ⬭ Use her lunch money to buy chips and cookies
- ⬭ Eat a healthy lunch, then buy a cookie
- ⬭ Trade her sandwich for two cookies

2 Zahara's grandpa paid her $2 for raking leaves. Kelly's grandpa gave her $2 for her birthday. Maggie found $2 on the sidewalk. Which girl earned income?

- ⬭ Zahara
- ⬭ Kelly
- ⬭ Maggie

3 Billy needs a new pair of sneakers. His mom gives him $15 to buy a pair.

How much money will Billy have left?

Answer ____________________

4 Draw or write two ways that you can give to charity.

5 Tiffany washes dishes in a diner on the weekends. Which word does NOT describe the money Tiffany makes?

- ⬭ Charity
- ⬭ Income
- ⬭ Earnings

Assessment

Name: ____________________

Concept Check

Standards 1.9(A), 1.9(B), 1.9(C), 1.9(D) – **Unit 35**

6 Quincy's dad gives him 3 dimes each week.
Quincy puts 1 dime in each box every week.

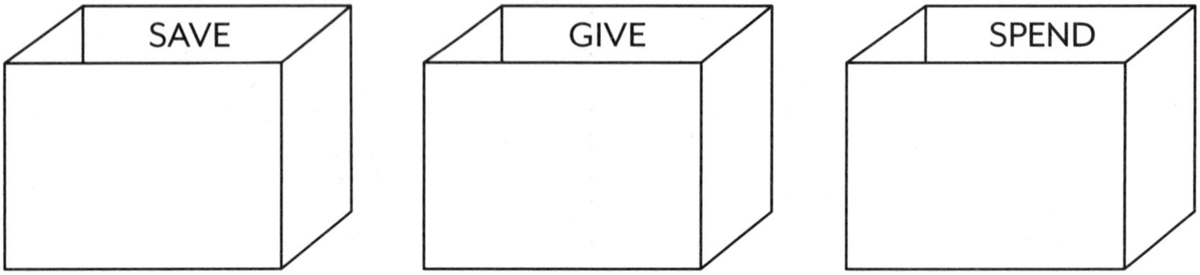

Draw the coins Quincy will have in his boxes after 4 weeks.

How much money does Quincy have to give after 4 weeks?

____

7 Terry earns 25¢ for making his bed. He buys 2 packs of gum.

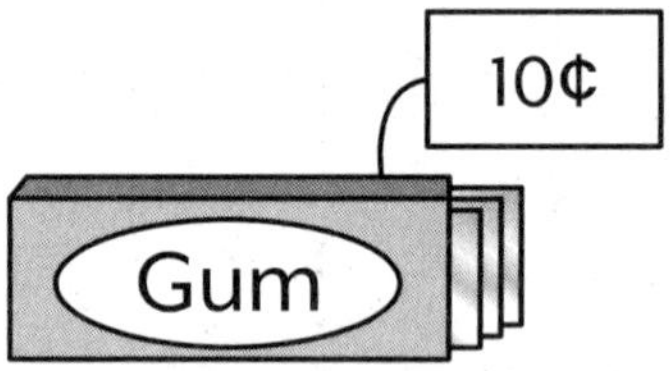

Does Terry spend or save money at the store?

Answer ____________________

Is the gum a need or a want? Explain your answer.

____

____

Illegal to Copy

Chart Your Success

Shade the square if your answer is correct.

Unit 1: 1.2(A) – Recognize the Quantities of Structured Arrangements (pages 15 and 16)

1	2	3	4	5	6	7	8	9	Total Correct
									/9

Unit 2: 1.2(B) – Compose and Decompose Numbers to 120 (pages 25 and 26)

1	2	3	4	5	6	7	8	Total Correct
								/8

Unit 3: 1.2(C) – Represent Numbers to 120 in Different Forms (pages 35 and 36)

1	2	3	4	5	6	7	8	Total Correct
								/8

Unit 4: 1.2(D) – Generate Numbers to 120 (pages 45 and 46)

1	2	3	4	5	6	7	Total Correct
							/7

Unit 5: 1.2(E) – Compare Numbers to 120 (pages 55 and 56)

1	2	3	4	5	6	7	8	Total Correct
								/8

Unit 6: 1.2(F) – Order Whole Numbers (pages 65 and 66)

1	2	3	4	5	6	7	8	Total Correct
								/8

Unit 7: 1.2(G) – Compare Whole Numbers (pages 75 and 76)

1	2	3	4	5	6	7	8	Total Correct
								/8

Unit 8: 1.3(A) – Find Sums of Multiples of 10 and One-Digit Numbers (pages 85 and 86)

1	2	3	4	5	6	7	8	9	Total Correct
									/9

Unit 9: 1.3(B) – Solve Word Problems: Addition and Subtraction Within 20 (pages 95 and 96)

1	2	3	4	5	6	7	8	Total Correct
								/8

Unit 10: 1.3(C) – Compose 10 with Two or More Addends (pages 105 and 106)

1	2	3	4	5	6	7	8	9	Total Correct
									/9

Chart Your Success

Shade the square if your answer is correct.

Unit 11: 1.3(D), 1.3(E) – Apply and Explain Fact Strategies: +/– Within 20 (pages 115 and 116)

1	2	3	4	5	6	7	8	Total Correct
								/8

Unit 12: 1.3(F) – Generate and Solve Problems Given a Number Sentence (pages 125 and 126)

1	2	3	4	5	6	7	Total Correct
							/7

Unit 13: 1.4(A) – Identify Coins and Their Values (pages 135 and 136)

1	2	3	4	5	6	7	8	Total Correct
								/8

Unit 14: 1.4(B), 1.4(C) – Determine the Value of a Set of Coins and Use the Cent Symbol (pages 145 and 146)

1	2	3	4	5	6	7	8	Total Correct
								/8

Unit 15: 1.5(A) – Recite Numbers Between 1–120 (pages 155 and 156)

1	2	3	4	5	6	7	8	Total Correct
								/8

Unit 16: 1.5(B) – Skip Count by Twos, Fives, and Tens (pages 165 and 166)

1	2	3	4	5	6	7	8	Total Correct
								/8

Unit 17: 1.5(C) – Determine Numbers 10 More/Less Than a Given Number (pages 175 and 176)

1	2	3	4	5	6	7	8	9	Total Correct
									/9

Unit 18: 1.5(D) – Represent Word Problems with Addition and Subtraction (pages 185 and 186)

1	2	3	4	5	6	7	Total Correct
							/7

Unit 19: 1.5(E) – Understand the Meaning of the Equal Sign (pages 195 and 196)

1	2	3	4	5	6	7	8	9	Total Correct
									/9

Unit 20: 1.5(F) – Determine the Unknown Number in Equations (pages 205 and 206)

1	2	3	4	5	6	7	8	9	Total Correct
									/9

Illegal to Copy

Chart Your Success

Shade the square if your answer is correct.

Unit 21: 1.5(G) – Apply Properties of Operations to Add and Subtract Numbers (pages 215 and 216)

1	2	3	4	5	6	7	8	Total Correct
								/8

Unit 22: 1.6(A) – Classify and Sort Two-Dimensional Shapes (pages 225 and 226)

1	2	3	4	5	6	7	8	Total Correct
								/8

Unit 23: 1.6(B) – Distinguish Attributes of Two- and Three-Dimensional Shapes (pages 235 and 236)

1	2	3	4	5	6	7	8	Total Correct
								/8

Unit 24: 1.6(C) – Create Two-Dimensional Shapes (pages 245 and 246)

1	2	3	4	5	6	7	8	Total Correct
								/8

Unit 25: 1.6(D) – Use Attributes to Identify Two-Dimensional Shapes (pages 255 and 256)

1	2	3	4	5	6	7	8	Total Correct
								/8

Unit 26: 1.6(E) – Identify and Describe Three-Dimensional Solids (pages 265 and 266)

1	2	3	4	5	6	7	8	9	10	Total Correct
										/10

Unit 27: 1.6(F) – Compose Two-Dimensional Shapes (pages 275 and 276)

1	2	3	4	5	6	7	8	Total Correct
								/8

Unit 28: 1.6(G), 1.6(H) – Identify Halves and Fourths in Two-Dimensional Shapes (pages 285 and 286)

1	2	3	4	5	6	7	8	Total Correct
								/8

Unit 29: 1.7(A), 1.7(B) – Use Tools to Measure and Explain Length (pages 295 and 296)

1	2	3	4	5	6	7	8	Total Correct
								/8

Unit 30: 1.7(C), 1.7(D) – Measure and Report Length with Appropriate Units (pages 305 and 306)

1	2	3	4	5	6	Total Correct
						/6

Chart Your Success

Shade the square if your answer is correct.

Unit 31: 1.7(E) – Tell Time to the Hour and the Half Hour (pages 315 and 316)

1	2	3	4	5	6	7	Total Correct
							/7

Unit 32: 1.8(A) – Collect, Sort, and Organize Data (pages 325 and 326)

1	2	3	4	5	6	Total Correct
						/6

Unit 33: 1.8(B) – Create Picture Graphs and Bar Graphs (pages 335 and 336)

1	2	3	4	5	6	Total Correct
						/6

Unit 34: 1.8(C) – Answer Questions Based on Picture Graphs and Bar Graphs (pages 345 and 346)

1	2	3	4	5	6	7	Total Correct
							/7

Unit 35: 1.9(A), 1.9(B), 1.9(C), 1.9(D) – Manage Financial Resources (pages 355 and 356)

1	2	3	4	5	6	7	Total Correct
							/7

Illegal to Copy

Math Glossary

add/addition

to join 2 groups

2 plus 4 equals 6

amount

the number of things; the quantity

The **amount** of money shown is 7¢.

addends

numbers that are added

3 + 6 = 9

↑ **addend** ↑ **addend**

analog clock

a clock with a minute hand and an hour hand

addition sentence

an equation showing the sum of two or more numbers

2 + 5 = 7

2 plus 5 equals 7.

attribute

a characteristic that describes a shape

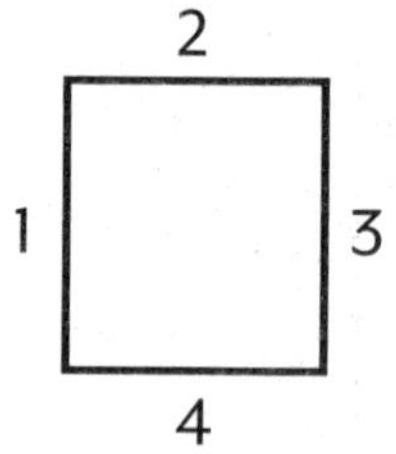

An **attribute** of a square is that it has 4 sides.

after

to be behind or to the right of a number on the number line

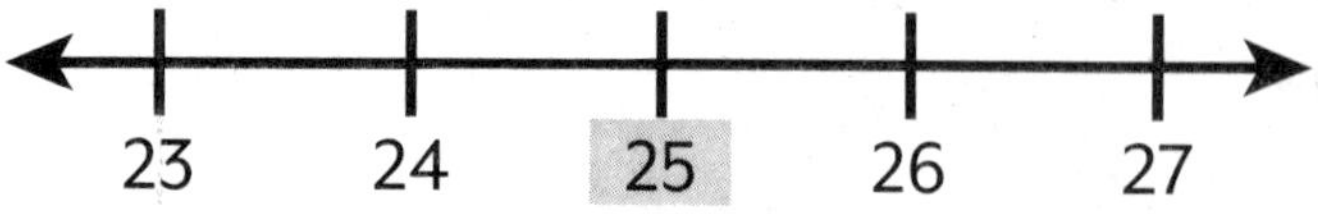

25 is **after** 24.

bar graph

a graph that uses bars to show data

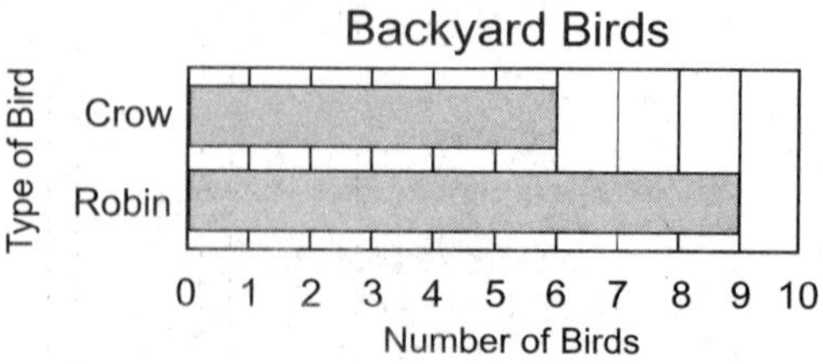

Illegal to Copy

before

to be in front of or to the left of a number on the number line

25 is **before** 26.

chart

Number of Bicycles	Number of Wheels
1	2
2	4
3	6
4	8

a table or diagram that shows recorded data

between

in the middle of

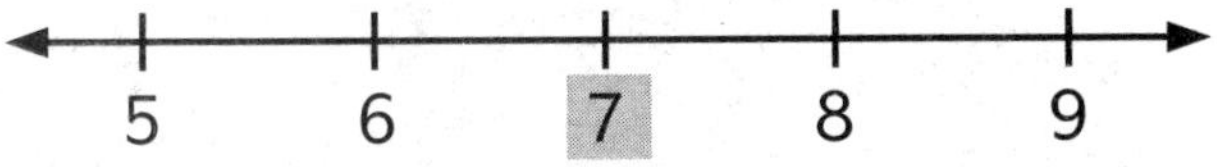

7 is **between** 6 and 8.

circle

a round, two-dimensional shape

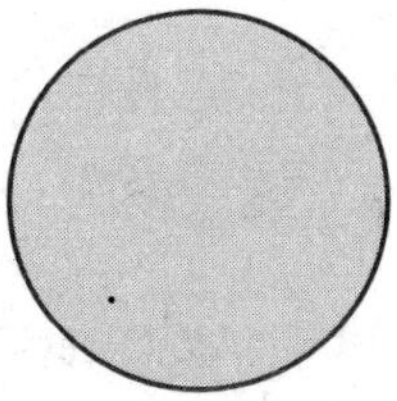

cent (¢)

a unit of money; a penny

1¢

1 **cent**

closed figure

a figure with ends that touch and no openings

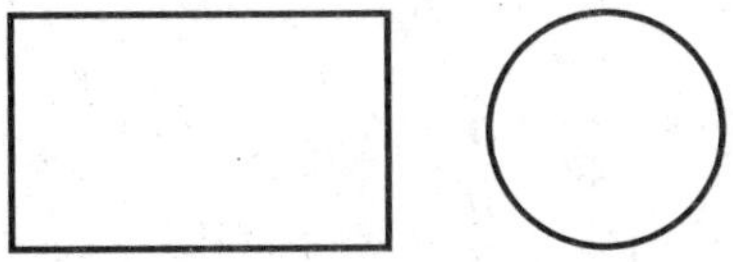

charity

an organization that helps people in need

I give part of my allowance to **charity**.

coins

flat pieces of metal used as money

penny	nickel	dime	quarter
1¢	5¢	10¢	25¢

compare

to determine how numbers, objects, or shapes are alike or different

compose

to put together or combine

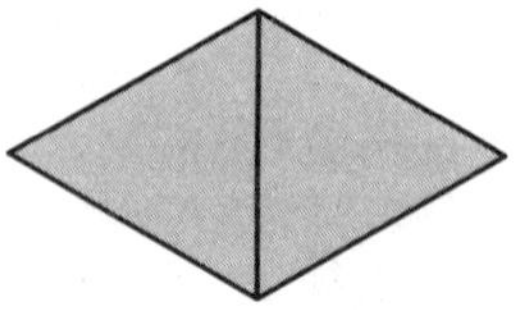

Two triangles **compose** the rhombus.

cone

a three-dimensional solid with a circle for a base and one vertex

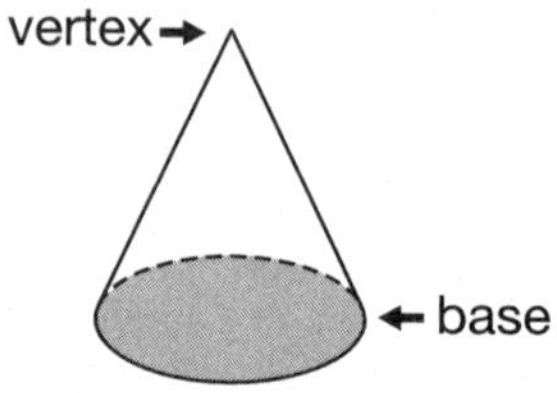

corner (vertex)

the point where two lines or surfaces meet

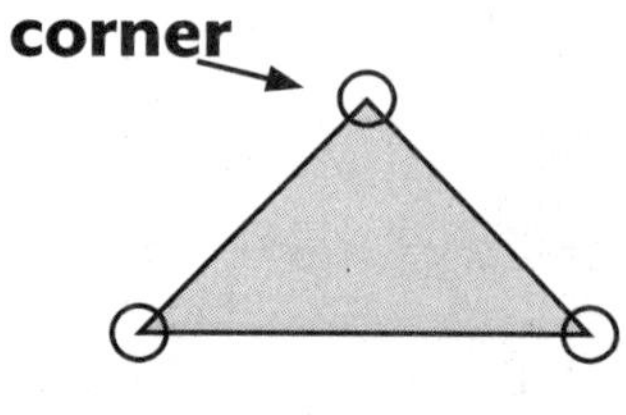

This triangle has 3 **corners**.

count

to name numbers in order

count back

a method used to subtract

(9), 8, 7, 6, 5

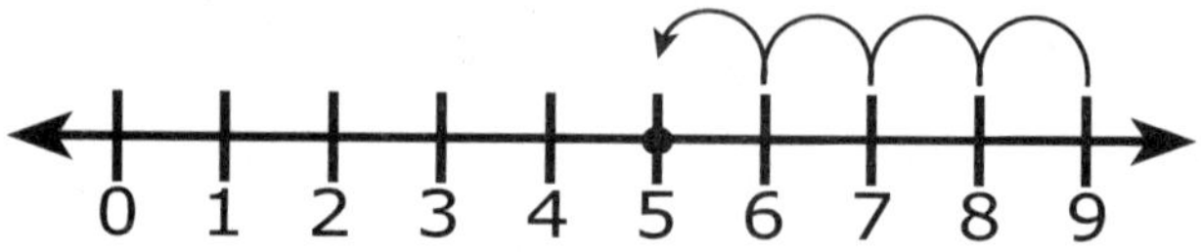

$9 - 4 = 5$

count on

a method used to add

(5), 6, 7, 8, 9

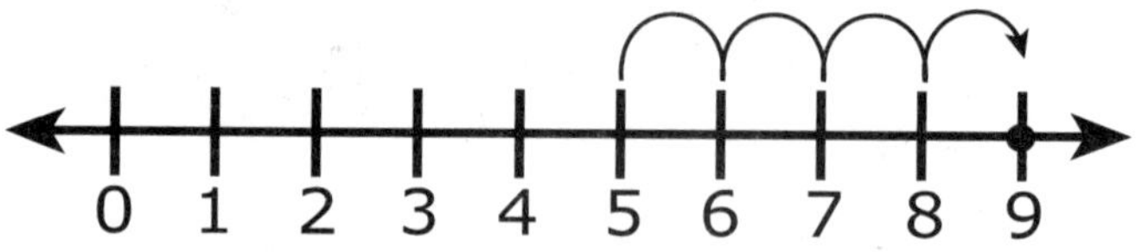

$5 + 4 = 9$

cube

a special rectangular prism

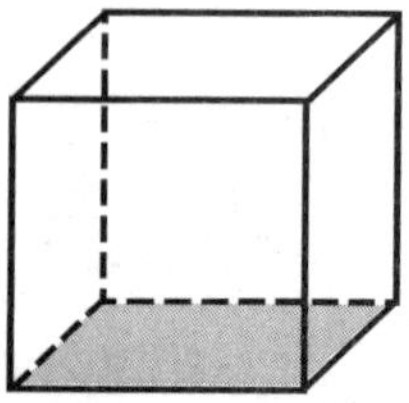

Illegal to Copy

cylinder

a three-dimensional solid with two circular bases

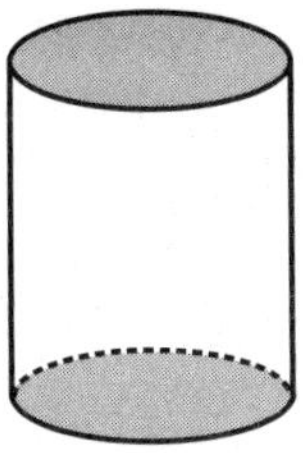

examples of cylinders
- soda can
- drinking glass
- drum

digit

one of the symbols used to write numbers

The **digits** used to write numbers are 0, 1, 2, 3, 4, 5, 6, 7, 8, and 9.

data

facts or information used to make a chart or graph

We gathered **data** about our favorite flavors of ice cream.

digital clock

a clock that shows time in numbers

decompose

to take apart or separate

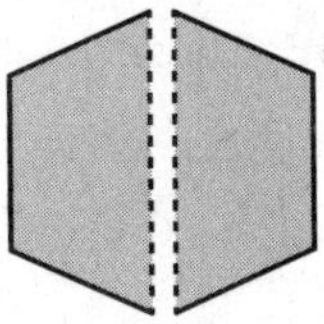

The hexagon was **decomposed** to form 2 trapezoids.

dime

a coin with a value of 10¢

10¢ 10 cents

difference

the answer to a subtraction problem

7 − 3 = 4

↑

difference

doubles

an addition fact with two addends that are the same

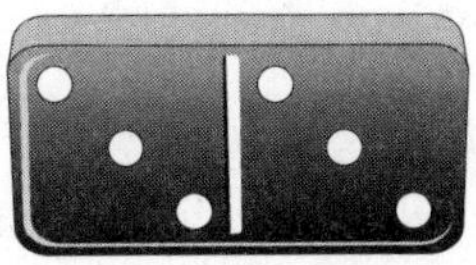

3 + 3 = 6

dozen

a group or set of 12

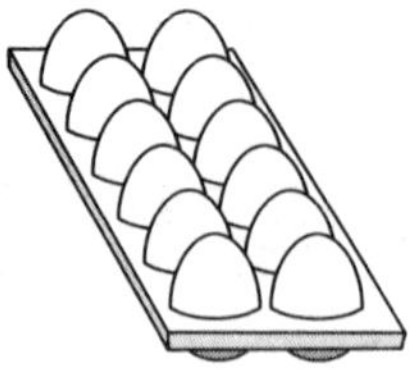

The carton holds a **dozen** eggs.

earn

to receive money for work

I **earn** money when I babysit my sister.

eight

a counting number; the next number after seven

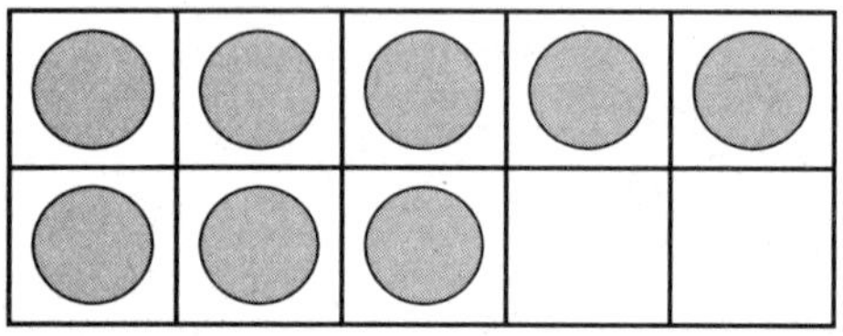

8

eleven

a counting number composed of 1 ten and 1 one; the next number after ten

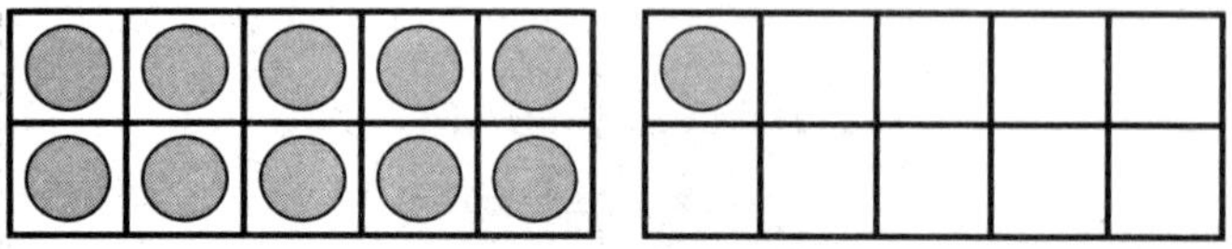

11

equal/equals (=)

a symbol that means is the same as

equal parts

pieces of a whole that are all the same size

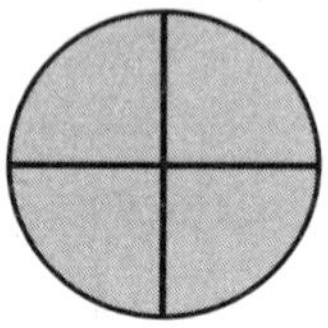

This circle is divided into 4 **equal parts**.

equation

a number sentence that uses the equal sign

$3 + 3 = 6$ $4 - 3 = 1$

estimate

to guess about how many

There are about 20 grapes.

Illegal to Copy

expanded form

a way to write a number that shows the value of each digit

100 + 10 + 3 is the **expanded form** of 113.

five

a counting number; the next number after four

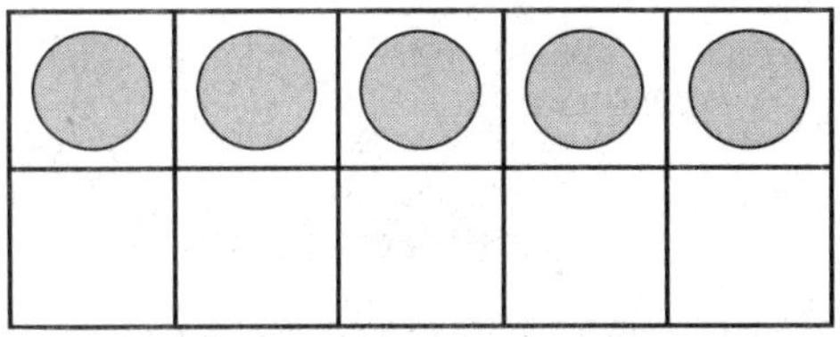

5

expression

a math phrase with numbers and symbols

7 + 3

11 - 8

four

a counting number; the next number after three

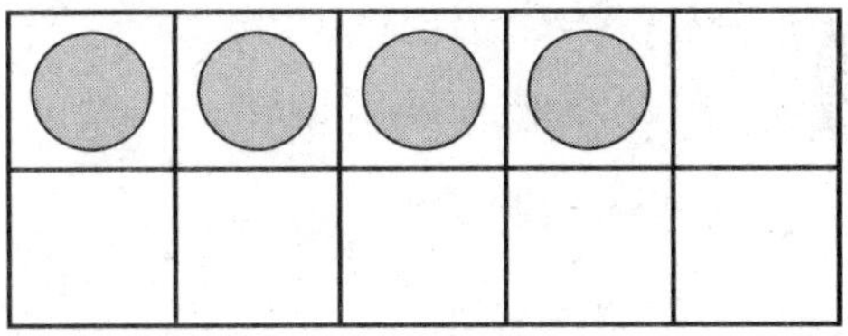

4

face

a flat surface of a solid shape

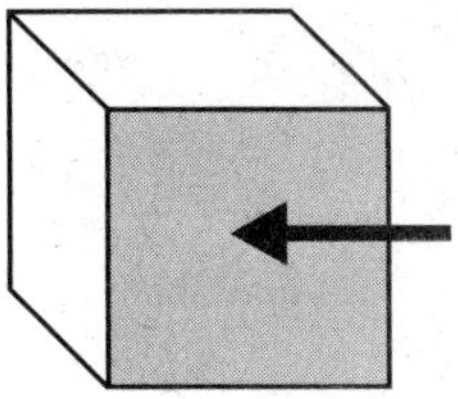

face
A cube has 6 **faces**.

fourth

one of four equal parts that make a whole

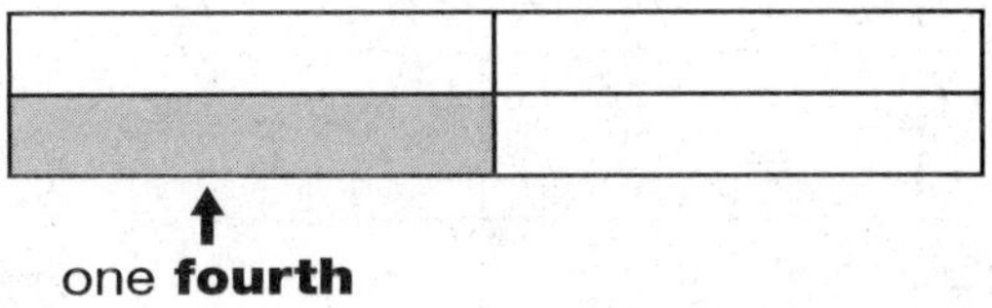

One **fourth** of the rectangle is shaded.

fact family

a set of related number sentences

This is the **fact family** for 2, 3, and 5.

2 + 3 = 5   3 + 2 = 5

5 - 3 = 2   5 - 2 = 3

goods

things that are made to be sold

The toy store sells many different **goods**.

greater than (>)

a symbol used
to compare two numbers

21 > 13

21 is **greater than** 13.

greatest

the largest in number or size

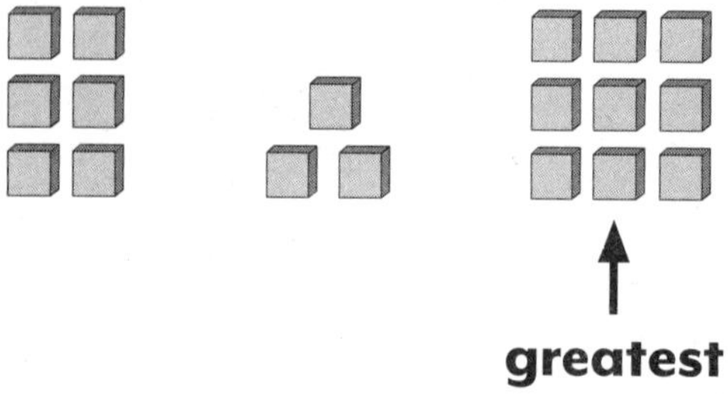

half/halves

two equal parts
that make a whole

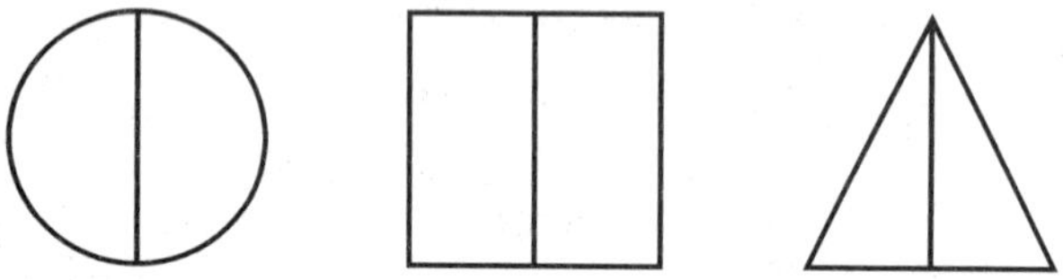

Each shape is divided into **halves**.

half hour

an amount of time
equal to 30 minutes

hexagon

a two-dimensional shape
with 6 straight sides

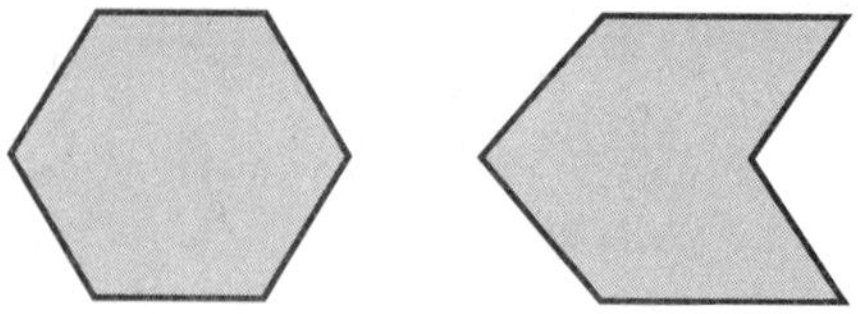

hour

a unit of time

60 minutes = 1 **hour**

hour hand

the shorter hand
on an analog clock

hundreds

the place value to the left of the
tens place; a whole number
equal to 10 tens

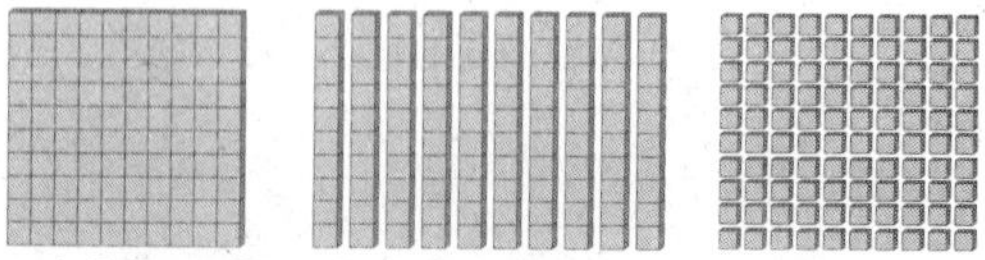

1 **hundred** = 10 tens = 100 ones

Illegal to Copy

income

money earned from working

My **income** from chores is $5 each week.

join

to put together

1 bird **joins** the group.

2 + 1 = 3

key

the part of a graph that shows what the symbols mean

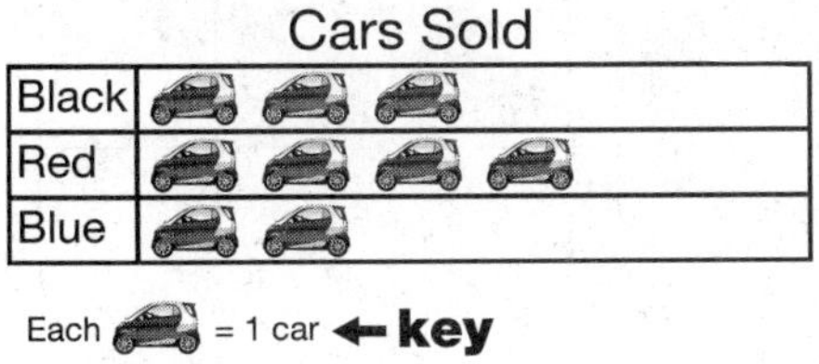

least

the smallest in number or size

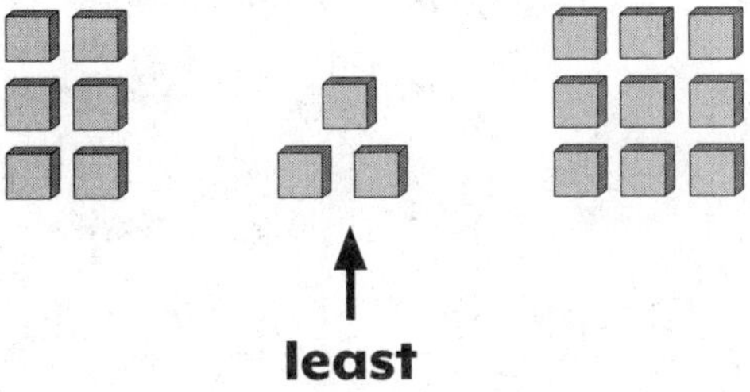

length

the distance from one end of an object to the other

less than (<)

a symbol used to compare two numbers

18 < 24

18 is **less than** 24.

longer/shorter

words used to compare length

The paintbrush is **longer** than the pencil.

The pencil is **shorter** than the paintbrush.

measure

to find the size, weight, or capacity

minus (–)

to take away or subtract

$6 - 2 = 4$

↑

6 **minus** 2 equals 4.

minute

a unit of time

There are 60 **minutes** in 1 hour.

minute hand

the longer hand
on an analog clock

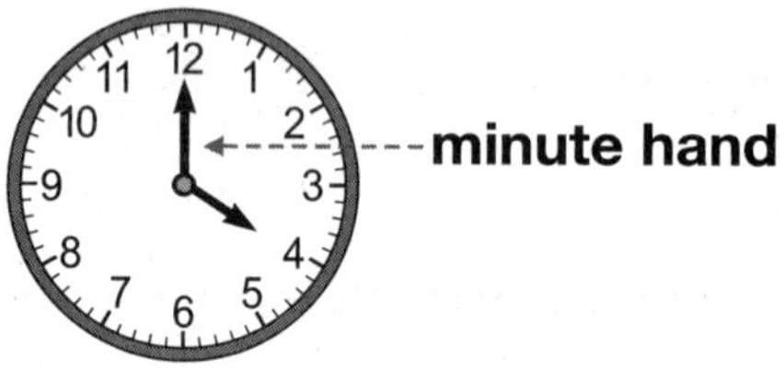

multiple of 10

a number that results from
skip counting by 10

Some **multiples of 10** are
10, 20, 30, 40, 50,
60, 70, 80, 90, and 100.

needs

things a person must
have to live

Food, shelter, and clothing
are **needs**.

nickel

a coin with a value of 5¢

5¢ 5 cents

nine

a counting number;
the next number after eight

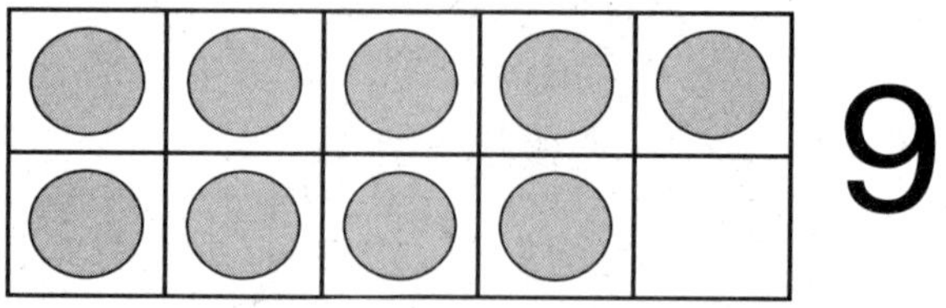

number

a way to describe how
many or how much

The **number** of apples is 6.

 Illegal to Copy

number line

a line on which points correspond to numbers

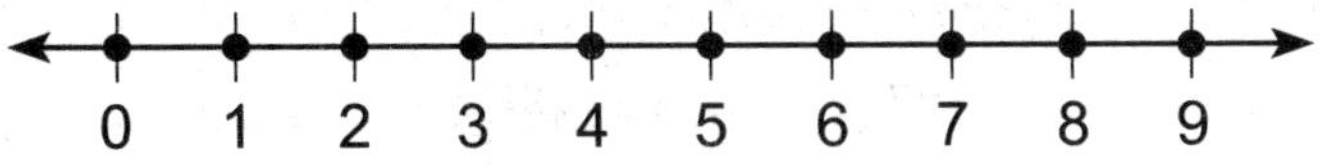

one

the first counting number; the next number after zero

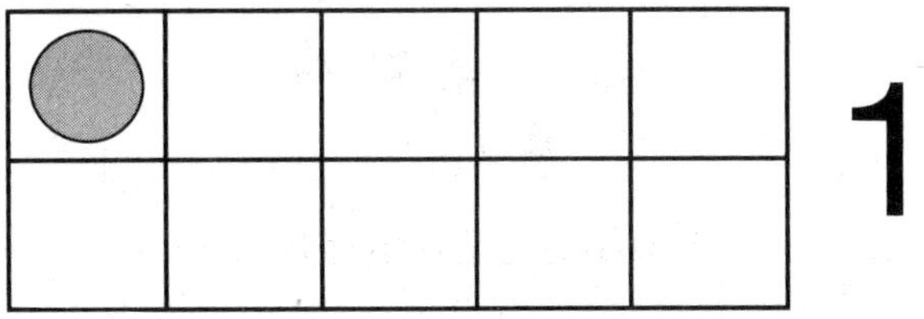

number sentence

a mathematical sentence using numbers and symbols

3 + 3 = 6   9 > 6

4 - 3 = 1   3 < 5

ones

the place value to the right of the tens place; a single item

5 **ones**

numeral

a symbol that represents a number

eight = 8
two = 2
six = 6

open figure

a figure with two ends that do not touch

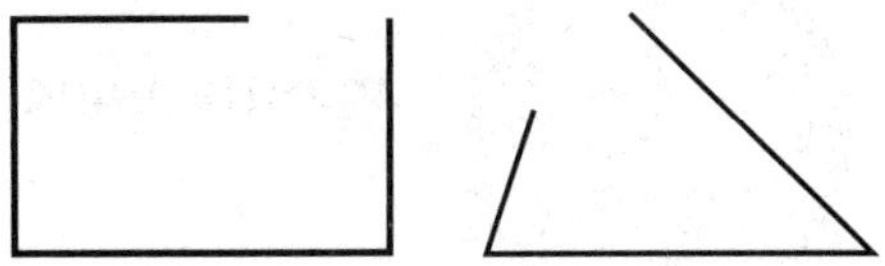

o'clock

of the clock

The time is 5 **o'clock**.

order

an arrangement according to size, amount, or value

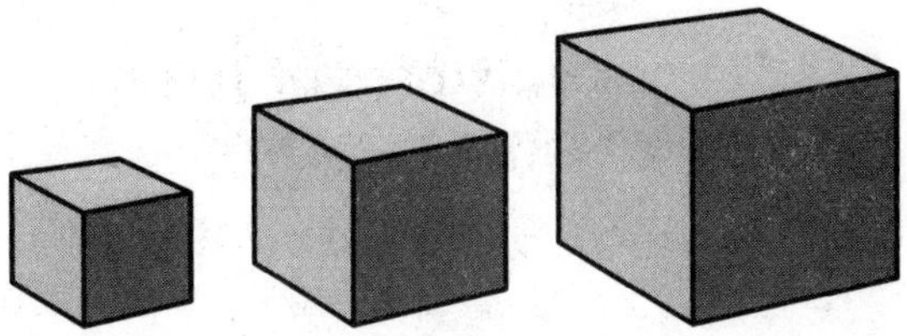

Illegal to Copy

part

a portion of a whole

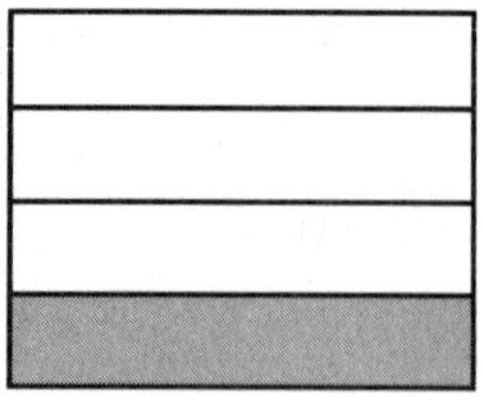

One **part** of the box is shaded.

picture graph

a graph that uses pictures or symbols to represent data

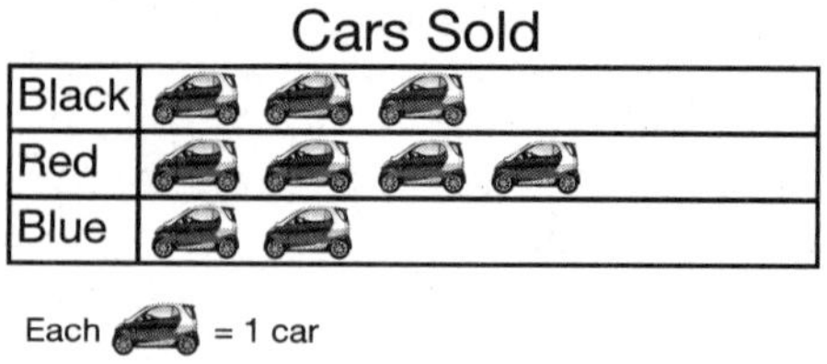

partition

to divide a figure into groups or smaller parts

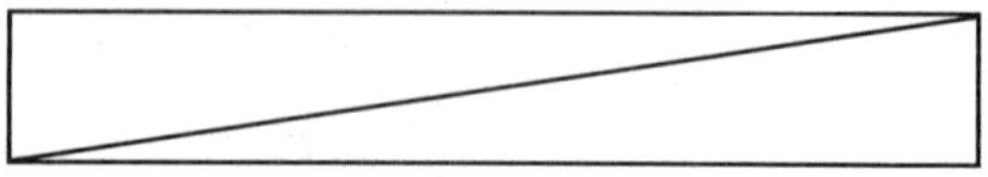

Sam drew a line to **partition** the rectangle into 2 triangles.

place value

the value of a digit based on its position in a number

48 = 4 tens and 8 ones

The digit 4 in the tens place has a value of 40.

pattern

a repeated design or sequence

shape **pattern**

number **pattern**

5, 10, 15, 20, 25, 30, ...

plus (+)

add or join

2 + 6 = 8

↑

2 **plus** 6 equals 8.

penny

a coin with a value of 1¢

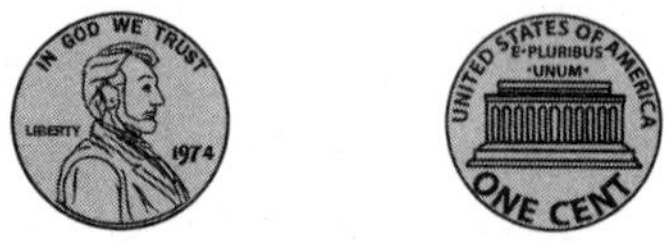

1¢ 1 cent

quarter (fraction)

one of four equal parts

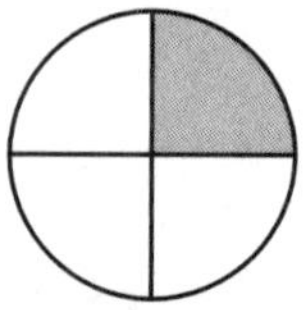

One **quarter** of this circle is shaded.

Illegal to Copy

quarter (money)

a coin with a value of 25¢

25¢ 25 cents

rectangle

a two-dimensional shape with
4 straight sides and
4 square corners

rectangular prism

a three-dimensional solid with
6 rectangular faces

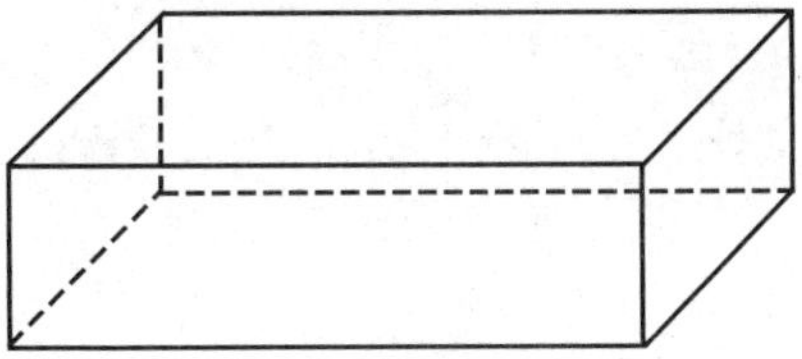

rhombus

a two-dimensional shape with
4 straight sides of equal length

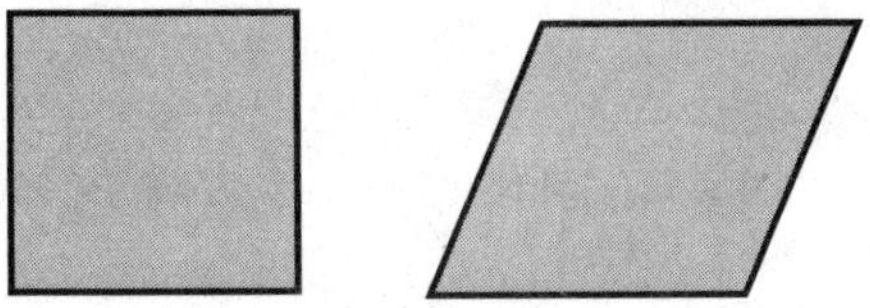

save

to keep money instead of
spending it

I want to **save** my money so
I can buy a video game.

services

work done by a person who
does not produce goods

Firefighters and policemen
provide important **services**.

seven

a counting number;
the next number after six

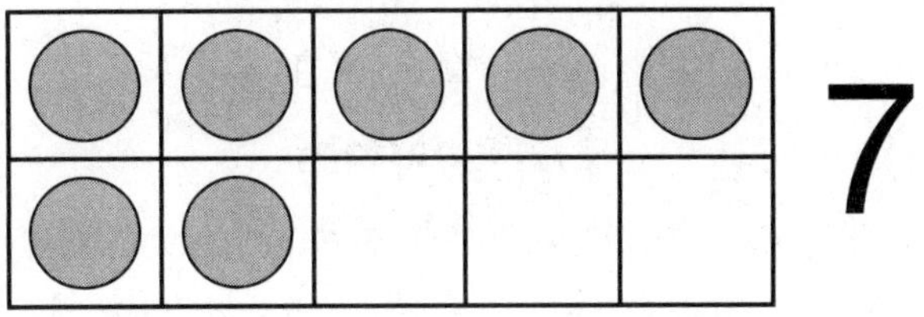

sides

the line segments that form
a two-dimensional shape

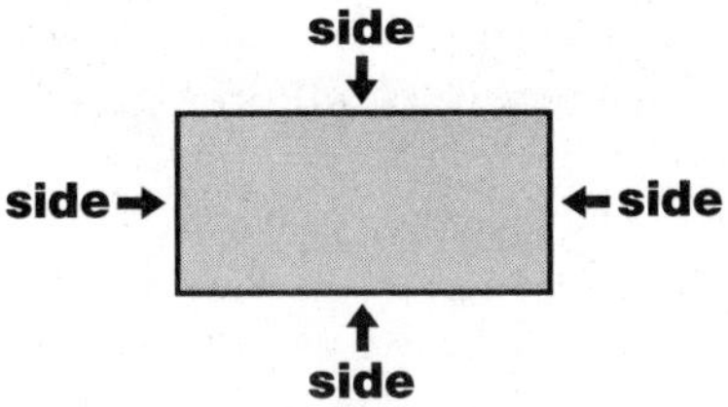

six

a counting number;
the next number after five

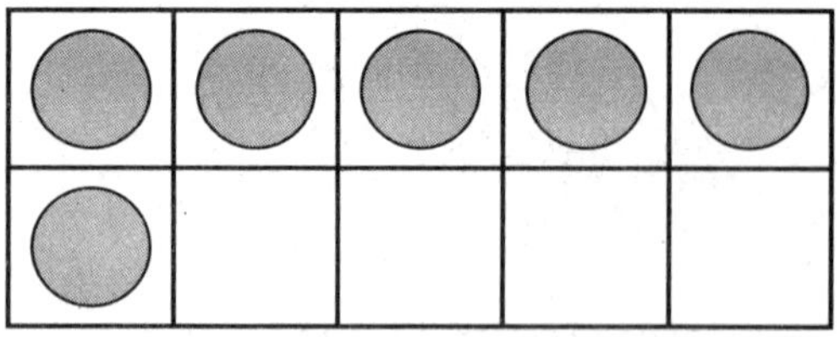

6

sphere

a three-dimensional solid

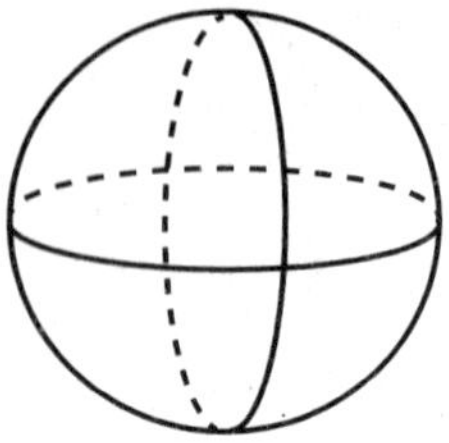

examples of **spheres**

- basketball
- orange
- globe

skip count

to count by a given number

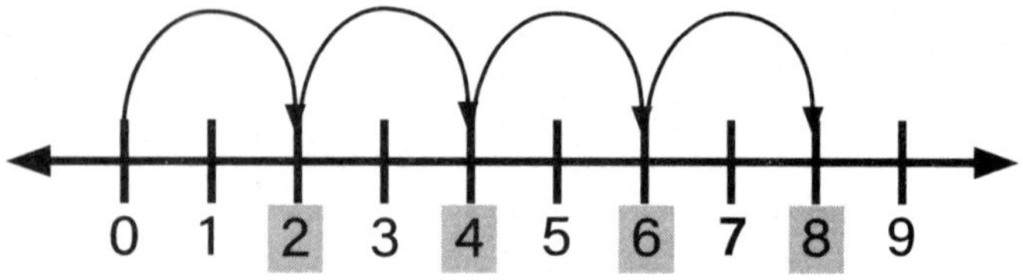

square

a special rectangle with
4 sides of equal measure

sort

to put things together using
an attribute

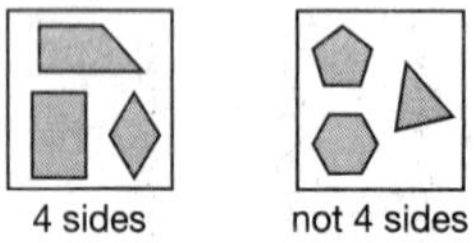

These shapes have been **sorted** into two groups by the number of sides.

standard form

a way to write numbers using
the digits 0 – 9

5 tens and 3 ones is written as
53 in **standard form**.

spend

to use money to pay for
things you want or need

I will **spend** $10 to buy a
present for my mother.

subtract/ subtraction

to take away part of a group or
to compare the sizes of 2 groups

$7 - 3 = 4$

Illegal to Copy

subtraction sentence

an equation showing the difference of two numbers

7 - 4 = 3

7 minus 4 equals 3.

take away

to subtract

5 **take away** 2 equals 3.

sum

the answer to an addition problem

3 + 6 = 9

↑

sum

tally chart

a chart used to keep track of data being counted

Our Pets

Student Name	Number of Pets
Caroline	|||
Jackson	卌
Preston	||
Tori	卌 ||

symbol

a letter or picture used in place of words

The **symbol** for "greater than" is >.

tally marks

marks used to keep track of data being counted

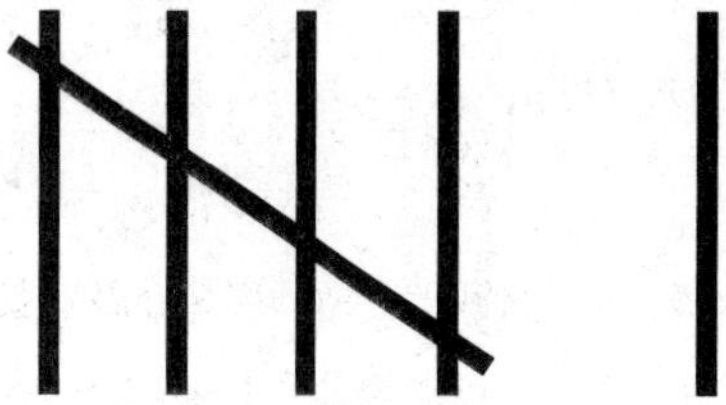

table

information organized in columns and rows

Tricycle Wheels

Number of Tricycles	Number of Wheels
1	3
2	6
3	9
4	12

T-chart

a chart used to organize data

Number of Dogs	Number of Legs
1	4
2	8
3	12
4	16

ten

a counting number;
the next number after nine

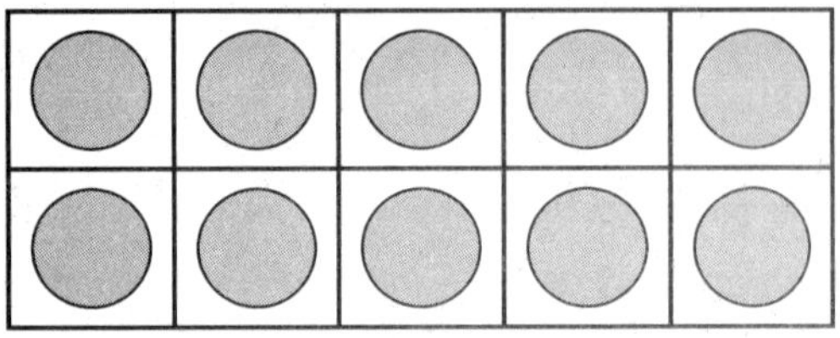

10

ten frame

a rectangle with 10 spaces
used to build numbers

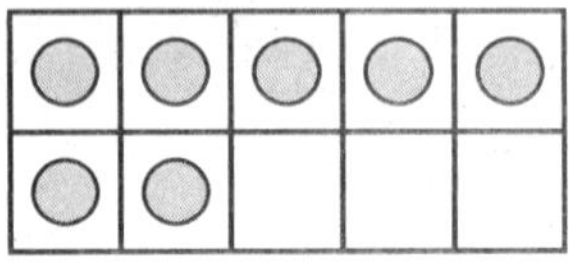

tens

the place value to the left of the ones
place; groups of 10 ones

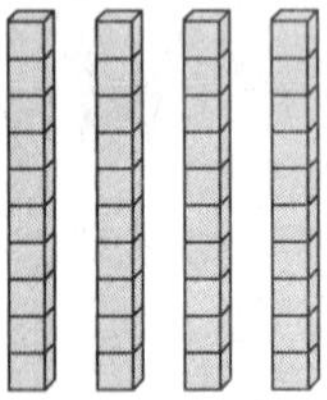

4 **tens** or 40

three

a counting number;
the next number after two

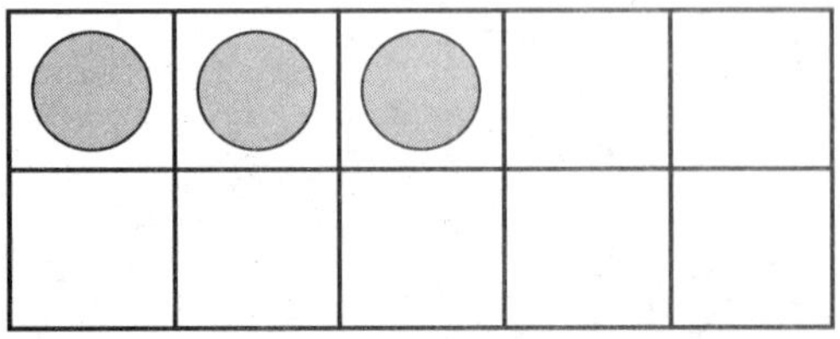

3

three-dimensional solid

a solid figure that has
length, width, and height

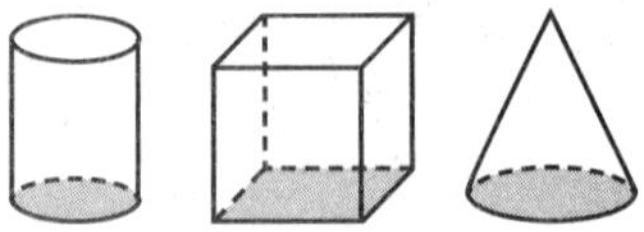

total

a sum of objects or numbers

The **total** number of
milk cartons is 4.

triangle

a two-dimensional
shape with 3 straight sides

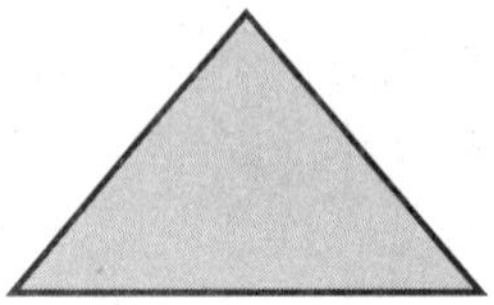

triangular prism

a three-dimensional solid
with 2 triangular bases

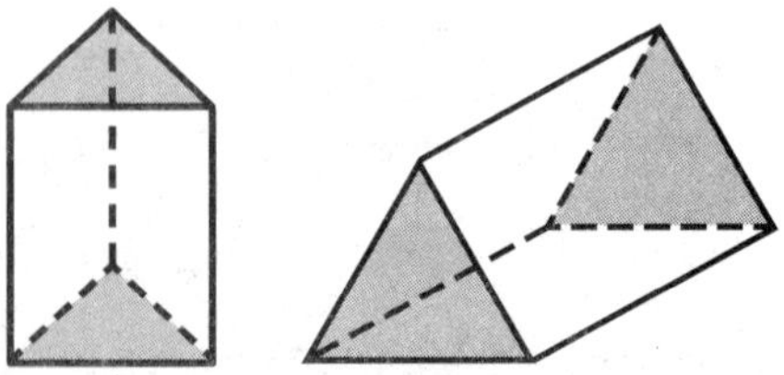

Illegal to Copy

twelve

a counting number composed of 1 ten and 2 ones; the next number after eleven

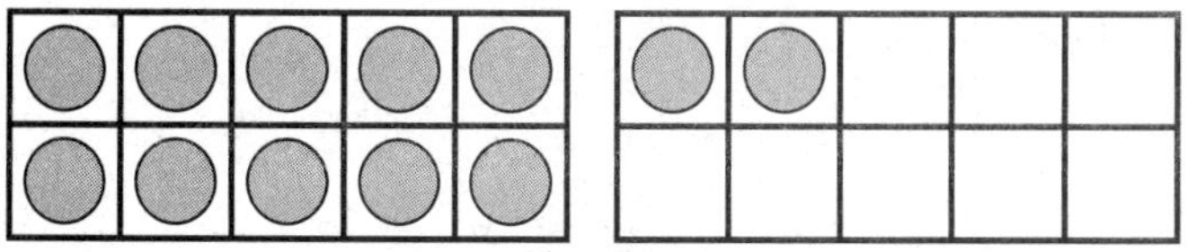

12

two

a counting number; the next number after one

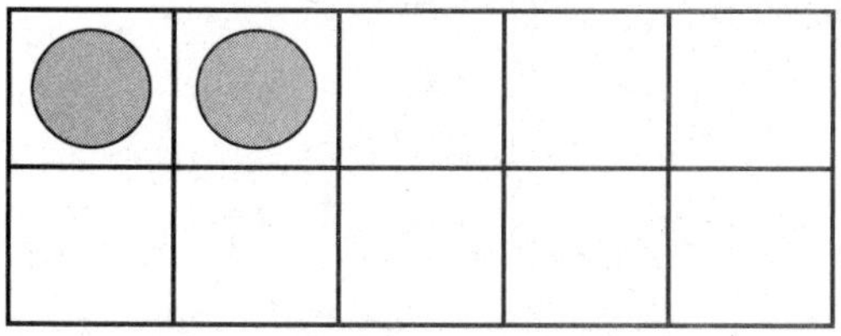

2

two-dimensional shape

a shape that has length and width

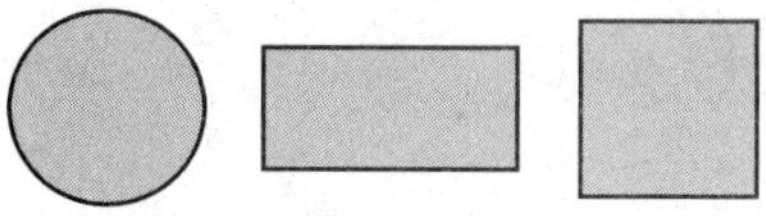

unknown

the missing number in a number sentence

5 + ☐ = 7

↑

unknown

value

how much something is worth

These coins have a **value** of 48¢.

vertex/vertices

a corner of a two- or three-dimensional shape

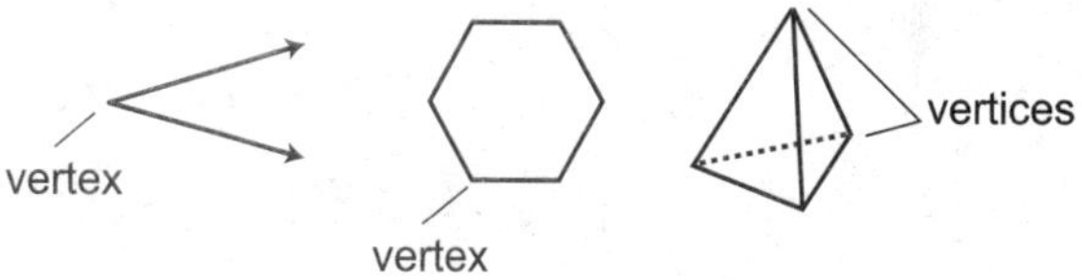

wants

things a person would like to have

Candy and toys are **wants**, not needs.

whole

a shape or a set that is complete with no parts missing

1 **whole** pizza

whole numbers zero and all counting numbers **0, 1, 2, 3, 4, 5, ...**	
zero the number which indicates no quantity **0**	

Illegal to Copy